Social Suffering

Social Suffering

Edited by

ARTHUR KLEINMAN, VEENA DAS,
AND MARGARET LOCK

University of California Press

BERKELEY   LOS ANGELES   LONDON

The following essays were originally published in *Dædalus: Journal of the American Academy of Arts and Sciences,* Winter 1996, volume 125, no. 1:

Arthur Kleinman and Joan Kleinman, "The Appeal of Experience; The Dismay of Images: Cultural Appropriations of Suffering in Our Times"

David B. Morris, "About Suffering: Voice, Genre, and Moral Community"

Lawrence L. Langer, "The Alarmed Vision: Social Suffering and Holocaust Atrocity"

Veena Das, "Language and Body: Transactions in the Construction of Pain"

Stanley Cavell, "Comments on Veena Das's Essay 'Language and Body: Transactions in the Construction of Pain'"

Mamphela Ramphele, "Political Widowhood in South Africa: The Embodiment of Ambiguity"

Vera Schwarcz, "The Pane of Sorrow: Public Uses of Personal Grief in Modern China"

Tu Wei-ming, "Destructive Will and Ideological Holocaust: Maoism as a Source of Social Suffering in China"

Anne Harrington, "Unmasking Suffering's Masks: Reflections on Old and New Memories of Nazi Medicine"

Margaret Lock, "Displacing Suffering: The Reconstruction of Death in North America and Japan"

Allan Young, "Suffering and the Origins of Traumatic Memory"

Paul Farmer, "On Suffering and Structural Violence: A View from Below"

University of California Press
Berkeley and Los Angeles, California

University of California Press, Ltd.
London, England

Library of Congress Cataloging-in-Publication Data
Social suffering / edited by Arthur Kleinman, Veena Das, and Margaret Lock.
   p. cm.
   Some of the essays originally appeared in the journal Dædalus, Winter 1996, v. 125, no. 1.
   Includes bibliographical references and index.
   ISBN 0–520–20993–1 (cloth : alk. paper).—ISBN 0–520–20995–8 (pbk. : alk. paper)
   1. Suffering—Social aspects. 2. Violence. 3. Power (Social sciences). 4. Victims.
5. Social medicine. 6. Body, Human—Social aspects. I. Kleinman, Arthur. II. Das, Veena. III. Lock, Margaret M.
HM291.S5889   1997
306.4—dc21
                                       97–201
                                         CIP

Printed in the United States of America
9 8 7 6 5 4 3 2

The paper used in this publication meets the minimum requirements of American National Standard for Information Sciences—Permanence of Paper for Printed Library Materials, ANSI Z39.48–1984.

Contents

Acknowledgments

These essays (except for Paul Farmer's) were discussed at a conference held at the Rockefeller Foundation's Bellagio Center in July 1994. The conference was organized as part of the Social Science Research Council's Committee on Culture, Health, and Human Development, which sponsors a program on Culture, Suffering, and Social Change. The funding for the committee's work came from the MacArthur Foundation. The editors acknowledge with pleasure their appreciation for the support received from the MacArthur Foundation, from the Rockefeller Foundation, from the Bellagio Conference Center staff, and from the Social Science Research Council. They thank in particular Dr. Robert Lawrence, Dr. Denis Prager, Dr. Robert Rose, and especially Dr. David Featherman, Dr. Frank Kessel, and Ms. Diana Colbert. They also thank all the participants in the conference, including especially Dr. Stephen Graubard, whose influence is felt both in the issue of *Dædalus* and here. We also thank Joan Gillespie, Phyllis Bendell, Robin Root, and Don Seeman for their assistance in the preparation of the manuscript.

This book is composed of twelve chapters that were published in *Dædalus* (Winter 1996) as well as three others (those by Talal Asad, E. Valentine Daniel, and J. W. Bowker) that are new to this volume. The editors are grateful for permission from the American Academy of Arts and Sciences to republish the *Dædalus* essays. We also extend our thanks to the contributors for their loyalty, patience, and commitment to the endeavor.

Arthur Kleinman
Veena Das
Margaret Lock

Introduction

SOCIAL SUFFERING, THE TOPIC OF THIS VOLUME, brings into a single space an assemblage of human problems that have their origins and consequences in the devastating injuries that social force can inflict on human experience. Social suffering results from what political, economic, and institutional power does to people and, reciprocally, from how these forms of power themselves influence responses to social problems. Included under the category of social suffering are conditions that are usually divided among separate fields, conditions that simultaneously involve health, welfare, legal, moral, and religious issues. They destabilize established categories. For example, the trauma, pain, and disorders to which atrocity gives rise are health conditions; yet they are also political and cultural matters. Similarly, poverty is the major risk factor for ill health and death; yet this is only another way of saying that health is a social indicator and indeed a social process.

The clustering of substance abuse, street violence, domestic violence, suicide, depression, posttraumatic stress disorder, sexually transmitted disorders, AIDS, and tuberculosis among people living in disintegrating communities runs against the professional medical idea that sufferers experience one or at most two major problems at a time. That grouping of human problems also defeats categorization of such issues as principally psychological or medical and, therefore, *individual*. Instead, it points to the often close linkage of personal problems with societal problems. It reveals too the interpersonal grounds of suffering: in other words, that suffering is a social experience. That social experience occurs not only in the slums of cities in poor societies, like Kibera in Nairobi, or in shantytowns surrounding Johannesburg or Mexico City; it also flourishes in inner-city Chicago, the South Bronx, and the ethnic *banlieue* of Paris. Social suffering is shared across high-income and low-income societies, primarily affecting, in such different settings, those who are desperately poor and powerless. This is not merely a statistical correlation, but a causal web in the global political economy. Many of the same sources of breakdown, violence, emerging infectious diseases, and mental and social health problems are at work among poor populations worldwide.[1]

The vicious spiral of political violence, causing forced uprooting, migration, and deep trauma to families and communities, while intensifying domestic abuse and personal suffering, spins out of control across a bureaucratic landscape of health, social welfare, and legal agencies.[2] The gathering cycle churns through domestic and international agendas and threatens both local and global structures of security. At its brutal extremity in the Holocaust, or when it results from the "soft knife" of routine processes of ordinary oppression, social suffering ruins the collective and the intersubjective connections of experience and gravely damages subjectivity.

The cultural processes of rational-technical analysis that describe these human defeats and the technological interventions they authorize as "treatments" at times are effective, but all too regularly bureaucratic responses to social violence intensify suffering. This is caused by unforeseen and untoward moral, economic, and gender effects of policies and programs, and also by actions that end up normalizing social pathology or pathologizing the psychophysiology of terror. Cultural responses to the traumatic effects of political violence often transform the local idioms of victims into universal professional languages of complaint and restitution—and thereby remake both representations and experiences of suffering. Existential processes of pain, death, and mourning are metamorphosed by these historically shaped rationalities and technologies, which, again all too regularly, are inattentive to how the transformations they induce contribute to the suffering they seek to remedy.

The essays in this volume approach these ominous problems in a different way. They collapse old dichotomies—for example, those that separate individual from social levels of analysis, health from social problems, representation from experience, suffering from intervention. From these perspectives—the perspectives of anthropology, social history, literary criticism, religious studies, and social medicine—the standard dichotomies are in fact barriers to understanding how the forms of human suffering can be at the same time collective and individual, how the modes of experiencing pain and trauma can be both local and global. Prior to forging new policies or lubricating creaky policy discourses, these essays argue, we need first to examine the most basic relationships between language and pain, image and suffering. The authors discuss why a language of dismay, disappointment, bereavement, and alarm that sounds not at all like the usual terminology of policy and programs may offer a more valid means for describing what is at stake in human experiences of political catastrophe and social structural violence, for professionals as much as for victims/perpetrators, and also may make better sense of how the clash among globalizing discourses and localized social realities so often ends up prolonging personal and collective tragedy.

The essays critically explore the ways our historically and culturally shaped commitments to particular versions of modernization construct moral quandaries and how our usual practices of casting social experience as "natural" or "normal" obscure the greatly consequential workings of "power" in social life. Pursuing these destabilizing, interdisciplinary themes, the authors show the permeability between the borders of moral imagination, bodily affect, and social processes. They demonstrate that both the varieties of human misery and the various social scientific and literary analyses of these truly dangerous problems *interfuse,* so that it is no longer useful to insist upon artificial boundaries that divide an unruly world into tidy analytic chambers. The most interesting questions for theory and practice concerning social suffering are in the cracks between our categories and in the discursive processes that traverse our disciplines.

The chapters converge on three overlapping themes: cultural representations, social experiences, political and professional processes. *Cultural representations* of suffering—images, prototypical tales, metaphors, models—can be (and frequently are) appropriated in the popular culture or by particular social institutions for political and moral purposes. For this reason, suffering has social use. Historical memories of suffering—e.g., slavery, the destruction of aboriginal communities, wars, genocide, imperialistic and post-imperialistic oppression—have present uses, for example, to authorize nationalism or class and ethnic resistance. Collective suffering is also a core component of the global political economy. There is a market for suffering: victimhood is commodified.

The cultural representations of suffering shape it as a form of *social experience.* Norms do somehow enfold into normality (and pathology).[3] Experience is learned, shared, and, not infrequently, contradicted. Even what we so easily assume to be the existential ground of the human condition (its defining panhuman core, its "nature") may undergo change in keeping with epochal transformations in the nexus of symbolic-moral systems and the political economy, such as those of our postmodern period. Social experience as a theoretical construct encourages the view (to our minds a critical and destabilizing one) that changing societal practices transform individual lives and ways of being-in-the-world.

Political and professional processes powerfully shape the responses to types of social suffering. These processes involve both authorized and contested appropriations of collective suffering. A central activity described later in this volume is *medicalization.* The state, its institutions, and groups that contest state control press medicalization for its advantages in regulating persons, their bodies, and networks. But this is not the only form that political and professional processes of constructing and contesting social order take. Public policies and programs have created some of the worst instances of social sufferings (see Tu Wei-ming's account of Maoism in his essay); even in seeking to manage social suffering, they have, through intended and unintended effects, intensified human misery. The following chapters, with varying degrees of emphasis, fill out these themes as the deep architecture of this volume.

That ours is an age of the picture is more than a cliché. Experience, including experiences of social suffering, has been *mediatized.* Wars, plague, street violence, AIDS, and famine are all captured in their raw immediacy by the ubiquitous video camera. The devastating conflicts in Bosnia, Rwanda, Zaire, Somalia, and Afghanistan are made over from national and regional disasters into transnational tragedies that are "seen" and "felt" as part of the stream of everyday experience in the intimacy of homes thousands of miles away, at a safe distance. Social suffering is a feature of cultural representation both as spectacle and as the presentation of the real. But cultural technologies now exist to fashion the "real" in accord with the interests of power to a degree hardly imagined in the past. What W. J. T. Mitchell calls the gap between representation and responsibility is a master moral dilemma.[4] How we "picture" social suffering becomes that experience, for the observers and even for the sufferers/perpetrators. What we represent and how we represent it prefigure what we will, or will not, do to intervene. What is not pictured is not real. Much of routinized misery is invisible; much that is made visible is not ordinary or routine. The very act of picturing distorts social experience in the popular media and in the professions under the impress of ideology and political economy. So entailed, even personal "witnessing" is compromised. We are living through a great historical transformation in the imaging, and therefore perhaps also in the experience, of social adversity. Is that transformation *anamorphic* in the sense of a greater experience of complexity, or is it anamorphic in the sense that the global lenses of the media and other transnational institutions distort local images while providing the optical system for regularizing (normalizing) the global recovery of images and experiences?

A major preoccupation in the Western tradition has to do with the incommunicability of pain, its capacity to isolate sufferers and strip them of cultural resources, especially the resource of language. This incommunicability of pain arises from the asymmetry of access to experiential knowledge that it gives us. According to this view, to be in pain is to be certain about this knowledge. To be asked to react to another person's pain is to be in doubt about its existence.[5] From the perspective of theories of *social* suffering, such a preoccupation with individual certainty and doubt simply seems a less interesting, less important question to ask than that of how such suffering is produced in societies and how acknowledgment of pain, as a cultural process, is given or withheld. After all, to be ignorant or incapable of imagining another person's pain does not signal blindness in moral sensibility in the same way in which the incapacity to *acknowledge* that pain does.[6] Yet this latter failure is at the bottom of the cultural process of political abuse.

Many of the essays in this volume formulate questions of social suffering in relation to the problem of language. Only an excessive allegiance to the referential theory of language would lead us to privilege its pointing function in relation to experiences like pain. For one thing, that would construct the inner geography of a person as if it were a replica of the external geography of the physical world. But more than that, such a theory would have no place for the performative aspects of language or for the role of the speech genre of a society in molding the experience of suffering so that certain experiences of pain and grieving become expressible while others are shrouded in silence. And, furthermore, while experience is shaped by representations, it can also push against these representations—resisting language, bending it in new directions, and distorting the received ways of expressing distress and desperation so that these distortions themselves transform the experience of suffering.

These essays illustrate great variation in historical and cultural styles of suffering. But they are not content to simply describe differences—for instance, the value placed on "enduring" hardship as a moral practice in China, the passionate pronouncements on the incoherent, chaotic nature of the gods in mourning laments in India, or the resistance to redefining "death" in Japan. One could multiply examples of variation endlessly. Instead, the essays tell of cultural ruptures and new, globalized suturings.

For example, Vera Schwarcz describes the vicissitudes of silent endurance and indirect expression of the trauma of political oppression as traditional moral modes of suffering among Chinese intellectuals engaged in the project of modernization. The cultural mode of directly "speaking bitterness," through which, for example, abused peasant women were liberated by their new Communist masters to hurl the residue of that experience of abuse back at erstwhile landlords and patriarchs, hundreds of thousands of whom subsequently were put to death, occurred in an era of radical change that Tu Wei-ming regards as one of unprecedented "destruction of life, property, institutions, traditions, and values." The new discourse community that crystallized around Maoism created, for the first time in the Chinese tradition, a union between diffused processes of political control, an inversionary ideology that reversed the Confucian order, and control over the language of moral approbation and critique, which had traditionally belonged to scholar-bureaucrats. Under the guise of rationality and democracy, Tu shows, this union of discursive and nondiscursive practices mobilized scientism and populism to create the moral-political instruments of immense societal suffering. Schwarcz demonstrates that under the vast pressure of suffering, sensibility and urgency also transmute, though not so greatly that the past loses its influence on present experience.

In a different context, Veena Das describes the magnification of the images of nation in the anticolonial movements in India, where men came to appropriate the bodies of women as cultural media through which new political programs would be expressed. The Partition in 1947, on the eve of India's independence, is considered the most cataclysmic event in the history of twentieth-century India. Traditionally, the historiography of the dramatic politics of Partition has been strongly rooted in two assumptions. The first is the assumption that the Muslim League stood for Partition on the grounds of the "two nation theory," which held that Hindus and Muslims belonged to two different social orders and therefore could not evolve into a single nation. The second assumption is that the Congress stood for national unity but was forced to concede the demand for Partition because it was the only condition under which the British would agree to a transfer of power and freedom for India. Recent historiography has questioned these assumptions. It now seems clear that the pressures and counterpressures on both the Muslim League and the Congress were much more subtle. The real motives behind the moves made by the League and the Congress were quite different from those stated publicly. According to most recent work, the Congress bore a far greater responsibility for the Partition than traditional historiography has been willing to grant.[7]

Although the politics of the Partition received renewed attention in the 1980s, the experiences of the common person began to be seriously documented in the social sciences only in the 1990s. In the arts, literature, and cinema, however, the Partition and its trauma have been the subject of many important works. From the perspective of the common man and woman, the period preceding the Partition was marked by large-scale civil violence, riots, and movements of population, especially in the north and east of India. Local administration collapsed. An estimated 200,000 to 250,000 persons on both sides of the border died in this civil violence. It was stated in India's Constituent Assembly in December 1949 that 33,000 Hindu or Sikh women had been abducted by Muslims, and the government of Pakistan held that 50,000 Muslim women had been abducted by Hindu or Sikh men. Precise estimates are not possible, but we can imagine the magnitude of this tragedy from the fact that the Constituent Assembly listed the number of women "recovered" through the army evacuation services as 12,000 from India and 6,000 from Pakistan. In his memoir of the period, the Raja of Mahmudabad, a close associate of Jinnah and a member of the Muslim League, wrote: "I can well recall the general sense of gloom and despondency that pervaded the two newly created nation states; instead of joy and expectancy which should have been ours after those years of struggle there were only premonitions of impending conflicts and a promise of future struggle."[8]

Of the cultural processes of destruction unleashed by the Partition of India, Das finds ghostly apparitions in the register of the social imaginary. If the cultural project of modernity led to disappointment about the possibilities of human emancipation, so did projects of conserving tradition fail to promise deliverance. This experience of disappointment with cultural resources, with language, with culture itself, a sensibility of a grand illusion recognized, perhaps even of a deception, Das suggests, defines a key dimension of human societies in our bloody times, because experiences of social suffering in the middle of massive human destruction thrust against the limits of representations, received or newly created. Paradoxically, Das observes, cultural disappointment is not without rewards. It becomes possible in the ethos of disappointment for persons to acknowledge the pain of the other. This cultural opening is made possible not through the mediation of established genres. Rather, it is the failure of those genres and the dismay of the moral communities anchoring them that sometimes enable acknowledgment of the uniqueness of being, of the suffering of the other.

Stanley Cavell's philosophical reading of Das's essay in social theory suggests why the relationship of suffering to meaning-making must be worked through if interventions (academic and practical) are to be adequate to the complexity of human problems and not romanticize or trivialize human conditions. For Cavell, withholding acknowledgment of pain is a societal failure: "the study of social suffering must contain a study of a society's silence toward it . . . the study of that suffering and that silence must contain an awareness of its own dangers in mimicking the social silence that perpetrates the suffering." Philosophy's silence about the social condition of suffering is also an obvious part of Cavell's concerns. The study of suffering, therefore, needs to interrogate this failure of theory, just as it needs to examine the long stream of exploration of men's and women's pain and tribulations in literature and social science.

Lawrence Langer, however, cautions against the temptation of finding meaning (large or small) and thereby humanizing extreme atrocity. Writing on the Holocaust, he is concerned not so much with the uniqueness of the historical event of the bureaucratized destruction of European Jewry but with the fact that to find models in religious or literary texts (or professional discourse) to make sense of the suffering of the Jews "normalizes" that which can never be normalized, never rationalized. He finds attempts to explain extreme atrocity naive, as he does the understandable but, to his way of thinking, misguided efforts to cure survivors of their trauma. Massive social suffering does not lend itself to metaphors of rescue or remedy. (In any case, the six million who were murdered are beyond healing.) For Langer, survivors live in the chronological time of ordinary life experience, but they also still inhabit, and are inhabited by, durational time, a frozen time, a continuously experienced duration of atrocity that can be neither transcended nor generalized. All efforts at interpreting atrocity, for Langer, must begin with individual narratives of the "unappeasable experience" of durational time. He advocates cultivation of a language of diminished possibility, a rhetoric of consternation that eschews teleology and especially salvational longings. But above all, he argues for an alarmed vision, an alerted way of looking at the world that expects danger, a vision that would constantly look out for atrocity and prepare people to respond. If it sounds like survivalist tactics on the collective level, that is indeed part of the only moral (or social policy) lesson Langer seems willing to accept from the extreme suffering of victims of the Holocaust: disheartenment and alarm.

The theme of disappointment with both tradition and modernity arises again, in a troubling irony, in Anne Harrington's discussion of the relationship between holism and Nazi medicine. That a humanistic critique of scientific objectification in biomedicine was appropriated by National Socialism may not destabilize our picture of the Nazis nearly as much as it does the idea of cultural critique as a means of unmasking the sources of human suffering. For Harrington, the products of our moral imagination—in this case, the critique of objectification in biomedicine—can be politically appropriated by the very forces that produce social suffering to hide immediate horror under the seductive ideology of a distant ideal. Cultural critique and reform of biomedicine came to legitimate a new social order in Nazi Germany rather than challenge that order. Both tradition and modernity failed to offer effective resistance to cultural appropriation by the most dangerous of political programs.

Political-moral misadventures involving social appropriations of cultural representations of suffering are the subject of several other essays. The Kleinmans examine the processes through which popular, professional, and political appropriations of images of suffering appeal to the experiences of distant audiences. In so doing, those representations authorize transformations of core symbol systems and cultural discourses and thereby alter social experience, inducing ominous historical change in experiences of suffering in our own epoch. What is the effect upon cultural representations and social experience when the corporative media trivializes suffering or hypocritically distorts it by marketing the victim as a sentimentalized hero? Voyeurism is another outcome of construing suffering at a safe distance, without the social responsibility of real engagement. As this chapter illustrates, the three themes of this volume are so intimately interconnected that examination of one is merely a matter of relative emphasis. The other two are called forth as part of what might be termed the circle of social structural processes involved in continuity and transformation of everyday experience. That circle connects the stuff of humanistic and social science analysis—meanings, relationships, structures—to health and social policy. It also makes the moral and the political inseparable from the medical; the cultural processes of global social change that are altering health outcomes are also transmuting subjectivity, so that what we have, perhaps naively, taken to be panhuman existential conditions are changing too.

Mamphela Ramphele's autobiographical account, an analysis of the political uses to which the experiences of bereavement of political widows are put, examines a telling ethnographic instance of the appropriation of social suffering. Here, the dialectics of social life that remake the heterogeneity of private grief into homogenized stereotypes of public mourning are shown to damage women's experience. Neither programs of modernization nor the reinvention of tradition succeed in resolving a tension that comes close to an existential limit condition. In this essay and in others in this volume, the problem of suffering appears very different when we do away with the classic dualisms of social analysis. Suffering becomes a process of social mediation *and* transformation. It is experienced within nested contexts of embodiment: collective, intersubjective, individual. It absorbs into the body-self the moral world's contradictory obligations/rights and the norms/contestations of the body politic.

Margaret Lock reminds us of the profound diversity of what is fundamentally at stake in those different cultural nexuses that can generate and sustain greatly different responses to suffering. Thus, debates over the experience of dying and the definition of death in Japan and North America may be driven by certain of the same global processes of technological rationalization and political economy, yet they differ enormously owing to the particularities of history, religion, and local traditions of conceiving and doing biomedicine. As we "master" nature, Lock demonstrates, the form that suffering takes, the construction of needs and deficiencies, is actually created by the very technology designed to alleviate suffering. The cultural appropriation through technology of what was formerly taken as "natural," and therefore largely beyond our control, has changed our expectations about, for example, events such as birth, illness, and death. Increasingly we assume that the production of perfect babies, an extended life span, and the elimination of disease is within our grasp; anything short of this incites suffering. This tendency is particularly dangerous because such suffering is hypothetical and not grounded in either critical politics or everyday reality.

Lock's essay, and Allan Young's as well, builds upon an understanding of the infiltration of the concept of normality, under the rationalized bureaucratic apparatus of the modern state, from medicine into many other domains of ordinary life.[9] "People, behavior, states of affairs, diplomatic relations, molecules: all these may be normal or abnormal."[10] The concept of normality closes the gap between "is" and "ought." Two ideas are contained in our concept of the normal: preservation and amelioration. There can be little doubt that technologies applied today purportedly to reduce suffering, such as those aimed at controlling female reproductive physiology and the genome, are often at the same time designed to create or reassert the normal. The normal, instated through bureaucratized norms and institutional practices of regulating bodies and behavior, advances the bureaucratic state's quest for order, control,

and efficiency. Technical rationality excludes other forms of knowledge and practice by generalizing, quantifying, in a word, normalizing experiences (collective and personal). Besides medical discourse, legal, scientific, regulatory, and policy discourses carry the
technical rational weight of the modern and postmodern state.

Lock traces the normalization/pathologization of death and
transplantation; Young reviews the history of the pathological
memory as a cultural process for making people as much as for
constructing disease entities. Fear, Young shows, was central to the
kind of memory, person, and disorder being constructed at the turn
of the nineteenth century. And it is still central to the kind of
memory, person, and disorder being constructed in our own age of
posttraumatic stress. Death and fear point to the connections between politics and experience that lie at the very heart of social life,
connecting social memory and individual practice, suffering and
society. Increasingly, however, such "connecting" is accomplished
through bureaucratic mediation, which remakes suffering much as
it remakes social life. Medicine is a powerful bureaucratic trans-
former of the existential, the moral, the aesthetic, even the religious
sides of suffering. And in the 1990s, especially, the kind of bureaucratic transformation medicine enacts is to remake sufferers as con-
sumers and to transform death and fear into commercial stakes and
financial opportunities.

Paul Farmer's essay shows how the politics of culture and ethnicity can obscure the workings of poverty and international relations in the transmission of AIDS and tuberculosis in Haiti. Globally, poverty is the major risk factor for these disorders, as it is for
most other forms of social suffering. An unjust distribution of disease and health care characterizes both the old and the new world
order, and that gap between rich and poor is worsening. Health
gradients of premature mortality and excess morbidity separate
rich from poor, both between and within societies. Health policy
and social policy are inseparable. As Farmer's case histories also
disclose, the brutal local effects of global political and economic
forces coerce the moral economy of policies and programs as well
as the distribution of adversity and woe.

Farmer will not, however, allow political-economic analysis to
overwhelm and silence the local idioms in which human distress is
experienced. Rather, he argues that the immense pressure of the

global and the national on the local is the appropriate space for anthropological and clinical engagement with the social sources of human misery and with the social experiences of adversity such as that brought by AIDS, tuberculosis, infant mortality, and the abuse of those in extreme poverty.

The question of social suffering brings a stubbornly moral orientation to social analysis. It has been a foundational question for religions, political movements, the helping professions, and social policy. As David Morris observes in his review of its place and its uses in the Western literary tradition, suffering is about the voices (and silences) as well as the genres of moral communities that range from the local to the global. In a plot-centered view of suffering, Morris contends, the viewer is able to see how a matrix of related actions comes to bear upon an individual event. Both Morris and Farmer are impressed by a view of suffering that sees the historical injustices through which such individual events as hunger, sickness, and early mortality are produced in urban slums or among economically displaced rural peoples. For both Morris and Farmer, the reformulation of the meaning of suffering in liberation theology holds important lessons. Morris draws the conclusion that membership in a moral community gives direction to the way in which entitlements can be claimed: "We do not acknowledge the destruction of beings outside our moral community as suffering. . . . Within a moral community, we employ names like *martyr* or *hero* and inscribe the suffering of our own people within narratives of hallowed sacrifice and epic achievement." This leads Morris to call for an expansion of the borders of moral community so that we may extend recognition to those whose suffering is otherwise excluded (e.g., the enemy, the mad, the marginal, the foreign, the other).

Paul Farmer, on the other hand, sees a great danger in this move to extend the definition of suffering. His view stems in part from the perspective of a physician who must consider limited resources and hence must bring judgment to bear in deciding which persons are most deserving of these scarce resources. His view gains support from the dominant trend in the contemporary world, which sees justice as fair distribution of resources. As he states: "The capacity to suffer is, clearly, part of being human. But not all suffering is equal, in spite of pernicious and often self-serving identity politics

that suggest otherwise. . . . Careful assessment of severity is important, at least to physicians, who must practice triage and referral
daily."

While Farmer is surely correct to say that the physician who
must make decisions about the distribution of scarce resources
must also practice triage and ask which lives are worth spending
more resources to preserve, he may slip too easily into the position
that not all suffering is equal. The physician and eventually society
must struggle to decide who should be given priority for the use of
a limited number of dialysis machines, but they cannot conclude
that those denied the scarce resources are suffering *less*—only that
at the bedside or in the logic of societal judgment about priorities,
others are deemed likely to make better use of the scarce resources.
It is when principles of triage have been applied to populations considered useless or less capable of the human experience of suffering
that we see the truly pernicious consequences of a doctrine that re-
configures suffering to questions of resource allocation.[11] The principle of suffering that counts for less can be a slippery slope that,
even when it results from a deep commitment to social justice, creates inadvertent yet nonetheless dangerous moral slides.

Talal Asad's essay on misapplications of the liberal discourse on
pain, torture, and trauma in transcultural contexts shows how the
claims of moral community, once restricted by the political processes of colonialism and the postcolonial world order to posit a
liberalist Europe and a despotic other, selectively legitimate those
forms of pain that the state can inflict and those that are proscribed.
Modern torture, Asad summarizes, is not an "inseparable part of a
disciplinary society." What it is, he remarks, is "a practical logic
integral to the maintenance of the nation state's sovereignty" in the
bureaucratic arena of policing, where "national security" overrides
most other social values and legal rights. This practical logic becomes additionally sinister because the secretive cloak under which
torture is carried out creates a state of fear in everyday life.

Asad makes the strong claim not only that the philosophical
basis of the *Universal Declaration of Human Rights* is bound by
a culture and history which may (or may not) preclude its universal applicability but also that a fundamental hypocrisy exists in
eliminating punishments considered brutally inhuman while saying
nothing about practices such as war that result in massive imposi-

tion of pain and suffering on whole populations. That hypocrisy also underlies and perhaps grew out of the colonialist practice of imposing on colonized peoples "civilized standards of justice and humanity" as a new form of disciplinary effects, rather than as a means of relieving suffering and making life more bearable. Suffering was to be made useful for societal "progress." National interest, in the liberal convenant, can (and regularly does) legally endorse acts that lead to pain and trauma because, as the apex of societal values, national interest comes to define liberal modernity. Asad argues for analyzing on a case-by-case basis any society's political processes and its purported values and the contradictory policies that issue forth in order to understand the calculus of authority that sustains some manner of social suffering in nearly every society. He also argues for appreciation of the liberal implications for "policing" interpersonal relationships, where again, he shows, contradictory values and a hypocrisy of practice preside. Torture and social suffering exist, then, not because of the absence of modernity, but because of modernity's very tenets and technologies and tactics of bureaucratic order for asserting national interest. Yet, because that same program of modernity calls into question the indigenous "defense" of cultural practices of oppression as self-interested, we find irony as well as tragedy in the clash of symbolic-political programs of conservation and change.

National memories and nationalism are explored further in E. Valentine Daniel's essay on Tamil immigrants in the United Kingdom. In the politics of Tamil immigrant suffering, Daniel looks at what happens when the image of the nation is lost so that alienation from the political present is matched by alienation from the imagined past. In this moment, relations among immigrants from three different phases of migration are reshaped away from ethnic alliances to class-based ones. For Daniel, these three cohorts experience different "comportments," ways of being-in-the-world, in which national memory and nationalism lend very different degrees of existential support. Drawing from the phenomenological vocabulary that Heidegger innovated to access the "felt" quality of experience, Daniel interprets various types of chronic suffering—e.g., statelessness, double alienation—that immigrants and refugees experience as they are caught up in the political-moral-psychological processes of diasporic coping created by fundamental cultural transformations in their country of origin, in their host country, and in their own cohorts.[12] This meditation on suffering from perspectives in diaspora also will return readers to the theme of "indifference" by the host culture and its bureaucracies toward the cultural other and his or her search for affirmation.

Suffering is, of course, an absolutely central subject for theology. The last essay in this collection, "Religions, Society, and Suffering," is written by John Bowker, a long-term student of the comparative study of religion and the author of a major work on the problems suffering poses for the world's major religions.[13] Seeking to find a bridging language between the study of religion, medicine, and the social sciences, Bowker analogizes the approach to the human soma in medicine to somatic exegesis in religious writings. This analogy fosters an interdisciplinary language of a "network of constraints controlling eventualities into their outcomes" and producing instances of suffering.

Bowker sees the incorporation of issues such as poverty, inequality, violence, and social breakdown into medicine and public health as a movement that recovers a much wider experience of suffering, one that links the medical with the religious and that brings to the fore the hermeneutical tasks in both domains. "The exegeses of the somatic text," as Bowker puts it, also connect medicine and religion through "interrelatedness" as the social grounds of meaning-laden experience. World religions have been unwilling to isolate illness and other forms of suffering from this complex of social factors—relationships, meanings, the interrelatedness of somatic experiences. Medicine has lost its way in the recent past by denying the centrality of these connections. The socio-logic of "sets of constraints on eventualities and outcomes"—a response to sociodicy as much as theodicy—is a way of thinking that enables both religion and medicine to engage suffering in the broadest form of social experience. This, Bowker concludes, is the human grounds of experience (social and individual) where both fields should operate.

The essays in this book demonstrate that we have gone beyond the point where the subject of suffering can be examined as a single theme or a uniform experience.[14] That an abiding human concern about an interpersonal process also contributes to the definition of what being human is about means that suffering is profoundly *social* in the sense that it helps constitute the social world. That this social process carries an existential resonance today means that it is part of the constitution of *our* world. Social suffering possesses these meanings, among others. Our intention has been to deepen a conversation, from the perspectives of ethnography, social history, critical humanities, comparative religion, and social medicine, in order to come to a more complexly human understanding of the relationship of theory to policy. To engage human problems, we hold, is to engage this moral, political, and cultural nexus.

It is not that concern with discrete issues such as disease eradication, control of crime and violence, and intervention in poverty has been lacking in the administrative discourses of planning and policy or in the research that informs them. (Far from it!) But because of the manner in which knowledge and institutions are organized in the contemporary world as pragmatically oriented programs of welfare, health, social development, social justice, security, and so on, the phenomenon of suffering as an experiential domain of everyday social life has been splintered into measurable attributes. These attributes are then managed by bureaucratic institutions and expert cultures that reify the fragmentation while casting a veil of misrecognition over the domain as a whole (because if seen as a whole it would be too threatening?). As a result, neither a transsectoral framework of analysis nor interdisciplinary theories are made visible. By returning to the primacy of the phenomenological domain of experiences of suffering in a broad social context, we seek to show that what one expert defines as the object of health policy and another as the object of economic policy can and must be viewed in a frame that integrates these and yet other human problems—a frame that names a large domain of the sources, forms, and consequences of social life. In order to intervene in that domain, we need to ground responses, with the aid of social maps and social theories, in new and more humanly valid ways of refiguring the predicaments of our time.[15]

Arthur Kleinman
Veena Das
Margaret Lock

ENDNOTES

[1] Robert Desjarlais, Leon Eisenberg, Byron Good, and Arthur Kleinman, eds., *World Mental Health: Problems and Priorities in Low-Income Countries* (New York: Oxford University Press, 1995).

²Ibid.

³See, for example, Georges Canguilhem, *The Normal and the Pathological,* trans. Carolyn R. Fawcett and Robert S. Cohen (New York: Zone Books, 1989); Michel Foucault, *Discipline and Punish: The Birth of the Prison,* trans. Alan Sheridan (New York: Vintage, 1979); Ian Hacking, *The Taming of Chance* (Cambridge: Cambridge University Press, 1990).

⁴W. J. T. Mitchell, *Picture Theory: Essays on Verbal and Visual Representation* (Chicago, Ill.: University of Chicago Press, 1994), 421–25.

⁵Elaine Scarry, *The Body in Pain* (New York: Oxford University Press, 1985).

⁶Stanley Cavell, *Must We Mean What We Say?* (Cambridge: Cambridge University Press, 1976), 242–66.

⁷A. Jalal, *The Sole Spokesman: Jinnah, The Muslim League, and the Demand for Pakistan* (Cambridge: Cambridge University Press, 1985); S. Wolpert, *Jinnah of Pakistan* (Delhi: Oxford University Press, 1984); M. Hasan, ed., *India's Partition: Process, Strategy, and Mobilization* (Delhi: Oxford University Press, 1994).

⁸A. K. Gupta, ed., *Myth and Reality: The Struggle for Freedom in India* (Delhi: Oxford University Press, 1987); G. D. Khosla, *Stern Reckoning* (Delhi: Oxford University Press, 1989; first published in 1951); V. Das, *Critical Events: An Anthropological Perspective on Contemporary India* (Delhi: Oxford University Press, 1995), chap. 3.

⁹See the sources cited in note 3 above.

¹⁰Hacking, *The Taming of Chance,* 160.

¹¹See Anne Harrington's essay in this volume, 181–205. See also Daniel Jonah Goldhagen, *Hitler's Willing Executioners* (New York: Knopf, 1996).

¹²There is, of course, a troubling irony in making use of Heidegger's work in a book on social suffering, given Heidegger's pro-Nazi statements and actions as rector of a major German university under Hitler. That sad irony points us all toward the crucial discipline of self-reflective scrutiny as a critical strategy in ethnography. In Thomas Buckley's useful piece "Suffering in the Cultural Construction of Others: Robert Spott and A. L. Kroeber," *American Indian Quarterly* (Fall 1989): 437–45, we learn how a famous American ethnographer participated in this practice of indifference to the suffering of the other and the appropriation of local Amerindian voices, thereby denying the other's affirmation of self (personal and ethnic). In one sense, all writing about suffering is an appropriation for self-interested reasons. But the uses of suffering include giving testimony and assistance as well—a very different moral response. The complexities—moral and professional—of these antinomian human responses are illustrated in Arthur Kleinman and Joan Kleinman, "Suffering and Its Professional Transformation," *Culture, Medicine and Psychiatry* 15 (3) (1991): 275–301; and in Shoshana Feldman and Dori Laub, *Testimony* (New York and London: Routledge, 1991).

¹³John W. Bowker, *Problems of Suffering in Religions of the World* (Cambridge: Cambridge University Press, 1970).

¹⁴In the recent past, the dominant mode of representing suffering has come from medicine. Illness viewed as the contingent misfortune of an individual acutely

beset is the archetype. Without at all attempting to cover the variety of forms of suffering, we have chosen to emphasize catastrophes, chronic states, routinized misery, and direct abuse that result from the international political economy, state policies, bureaucratic practices, and cultural forces. We do this to change the object of inquiry and also to suggest that the medical archetype is seriously misleading. Indeed, it is so even for health problems such as cancer, heart disease, diarrheal disease, and depression, whose sources frequently are located (at least in part) in the social world and whose consequences have powerful effects there too, effects that stamp all chronic illnesses with a social course. But this is a topic that goes beyond the limits of this volume; see the Introduction in Arthur Kleinman, *Writing at the Margin: Discourse Between Anthropology and Medicine* (Berkeley, Calif.: University of California Press, 1996). For our purposes here, it is enough to emphasize the varieties of social suffering. By doing so, we do not seek to diminish attention to subjectivity and agency: suffering evokes individual lives. Instead, we wish to redirect the pathway to personal accounts so that their inextricable embeddedness in social context is highlighted. The relationship between the varieties of human misery and the varieties of subjective experiences is still a huge question for future work.

[15] The editors wish to thank Robin Root for her contribution to the descriptions of the essays by Asad, Daniel, and Bowker.

Arthur Kleinman and Joan Kleinman

The Appeal of Experience; The Dismay of Images: Cultural Appropriations of Suffering in Our Times

ORIENTATION

S UFFERING IS ONE OF THE EXISTENTIAL GROUNDS of human experience; it is a defining quality, a limiting experience in human
conditions.[1] It is also a master subject of our mediatized
times. Images of victims of natural disasters, political conflict,
forced migration, famine, substance abuse, the HIV pandemic,
chronic illnesses of dozens of kinds, crime, domestic abuse, and
the deep privations of destitution are everywhere. Video cameras
take us into the intimate details of pain and misfortune.

Images of suffering are appropriated to appeal emotionally and
morally both to global audiences and to local populations. Indeed,
those images have become an important part of the media. As
"infotainment" on the nightly news, images of victims are commercialized; they are taken up into processes of global marketing
and business competition. The existential appeal of human experiences, their potential to mobilize popular sentiment and collective
action, and even their capability to witness or offer testimony are
now available for gaining market share. Suffering, "though at a

*Arthur Kleinman is Maude and Lillian Presley Professor of Medical Anthropology, Chair-
man of the Department of Social Medicine, and Professor of Psychiatry at Harvard
Medical School; and Professor of Anthropology at Harvard University.*

*Joan Kleinman, a sinologist, is Research Associate, Medical Anthropology Program at
Harvard University.*

1

distance," as the French sociologist Luc Boltanski tellingly expresses it, is routinely appropriated in American popular culture, which is a leading edge of global popular culture.[2] This globalization of suffering is one of the more troubling signs of the cultural transformations of the current era: troubling because experience is being used as a commodity, and through this cultural representation of suffering, experience is being remade, thinned out, and distorted.

It is important to avoid essentializing, naturalizing, or sentimentalizing suffering. There is no single way to suffer; there is no timeless or spaceless universal shape to suffering. There are communities in which suffering is devalued and others in which it is endowed with the utmost significance. The meanings and modes of the experience of suffering have been shown by historians and anthropologists alike to be greatly diverse.[3] Individuals do not suffer in the same way, any more than they live, talk about what is at stake, or respond to serious problems in the same ways. Pain is perceived and expressed differently, even in the same community.[4] Extreme forms of suffering—survival from the Nazi death camps or the Cambodian catastrophe—are not the same as the "ordinary" experiences of poverty and illness.[5]

We can speak of suffering as a social experience in at least two ways that are relevant to this essay: *1)* Collective modes of experience shape individual perceptions and expressions. Those collective modes are visible patterns of how to undergo troubles, and they are taught and learned, sometimes openly, often indirectly. *2)* Social interactions enter into an illness experience (for example, a family dealing with the dementia of a member with Alzheimer's disease or a close network grieving for a member with terminal cancer). As these examples suggest, relationships and interactions take part, sometimes a central part, in the experience of suffering.[6] Both aspects of social experience—its collective mode and intersubjective processes—can be shown to be reshaped by the distinctive cultural meanings of time and place. Cultural representations, authorized by a moral community and its institutions, elaborate different modes of suffering. Yet, local differences—in gender, age group, class, ethnicity, and, of course, subjectivity—as well as the penetration of global processes into local worlds make this social influence partial and complex.

It is this aspect of suffering that this essay addresses by way of an analysis of the cultural and political processes that contribute to professional appropriations of suffering, processes that have important moral implications. To what uses are experiences of suffering put? What are the consequences of those cultural practices for understanding and responding to human problems? And what are the more general implications of the cultural appropriations of suffering for human experience, including human experiences of suffering?

PROFESSIONAL APPROPRIATIONS OF THE IMAGES OF SUFFERING: PHOTOJOURNALISM AND PUBLIC HEALTH

Source: Kevin Carter, *The New York Times*, 26 March 1993. © 1993 by Sygma.

This photograph won a Pulitzer Prize for *The New York Times*. In the April 13, 1994 issue of the *Times*, there was a full-page advertisement taken out by the *Times'* owners in recognition of the three Pulitzer Prizes that it won that year. The *Times* described this award-winning picture in the following way:

> To *The New York Times*, for Kevin Carter's photograph of a vulture perching near a little girl in the Sudan who has collapsed from hunger, a picture that became an icon of starvation.

When the photograph first appeared, it accompanied a story of the famine that has once again resulted from political violence and the chaos of civil war in the southern Sudan.[7] The *Times'* self-congratulatory account fails to adequately evoke the image's shocking effect. The child is hardly larger than an infant; she is naked; she appears bowed over in weakness and sickness, incapable, it would seem, of moving; she is unprotected. No mother, no family, no one is present to prevent her from being attacked by the vulture, or succumbing to starvation and then being eaten. The image suggests that she has been abandoned. Why? The reader again is led to imagine various scenarios of suffering: she has been lost in the chaos of forced uprooting; her family has died; she has been deserted near death in order for her mother to hold on to more viable children. The image's great success is that it causes the reader to want to know more. Why is this innocent victim of civil war and famine unprotected? The vulture embodies danger and evil, but the greater dangers and real forces of evil are not in the "natural world"; they are in the political world, including those nearby in army uniforms or in government offices in Khartoum. Famine has become a political strategy in the Sudan.[8]

The photograph has been reprinted many times, and it has been duplicated in advertisements for a number of nongovernmental aid agencies that are raising funds to provide food to refugees. This is a classic instance of the use of moral sentiment to mobilize support for social action. One cannot look at this picture without wanting to do something to protect the child and drive the vulture away. Or, as one aid agency puts it, to prevent other children from succumbing in the same heartlessly inhuman way by giving a donation.

The photograph calls for words to answer other questions. How did Carter allow the vulture to get so close without doing something to protect the child? What did he do after the picture was taken? Was it in some sense posed? Inasmuch as Kevin Carter chose to take the time, minutes that may have been critical at this point when she is near death, to compose an effective picture rather than to save the child, is he complicit?

Those moral questions particular to Carter's relationship (or nonrelationship) to the dying child were only intensified when, on July 29, 1994, a few months after the Pulitzer Prize announcement, *The New York Times* ran an obituary for Kevin Carter, who had committed suicide at age thirty-three. That shocking notice of his death, written by Bill Keller, the *Times'* Johannesburg correspondent, as well as a longer article by Scott Mac Leod in *Time* magazine on September 12, reported Carter's clarifications about how he took the photograph and what followed:[9]

> ...he wandered into the open bush. He heard a soft, high-pitched whimpering and saw a tiny girl trying to make her way to the feeding center. As he crouched to photograph her, a vulture landed in view. Careful not to disturb the bird, he positioned himself for the best possible image. He would later say he waited about 20 minutes, hoping the vulture would spread its wings. It did not, and after he took his photographs, he chased the bird away and watched as the little girl resumed her struggle. Afterwards he sat under a tree, lit a cigarette, talked to God and cried. He was depressed afterward. . . .He kept saying he wanted to hug his daughter.[10]

The *Times'* obituary ends with a section entitled "The Horror of the Work," in which Jimmy Carter, Kevin's father, observes that his son "Always carried around the horror of the work he did." Keller implies that it was the burden of this "horror" that may have driven Carter to suicide. The article by Scott Mac Leod in *Time* shows that Kevin Carter had lived a very troubled life, with drug abuse, a messy divorce, deep financial problems, brushes with the police, and was a manic-depressive. We also learn that he had spent much of his career photographing political repression and violence in South Africa, and that he had been deeply affected by the shooting of his best friend and coworker, Ken Oosterbrock, for whom, he told friends, he "should have taken the bullet."[11] His suicide note, besides mentioning these other problems, comes back to the theme of the burden of horror: "I am haunted by the vivid memories of killings and corpses and anger and pain. . .of starving or wounded children, of trigger-happy madmen, often police, of killer executioners. . . . "[12]

From Scott Mac Leod we also learn that Carter had been present at the execution of right-wing paramilitary men in Bophuthatswana; much to his annoyance he had missed the master image snapped by his colleagues of a white mercenary pleading for his life before being executed—a picture that also was reprinted by newspapers around the globe. The article in *Time* reports that Carter was painfully aware of the photojournalist's dilemma:

> "I had to think visually," he said once, describing a shoot-out. "I am zooming in on a tight shot of the dead guy and a splash of red. Going into his khaki uniform in a pool of blood in the sand. The dead man's face is slightly grey. You are making a visual here. But inside something is screaming, 'My God.' But it is time to work. Deal with the rest later. . . ."[13]

Time magazine's writer discovered that some journalists questioned Carter's ethics: "The man adjusting his lens to take just the right frame of her suffering. . .might just as well be a predator, another vulture on the scene." Scott Mac Leod notes that even some of Carter's friends "wondered aloud why he had not helped the girl."[14]

It is easy to moralize about how Carter's professional success was a result of his failure to act humanely. To balance the account, we need to remember that many photographers and journalists have been killed this year covering some of the more violent political conflicts around the world. "Hardly career advancement," cautioned Bill Kovach, Curator of Harvard's Nieman Foundation, in response to an earlier version of this paper. Kevin Carter's career is as much a story of courage and professionalism as it is a tale of moral failure. Moreover, the photograph he created provided political testimony and drove people to act. Photojournalists, like Kevin Carter, contribute to a global humanitarian effort to prevent silence. That is a considerable contribution.

Having learned about Carter's suicide, the prize-winning image, an anonymously public icon of suffering at a distance, becomes part of close experience. Kevin Carter is transformed from a name on the side of the photograph to a narrative, a story that is emplotted with a classic example of Joseph Conrad's depiction of Africa as the heart of darkness, the site of social horror. Carter becomes a subject in the cultural story his photograph helped write by being transformed, infected more than affected, by what he had to bear.

But what of the horrors experienced by the little Sudanese girl, who is given neither a name nor a local moral world? The tension of uncertainty is unrelieved. Only now, with the story of Carter's suicide, the suffering of the representer and the represented interfuses. Professional representation as well as popular interpretations would have us separate the two: one a powerless local victim, the other a powerful foreign professional.[15] Yet, the account of Carter's suicide creates a more complex reality. The disintegration of the subject/object dichotomy implicates us all. The theories of a variety of academic professions may help explain how Carter got us into this situation of bringing the global into the local, but they fail to explain how we will get ourselves out of the moral complexities he has intensified for us by projecting the local into the global.[16] We are left only with the unsentimentalized limits of the human condition—a silence seemingly without meaning, possibly without solace. And still the world calls for images: the mixture of moral failures and global commerce is here to stay.[17]

Without disputing the photograph's immense achievement, it is useful to explore its moral and political assumptions.[18] There is, for example, the unstated idea that this group of unnamed Africans (are they Nuer or Dinka?) cannot protect their own. They must be protected, as well as represented, by others. The image of the subaltern conjures up an almost neocolonial ideology of failure, inadequacy, passivity, fatalism, and inevitability.[19] Something must be done, and it must be done soon, but *from outside* the local setting. The authorization of action through an appeal for foreign aid, even foreign intervention, begins with an evocation of indigenous absence, an erasure of local voices and acts.

Suffering is presented as if it existed free of local people and local worlds. The child is alone. This, of course, is not the way that disasters, illnesses, and deaths are usually dealt with in African or other non-Western societies, or, for that matter, in the West. Yet, the image of famine is culturally represented in an ideologically Western mode: it becomes the experience of a lone individual.[20] The next step, naturally, is to assume that there are no local institutions or programs. That assumption almost invariably leads to the development of regional or national policies that are imposed on local worlds. When those localities end up resisting or not complying with policies and programs that are meant to assist them, such acts are then labeled irrational or self-destructive. The local world is deemed incompetent, or worse.

This may seem too thoroughgoing a critique. Clearly, witnessing and mobilization can do good, but they work best when they take seriously the complexity of local situations and work through local institutions. Moral witnessing also must involve a sensitivity to other, unspoken moral and political assumptions. Watching and reading about suffering, especially suffering that exists some-where else, has, as we have already noted, become a form of entertainment. Images of trauma are part of our political economy. Papers are sold, television programs gain audience share, careers are advanced, jobs are created, and prizes are awarded through the appropriation of images of suffering. Kevin Carter won the Pulitzer Prize, but his victory, substantial as it was, was won because of the misery (and probable death) of a nameless little girl. That more dubious side of the appropriation of human misery in the globalization of cultural processes is what must be addressed.

One message that comes across from viewing suffering from a distance is that for all the havoc in Western society, we are some-how better than this African society. We gain in moral status and some of our organizations gain financially and politically, while those whom we represent, or appropriate, remain where they are, moribund, surrounded by vultures. This "consumption" of suffer-ing in an era of so-called "disordered capitalism" is not so very different from the late nineteenth-century view that the savage barbarism in pagan lands justified the valuing of our own civiliza-tion at a higher level of development—a view that authorized colonial exploitation. Both are forms of cultural representation in which the moral, the commercial, and the political are deeply involved in each other. The point is that the image of the vulture and the child carries cultural entailments, including the brutal historical genealogy of colonialism as well as the dubious cultural baggage of the more recent programs of "modernization" and globalization (of markets and financing), that have too often wors-ened human problems in sub-Saharan Africa.[21]

Another effect of the postmodern world's political and eco-nomic appropriation of images of such serious forms of suffering at a distance is that it has desensitized the viewer. Viewers are overwhelmed by the sheer number of atrocities. There is too much to see, and there appears to be too much to do anything about. Thus, our epoch's dominating sense that complex problems can be neither understood nor fixed works with the massive globalization of images of suffering to produce moral fatigue, exhaustion of empathy, and political despair.

The appeal of experience is when we see on television a wounded Haitian, surrounded by a threatening crowd, protesting accusations that he is a member of a murderous paramilitary organization. The dismay of images is when we are shown that the man and the crowd are themselves surrounded by photographers, whose participation helps determine the direction the event will take.[22] The appeal of experience and the dismay of images fuse together in Kevin Carter's photograph, and in the story of his suicide. The photograph is a professional transformation of social life, a politically relevant rhetoric, a constructed form that ironically naturalizes experience. As Michael Shapiro puts it,

> . . .representation is the absence of presence, but because the real is never wholly present to us—how it is real for us is always mediated through some representational practice—we lose something when we think of representation as mimetic. What we lose, in general, is insight into the institutions and actions and episodes through which the real has been fashioned, a fashioning that has not been so much a matter of immediate acts of consciousness by persons in everyday life as it has been a historically developing kind of imposition, now largely institutionalized in the prevailing kinds of meanings deeply inscribed on things, persons, and structures.[23]

This cultural process of professional and political transformation is crucial to the way we come to appreciate human problems and to prepare policy responses. That appreciation and preparation far too often are part of the problem; they become iatrogenic.

PATHOLOGIZING SOCIAL SUFFERING

When those whose suffering is appropriated by the media cross over to places of refuge and safety, they often must submit to yet another type of arrogation.[24] Their memories (their intimately interior images) of violation are made over into *trauma stories*. These trauma stories then become the currency, the symbolic capital, with which they enter exchanges for physical resources and achieve the status of political refugee. Increasingly, those complicated stories, based in real events, yet reduced to a core cultural image of *victimization* (a postmodern hallmark), are used by health professionals to rewrite social experience in medical terms. The person who undergoes torture first becomes a victim, an image of innocence and passivity, someone who cannot represent himself, who must be represented. Then he becomes a patient, specifically a patient with a quintessential fin de siècle disorder (i.e., posttraumatic stress disorder).[25] Indeed, to receive even modest public assistance it may be necessary to undergo a sequential transformation from one who experiences, who suffers political terror to one who is a victim of political violence to one who is sick, who has a disease. Because of the practical political and financial importance of such transformations, the violated themselves may want, and even seek out, the re-imaging of their condition so that they can obtain the moral as well as the financial benefits of being ill. We need to ask, however, what kind of cultural process underpins the transformation of a victim of violence to someone with a pathology? What does it mean to give those traumatized by political violence the social status of a patient? And in what way does the imagery of victimization as the pathology of an individual alter the experience—collective as well as individual—so that its lived meaning as moral and political memory, perhaps even resistance, is lost and is replaced by "guilt," "paranoia," and a "failure to cope"?

There is an uncomfortable irony here. There is an uncanny and unnecessary correlation between the aesthetics of murder in Guatemala, Rwanda, and Bosnia and the way in which those deaths are reported in the news. We are shown close-ups of limbs blown off by mortars and landmines. In low intensity warfare directed at terrorizing populations, people are not just killed; they are hacked into pieces, blown up, torn apart, burned, and broken. And all the details are dramatically displayed for us. Thus, the cultural capital of trauma victims—their wounds, their scars, their tragedy—is appropriated by the same popular codes through which physical and sexual violence are commodified, sold in the cinema, marketed as pornography, and used by tabloids and novelists to attract readers. Spectacular forms of trauma from abroad hold another significance as well: they consume our interest and deflect attention from routinized misery at home.

The aesthetization of child sexual abuse is another case in point. Appearing in *The New York Times* of April 9, 1993 was a picture of a child prostitute in the red-light district of old Dhaka, Bangladesh. The prepubescent girl is shown bare-chested, wearing a Lolita smile, a tousled adult hairstyle, many bangles on her arms, earrings, and a necklace. Behind her small, thin figure looms someone who appears to be her brothel-keeper, grim, mustached, one hand near his groin. Behind them are the filthy walls of an alley; another prostitute or a customer stands off to one side. The accompanying story is titled, "The Sex Market: Scourge on the World's Children." Outside the context of a major newspaper, this picture would qualify as child pornography. The purpose of the picture and the accompanying story is to expose the degradation of child prostitution, a phenomenon greatly increasing in the era of AIDS. But the picture simultaneously appeals, probably not entirely without intention, to a prurient sensibility. It is clearly not enough to picture a child's body for sale; the picture needs to recreate the atmosphere of sexual desire. Thus, the media, by the success of its artistry, gets caught up in the very processes it seeks to criticize.

We now turn to explore a different form of the transformation of social suffering. In recent years, experts in international health and social development, for very appropriate reasons, have sought to develop new ways of configuring the human misery that results from chronic disease and disability. Faced with the problem of increasing numbers of cases of chronic illness—diabetes, heart disease, cancer, asthma, depression, schizophrenia—as populations live long enough to experience degenerative diseases and other health conditions of later life, health professionals have realized that mortality rates are unable to represent the distress, disablement, and especially the *cost* of these conditions. Therefore, they have sought to construct new metrics to measure the suffering from chronic illness, which in medical and public health argot is called "morbidity." These metrics can be applied, the experts claim, to measure the burden of suffering in "objective" terms that can enable the just allocation of resources to those most in need.[26]

One metric of suffering recently developed by the World Bank has gained wide attention and considerable support.[27] *Image II* describes what the World Bank's health economists mean by the term Disability Adjusted Life Years (DALYs). *Table 1* shows the result of the application of DALYs to measure the cost of suffering from illnesses globally. It emphasizes the significant percentage of loss in DALYs due to mental health problems. This finding, one would suppose, should help make the case for giving mental health problems—suicide, mental illnesses, trauma due to violence, substance abuse—higher priority so that greater resources can be applied to them. In fact, the cost of mental health problems are placed by the World Bank in the discretionary category so that the state is not held responsible for that burden. This is a serious problem that requires fundamental change in the way suffering from mental health problems is prioritized by the World Bank. But here we ask a different question: What kind of cultural representation and professional appropriation of suffering is this?

Image II. Disability Adjusted Life Years

The World Bank's estimates of lost years of quality life hinges on the concept of Disability Adjusted Life Years (DALYs), which is a measure of the burden produced by specific diseases; it combines the impact of the premature deaths and of the disablements that result from those diseases. In taking death at a given age into account, the number of *years of life lost* is evaluated by using the expectation of life remaining at that age to individuals in low mortality countries. Years of life do not have the same value throughout the life span; thus, most people value a year in their twenties as worth three or four times what a year in the eighties is worth. This differential evaluation is taken into account in the calculation. To measure the disability resulting from disease, each surviving year is modified according to the expected *duration* and *severity* of the disability. Duration is simply the years (or fractions thereof) that the disability lasts. Severity represents the comparative disadvantage of a given handicap on a scale from 0, for perfect health, to 1, for death. For example, expert panels have rated blindness at a severity of 0.6, and disease of the female reproductive system at a severity of 0.22. Losses from death and disability are combined. In calculating DALYs, the formula takes into account the age at which the specific disease is acquired, the years of life expectancy lost (and the relative value of those years), and the years compromised by handicap.

Source: Robert Desjarlais et al., *World Mental Health: Problems and Priorities in Low-Income Countries* (New York: Oxford University Press, 1995), 295.

Table 1. Distribution of DALY Loss by Cause and Demographic
Region, 1990 (percent)

Cause	World	Sub-Saharan Africa	India	China	Other Asia & Islands	Latin America & Caribbean	Middle Eastern Crescent	Former Socialist Economies of Europe	Established Market Economies
Population (millions)	5,267.0	510.0	850.0	1,134.0	683.0	444.0	603.0	346.0	798.0
Noncommunicable diseases	*42.2%*	*19.4%*	*40.4%*	*68.0%*	*40.1%*	*42.8%*	*36.0%*	*74.8%*	*78.4%*
Neuropsychiatric disease	6.8	3.3	6.1	8.0	7.0	8.0	6.6	11.1	16.0
Cancer	5.8	1.5	4.1	9.2	4.4	6.2	3.4	14.8	19.1
Nutritional deficiencies	3.9	2.8	6.2	3.3	4.6	4.6	3.7	1.4	1.7
Cerebrovascular disease	3.2	1.5	2.1	6.3	2.1	2.6	2.4	8.8	6.3
Ischemic heart disease	3.1	0.4	2.8	2.1	3.5	2.7	1.8	13.7	10.0
Pulmonary obstruction	1.3	0.2	0.6	6.6	0.5	0.7	0.6	1.6	1.7
Other	18.0	9.7	18.5	23.6	17.9	19.1	18.7	23.4	26.6
Injuries	*11.9%*	*9.3%*	*9.1%*	*16.7%*	*11.3%*	*16.0%*	*13.0%*	*16.6%*	*11.9%*
Motor vehicle	2.3	1.3	1.1	2.3	2.3	5.7	3.3	3.7	3.6
Intentional	3.7	4.2	1.2	6.1	3.2	4.3	6.2	4.8	4.0
Other	5.9	3.9	6.8	9.3	5.8	6.0	4.6	8.1	4.3
Communicable diseases	*45.8%*	*71.3%*	*50.3%*	*25.3%*	*48.6%*	*42.2%*	*51.0%*	*8.6%*	*9.7%*
Tuberculosis	3.4	4.7	3.7	2.9	6.1	2.5	2.8	0.6	0.2
STDs & HIV	3.8	8.8	2.7	1.7	1.6	6.6	0.7	1.2	3.4
Diarrhea	7.3	10.2	9.6	2.1	8.3	5.7	10.7	0.4	0.3
Vaccine-preventable childhood infections	5.0	9.6	6.7	0.9	4.5	1.6	6.0	0.1	0.1
Malaria	2.6	10.8	0.3		1.4	0.4	0.2		
Worm infections	1.8	1.8	0.9	3.4	3.4	2.5	0.4		
Respiratory infections	9.0	10.8	10.9	6.4	11.1	6.2	11.6	2.6	2.6
Maternal causes	2.2	2.7	2.7	1.2	2.5	1.7	2.9	0.8	0.6
Perinatal causes	7.3	7.1	9.1	5.2	7.4	9.1	10.9	2.4	2.2
Other	3.5	4.6	4.0	1.4	3.3	6.8	4.9	0.6	0.5
Total	*100.0%*	*100.0%*	*100.0%*	*100.0%*	*100.0%*	*100.0%*	*100.0%*	*100.0%*	*100.0%*
DALYs (millions)	1,362.0	293.0	292.0	201.0	177.0	103.0	144.0	68.0	94.0
Equivalent infant deaths (millions)	42.0	9.0	9.0	6.2	6.5	3.2	4.4	1.8	2.9
DALYs per 1000 population	259.0	575.0	344.0	178.0	260.0	233.0	286.0	168.0	117.0

Source: Adapted from World Bank, *World Development Report 1993: Investing in Health* (New York: Oxford University Press, 1993), 27.

This metric of suffering was constructed by assigning degrees of suffering to years of life and types of disability. The assumption is that values will be universal. They will not vary across worlds as greatly different as China, India, sub-Saharan Africa, and North America. They will also be reducible to measures of economic cost. That expert panels rate blindness with a severity of 0.6, while female reproductive system disorders are evaluated at one third the severity is surely a cause for questioning whether gender bias is present, but more generally it should make one uneasy with the means by which evaluations of severity and its cost can be validly standardized across different societies, social classes, age cohorts, genders, ethnicities, and occupational groups.

The effort to develop an objective indicator may be important for rational choice concerning allocation of scarce resources among different policies and programs. (It certainly should support the importance of funding mental health programs, even though as it is presently used in the World Bank's *World Development Report* it does not lead to this conclusion.) But it is equally important to question what are the limits and the potential dangers of configuring social suffering as an economic indicator. The moral and political issues we have raised in this essay cannot be made to fit into this econometric index. Likewise, the index is unable to map cultural, ethnic, and gender differences. Indeed, it assumes homogeneity in the evaluation and response to illness experiences, which belies an enormous amount of anthropological, historical, and clinical evidence of substantial differences in each of these domains.[28] Professional categories are privileged over lay categories, yet the experience of illness is expressed in lay terms.

Furthermore, the index focuses on the individual sufferer, denying that suffering is a social experience. This terribly thin representation of a thickly human condition may in time also thin out the social experience of suffering. It can do this by becoming part of the apparatus of cultural representation that creates societal norms, which in turn shapes the social role and social behavior of the ill, and what should be the practices of families and health-care providers. The American cultural rhetoric, for example, is changing from the language of caring to the language of efficiency and cost; it is not surprising to hear patients themselves use this rhetoric to describe their problems. Thereby, the illness experience, for some, may be transformed from a consequential moral experience into a merely technical inexpediency.

This slow transmutation of experience is what Czeslaw Milosz, himself a refugee from political violence, presses us to come to grips with in taken-for-granted cultural processes of representation in the popular culture that infiltrate the ordinary practices of living:

> Almost every day, Public Television airs nature programs mainly for young people. About spiders, fish, lizards, coyotes, animals of the desert or of alpine meadows, and so on. The technical excellence of the photography doesn't prevent me from considering these programs obscene. Because what they show offends our human, moral understanding—not only offends it, but subverts it, for the thesis of these programs is: You see, that's how it is Nature; therefore, it is natural; and we, too, are a part of Nature, we belong to the evolutionary chain, and we have to accept the world as it is. If I turn off the television, horrified, disgusted by the images of mutual indifferent devouring. . .is it because I am capable of picturing what this looks like when translated into the life of human society? But the children, those millions of young minds, are they able to watch this with impunity since they don't associate anything with the blind cruelty of Nature? Or, without realizing it, are they being slowly and systematically poisoned by those masters of photography who also do not know what they are doing?[29]

DALYs and other economic indexes of health conditions have their appropriate uses, of course. We need to formulate health and social policy with respect to priorities for limited resources. We need valid economic indexes of illnesses and their social consequences. DALYs can be useful in health-care reform and public health planning. Yet, economic indexes should not become, as they seemed in much of the recent debate on health-care reform in the United States, the only authorized construction of suffering for policy and programs. These economic measures need to be complemented by narratives, ethnographies, and social histories that speak to the complex, even contradictory, human side of suffering. Absent this other side, the economistic measurement of suffering leaves out most of what is at stake for peoples globally.

ABSENT IMAGES: THE POLITICAL RHETORIC OF OPPRESSION

It is necessary to balance the account of the globalization of commercial and professional images with a vastly different and even more dangerous cultural process of appropriation: the totalitarian state's erasure of social experiences of suffering through the suppression of images. Here the possibility of moral appeal through images of human misery is prevented, and it is their absence that is the source of existential dismay.

Such is the case with the massive starvation in China from 1959 to 1961. This story was not reported at the time even though more than thirty million Chinese died in the aftermath of the ruinous policies of the Great Leap Forward, the perverse effect of Mao's impossible dream of forcing immediate industrialization on peasants. Accounts of this, the world's most devastating famine, were totally suppressed; no stories or pictures of the starving or the dead were published.

An internal report on the famine was made by an investigating team for the Central Committee of the Chinese Communist Party. It was based on a detailed survey of an extremely poor region of Anwei Province that was particularly brutally affected. The report includes this numbing statement by Wei Wu-ji, a local peasant leader from Anwei:

> Originally there were 5,000 people in our commune, now only 3,200 remain. When the Japanese invaded we did not lose this many: we at least could save ourselves by running away! This year there's no escape. We die shut up in our own houses. Of my 6 family members, 5 are already dead, and I am left to starve, and I'll not be able to stave off death for long.[30]

Wei Wu-ji continued:

> Wang Jia-feng from West Springs County reported that cases of eating human meat were discovered. Zhang Sheng-jiu said, "Only an evil man could do such a thing!" Wang Jia-feng said, "In 1960, there were 20 in our household, ten of them died last year. My son told his mother 'I'll die of hunger in a few days.'" And indeed he did.[31]

The report also includes a graphic image by Li Qin-ming, from Wudian County, Shanwang Brigade:

In 1959, we were prescheduled to deliver 58,000 jin of grain to the State, but only 35,000 jin were harvested, hence we only turned over 33,000 jin, which left 2,000 jin for the commune. We really have nothing to eat. The peasants eat hemp leaves, anything they can possibly eat. In my last report after I wrote, "We have nothing to eat," the Party told me they wanted to remove my name from the Party Roster. Out of a population of 280, 170 died. In our family of five, four of us have died leaving only myself. Should I say that I'm not broken hearted?[32]

Chen Zhang-yu, from Guanyu County, offered the investigators this terrible image:

> Last spring the phenomenon of cannibalism appeared. Since Comrade Chao Wu-chu could not come up with any good ways of prohibiting it, he put out the order to secretly imprison those who seemed to be at death's door to combat the rumors. He secretly imprisoned 63 people from the entire country. Thirty-three died in prison.[33]

The official report is thorough and detailed. It is classified *neibu*, restricted use only. To distribute it is to reveal state secrets. Presented publicly it would have been, especially if it had been published in the 1960s, a fundamental critique of the Great Leap, and a moral and political delegitimation of the Chinese Communist Party's claim to have improved the life of poor peasants. Even today the authorities regard it as dangerous. The official silence is another form of appropriation. It prevents public witnessing. It forges a secret history, an act of political resistance through keeping alive the memory of things denied.[34] The totalitarian state rules by collective forgetting, by denying the collective experience of suffering, and thus creates a culture of terror.

The absent image is also a form of political appropriation; public silence is perhaps more terrifying than being overwhelmed by public images of atrocity. Taken together the two modes of appropriation delimit the extremes in this cultural process.[35]

CODA

Our critique of appropriations of suffering that do harm does not mean that no appropriations are valid. To conclude that would be to undermine any attempt to respond to human misery. It would be much more destructive than the problem we have identified; it would paralyze social action. We must draw upon the images of human suffering in order to identify human needs and to craft humane responses.

Yet, to do so, to develop valid appropriations, we must first make sure that the biases of commercial emphasis on profit-making, the partisan agendas of political ideologies, and the narrow technical interests that serve primarily professional groups are understood and their influence controlled. The first action, then, is critical self-reflection on the purposes of policies and the effects of programs. We take that to be a core component of programs of ethics in the professions. Perhaps a more difficult action is to lift the veil on the taken-for-granted cultural processes within which those policies and programs, no matter how well intended, are inevitably, and usually unintentionally, taken up and exploited. The idea that the first impulse of social and health-policy experts should be to historicize the issue before them and to critique the cultural mechanisms of action at hand goes against the grain of current practice. Nonetheless, that is a chief implication of our analysis. The starting point of policymakers and program builders needs to be the understanding that they can (and often unwillingly do) do harm. Because that potential for harm lies latent in the institutional structures that have been authorized to respond to human problems, that work behind even the best intentioned professionals, "experts" must be held responsible to define how those latent institutional effects can be controlled.

Humanizing the level at which interventions are organized means focusing planning and evaluation on the interpersonal space of suffering, the local, ethnographic context of action. This requires not only engagement with what is at stake for participants in those local worlds, but bringing those local participants (not merely national experts) into the process of developing and assessing programs. Such policy-making from the ground up can only succeed, however, if these local worlds are more effectively projected into national and international discourses on human problems. (This may represent the necessary complement to the globalization of local images. Perhaps it should be called the global representation of local contexts.) To do so requires a reformulation of the indexes and instruments of policy. Those analytic tools need to authorize deeper depictions of the local (including how the global—e.g., displacement, markets, technology—enters into the local). And those methodologies of policy must engage the existential side of social life. How to reframe the language of policies and programs so that large-scale social forces are made to relate to biography and local history will require interdisciplinary engagements that bring alternative perspectives from the humanities, the social sciences, and the health sciences to bear on human problems. The goal is to reconstruct the object of inquiry and the purposes of practice.

Ultimately, we will have to engage the more ominous aspects of globalization, such as the commercialization of suffering, the commodification of experiences of atrocity and abuse, and the pornographic uses of degradation.[36] Violence in the media, and its relation to violence in the streets and in homes, is already a subject that has attracted serious attention from communities and from scholars.[37] Regarding the even more fundamental cultural question of how social experience is being transformed in untoward ways, the first issue would seem to be to develop historical, ethnographic, and narrative studies that provide a more powerful understanding of the cultural processes through which the global regime of disordered capitalism alters the connections between collective experience and subjectivity, so that moral sensibility, for example, diminishes or becomes something frighteningly different: promiscuous, gratuitous, unhinged from responsibility and action.[38] There is a terrible legacy here that needs to be contemplated. The transformation of epochs is as much about changes in social experience as shifts in social structures and cultural representations; indeed, the three sites of social transformation are inseparable. Out of their triangulation, subjectivity too transmutes. The current transformation is no different; yet perhaps we see more clearly the hazards of the historical turn that we are now undertaking. Perhaps all along we have been wrong to consider existential conditions as an ultimate constraint limiting the moral dangers of civilizational change.

> At the end of this century it has for the first time become possible to
> see what a world may be like in which the past, including the past

in the present, has lost its role, in which the old maps and charts which guided human beings, singly and collectively, through life no longer represent the landscape through which we move, the sea on which we sail. In which we do not know where our journey is taking us, or even ought to take us.[39]

ENDNOTES

[1]This essay is drawn from a larger project concerning the social experience of suffering. Readers may wish to read Arthur Kleinman and Joan Kleinman, "Suffering and its Professional Transformation," *Culture, Medicine and Psychiatry* 15 (3) (1991): 275–301; Arthur Kleinman, "Pain and Resistance," in Mary-Jo DelVecchio Good et al., eds., *Pain as Human Experience: Anthropological Perspectives* (Berkeley, Calif.: University of California Press, 1991), 169–97; Arthur Kleinman et al., "The Social Course of Epilepsy in China," *Social Science and Medicine* 40 (10) (1995): 1319–330; Arthur Kleinman and Joan Kleinman, "How Bodies Remember: Social Memory and Bodily Experience of Criticism, Resistance, and Delegitimation following China's Cultural Revolution," *New Literary History* 25 (1994): 707–23; and Arthur Kleinman, *Writing at the Margin: Discourse Between Anthropology and Medicine* (Berkeley, Calif.: University of California Press, 1995).

[2]Luc Boltanski, *La Souffrance a Distance* (Paris: Metailie, 1993).

[3]On the heterogeneity of meanings and modes of suffering, see, for example, John Bowker, *Problems of Suffering in Religions of the World* (Cambridge: Cambridge University Press, 1970); Veena Das, "Moral Orientations to Suffering," in L. C. Chen, N. Ware, and A. Kleinman, eds., *Health and Social Change* (Cambridge, Mass.: Harvard University Press, 1994), 139–67; Arthur Kleinman, *The Illness Narratives: Suffering, Healing and Human Experience* (New York: Basic Books, 1988); Arthur Kleinman and Byron Good, eds., *Culture and Depression: Studies in the Anthropology and Cross-Cultural Psychiatry of Affect and Disorder* (Berkeley, Calif.: University of California Press, 1985); Paul Farmer, *AIDS and Accusation: The Geography of Blame in Haiti* (Berkeley, Calif.: University of California Press, 1992); T. N. Madan, "Living and Dying," in T. N. Madan, ed., *Non-renunciation Themes and Interpretations of Hindu Culture* (New Delhi: Oxford University Press, 1987), 118–41; Phillipe Ariès, *The Hour of Our Death*, trans. Helen Wever (New York: Knopf, 1981); Piero Camporesi, *Bread of Dreams: Food and Fantasy in Early Modern Europe*, trans. David Gentilcore (Chicago, Ill.: University of Chicago Press, 1989); Carlos Ginzburg, *The Cheese and the Worms: The Cosmos of a Sixteenth-Century Miller,* trans. John and Anne Tedeschi (New York: Penguin Books, 1980); Ivan Morris, *The Nobility of Failure: Tragic Heroes in the History of Japan* (New York: New American Library, 1976); and Ann F. Thurston, *Enemies of the People: The Ordeals of the Intellectuals in China's Great Cultural Revolution* (New York: Knopf, 1987).

[4]See DelVecchio Good et al., eds., *Pain as Human Experience: Anthropological Perspectives*; David Morris, *The Culture of Pain* (Berkeley, Calif.: University of

California Press, 1991); and Elaine Scarry, *The Body in Pain* (New York: Oxford University Press, 1985).

[5]Lawrence Langer, *Holocaust Testimonies: The Ruins of Memory* (New Haven, Conn.: Yale University Press, 1993); Nancy Sheper-Hughes, *Death Without Weeping: The Violence of Everyday Life in Brazil* (Berkeley, Calif.: University of California Press, 1993); and Pierre Bourdieu, ed., *La Misere du Monde* (Paris: Editions du Seuil, 1993).

[6]Kleinman and Kleinman, "Suffering and its Professional Transformations."

[7]*The New York Times*, 26 March 1993, A3.

[8]Jean Dreze and Amartya Sen, *Hunger and Public Action* (New York: Oxford University Press, 1991), show that famines in sub-Saharan Africa occur as a result of political disorder, not crop failure per se.

[9]Bill Keller, "Kevin Carter, a Pulitzer Winner for Sudan Photo, is Dead at 33," *The New York Times*, 29 July 1994, 138; Scott Mac Leod, "The Life and Death of Kevin Carter," *Time*, 12 September 1994, 70–73.

[10]*Time*, 12 September 1994, 72.

[11]Ibid., 73.

[12]Ibid.

[13]Ibid.

[14]Ibid.

[15]For this view of the "taking" of victimized social subjects by the more powerful photographer, "a privileged observer"—the "eyes of power" idea—see W. J. T. Mitchell, *Picture Theory* (Chicago, Ill.: University of Chicago Press, 1994), 288, 324, 365, 420–21. Mitchell also introduces the fundamental moral issue of the relationship between representation and responsibility. See Ibid., 421–25.

[16]On the dilemmas for cultural analysis of globalization, see Ulf Hannerz, "Mediations in the Global Ecumene," in Gisli Palsson, ed., *Beyond Boundaries: Understanding Translation and Anthropological Discourse* (Providence: BERG, 1993), 41–57; and Ulf Hannerz, "When Culture is Everywhere: Reflections on a Favorite Concept," *Ethnos* 58 (1993): 95–111.

[17]Stanley Cavell writes that philosophical knowledge is ultimately disappointing because it is incapable of decisively sorting out such "ordinary" human complexities. Stanley Cavell, *In Quest of the Ordinary* (Chicago, Ill.: University of Chicago Press, 1988), 88, 147, 149; he goes on to assert, in Stanley Cavell, *A Pitch of Philosophy* (Cambridge, Mass.: Harvard University Press, 1994), 116, "the world calls for words, an intuition that words are, I will say, world-bound, that the world, to be experienced, is to be answered, that this is what words are for."

[18]The analysis that follows in this section draws on materials, and contains several paragraphs, in Arthur Kleinman and Robert Desjarlais, "Violence, Culture and the Politics of Trauma," in Arthur Kleinman, *Writing at the Margin*, chap. 8; Robert Desjarlais and Arthur Kleinman, "Violence and Demoralization in the New World Disorder," *Anthropology Today* 10 (5) (1994): 9–12; and Arthur

Kleinman and Robert Desjarlais, "Ni patients ni victimes: Pour une ethnographie de la violence politique," *ACTES De La Recherche en sciences sociales* (ISSN 0355–5322) 104 (1994): 56–63.

[19]Compare the cover picture of *The Economist* of 23 July 1994, which, in the midst of the Rwandan crisis, is of a frightened Rwandan child. The picture is entitled "Helpless."

[20]On the uses of personification of collective catastrophe in the Western tradition of cultural representation, see Alan Mintz, *Hurban: Response to Catastrophe in Hebrew Literature* (New York: Columbia University Press, 1984).

[21]See the chapter on global social change in Robert Desjarlais et al., *World Mental Health: Problems and Priorities in Low-Income Countries* (New York: Oxford University Press, 1995), for a discussion of how the World Bank and the International Monetary Fund's rigorously-applied program of economic restructuring has worsened the health of women in sub-Saharan Africa. This volume also shows how the end of the Cold War and other global, political, and economic changes have often worked either to worsen social and mental health problems or to constrain health and social policy responses to those problems.

[22]See Alex Webb and David C. Unger, "Taking Haiti," *The New York Times Magazine,* 23 October 1994, 50–53.

[23]Michael J. Shapiro, *The Politics of Representation: Writing Practices in Biography, Photography, and Policy Analysis* (Madison, Wis.: University of Wisconsin Press, 1988), xii.

[24]The following section draws on materials in Arthur Kleinman and Robert Desjarlais, "Violence, Culture and the Politics of Trauma."

[25]See Allan Young, *The Harmony of Illusion: An Ethnography of Traumatic Memory* (Princeton, N.J.: Princeton University Press, forthcoming); and Allan Young, "Suffering and the Origins of Traumatic Memory," in this issue of *Dædalus.* Recent surveys of populations of people who have experienced political violence report that between 25 and 75 percent experience posttraumatic stress disorder. See the chapter on violence in Desjarlais et al., *World Mental Health: Problems and Priorities in Low-Income Countries.*

[26]Arthur Kleinman, "A Critique of Objectivity in International Health," in Chen, Ware, and Kleinman, eds., *Health and Social Change.*

[27]See World Bank, *World Development Report 1993: Investing in Health* (New York: Oxford University Press, 1993).

[28]See, for example, Sheila Rothman, *Living in the Shadow of Death: Tuberculosis and the Social Experience of Illness in America* (New York: Basic Books, 1994); and Morris, *The Culture of Pain.*

[29]Czeslaw Milosz, "The State of Nature: Notes from a Diary," *New York Review of Books,* 11 August 1994, 41.

[30]Central Committee, Chinese Communist Party, *Internal Report, Annals for Feng Yang County, 1961,* 188–91.

[31]Ibid.

[32]Ibid.

[33]Ibid.

[34]See James C. Scott, *Domination and the Arts of Resistance* (New Haven, Conn.: Yale University Press, 1992); and Rubie Watson, "Memory, History and Opposition Under State Socialism: An Introduction," in Rubie Watson, ed., *Memory, History and Opposition Under State Socialism* (Santa Fe, N.Mex.: School of American Research Press, 1994), 1–20.

[35]It is not only the totalitarian state that makes use of the weight of silence, of course. In the Gulf War, the US media often disregarded Iraqi casualties on the battlefield, and told the story largely from the American perspective, in spite of the fact that there were several dozen Western journalists in Baghdad.

[36]Ian Palmer, a British military psychiatrist in Rwanda, is reported in *The New York Times* to have said: "A fascination with death has created a voyeurism among Westerners here—the relief agencies, the United Nations and the journalists. . . ." *The New York Times,* 7 November 1994, A4. The *Times*' reporter continues: "Western visitors regularly tour massacre sites where bodies are rotting and still unburied. Visiting diplomats have driven for hours to see bodies washed up in the eddies of the Akagera River on the Tanzanian border." Ibid. This deepening voyeuristic sensibility may be another side of the cultural process we have identified.

[37]With relation to the Carter picture, see, for example, Richard Harwood, "Moral Motives," *The Washington Post,* 21 November 1994, A25, which offers a defense of the ethical motivation of journalists who report on violence and atrocities, yet still registers the complexity of the moral issue of cultural representation.

[38]That there are limits to the commercial uses to which images of suffering can be put is shown by the responses, in Germany especially, to Benetton's provocative advertising campaign in which pictures of bodies tattooed with "HIV-positive," a war cemetery, an oil-soaked bird, child labor in South America, and the bloody uniform of a Croatian soldier are used, in a strange paradox even by postmodern terms, to sell clothing. See Nathaniel Nash, "Benetton Touches a Raw Nerve," *The New York Times,* 2 February 1995, D1, 18.

[39]Eric Hobsbawm, *The Age of Extremes: A History of the World, 1914–1991* (New York: Pantheon, 1994), 16.

What difference does it make—for theory, for research, for policy, and for societal ethics—to change the border between a social and a health problem. Now pulling the edge toward the social side, later on pushing it toward the medical margin—does that disclose a comparative advantage for "medicalization" of human misery under certain conditions, or for "socialization" under others? The moral, the political, and the medical are culturally interrelated, but how do we best interpret that relationship and its implications?

Arthur Kleinman

From *Writing at the Margin: Discourse Between Anthropology and Medicine*

Berkeley, Calif.: University of California Press, 1995

David B. Morris

About Suffering: Voice, Genre, and Moral Community

"About suffering, they were never wrong,
The Old Masters: how well they understood
Its human position. . . ."

—*W. H. Auden*
"Musée des Beaux Arts"

W HAT CAN THE STUDY OF LITERATURE tell us about suffering? It is, of course, an impossible question, a sinkhole, a yawning chasm that dissertation directors warn against. It is also a question that opens up special difficulties because debates in contemporary theory have forced us to ask hard questions about such basic issues as the nature of interpretation, the boundaries of literature, and the relations between texts and the world. Literature, for example, is now routinely described as an ideological category that did not exist before the Enlightenment— its status threatened by such postmodern upstarts as discourse, *écriture*, and grammatology.[1] A loose alliance of new academic disciplines has shown how once-canonical works of Western literary tradition relegate minority figures—i.e., women, blacks, and Asians—to, at best, marginal status. What literature has to tell us about suffering, in short, depends on basic decisions about what counts as literature and whose suffering matters.

The difficulties mount because current theory makes it often hard to say what literature has to tell us about *anything*. Some

---

David B. Morris is a writer.

theorists hold that all texts are inherently undecidable or receive temporarily stable meaning only through their changing historical receptions by different interpretative communities. A move from theory to practice does not promise firmer ground. The individual texts to consider are numberless. "It is probably no exaggeration to say that the single most common subject of art," writes Walter Slatoff, "is some form of human suffering."[2] Practical critics in the analysis of specific texts often simply replicate contested theoretical assumptions. We can expect that Marxist critics will show how suffering is bound up with social class and with the means of production; psychoanalytic critics will show how it taps into mechanisms of desire; feminist critics will show how it follows the fault lines of gender. While recent literary debates have left us in no danger of oversimplifying a discussion of suffering, they may appear at times as merely a conflict among partisans of wholly incompatible ways of reading.[3]

A final difficulty—the presumed need to define suffering and to distinguish it from related or overlapping states such as grief and pain—would seem to constitute an impassable barricade. Yet, some impassable barriers can be safely sidestepped. Suffering is currently undergoing vigorous redefinition within the biomedical community in a process that still seems rather fluid.[4] Moreover, literature has long served as an arena for explorations into the unknown and the indefinite; accounts of suffering should therefore include whatever literature (or its postmodern successor) reveals. Sidestepping specialized or essentialist definitions, I prefer to invoke an exploratory spirit and a provisional vocabulary as a means of respecting both the diversity of materials on suffering and the urgent need for dialogue among disparate disciplines, which always tend to see things a bit differently.

VOICE AND SILENCE

Voice is a concept familiar both in grammar and in poetics. It is often said that writing well means finding one's own voice. T. S. Eliot, in his essay "The Three Voices of Poetry," argued that poetry demands an encounter with intricately layered nuances of human speech expressing tone, attitude, and character.[5] A less common but useful way to think about voice is to consider its opposite: silence. Silence stands in opposition to every voice, weak or strong, ordinary or unique, prosaic or poetic. The basic opposition between voice and silence matters here because suffering, like pain, with which it so often intermingles, exists in part beyond language.

The silence of suffering has, oddly, turned into something of a modern cliché—despite the contrary evidence of an almost interminable discourse of complaint, lament, litigation, symptom-mongering, and public confession. The cliché may simply acknowledge the power that most people possess to tune out unwelcome news, but it also captures a complex and basic fact about suffering.[6] Suffering is voiceless in the metaphorical sense that silence becomes a sign of something ultimately unknowable. It implies an experience not just disturbing or repugnant but inaccessible to understanding. In this sense, suffering encompasses an irreducible nonverbal dimension that we cannot know—not at least in any normal mode of knowing—because it happens in a realm beyond language. The quality of such suffering remains as blank to thought as the void opened up by a scream.

Paradoxically, the scream might serve as a potent image for the metaphorical silence at the heart of suffering. A scream is not speech but the most intense possible negation of language: sound and terror approaching the limits of absolute muteness. Like the ceremonial wailing of grief, it seems to come from a region where words fail. A typical Hollywood scream, while it often shatters a preceding silence or calm, also deepens the silence it shatters, as if gesturing toward something radically inexpressible. Indeed, one function of literature is to give this deeper silence a voice. Literary works from *Philoctetes* to *Krapp's Last Tape* labor to make such silences "speak" by extending our awareness of an irreducible, nonverbal dimension of suffering that can never be put into words. The impossible project of giving "speech" to silence is important especially because it exposes how we simplify and betray suffering whenever we ignore its power to elude every linguistic and conceptual tool that humans can marshal to understand it.

Silences are not all identical, of course, but convey a wide range of significance, from the contemplative depth of a pregnant pause to outrage, disbelief, and stunned wonder. In addition to metaphorical links with an inexpressible or unknowable experience, the silence of suffering also points to very practical breakdowns of speech. Its silence, that is, reflects something not ultimately ungraspable but merely resistant to description. Suffering tends to make people inarticulate, and in this sense the voicelessness of suffering often resembles the quiet retreat of people who live with chronic pain, who discover that months or years of unremedied complaint finally exhaust care-givers and even family. Such patients withdraw into an uncommunicative isolation, constructed in response to an environment where effective help and concern have all but vanished.

The silence of the patient, however, differs significantly from the voicelessness of many who suffer in other ways. Patients at least possess a recognized status within the social world of medicine, a status that confers rights and obligations, connecting the sufferer with an entire health-care system and with its attendant, language-rich field of physicians, nurses, therapists, insurance agents, and attorneys. Many people who suffer the routine misery of famine, civil conflict, and industrialized poverty have almost no status beyond the role of victim. An occasional grim picture flashed across millions of television screens merely intensifies the silence: it is axiomatic that the victims do not speak.

A loss of voice, further, proves to be almost built-in to the interpersonal structure within which suffering usually occurs. That is, even when words prove at least partially adequate, even when speech occurs, communication fails. W. H. Auden observes in his famous poem "Musée des Beaux Arts" that suffering is inextricably embedded in a social world where nonsufferers always find their own lives more immediate and absorbing, like the torturer's horse scratching its rump against a tree.[7] The problem, as Auden poses it, is not that witnesses deliberately turn away from disaster, unable to bear it or refusing to assist, although in fact people often do turn away. While suffering regularly disturbs and threatens us, which helps to explain why many people recoil or resist the ethical claims it makes upon us, Auden does not represent an aversion to suffering as moral failure, a lapse, say, of charity or courage. He depicts aversion or detachment, rather, as the outcome of a structural position we cannot help but occupy.

Suffering, in Auden's almost structuralist view, is an event that we witness always and only once-removed, as if through a pane of thick glass. The ploughman never looks up; the expensive ship always sails on. Should an act of suffering fall unavoidably within our field of vision, Auden insists that we cannot escape our built-in estrangement; it might as well occur in silence. Not even the Old Masters, he implies, could somehow shatter the glass and place us in direct relation to another's suffering. Instead, their triumph— perhaps straining the limits of art—lies in forcing us to recognize and to contemplate our fated detachment.

We need not wholly accept Auden's view that the structure of suffering contains at its heart an absolute and insurmountable otherness. His view, however, provides a helpful corrective to the widespread modern pieties based, say, in the parable of the Good Samaritan. The Good Samaritan represents a belief that suffering is an occasion for religious acts of virtue and compassion. The great strength of the parable is to insist that right action can take place despite the incomprehensible silence and otherness at the heart of suffering. Still, the parable also depends for its impact on our awareness that acts of virtue and compassion are, unfortunately, rare, and it thus indirectly supports Auden's view that our normal "human position" in relation to suffering mandates a glasslike separation and detachment. If abruptly our role changes from witness to victim, forcing us to endure affliction firsthand, then our position in the structure will correspondingly change, and we pass at once into an unfamiliar dimension where others view *us* with detachment and incomprehension, as if through a thick glass.

The irreducible otherness of suffering that Auden evokes so well is what gives special resonance to the concept of voice. Voice matters precisely because suffering remains, to some degree, inaccessible. Voice is what gets silenced, repressed, preempted, denied, or at best translated into an alien dialect, much as clinicians translate a patient's pain into a series of units on a grid of audiovisual descriptors. Indeed, voice ranks among the most precious human endowments that suffering normally deprives us of, removing far more than a hope that others will understand or assist us. Silence and the loss of voice may eventually constitute or represent for some who suffer a complete shattering of the self.

Certainly literature attests, often in paradoxical ways, to the loss of voice in suffering. Samuel Beckett spent a lifetime creating minimalist texts in which, like the Cheshire cat, voice seems caught

in the process of imminent disappearance.[8] Either the human state
in its seriocomic bleakness leaves almost nothing to say, as in
Waiting For Godot, or stable personal identity crumbles toward
anonymous incoherence, as in *Not I,* where a spotlight shines on
a mouth-sized hole in the closed curtain through which a nameless
voice utters its nonstop woe. Images of linguistic breakdown and
futile interchange express Beckett's view that suffering is not a trial
of faith or a noble burden—as in Christian tradition—but an
almost meaningless charade in the cosmic theater of the absurd.
Beckett's art is to represent this diminished, nullified state of being
with such droll precision that it seems almost tolerable. "I can't go
on. I'll go on."

Yet, literature also contains more potent employments of voice
in the face of affliction. As if in resistance to the detachment and
bleakness that Auden and Beckett describe, other writers explore
ways to readjust the structure of suffering. That is, they seek out
means of expression that might approximate or at least respect an
experience ordinarily beyond language. Like silence, voice is really
a plural concept. The diverse voices transmitted in literary texts, of
course, are far from always wise or composed. As in the Book of
Job or in the voluminous writing that responded to the unprecedented disaster of World War I, readers may confront halting and
troubled voices, voices that are angry and confused, hurt, exhausted, foolish, or blasphemous.[9] The content of the utterance,
while crucial to its writer or speaker, matters less in suggesting
what literature can tell us about suffering than the sheer act of
speech itself: affliction has at last broken through into language.
We are finally in the presence of words that cross over from the
other side of torment.

Literary voices indeed convey such an enormous diversity of
views that—taken together—they might approach or approximate
a kind of encyclopedia of suffering. No single voice is sufficient.
Women's voices will convey a different experience of suffering
than the voices of men; black voices speak differently than white
voices; martyrs' voices will not match the voices of inquisitors;
Protestant martyrs will differ from Catholic martyrs; medieval
voices, steeped in beliefs that link suffering to sin and damnation,
will differ from modern voices.[10] In *King Lear,* for example, the
treacherous, self-serving Edmund attributes suffering both to the

influence of malign gods and to brutal human appetites. Blind, foolish Gloucester blames his suffering on fortune, while pious Kent invokes the mystery of an all-seeing divine providence. Lear, in moods ranging from compassion to madness, offers still more variations on the question of what it is to suffer. And all in one play.

In addition to the encyclopedic diversity of voices that it contains, literature makes two other significant contributions to a knowledge of suffering. Writers can open up the interior or private life of a character in ways often difficult or impossible outside of texts, revealing a personal side of affliction that we rarely see. Moreover, they can infuse the voices of suffering with an unusual power to move emotion and compel attention. In both ways, writers create the occasion for an empathetic reader-response that might counteract the structural detachment observed by Auden. Literature, in short, holds a power to address, or even reverse, the inherent pressure within affliction toward isolation and silence.

"The use of language," Joyce Carol Oates noted when accepting the National Book Award in 1970, "is all we have to pit against death and silence."[11] Writers, of course, have much to say about the limitations and misuses of language. Half the characters in world literature seem engaged in telling lies to the other half, and Oates never guarantees that the opposite of silence is truth. Yet, in giving voice to affliction, however imperfectly, writers also struggle to alter and improve our difficult relation to suffering. William Faulkner, accepting the Nobel Prize, argued that literature holds a special duty to lift the human heart by reminding us of our capacity for "compassion and sacrifice and endurance." It is suffering that traditionally requires these powers, and literature may thus develop and sustain a resource desperately needed in times of trouble. As Faulkner said in the final sentence of his acceptance speech, invoking poetry as a figure for all great literature, "The poet's voice need not merely be the record of man, it can be one of the props, the pillars to help him endure and prevail."[12]

Although award ceremonies may call forth suspiciously high-minded statements, the belief that literature can oppose suffering has a long history. In the Middle Ages, literature was sometimes defended against its pious detractors as therapeutic and restorative, a necessary tonic for renewed spiritual struggle. Medieval doctors openly prescribed laughter and comic tales as an effective medicine against plague.[13] Renaissance physicians continued to prescribe mirth as a therapy useful against the epidemic illness called melancholy, and thus the noted writer-editor Norman Cousins in 1976 was simply invoking an ancient tradition when he described how Marx Brothers' films and comic television reruns helped him recover from a debilitating illness.[14] Like tragedy, comedy seems to be an enduring response to the dehumanizing powers of pain and suffering.

Certainly, as Western medicine has grown increasingly dependent on high-tech machines and complex pharmacokinetics, the uses of an instrument as basic and inexpensive as the human voice seem greatly underestimated. Evidence from support groups and psychoanalysis strongly suggests that language, under the right conditions, can have healing powers. Words can demonstrably trigger a painkilling placebo effect. Yet, the vast biomedical library on pain contains only a few slim booklets in which patients speak in their own voices—free from appropriation via commentary or analysis.[15] The distinguished American novelist Reynolds Price recently lamented the absence of helpful voices when he suddenly faced a personal struggle against spinal cancer. "I needed to read some story that paralleled, at whatever distance, my unfolding bafflement," he writes, "—some honest report from a similar war, with a final list of hard facts learned and offered unvarnished— but...I never found it."[16] His own account, *A Whole New Life: An Illness and a Healing,* is a compelling example of how writers can help others by empowering and amplifying the individual human voice: soon after publication he was receiving some forty letters each week from people seeking his assistance. The need to hear a voice is rarely stronger than when a person endures suffering. Letters, diaries, and journals written by sufferers both famous and remote—from John Keats to unknown slaves or soldiers— attest to a value implicit in the act of writing. Many who today suffer silently and in confusion might be helped if we learned how to tap the resources of literature in restoring significance to an individual human voice.

GENRE AND THE SHAPE OF SUFFERING

Voices are never simply the medium of individual speech. With the help of theorists from Wittgenstein and Austin to Foucault and Bakhtin, recent literary studies have argued that individual voices are always engaged in (often unnoticed) dialogue that links them to other speakers in the encompassing social network of language. Each voice speaks with a distinctive timbre, of course. Yet, no one can communicate in language without employing the innumerable speech acts—asking, telling, promising, begging, urging, praising—that typify the intricate cultural and linguistic codes underlying even the most simple utterance. Analysis of such ordinarily unnoticed codes makes it clear that we communicate by means of widely-shared social patterns that Bakhtin calls "speech genres."[17] Speech genres denote all the formal or informal—pure or mixed—codes that allow us to understand and to construct individual utterances, from legal briefs and government documents to jokes, postcards, papal bulls, football cheers, and letters of recommendation.

Jacques Derrida makes the crucial point when he writes that "there is no genreless text." "A text," he insists, "cannot belong to no genre, it cannot be without or less a genre."[18] Like texts, voices communicate only by means of genres that impose loose or strict demands on speakers. Speech genres depend, moreover, on the existence of specific discourse communities. A football cheer is meaningless in a culture without sport. An Islamic call to prayer makes no sense in a world devoid of Muslims. Yet, speech genres do more than assure that there is never simply a voice speaking. They help to shape the substance of what is said. For example, Ralph Cohen shows how a single narrative (about the murderous apprentice George Barnwell) undergoes crucial changes as it is retold in the differing genres of oral ballad, domestic tragedy, chapbook, and novel.[19]

Why does it matter that every voice is shaped and constrained by speech genres? How we talk about suffering and how we talk when suffering is always shaped and constrained by the speech genres of specific discourse communities. In a scholarly journal, discourse about suffering will normally take the form of twenty-five-page essays. There will be footnotes to contemporary thinkers, correct grammar, titles with colons. Obscenities and profanities will be expunged. Readers may notice that the essays place an invisible premium on intelligence, employ difficult or specialized diction, avoid familiar ideas, and strive to appear original. Methodist hymns, by contrast, treat suffering within a speech genre where almost none of the assumptions about scholarly essays apply.

Subtly or overtly, then, genre molds facts and events to fit its contours, and a narrative of suffering will undergo subtle changes depending on whether it takes the form of a documentary film, a television miniseries, or a comic book. Even such deeply personal utterances as the testimony of Holocaust survivors will fall under the sway of generic patterns no doubt invisible to the speakers. Indeed, "survivor testimony" is now a distinctive modern subgenre, with informal conventions governing content, setting, camera angle, gesture, and displays of emotion. Scholars who ignore how speech genres shape any utterance or representation of suffering risk making the same error as visitors to a museum who see an African ritual mask—torn from its context of social life—hung up on the wall like Western artwork.

The shaping force of genre extends beyond form to meaning. In fact, audiences depend on generic patterns to provide a framework for interpretation. Such frames, for example, let us know whether we are reading a sacred scripture or a blasphemous parody: the words may be almost identical. An utterance that would seem incoherent within a tragedy may make perfect sense in a farce. The way we understand the meaning of any utterance, writes E. D. Hirsch, Jr. in his chapter on genre, is "like learning the rules of a game."[20] The rules may change and new games may appear. It is important to remember that genres are historical creations and, like tragedy, change over time. It is genre, however, in every age, that tells us what language-game we are playing.

The power of genre reaches even beyond meaning to influence the very possibility of speech. As in traditions of courtroom testimony, genre not only shapes content and sways understanding but it constrains what we are *permitted* to say. A fact so obvious may go without saying, but its implications are far-reaching. Specific literary genres often carry within them explicit or unspoken ideological values.[21] Suffering, thus, will be infused with specific values depending on the speech genre in which it is communicated. Further, generic values do not somehow stop short at the (porous) borders of literature. Hayden White has mounted a strong argument that historians write history—and hence we know our own past—only within the conventions of literary genre.[22] It is highly relevant that two powerful literary genres—tragedy and the novel—have dominated Western discourse on suffering. The unavoidable question might be put this way: What values, constraints, or conditions do tragedy and the novel impose on our knowledge of suffering?

Tragedy indeed is the one genre so basic to Western thought on suffering that newspapers still call almost any large misfortune *tragic*. Behind this casual usage lies a tradition that stretches back to Aristotle. Two thousand years of theory and practice make any search for an unchanging essence of tragedy more than ordinarily futile. Northrop Frye observed that most theories of tragedy focus on a single great drama as the norm, much as Hegel's emphasis on the clash of opposing systems of value is keyed to the *Antigone*.[23] Aristotle's account, centered mostly on *Oedipus Tyrannus,* is no less partial than other theories, but its status as the origin of Western discourse on tragedy makes the *Poetics* an important test case for examining the influence of genre on our knowledge of suffering.

Suffering (*pathos*) is, for Aristotle, indispensable to tragedy. Drama without *pathos*, he writes, cannot be tragic. Unknown before the fifth century B.C., the term *pathos* indicated not just misery or misfortune but what classicist Thomas Gould calls "catastrophic suffering, undergone by some great figure, man or god, far in excess of the sufferer's deserts."[24] Aristotelian tragedy, in its implicit ideological assumptions, thus involves a view that not all suffering (and not everyone who suffers) is equal. In effect reproducing Greek assumptions about social worth, it holds at its core the values of aristocratic privilege, whereas ordinary suffering and ordinary people lie beyond its scope, pushed to the margins or personified in a passive, hapless chorus. These social values, in turn, are reflected in Aristotle's insistence that the tragic poet writes in an elevated style appropriate to powerful individuals and great acts. The catastrophe befalling a person of high rank likely involves the fate of whole families, armies, or cities so that Aristo-

telian tragedy helps confirm our assumption that suffering is invariably serious. Yet, a belief that suffering is always serious—
tragic—belongs to the history of Western thought. Other cultures
do not uniformly share it.[25]

The novel—the second dominant genre that helps to shape
Western knowledge of suffering—complicates but also reinforces
the emphasis in tragic drama on individuality and seriousness. One
complication lies in novelistic techniques for achieving the mixture
of distinct styles, voices, and discourses that Bakhtin calls
"heteroglossia."[26] Heteroglossia—the dynamic clash of differing
dialects and diction—for Bakhtin is what distinguishes the novel
from more homogeneous and elevated genres such as tragedy.
Novels, in his view, extend heteroglossia beyond language to a
mixture that encompasses action, character, social status, and
belief systems such that no single voice can emerge from the text
as delivering the authorized version. Where tragedy for Aristotle is
implicitly aristocratic, the novel for Bakhtin implicitly subverts
established hierarchies. Where Aristotle sees tragedy as always
serious, Bakhtin views the novel as inherently comic, a prose
carnival or marketplace, where laughter and a license to speak
freely across traditional lines of authority call into question every
solemn or single-minded view.

It is useful to examine further the ways in which Bakhtinian
novels complicate the view of suffering implicit in Aristotelian
tragedy. Just as novels mostly explore instances of suffering that
are less than catastrophic, they extend the role of hero to figures
whose low or middling birth would exclude them from classical
tragedy. The comic spirit native to the novel tends to undermine
tragic seriousness. In Beckett's work, for example, the novel may
even embrace a sense that suffering is absurd—or absurdly comic.
Further, the novel often vastly expands its focus on the social
world; Zola, for example, forces us to recognize the suffering of
whole masses of common people. There is, thus, good reason to
think that tragedy and the novel offer quite different outlooks on
human suffering. Yet, allowing for important differences, in two
respects tragedy and the novel both reinforce an implicitly unified
view of suffering: high value is placed on the individual, and both
rely on the fascinations of plot.

Plot, for Aristotle, is the soul of tragedy. While he insists that tragedies must include *pathos*, suffering alone does not create tragedy. It is the action, or plot, that creates a structure within which the *pathos* makes sense. Plot, then, for Aristotle, is what imparts to suffering its tragic status. With some obvious and quirky exceptions, plot is likewise so central to the novel that many popular novelists seem little more than machines for its mass production. Novelistic suffering, whatever its forays into stream-of-consciousness or meditative stasis, fundamentally demands the construction of plot. Plot, we might say, is somehow crucial to the generic framework within which both novels and tragedies place human suffering.

What does suffering have to do with plot? Through their emphasis on plot, tragedy and the novel implicitly represent suffering not as a mere state of being—persisting like a viral infection almost independent of human agency—but rather as an event embedded within a matrix of related actions. Further, plots illuminate the ways in which individual events are connected. One reason why Aristotle values plot so highly is because it offers cognitive clarifications that make tragedy, in his words, more philosophical than history.[27] History, for Aristotle, provides a mere record of actual happenings, whereas tragedy employs its artfully constructed plot to show us not what is actual or merely possible but rather *probable*. It demonstrates, almost like a theorem in geometry, that suffering is an unavoidable outcome given a sequence of specific, connected actions.

In short, in tragedy and the novel, suffering is represented as more than a persistent theme in the human condition. It implies that suffering is less a condition—a state of being—than an event: an event within the context of a larger, surrounding plot. Despite the frequent invocation of fate by characters in Greek tragedies, suffering in tragedy and the novel loses its ancient aura of fatalism because it is never merely the experience of a debilitating passivity. Suffering is an action. It is the outcome of a series of preceding acts. Indeed, this plot-centered view holds the promise of cognitive clarifications that may lead to the possibility of personal and social change. Although the protagonist of a tragedy or novel may be inextricably trapped within a structure of action too intricate or complex to reverse, the reader or audience occupies a position in which the detachment that Auden observed in "Musée des Beaux Arts" offers a crucial vantage point for securing knowledge and directing relief.

A plot-centered view of suffering certainly holds important consequences in the world outside literature. Gustavo Gutiérrez, Peruvian founder of liberation theology, views the suffering of the Lima slum-dwellers and of the impoverished masses in Latin America not as a changeless state of being rooted in original sin or in the human condition. He understands it instead as embedded in an extended and ongoing historical action: in this case, the political and economic oppression sponsored by an elite class (including leaders of the Church) who secured power through an appalling series of historical injustices.[28] Suffering in the slums of Lima, Gutiérrez implies, will be reversed not by medicines, compassion, or improved services, however welcome these might be, but only by material social change—action—that signifies the creation of a new and just historical plot.

SUFFERING AND MORAL COMMUNITY

The massive suffering in Latin America and elsewhere raises the question of how far we may perceive suffering as purely an individual matter. C. S. Lewis once claimed that, at any moment, there is never more pain in the universe than a single person experiences.[29] Pain, so the argument goes, exists only within an individual nervous system. I cannot feel your pain; you cannot feel mine; together we cannot feel the pain of a whole battlefield of casualties. This argument disregards the claim of non-Western spiritual traditions to transcend the isolated ego. It also completely misses the point. The Holocaust cannot accurately be described as the suffering of a single Jew repeated six million times. The fact remains that the suffering of groups or entire populations is an experience that most people, writers included, find extremely difficult to grasp.

Literature, in its reliance on individual characters, reflects and augments our difficulties in grasping the affliction of large groups of people.[30] Such reliance is historical and cultural in the sense that writers—always situated within a specific social landscape—necessarily work with the materials of a bounded world. It is hardly surprising that the emphasis on individual suffering reinforced through tragedy and the novel is saturated with the distinctive values of Western culture. Despite its deeper roots in Dionysian mysteries or fertility cults, tragedy takes its social origin in the aristocratic, slave-owning, heroic culture of ancient Greece, while the novel famously emerges during the early modern era when European feudal hierarchies began to crumble under the new pressure of bourgeois individualism. There are sound reasons why tragedy and the novel would reinforce an implicit belief that suffering, whatever its wider resonance, is ultimately an individual matter.

Certainly tragedy and the novel, however much preoccupied with metaphysics or the social world, tend to focus on the crisis of a single hero or heroine: *Oedipus Rex, Macbeth, King Lear, Robinson Crusoe, Tom Jones, Hedda Gabler.* Although some writers subordinate character to theme, setting, or sheer linguistic exuberance, even in novels that describe immense casts and huge catastrophes—such as *War and Peace*—the affliction of entire groups appears mostly as a vague background against which we view in sharp detail the lives of a few main characters. Despite the famous panoramic shot of Civil War casualties in David O. Selznick's film *Gone With the Wind,* it is Rhett and Scarlett who occupy the center of attention. We see but in another sense do not see—do not truly experience—the suffering of multitudes.

The affliction of large groups is often not just difficult to see but impossible to find. The text simply cannot recognize the suffering of groups whose misery it represses, as in the common run of cowboy films or colonial novels.[31] This ideological blindness to suffering operates on a principle very different from the structure of detachment that Auden identified. Auden traces our detachment to a normal human self-absorption and inability to share the consciousness of a fellow creature. An ideological blindness to suffering, by contrast, depends largely on the operation of what philosopher Tom Regan has termed "moral communities."

Moral communities differ immensely in their beliefs, values, and cohesiveness but they always share a dependence on exclusion. In *The Thee Generation: Reflections on the Coming Revolution,* Regan proposes this geometrical analogy:

Suppose we imagine the moral community circumscribed by a circle. Individuals inside the circle are members of the moral community, individuals outside the circle are not. Those inside the circle, by virtue of their membership in the moral community, are entitled to a kind of consideration denied those outside. Of the former, but not the latter, we may say, "They are morally considerable."[32]

The boundaries of a moral community, of course, are flexible and often paradoxical. Animals, for example, are excluded from most Western moral communities, although Americans regularly make an exception for household pets and for a few charismatic species, like whales or dolphins. Certain criminals are excluded—mass murderers, for example, and serial rapists—but not bank robbers, stock manipulators, or repentant evangelists. Wartime propaganda shows how easy and convenient it is to exclude the enemy from a nation's moral community, just as earlier ages (without the pretext of war) found it possible to exclude the insane, the poor, women, blacks, and children.

Suffering, in short, is not a raw datum, a natural phenomenon we can identify and measure, but a social status that we extend or withhold. We extend or withhold it depending largely on whether the sufferer falls within our moral community. An Iraqi truck driver in the Persian Gulf War can die in a firestorm of laser-guided missiles, and the incident will play on American television as proof of superior United States technology. (Iraqi soldiers, in turn, seemed to find Kuwaiti civilians readily disposable.) We do not acknowledge the destruction of beings outside our moral community as suffering; we detach ourselves from their pain as if it were an incomprehensible behavior encountered on some Swiftian island. Within a moral community, we employ names like *martyr* or *hero* and inscribe the suffering of our own people within narratives of hallowed sacrifice and epic achievement. Literature clearly plays a significant role in orchestrating the language that validates or invalidates certain experiences as suffering.

Literary inclusions and exclusions usually reflect dominant values of the community within which a text is written, but one important function of literature is to challenge and stretch—even to transgress—the boundaries of a moral community. The *Aeneid,* for example, while aspiring to the stance of national epic, places the Roman conquest of Italy in a tragic light that exposes the deep losses required by imperial success.[33] Virgilian pathos at the "tears of things" seeks to extend the borders of the Roman moral community to encompass even the death of an enemy and the loss of a former world. The implicit reader posited by the *Aeneid* cannot overlook or glorify the suffering imposed by national destiny. By their special skill in moving emotions and altering perceptions, writers can help create—as well as uncreate—suffering. That is, they can expand the borders of the moral community and force us to acknowledge suffering where we normally do not see it.

Charles Dickens and Harriet Beecher Stowe provide especially clear examples of this power to reinvent suffering. In adapting the earlier sentimental novel, they extend a Romantic concern for outcasts and marginal figures—slaves, chimney sweeps, orphans, and an almost forgotten subculture of the poor—into a focused social protest against the evils of slavery and industrialism. Their vivid characters, interconnected plots, and empathetic styles uncover suffering where it was earlier thought not to exist. In fact, Stowe in *Uncle Tom's Cabin; or, Life Among the Lowly*—the first American novel to sell over a million copies—so strongly engaged popular feeling that she has been cited among the causes of the Civil War. Contemporary readers not only wept at the ordeals of fictional slaves but, far more important, came to acknowledge the ordeals *as* suffering and felt moved enough to rearrange the existing social order that had denied it.

The power to reinvent suffering by extending or contracting the borders of a moral community can, like other powers, be used with differing degrees of blindness or insight. Neither Dickens nor Stowe could address the link between domestic injustice and colonial empire. The Marquis de Sade wrote vast pornographic novels that almost gleefully contract their moral community to a circle of pain-crazed aristocratic libertines, for whom suffering is transformed into a source of pleasure. On the other hand, a modern admirer of Sade, Michel Foucault, in 1971 helped found the "Prison Information Group"—a coalition that gave voice to a silent and powerless minority by publishing the firsthand accounts of prisoners who described conditions within the French penal system.[34] Few writers are more important than Foucault in exposing how, paradoxically, modern affliction is promoted by the same institutions—prisons, clinics, madhouses—that the state establishes in order to prevent suffering. It is a paradox that still remains potent in such ubiquitous modern institutions as disability insurance and welfare payments, which may often do as much harm as good.[35]

The point is not to celebrate or condemn specific writers but to recognize how writing helps to create and to uncreate suffering. Moral community, genre, and voice are concepts that can help us think about suffering both within and beyond literature. They certainly raise questions that need to be pursued. To what extent is all suffering alike, or to what extent is it inescapably heterogeneous? How far can writers exploit techniques of detachment (as in the drama of Brecht) to permit a revaluation of suffering perhaps impossible through techniques of empathy? A response to such questions should indicate that writers do far more than describe or represent affliction: they can also, on occasion, reinvent suffering and, in the process, help to mobilize the will, passion, and intelligence needed to change the world.

Yet, we must be careful not to claim too much. Perhaps the most important thing that literature has to tell us about suffering concerns the need for respect in the face of an experience that always holds back part of its truth, inaccessible and alien. In London in 1972 a small company of Zulus from South Africa put on a performance of *Macbeth*. The fur-clad, spear-thrusting Zulu warriors devoted much of the performance to tribal dances; they paid no attention to the hero's inner drama. "O, full of scorpions is my mind, dear wife!" cries Macbeth in his torment after the murder of King Duncan (III.ii). The Zulus conveyed none of this. Instead, ignoring the psychology of individual distress, what they conveyed superbly through drumbeat and ritual dance was the unthinkable disaster that enfolds a small community when someone murders the king. The dances expressed the suffering of a close-knit group—not separate individuals but a moral community—and they also seemed to be a means of dealing with the disorder Macbeth had unleashed, much like formal prayers in times of grief. Efforts to help people in affliction cannot succeed if we fail to respect how different cultures construct distinctive social practices of suffering and how these practices may envision unique remedies or responses.[36] Here too, if we heed the Zulu dancers, literature has much to tell us about the possibilities for knowledge and action.

ENDNOTES

[1] Terry Eagleton, *Literary Theory: An Introduction* (Oxford: Basil Blackwell, 1983).

[2] Walter J. Slatoff, *The Look of Distance: Reflections on Suffering and Sympathy in Modern Literature—Auden to Agee, Whitman to Woolf* (Columbus, Ohio: Ohio State University Press, 1985), 233.

[3] See *Falling into Theory: Conflicting Views on Reading Literature,* ed. David H. Richter (New York: St. Martin's Press, 1994).

[4] For biomedical definitions, see *The Hidden Dimension of Illness: Human Suffering,* ed. Patricia L. Starck and John P. McGovern (New York: National League for Nursing Press, 1992); and C. Richard Chapman and Jonathan Gavrin, "Suffering and its Relationship to Pain," *Journal of Palliative Care* 9 (2) (1993): 5–13.

[5] T. S. Eliot, "The Three Voices of Poetry" (1953), in *On Poetry and Poets* (New York: Farrar, Straus and Cudahy, 1957).

[6] On silence, see Elaine Scarry, *The Body in Pain: The Making and Unmaking of the World* (New York: Oxford University Press, 1985), 42–45. Voice and representation are discussed in *Pain as Human Experience: An Anthropological Perspective,* ed. Mary-Jo DelVecchio Good et al. (Berkeley, Calif.: University of California Press, 1992).

[7] On suffering, see Thomas Dilworth, "Auden's 'Musée des Beaux Arts,'" *Explicator* 49 (3) (Spring 1991): 181–83.

[8] On suffering, see Cho-hee Joh, "Beckett's Capacity for Differentiation: Some Observations on Reading His Works," *Journal of English Language and Literature* 35 (4) (Winter 1989): 759–73.

[9] See Gustavo Gutiérrez, *On Job: God-Talk and the Suffering of the Innocent* (1985), trans. Matthew J. O'Connell (Maryknoll, N.Y.: Orbis Books, 1987); and Paul Fussell, *The Great War and Modern Memory* (New York: Oxford University Press, 1975).

[10] See Susan Sipple, "'Witness [to] the Suffering of Women': Poverty and Sexual Transgression in Meridel Le Sueur's *Women on the Breadlines,*" in *Feminism, Bakhtin, and the Dialogic,* ed. Dale M. Bauer and Susan Jaret McKinstry (Albany, N.Y.: SUNY Press, 1991): 135–53; John Knott, *Discourses of Martyrdom in English Literature, 1563–1694* (Cambridge: Cambridge University Press, 1994); and Katherine Heinrichs, "Love and Hell: The Denizens of Hades in the Love Poems of the Middle Ages," *Neophilologus* 73 (4) (October 1989): 593–604.

[11] Joyce Carol Oates, "Remarks...accepting the National Book Award in Fiction" (1970), in Mary Kathryn Grant, *The Tragic Vision of Joyce Carol Oates* (Durham, N.C.: Duke University Press, 1978), 164.

[12] William Faulkner, "Address upon Receiving the Nobel Prize for Literature" (1950), in *Essays, Speeches, and Public Letters,* ed. James B. Meriwether (New York: Random House, 1965), 120.

[13]Glending Olson, *Literature as Recreation in the Later Middle Ages* (Ithaca, N.Y.: Cornell University Press, 1982).

[14]Norman Cousins's *JAMA* essay was expanded into his best-selling book, *Anatomy of an Illness as Perceived by the Patient: Reflections on Healing and Regeneration* (New York: W. W. Norton, 1979). On comedy, see David B. Morris, *The Culture of Pain* (Berkeley, Calif.: University of California Press, 1991).

[15]See *People With Pain Speak Out,* ed. Christine Nyhane and Brian Sardeson (Ballarat East, Australia: The Writing Project Group, 1990); and *Living With Chronic Pain: Personal Experiences of Pain Sufferers,* ed. Laura S. Hitchcock (Bethesda, Md.: National Chronic Pain Outreach Association, 1992). Various newsletters and support groups, such as the American Chronic Pain Association, also seek to give voice to the experience of patients.

[16]Reynolds Price, *A Whole New Life: An Illness and a Healing* (New York: Atheneum, 1994), 181.

[17]M. M. Bakhtin, *Speech Genres and Other Late Essays,* ed. Caryl Emerson and Michael Holquist, trans. Vern W. McGee (Austin, Tex.: University of Texas Press, 1986).

[18]Jacques Derrida, "The Law of Genre," *Critical Inquiry* 7 (1) (Autumn 1980): 65. Derrida offers this view as a "hypothesis."

[19]On genre and narrative change, see Ralph Cohen, "History and Genre," *New Literary History* 17 (2) (Winter 1986): 203–18.

[20]E. D. Hirsch, Jr., *Validity in Interpretation* (New Haven, Conn.: Yale University Press, 1967), 70.

[21]See Thomas O. Beebee, *The Ideology of Genre: A Comparative Study of Generic Instability* (University Park, Pa.: Pennsylvania State University Press, 1994).

[22]Hayden White, *Metahistory: The Historical Imagination in Nineteenth-Century Europe* (Baltimore, Md.: Johns Hopkins University Press, 1974).

[23]Northrop Frye, *Anatomy of Criticism* (Princeton, N.J.: Princeton University Press, 1957), 212.

[24]Thomas Gould, *The Ancient Quarrel Between Poetry and Philosophy* (Princeton, N.J.: Princeton University Press, 1990), ix.

[25]For a non-Western view, see Gananath Obeyesekere, "Depression, Buddhism, and the Work of Culture in Sri Lanka," *Culture and Depression: Studies in the Anthropology and Cross-Cultural Psychiatry of Affect and Disorder,* ed. Arthur Kleinman and Byron Good (Berkeley, Calif.: University of California Press, 1985), 134–52.

[26]M. M. Bakhtin, *The Dialogic Imagination: Four Essays by M. M. Bakhtin,* ed. Michael Holquist, trans. Caryl Emerson and Michael Holquist (Austin, Tex.: University of Texas Press, 1981); and Tzvetan Todorov, *Mikhail Bakhtin: The Dialogical Principle* (1981), trans. Wlad Godzich (Minneapolis, Minn.: University of Minnesota Press, 1984).

[27]"Clarification" is one definition of the Aristotelian term *catharsis*. See *Aristotle's Poetics: A Translation and Commentary for Students of Literature,* trans. Leon Golden, commentary by O. B. Hardison, Jr. (Englewood Cliffs, N.J.: Prentice-Hall, 1968).

[28]Gustavo Gutiérrez, *A Theology of Liberation: History, Politics and Salvation* (1971), trans. Caridad Inda and John Eagleson (Maryknoll, N.Y.: Orbis Books, 1973).

[29]C. S. Lewis, *The Problem of Pain* (New York: Macmillan, 1944), 103–104.

[30]Marxist theorist Georg Lukács sees novelistic characters as infused with thoughts and emotions "typical" of large groups, yet even this access to large groups remains *through* individuals. Georg Lukács, "The Intellectual Physiognomy of Literary Characters" (trans. 1936), in *Radical Perspectives in the Arts,* ed. Lee Baxandall (Baltimore, Md.: Penguin Books, 1972), 89–141.

[31]See Terry Eagleton, *Criticism and Ideology: A Study in Marxist Literary Theory* (London: NLB, 1976); and Terry Eagleton, Fredric Jameson, and Edward Said, *Nationalism, Colonialism, and Literature* (Minneapolis, Minn.: University of Minnesota Press, 1990). On ideological blind spots in texts, see Pierre Macherey, *A Theory of Literary Production* (1966), trans. Geoffrey Wall (London: Routledge & Kegan Paul, 1978).

[32]Tom Regan, *The Thee Generation: Reflections on the Coming Revolution* (Philadelphia, Pa.: Temple University Press, 1991), 20.

[33]See Michael C. J. Putnam, *The Poetry of the Aeneid: Four Studies in Imaginative Unity and Design* (Cambridge, Mass.: Harvard University Press, 1965).

[34]James Miller, *The Passion of Michel Foucault* (New York: Doubleday, 1993), 64–65, 187–93.

[35]On disability, see Wilbert E. Fordyce, "Pain and Suffering: A Reappraisal," *American Psychologist* 43 (4) (April 1988): 276–83; and Mark D. Sullivan and John D. Loeser, "The Diagnosis of Disability: Treating and Rating Disability in a Pain Clinic," *Archives of Internal Medicine* 152 (September 1992): 1829–1835.

[36]See Arthur Kleinman and Joan Kleinman, "Suffering and its Professional Transformation: Toward an Ethnography of Interpersonal Experience," *Culture, Medicine and Psychiatry* 15 (3) (1991): 275–301.

To talk of suffering is to talk not of an academic problem but of the sheer bloody agonies of existence, of which all men are aware and most have direct experience. All religions take account of this; some, indeed, make it the basis of all they have to say. Whatever theoretical constructions may be built, the foundations are laid in the apparent realities of what it is like to be alive. Thus, what a religion has to say about suffering reveals, in many ways more than anything else, what it believes the nature and purpose of existence to be.

John Bowker

From *Problems of Suffering in Religions of the World*

Cambridge: Cambridge University Press, 1970
Reprinted by permission of Cambridge University Press.

Lawrence L. Langer

The Alarmed Vision: Social Suffering and Holocaust Atrocity

NTIL WE FIND A WAY OF TOPPLING THE BARRIER that sequesters mass suffering in other regions of the world from the comfort and safety we enjoy far from its ravages, little will be done to rouse the attention of our political or professional leaders, to say nothing of our own. Domestic calm encourages distancing from foreign pain. Past episodes of catastrophe have taught us how difficult it is for the distress of others to disrupt the tranquil rhythms of our daily lives. We may be horror-struck by the chaos that starvation and civil strife inflict on victims in foreign places like Somalia or Sarajevo, but to be horror-struck is a frugal form of charity. We need a new kind of discourse to disturb our collective consciousness and stir it into practical action that moves beyond mere pity.

We will get nowhere with this problem until we admit that the familiar verbal modes for approaching it have been exhausted by centuries of repetition. Even a word like "suffering" does little to help us imagine the modern disasters we are challenged to confront. In fact, by calling the murder of European Jewry an example of mass suffering, we risk limiting its scope by merging it with prior models that are meager measures of the event. Job endured loss, but gained divine acknowledgment and a limited spiritual insight after refusing to let physical trial curtail his moral strength. Nothing could be further from the ordeal of the Holocaust victim than this prototype of unprovoked suffering, which is deemed redemptive only by those who misread Job's protest. The Gospel

Lawrence L. Langer is Professor of English Emeritus at Simmons College in Boston, Massachusetts.

accounts of the passion of Jesus are equally useless in aiding us to visualize the dilemma of the Holocaust. So too are the fictional visions of Tolstoy and Dostoyevsky that draw so heavily on those narratives. The notions of moral rebellion, punishment, and salvation that energize such Old and New Testament texts do not lead us to the outskirts of Auschwitz or Treblinka, nor indeed to the atrocities in Bosnia-Herzegovina. They steer us instead into friendly harbors, where neither conscience nor imagination is in any danger of running aground.

Holocaust literature is a major goad that urges us to reimagine atrocity and to rewrite the text of suffering in contemporary terms. The following poem, "Written in Pencil in the Sealed Boxcar," by Israeli writer Dan Pagis is a classic example of such artistic provocation:

> Here in this transport
> I am Eve
> With Abel my son
> If you should see my older son
> Cain son of man [or Adam]
> Tell him that I[1]

The journey from the Garden of Eden to the gas chambers of Auschwitz bears no scriptural authority, but since death camps need no biblical model to confirm their existence, it is scripture, not history, according to Pagis, that must alter its text. A Siamese bond now twins creation with destruction in a way that sabotages the narrative of Cain's primal crime and replaces it with a story of mass murder. This, in turn, imposes new burdens on our very notion of scripture and its role in the unfolding human saga.

But the poem does much more. Since Genesis is a completed tale, the reader is coaxed to demolish its frame and, through a kind of imaginative osmosis, to inject into its ancient nucleus a new vision more consistent with results it could not have foreseen. Who could have predicted for Eve and her issue the voyage that would turn Abel into a different kind of victim and fraternal violence into a vast catastrophe? The loss of a single son was the start of the Jewish narrative; the murder of an entire people was the beginning of something else, though we are left uncertain of what because Eve's unspoken message is buried in the challenge of her arrested voice. Whatever its content might have been, it would have included a summons to the alarmed vision, a call to Cain (and the rest of us) to rethink his assigned role and, through a retroactive gesture of spiritual insight, somehow to merge the dreadful end that awaits his mother and his brother with one of the archetypal chronicles of Jewish destiny.[2] A poem can no longer balance through its achieved form the void of discord that recent history seems to offer us. Deprived of this common solace from art, we are invited by Pagis to join in the perilous ritual of closure without any pledge that our search for meaning will uncover new comforts to blunt our grief.

The shift from fratricide to genocide as the norm of violence in the modern era is not easy to absorb. Not too long ago I engaged in a discussion with a historian who disputed my claim that America's lethargy in response to the plight of the Jews just prior to and during World War II resulted largely from a failure of imagination, a refusal or inability to etch on some internal monitor the details of the calamity that was consuming European Jewry. He argued that by 1942 Washington had "knowledge" of the death camps and "confirmed" reports of the mass murder under way. Actually, we had such information as early as the summer of 1941, when German mobile killing units in the Soviet Union began systematically executing the Jewish population in areas the army had conquered. "Confirmed knowledge," however, is a verbal expression that does little to threaten the repose of a mind outraged from a distance and privy only to the data that telegrams, communiques, and written summaries can convey.

It seems to me a little naive to expect governments and citizens to react with dispatch to accounts of disaster that are couched in general language, lacking specific facts. When Gerhardt Riegner, head of the Geneva office of the World Jewish Congress, learned on August 1, 1942 from a sympathetic German industrialist with connections in the Nazi hierarchy that a plan had been reviewed in Hitler's headquarters for the murder of all Jews in Nazi-occupied lands, he sent this information to Rabbi Stephen S. Wise in America, who passed it on to the US State Department. This was eight months *after* the first killing center had been opened at Chelmno in Poland. Would the State Department not have delayed interminably, "verifying" and then pigeonholing such stories, if Riegner had been able to describe how the Jews at Chelmno, who were gassed in vans with carbon monoxide on the way to the site of mass burial, sometimes arrived stunned instead of dead but were thrown into the graves anyway, and buried alive? Would the response have been different if he had been able to tell about the Jewish worker at Chelmno who, when he opened one of the vans, pulled out the corpses of his wife and two children and leaped into the grave beside their bodies asking to be shot and buried with them? (The Germans dragged him out, declaring that *they* decided when a Jew was to die.)[3] Of course, Riegner did not have these details, though similar evidence was given to the Polish underground by two women who had escaped from Chelmno, and it was transmitted to the Polish government in exile in London. It probably was not believed. But it seems clear that the meaning and the impact of an expression like "confirmed knowledge" depends on how that knowledge is being confirmed, and the language used to confirm it.[4]

Those who tried to summon Americans to action on behalf of the victims faced a double impasse: they lacked a vocabulary to portray the moments of atrocity I have just related; and they addressed an audience unable to hear because their mind-set was not tuned, and had never been tuned, to the kind of crisis that was unfolding in Europe. Even the Christian courier Jan Karski, who had visited the Warsaw ghetto twice and had also spent a few hours disguised as an Estonian guard in the Belzec death camp, and then was sent by the Polish underground to England and America to give an eyewitness account, could not impress on the skeptical minds of Anthony Eden, Felix Frankfurter, and Franklin Delano Roosevelt the enormity of the crimes being committed against the Jews and the absolute necessity of finding some way of limiting the murders.[5]

The system of values cherished by the American mind, with its stress on individual success and an infinitely improving future, nurtures a psychology of mental comfort that discourages encounters with tragedy, to say nothing of the atrocity that an event like the Holocaust requires us to absorb. But in the case of the Holocaust, this attitude was not confined to a particular culture. Even the victims were unprepared to handle the tales of slaughter drifting back to the ghettos from the killing centers. Abraham Lewin, in *A Diary of the Warsaw Ghetto,* drafts the dilemma of digesting "confirmed knowledge" of the unthinkable in the very heart of the maelstrom:

> Isolated refugees who arrive here literally by miracle from Treblinka bring reports that freeze the blood in the veins. The killing-machine there never rests. In the past few days Jews from Radomsko were brought there and murdered. News of this kind causes us hellish torments. Has anyone ever described the suffering of someone who has been condemned to death and who is to go to the gallows? Even the Russian artists, of whom the greatest is Dostoevsky, have not succeeded in giving a true description of what transpires in the depths of the soul of an innocent person who has been sentenced to death. When I hear these accounts of Treblinka, something begins to twist and turn in my heart. The fear of "that" which must come is, perhaps, stronger than the torments a person feels when he gives up his soul. Will these terrible agonies of the spirit call up a literary response? Will there emerge a new Bialik able to write a new Book of Lamentations, a new "In the Town of Slaughter"?[6]

In calling for a new Book of Lamentations, Lewin, like Dan Pagis, dismisses old scriptural models as sources of inspiration for portraying the murder of European Jewry. The quest for analogy, whether by literary artist or historian, is the task that bedevils anyone aiming to initiate the imagination of an audience into the singular realm of the unthinkable. The crime of our century, as Lewin predicts here, will be the chronic story of men, women, and children trying to stay alive in an environment that is moving them relentlessly toward an intrusive death that bears no relation to their previous lives. How does one describe the "fear of 'that' which must come" so as to differentiate it from ordinary dying?

In a desperate effort to make sense of his grim surroundings, Lewin himself is drawn in two directions at once. On the one hand, he lapses into the language of consolation, born of the psychology of mental ease, to deflect implications too horrible to admit: "It is impossible that so much innocent blood should be spilled without retribution. The day of judgement, the day of reckoning must and will come." But it never came. The habit of taking refuge in such rhetoric when one is left powerless to change one's situation is understandable, and Lewin seems aware that he is doing this, because virtually in the same breath he adds a contrary idea: "The level of Nazi brutality quite simply lies beyond our power to comprehend. It is inconceivable to us and will seem quite incredible to future generations, the product of our imagination, over-excited by misery and anger."[7] But the "inconceivable," in this case as well as in subsequent instances of mass violence in the post-Holocaust period, is nothing more than a name for a reality that we are unprepared to accept, because it either offends our sense of order or threatens to unravel the curtain before which we ply our daily lives.[8] If some forms of human misery do indeed still lie beyond our powers to comprehend, it would be irresponsible to allow our own psychological and intellectual hesitation to estrange us from that misery. The only alternative, a complex and difficult one, is to find ways of making the inconceivable conceivable, until it invades our consciousness without meeting protest or dismay. Drowning in daily episodes of atrocity, Lewin responds to the *experience* of his own muted tongue and stunned imagination, not to a rhetorical invocation of silence. A "new Bialik" would have to abandon, not rediscover, the literary techniques and imaginative vision of his predecessors. But such rejection might introduce a chaotic rupture into some of our most cherished views, like time as uninterrupted chronology or history as automatic progress—a rupture that many commentators are loath to embrace.[9]

In classical Greek literature the herald led a perilous life, because as a bearer of ill tidings he so often provoked the wrath of the recipient of his message. When the escaped messenger from Treblinka brought the evil news that the Germans were gassing all the Jews and throwing their bodies into flaming pits, he was not punished, but simply rebuffed as a madman by most members of the Jewish Council. Oddly, individuals and communities clamor for more stories of extraordinary *virtue,* no matter how exaggerated: holy sightings and unlikely miracles quickly rouse public enthusiasm, and the locales of the supposed events are soon turned into sacred shrines. But an unholy world with millions of victims and few heroes has little popular appeal, since it proves inhospitable to the romanticizing imagination. We need to defend ourselves against reports of such radical evil. "Inconceivable" becomes a frightful word chiefly when it refers to atrocities like the Holocaust that offer us no possibility for transcendence. Such verbal threats prompt us to build bunkers of inner security to shield us from their assault.

It may be useful to *classify* human misery in terms of social problems, but this rarely generates widespread concern. We need a special kind of portraiture to sketch the anguish of people who have no agency in their fate because their enemy is not a discernible antagonist but a ruthless racial ideology, an uncontrollable virus, or, more recently, a shell from a distant hillside exploding amid unsuspecting victims in a hospital or a market square. Before we can present a program for dealing with human misery, we need to *represent* that misery. This requires talents that will not flinch from physical outrages bearing no resemblance to the sufferings of an earlier era, or from horrors untempered by moral meaning, whether plague, poverty, or war, that were so often allied to a language of sanctity, virtue, or sentimental fervor.

Those talents include not only a verbal facility but frank consent to a philosophical shift about human expectation that allows us to work with limited aspirations, rather than the unlimited ones bequeathed by our Enlightenment and Romantic heritage. Unfortunately, what I call the alarmed vision feeds on a skimpy diet, one that fails to satisfy the appetite of those who "normalize" violence, disease, and other human abuses by placing them in the simple context of an agenda for improving the future. Few regard with enthusiasm the spectacle of diminished promise that the repeated abuses of our era have thrust upon us. The pragmatic decision to choose "reconciliation" over justice in places like Argentina, Chile, Haiti, and Israel (to be followed, perhaps, by Rwanda and Bosnia-Herzegovina) creates a dubious legacy for the worldwide victims of abuse and an even more doubtful precedent for those who would seize and misuse power in the future. Defusing alarm by deflecting atrocity may create a fragile peace in communities wearied by years of anguish, but it would be less than honest to ignore the price we pay for such a strategic form of avoidance.

Such avoidance resembles the attitude of those who use the texts of Holocaust testimonies as examples of "working through" past traumas toward a goal of reconciled understanding and liberating growth into the future. But the subtexts of those testimonies reveal a reality that is much more relevant to the issues we are exploring here. They reflect hundreds of instances of unredeemed and unredeemable loss, giving us a glimpse of how language shorn of a spiritual bond can shock the imagination into an alarmed vision— the only kind of vision that may goad us into interceding in situations of atrocity before they have spent their energy, leaving negotiated "reconciliation" as the only practical course of action. Such situations mock the good intentions of utopian hopes. They introduce us to a reversal of expectation that lies at the heart of any attempt to appreciate modern suffering. The Holocaust and subsequent large-scale atrocities exist in an orbit void of the usual consoling vocabulary: martyrdom, the dignity of dying, guilty conscience,[10] moral rigor, remorse, even villainy, which in literary tragedy so clearly distinguishes the victim from his or her persecutor. None of these verbal categories illuminate the devastation of the Holocaust, or for that matter the killing of millions by Stalin in the 1930s by enforced famine, the ravages in Cambodia, or the merciless destruction of civilian populations in Yugoslavia today.

In a world where the goal of life so often seems to be the death of others, we are forced to regard the reversal of expectations rather than the fulfillment of dreams as the model for being and behavior in some communities. Ironically, Nazi Germany nearly succeeded in establishing a prototype for this social paradigm, by equating its extermination policies with the dream of a Third Reich cleansed of Jews. A healthy community thus became, by definition, one in which the death of some was decisively tied to the life of the remainder. Because such a system violates our own moral and spiritual beliefs, we find it difficult, if not impossible, to imagine. But history pays little heed to what we find desirable or imaginable. The Holocaust and later atrocities have invaded our sense of stable living and normal dying, leaving us a legacy that colonizes the future with nightmares of frustration rather than dreams of fulfillment.

It would help to be able to call this condition a treatable trauma, but if the testimonies of hundreds of Holocaust survivors are to be trusted, that clinical formula simply will not serve the truth of their ordeal. As we shall see, their memories are not symptoms, nor in telling their tales do they seek some form of reintegration into their community—a goal they have long since achieved. Well-intentioned intervention after the fact is no substitute for strong action to prevent atrocities from occurring. Painful memories are not always disabling, and narratives about them—at least this is true of Holocaust testimony—rarely "liberate" witnesses from a past they cannot and do not wish to escape. For them, forgetting would be the ultimate desecration, a "cure" the ultimate illusion. As for renewal or rebirth, such monuments to hope cannot be built from the ruins of a memory crammed with images of flame and ash.

The myth that such a patient needs to be freed from his or her past originates in a number of questionable assumptions. The first is the designation "patient," which immediately creates a clinical relationship and transforms testimony into a form of therapy. The second is the premise that survivors of atrocities experience time only chronologically, so that the present appears to follow the past and precede the future. Testimony may *sound* chronological to an auditor or audience, but the narrator, a mental witness rather than a temporal one, is "out of time" as he or she tells the story. This is often the case in Holocaust discourse; we are led astray or baffled by the lack of a language to confront the difference between the chronological current, which flows until we channel it between the permanent banks of historical narrative, and durational persistence, which cannot overflow the blocked reservoir of its own moment in memory and hence never enters what we call the stream of time.

Anyone who hears these testimonies will understand that for the witnesses time is durational as well as chronological, and that durational time is experienced continuously, not sequentially as a memory from which one can be liberated. The notion that a Holocaust survivor—I suspect one might say this of any survivor of atrocity—can generalize his or her personal suffering and move beyond the role of victim derives from an unfamiliarity with how durational time assails the memory of a witness. That is why I believe that all attempts to investigate the effects of atrocity on a group or a community must begin with the narratives of individual victims, and especially with moments of durational time, which mock the very idea that traumas can be healed.

The speaker is Bessie K., a woman who is being interviewed with her present husband, also a survivor. Their chronological story is familiar: they met after the war, married, came to America, raised a family, and have led happy and successful lives. But this offers no compensation for what they are about to tell, which gives us a glimpse of the role durational time plays in their memories and their lives. During their testimony, they sit at opposite ends of the same couch, isolated and insulated, each dwelling in a series of durational moments that they share with no one. As so often in these testimonies, the crucial instants are not those when one explains how one survived, but how a member of one's family died. On their deepest level, these life stories are really death stories, which include the death of the self in ways we still need to interpret. In these instances, "suffering" seems a futile term, since its traditional associations with healing or a process for gaining moral maturity, to say nothing of conventional theological ideas like salvation and redemption, consign it to a lexicon of outmoded vocabulary. Any thought of legitimizing such "suffering" through treatment becomes an offense to the witness.

Bessie K.'s narrative is preceded by her husband's account of his farewell to his brother, ill with typhus, who was taken with other inmates from the camp infirmary and shot. She tries to enter into his distress by passing him a tissue, but he rejects it with a flick of the wrist, saying "I don't need it." Then he tells of his brother's last gesture—giving him his shirt after saying "I don't need it." The memory of his brother's death consumes him, shrouds him in a way that prevents intrusion, even from his wife. She then begins the story of her own unforgettable durational moment:

> I had a baby boy....They took us to the buses, they brought us to a big airfield. And nearby were the trains, the cattle trains. And...I look back: I think for a while I was in a daze; I didn't know what was happening actually. I saw they [were] taking away the men separate, the children separate, and the women separate. So I had the baby, and I took the coat what I had, the bundle, and I wrapped [it] around the baby and I put it on my left side, because I saw the Germans were saying left or right, and I went through with the baby. But the baby was short of breath, started to choke, and it started to cry, so the German called me back, he said in German "What do you have there?" Now: I didn't know what to do, because everything was so fast and everything happened so suddenly. I wasn't prepared for it.
>
> To look back, the experience was—I think I was numb, or something happened to me, I don't know. But I wasn't there. And he

stretched out his arms I should hand him over the bundle; and I hand him over the bundle. And this is the last time I had the bundle.

But as I look back, I don't think that I had anybody with me. I was alone, within myself. And since that time I think all my life I been alone. [Meanwhile, the camera pans to the other end of the couch on which she is sitting to settle on her present husband, Jack, whose face is a mask of grief and despair.] Even when I met Jack, I didn't tell Jack my past. Jack just find out recently. For me, I was dead. I died, and I didn't want to hear nothing, and I didn't want to know nothing, and I didn't want to talk about it, and I didn't want to admit to myself that this happened to me.

She is deported to Stutthof concentration camp, where she meets the doctor who had operated on her infected breast in the ghetto before her deportation. She continues:

And when [the doctor] saw me there she was so happy to see me, and right away she says "What happened, where's the baby, what happened to the baby?" And right there I said "What baby?" I said to the doctor "What baby? I didn't have a baby. I don't know of any baby."

Then she pauses for an instant, nods her head, taps her brow with a finger, and concludes, "That's what it did to me."[11]

This fragment of narrative illustrates why we must be cautious when trying to compare examples of individual or community suffering. Certainly there may be some overlap between the experience of this bereft mother and of parents who have lost children more recently through acts of extreme violence in other locales. But universalizing instances of atrocity only diminishes their private impact. Understanding the differences is crucial: the duration, nature, and extent of the violation, the role of the aggressor, the defensive resources available to the victims—issues like these enjoin us to view each atrocity within its own historical, geographical, cultural, and psychological context. Some victims may indeed respond to treatment, may find group discussion useful, may need to escape from the cocoon of remembering that traps them in a corrosive past. But Bessie K. fits none of these models. When she says "since that time I think all my life I been alone" while sitting next to her husband, she is not complaining or asking for sympathy; she is explaining that the passage of time cannot appease a durational memory. She is redefining the meaning of being "alone, within myself," making it a typical outgrowth of the disintegration of her first family, not to be undone by the emergence of a second one. The unappeasable experience is part of her inner reality, and though the optimistic American temperament winces at the notion, Bessie K. knows that what she has survived is an event to be endured, not a trauma to be healed.

But her narrative reveals even more. The Holocaust has collapsed conventional distinctions between living and dying as separate—indeed antithetical—states of being. We will never begin to understand the legacy of atrocity in the modern era until we realize what this means. When, after telling of surrendering her baby, Bessie K. insists, "For me I was dead. I died, and I didn't want to hear nothing, and I didn't want to know nothing," she invites us to reflect on a consequence of atrocity that surfaces in numerous survivor testimonies—the condition of having missed one's intended destiny by surviving one's own death.[12] The death of her child is her own death too, not in fantasy but in reality, a permanent intrusion on her post-Holocaust existence. It is also a form of verbal disturbance, since no language exists—certainly not a tame word like "suffering"—to describe the role of such durational moments in the lives of those who have lived them.

Bessie K.'s durational moment is part of the normal experience of the death-camp universe. If it seems abnormal or traumatic to us, that is because we approach it from our familiar perspective of chronological time. It is not part of her historical past, but of her durational present, and as such is both unforgotten and unforgettable. She is defined, not disabled, by her memory, a memory that can be told but not shared, because unlike loss through illness or accident, in her mind this was a "death" without parallel or analogy. It is neither desirable nor possible for her to "forget" it. Such expectations betray our own need for amnesia, because narratives like hers threaten our dependence on coherence, reason, and order, the moral and psychological balance that constitutes, for us, civilized being.

Testimony like this should not summon us to the healing of victims, but to a revision of the myth of civilized being. Human nature can no longer be set in opposition to inhuman nature, as if one were the norm and the other a correctable aberration. Atrocity in the form of violence that maims and kills others has become a "normal" rather than a pathological expression of the self—not of all selves, to be sure, but enough to cause us to question ancient premises about moral instincts and spiritual purpose. In its display of power, the act of atrocity brings a fulfillment similar to the one we usually associate with gestures of charity or love. The tiresome cliché about people who do not learn from the past being doomed to repeat it persists as our favorite buffer against facing human and historical truth. Perhaps it is time to admit that atrocity in the past does not discourage but in fact *invites* atrocity in the future. From the scandalous carnage of World War I to the innumerable murders of the Leninist and Stalinist regimes, the countless victims of the Holocaust (condensed into a single abstract figure, six million) to the bloody outrages in Bosnia and Rwanda, our age of atrocity slips into and out of consciousness with the casual appeal of a transient news item. We fail to decipher the clues that would rouse us to an alarmed vision.

I am not sure that we can find a way of sensitizing this numbness, in whose protective custody we live to avoid the unsettling spectacle of the deaths of others. But I am sure that one useful beginning is with the voices of those who were plunged into a death-in-life milieu from which survival did not bring escape. The roots of the quandary began to appear in the camps themselves. One survivor of the liquidation of the Vilna ghetto (eleven years old at the time), who was sent with her mother to Kaiserwald near Riga, tells of the kind of discussion she used to have with a friend in the camp:

> You kind of got laid back a little about being killed. The prime targets of our thoughts was always being killed. One of my friends. . .she and I went through—we met in Kaiserwald. She was from Liebau (people came there from Liebau too) and she and I were about the same age and conversations would be: "Let's see, how would you like to be killed? Would you like to be killed by the gas chamber? By being beaten? By hunger? Or the bullet?" And she and I agreed—the bullet. So our conversations were *not* building a future, what we are going to do when we grow up, you know how kids talk, I'm gonna be this and I'm gonna be that. Our hope was that when our time comes, that we will die by the bullet, so that we will suffer less.[13]

This is, of course, an extreme reaction to a death-stressed environment, but at the time other options for Jews seemed unlikely, and the witness is trying to recall her former state of mind honestly. It confirms the importance of reversal of expectation in contemporary thought, since the strategy focuses not on how to be more happy, but how to suffer less. The most dramatic examples of what I call durational time in these testimonies invariably terminate in death, real or imagined, imagined not as fantasy or illusion, but as the end of what *should have been,* that does not violate but grows logically out of the present situation. What we think of as chronology, with its investment in a long-term future, had already died. For many inmates, the shrunken margins of space in the camps were accompanied by a contraction in the boundaries of time, and within that area of constricted space and time the promise of death, the doom of dying at the hands of their persecutors, scarred the memories of those who would be lucky enough to outlive that doom.

How else are we to explain the testimony of a witness who, years after the event, remembers with apprehension the challenges of ordinary life when he reentered chronological time. After his release from the camps he came to America, where he tried to settle into a normal pattern of existence. But because his life had been so *unsettled* during the war, he was left with a legacy of unresolved conflict that emerges starkly from his testimony. Following more than five hours of reviewing the destruction of all but one member of his extensive family, he abruptly begins to speak of his fear of marriage and starting a new family after such ruin. "A home," he says, preparing for his narrative of how duration invades chronology, "is something you lose." This is a classic example of the reversal of expectation that an atrocity like the Holocaust has grafted onto our sense of modern reality. Nevertheless, he finds a job and marries. He has certainly earned an unimpeded future, but we are naive to anticipate this prospect. Unimpeded futures are now part of our nostalgia about the past. He reenacts in his dreams and even in certain physical responses during his waking hours the missed destiny of dying that still haunts him from the world of the death camps:

> We bought a home, and started to establish ourselves, and things were getting better—but I had some drawbacks. I was working

hard, trying to forget myself, forgetting the past, but it came back to me like a recording in my head. After we got married, for the longest time—we were already then in a family way, and things were looking up to me. During the day I was working hard, and studying, and trying to get ahead and establish myself—and at night, I was fighting the Germans, really fighting. And the SS were after me all the time, and I was trying to save my mother and my sister [gassed at Auschwitz]. I was jumping off from building to building, and they were shooting at me, and each time the bullet went through my heart. And I was sitting up not knowing at night in my bed, and I was screaming, you know it was hard on [my wife]. It must have been hard on her, and we didn't know how to handle it. I didn't know how to handle it. I was making believe. . .forgetting about it and going on during the day doing my things. And at night she was calming me down, she says "It's OK, it's OK, you're here, don't worry about it," and I was waking up and screaming at night and each time a bullet went through my heart.[14]

He returned to work, but his left arm began to pain him badly; he had difficulty driving the car, and one day a coworker rushed him to the hospital with the symptoms of a heart attack. The doctors found nothing physically wrong with him.

Is there such a feat as recharting your own death, or, perhaps more precisely, someone else's intention to kill you, so that the frustrated conclusion of durational time in the camps achieves some form of completion at a later date? The loneliness that surfaces as a theme in so many of these testimonies—like the mother who, after surrendering her infant to the Germans, declares "Since that time I think that all my life I been alone," while sitting next to her husband—results from a separation caused by the murder of members of one's family, and that in turn leads to an internal rewriting of the scenario of life to somehow include one's own death. Here, agency invades necessity, defiance replaces inertia, and the victim, by fighting the Germans and trying to save his mother and sister, embraces and *earns* the death that has already devoured them. But his waking life thwarts this, and his missed encounter with the destiny from which he escaped but so many others did not continues to exert its force as a subtext of his narrative.

Time does not close the gap between the text of his ongoing life and the subtext of his unpacified past, the unreconciled and unreconcilable stress between chronology and duration. The issue grows even more dramatic if we turn to a comparatively recent *New Yorker* article addressing the problem of preserving the ruins of Auschwitz-Birkenau that time and nature are gradually eroding. The remnants of mass murder are also disintegrating, the mountains of human hair and suitcases and prostheses that stun the visitor into imagining the huge number of victims consumed by the insatiable death-machinery of the place. But the author cites an even more perplexing question mentioned by the deputy director of the Auschwitz museum: "Recently," she tells him, "a number of Holocaust survivors have contacted us and asked that their remains be buried at Birkenau....Birkenau is a cemetery," she adds, "but not a cemetery where you can conduct funerals."[15]

For the moment, museum officials do not know what to do with this request, which seems grotesque only to those who ignore how the "missed destiny" of dying in Auschwitz continues to raid the memories of those who outlived their doom there. Together with George S.'s testimony, it reflects an ongoing need that many survivors feel to connect their lives to the death of others. This is the final reversal of expectation to disturb the serenity of our private consciousness, to say nothing of the smooth flow of chronological time. Few events have done more to create a tension between what we wish and what we know—if we allow ourselves to know it— than the atrocity of the Holocaust. The experience of its victims, those who survived and those who did not, permanently darkens the future by bequeathing us a legacy of unreconciled understanding. The passage of time heals many wounds, but this event leaves only a vexing and painful scab. No one is happy to discard the illusion that there is meaning in such suffering, that there is something to be learned from it, that the anguish of human cruelty can be minimized by calling it spiritual discipline. We live in an age haunted not by the kind of suffering that religion and literature have taught us to accept, but by a spectacle of atrocity, on smaller and larger scales, that no past traditions have prepared us to absorb. Thus, any effort to aid its victims, on an individual or community basis, must begin by acknowledging that the usual consolations may not apply, that efforts to heal by forgetting the past and bravely facing the future might only betray a misunderstanding of the effects of atrocity on the human body, mind, and spirit.

Taking or watching Holocaust testimony is a humbling experience. You begin with the hope of creating order out of chaos, finding patterns in the survival narrative that can be organized into what some call a "syndrome." You imagine you can design a new template of evil to gain insight into the motives that lead to mass murder. Then you hear the story of a young Jewish woman who was thrust alive into the crematorium by two SS men because she refused to follow their order to undress and scratched one of them on the cheek when he tried to force her to do so. And suddenly your faith in the logic of human nature collapses. Exasperated by my own inability to envision anecdotes like the ones I was hearing in the testimonies, I revised my assumptions about shareable memory and collective consciousness. Once we enter the tentative world of duration, leaving behind the security of chronology, we realize that life after atrocity is not a call to new unity but only a form of private and communal endurance, based on mutual toleration rather than mutual love. Though it is less than the utopia humanistic enlightenment once dreamed of achieving, all our efforts at rescue and remedy, nurture and renewal must grow from this insight.

ENDNOTES

[1]The translation is mine. For another version of this poem, as well as others by Dan Pagis, see *Points of Departure*, trans. Stephen Mitchell (Philadelphia, Pa.: Jewish Publication Society of America, 1981).

[2]A main thrust of Pagis's poem is what Harold Bloom calls the "anxiety of influence." Hebrew literature of catastrophe continues to shape subsequent writing in that tradition, but the Holocaust and the "deportation" of Abel and Eve forces on the literary imagination a re-visioning and hence a revisioning of Scripture. Holocaust and Scripture now conspire to alter each other's texts.

[3]This episode is recounted in Claude Lanzmann's film *Shoah* by one of the two survivors of the Chelmno death camp. Similar narratives may be found in Martin Gilbert, *Holocaust: A History of the Jews of Europe during the Second World War* (New York: Holt, Rinehart and Winston, 1985); Charlotte Delbo's trilogy, *Auschwitz and After*, trans. Rosette C. Lamont (New Haven, Conn.: Yale University Press, 1995), esp. vol. I; and Lawrence L. Langer, *Holocaust Testimonies: The Ruins of Memory* (New Haven, Conn.: Yale University Press, 1991). A comprehensive history of the Auschwitz death camp is *Anatomy of the Auschwitz Death Camp*, ed. Yisrael Gutman and Michael Berenbaum (Bloomington, Ind.: Indiana University Press, 1994). For further details about

the killing facilities, see Yitzhak Arad, *Belzec, Sobibor, Treblinka: The Operation Reinhard Death Camps* (Bloomington, Ind.: Indiana University Press, 1987). The full story of the Riegner telegram and the US State Department's response may be found in David S. Wyman, *The Abandonment of the Jews: America and the Holocaust, 1941–1945* (New York: Pantheon Books, 1984). In addition to the failure to imagine the disaster threatening European Jewry, Wyman lists Roosevelt's fear of alienating non-Jewish supporters as well as anti-Semitism among higher echelons of State Department officials as reasons for the sluggish response to the Jewish situation. The public, too, including parts of the American Jewish community, did not view with enthusiasm an expanded immigration policy during years of lingering economic depression.

[4]See Walter Laqueur, *The Terrible Secret: Suppression of the Truth about Hitler's "Final Solution"* (Boston, Mass.: Little, Brown, 1981) and Walter Laqueur and Richard Breitman, *Breaking the Silence* (New York: Simon and Schuster, 1988). Of course, even if Riegner could have provided intimate details of atrocity to convey the visceral horrors of the Final Solution, his more precise reports still might have been translated by the bureaucracy in Washington into technical memos shuffled from office to office, as was done with his original telegrams. The mentality prevailing in the State Department seemed more interested in managing the story than in responding to it with some form of prompt action.

[5]Karski tells part of his story in Lanzmann's film *Shoah*. The full narrative appears (well before the end of World War II, it should be noted) in Jan Karski, *Story of a Secret State* (Boston, Mass.: Houghton Mifflin, 1944).

[6]Abraham Lewin, *A Cup of Tears: A Diary of the Warsaw Ghetto*, ed. Antony Polonsky, trans. Christopher Hutton (New York: Basil Blackwell, 1989), 236–37. These questions are dated 9 January 1943, one week before the last entry in the diary, when Lewin and his daughter were presumably rounded up and deported to their deaths in Treblinka. Haim Nahman Bialik (1873–1934) was the leading poet of the modern Hebrew revival. His "In the Town [or City] of Slaughter" was a response to the Kishinev pogrom in tsarist Russia in 1903, when forty-nine Jews were killed.

[7]Ibid., 81.

[8]Perhaps the greatest threat of all to the stage on which we enact our existence is that behind the curtain nothing exists. But few of us are willing to contend with the possibility of meaninglessness in our lives.

[9]For a detailed discussion of the influence of traditional Jewish catastrophe writings on later Holocaust literature, see David G. Roskies, *Against the Apocalypse: Responses to Catastrophe in Modern Jewish Culture* (Cambridge, Mass.: Harvard University Press, 1984). Roskies argues that a direct line leads from one to the other, allowing for no permanent ideational rupture between, for example, depictions of pogroms and depictions of the destruction of European Jewry during World War II. All such efforts have common roots in a literature of lamentation. For an alternate point of view, see Lawrence L. Langer, *The Holocaust and the Literary Imagination* (New Haven, Conn.: Yale University Press, 1975).

[10]The question of "survivor guilt" continues to haunt us. The psychological community, especially in America, has made the idea an unchallenged premise about

the survival experience. But in an unpublished paper presented at a conference sponsored by the US Holocaust Memorial Museum Research Center in December 1993, Norwegian psychiatrist and Auschwitz survivor Leo Eitinger argued that "most survivors had the same self-reproaches one can hear in all cases of losses: 'If I had done this or that or if I had not done this or that, perhaps he or she would have lived today.'" Such "guilt," which Eitinger prefers to call self-reproach, is not specific to survivors but represents a common human response. Psychiatrist Anna Ornstein, also a Holocaust survivor, shrewdly refines this idea: "The frequently cited guilt in survivors, I believe, may not be related to having survived while others had died, but rather to the survivors' difficulty in reconciling their behavior and moral conduct during the Holocaust with their conduct and behavior under civilized conditions." See Anna Ornstein, "The Holocaust: Reconstruction and the Establishment of Psychic Continuity," in *The Reconstruction of Trauma: Its Significance in Clinical Work*, ed. Arnold Rothstein (Madison, Conn.: International Universities Press, 1986), 184–85.

[11]Fortunoff Video Archive for Holocaust Testimony, Yale University, composite tape A-67, testimony of Bessie K. and Jacob K.

[12]For a detailed discussion of the uniqueness of the Holocaust as an epistemological event (rather than as an illustration of comparative suffering), see Steven T. Katz, *The Holocaust in Historical Context (Volume One): The Holocaust and Mass Death Before the Modern Age* (New York: Oxford University Press, 1994). The concept of having missed one's "intended destiny" is born of the German intention to murder every living Jew with no exceptions, an intention that distinguishes the Holocaust from other atrocities, such as the ones in Cambodia and Rwanda. As Katz argues, the distinction is between historical events, not the quality or quantity of the suffering.

[13]Fortunoff Video Archive for Holocaust Testimony, Yale University, tape T-1879, testimony of Judith G.

[14]Ibid., tape 938, testimony of George S.

[15]See Timothy W. Ryback, "A Reporter at Large: Evidence of Evil," *The New Yorker*, 15 November 1993, 78.

It is simply unacceptable that, in the closing days of the twentieth century, in so many countries the chronically mentally ill are still abandoned in conditions of filth and brutality, without treatment or rehabilitation, so that their humanity is betrayed. It is unacceptable that tens of millions of patients with depressive disorder, a highly treatable condition, suffer the torment, the lost opportunities, the high costs, and the real risk for suicide because doctors and nurses are neither trained to diagnose this disorder nor encouraged to give its treatment priority. It is unacceptable that mothers, in all too many nations and cultures, are regularly beaten by alcoholic spouses, who steal the family's food monies at the same time that they deprive their wives of their safety and dignity. That those mothers often have no recourse in the community cannot continue. It is also intolerable that seven and eight year old girls face the horror of being sold into sexual slavery as part of a globally commercialized system of sexual abuse that fosters criminality and spreads AIDS. The abuses. . .are all unacceptable.

Robert Desjarlais, Leon Eisenberg, Byron Good, and
Arthur Kleinman, eds.

From Executive Summary to *World Mental Health:
Problems and Priorities in Low-Income Countries*

New York: Oxford University Press, 1995

Veena Das

Language and Body: Transactions in the Construction of Pain

I N REPEATEDLY TRYING TO WRITE the meaning(s) of violence against women in Indian society, I find that the languages of pain through which social sciences could gaze at, touch, or become textual bodies on which this pain is written often elude me.[1] The enormity of the violence is not in question. The very moment of the birth of India as a nation free from colonial domination was also the scene of unprecedented collective violence. One of the earliest studies of this violence stated that history had not known a fratricidal war of such dimensions: "Decrepit old men, defenseless women, helpless young children, infants in arms by the thousands were done to death by Muslim, Hindu and Sikh fanatics."[2] One of the signatures of this violence was the large-scale abduction and rape of women. The earliest estimates put the figure of abducted women from both sides of the border at close to one hundred thousand. In the legislative debates in the Constituent Assembly it was stated, on December 15, 1949, that thirty-three thousand Hindu or Sikh women had been abducted by Muslims, while the Pakistan Government had claimed that fifty thousand Muslim women had been abducted by Hindu or Sikh men. I have elsewhere analyzed the discourses of the State on abducted women and their recovery as well as the composition of the personal voice in accounts by women.[3] I want to reenter this scene of devastation to ask how one should inhabit such a world that has been made strange through the desolating experience of violence and loss. Stanley Cavell describes this as the Emersonian gesture of approaching the world through a kind of mourning for it.[4]

Veena Das is Professor of Sociology at the University of Delhi.

In the work of mourning in many societies it is the transactions between language and body, especially in the gendered division of labor, by which the antiphony of language and silence recreates the world in the face of tragic loss. It is not that in turning to these transactions I expect to find direct answers to the questions on violence and the problem of meaning, but I do want to reenter some of the texts with which I have engaged earlier to make the dialogue deeper on two questions:[5] *1)* How is it that the imaging of the project of nationalism in India came to include the appropriation of bodies of women as objects on which the desire for nationalism could be brutally inscribed and a memory for the future made? *2)* Did forms of mourning find a place in the re-creation of the world in, for instance, the discursive formations in post-Independence India?

In forming these questions I am borrowing a metaphor from Stanley Cavell—the metaphor of philosophy as a river that flows between the two shores of the metaphysical and the everyday. The river does not have to ask which of these two shores is more important for its existence.[6] But from the present position in which I write, one appears as the distant shore on which events of violence, brutal rape and abduction of women, and painful inscriptions of nationalist slogans on the bodies of women made sudden appearances. One is never certain whether the distance of these images is an optical illusion, for there is always the temptation, as in family and nationalist narratives, to cast away these images from the shore of everyday experience to some distant unseen horizon. Yet, one must ask what this brutalization did to the experiences of self, community, and nation. At the very least these scenes of violence constitute the (perhaps metaphysical) threshold within which the scenes of ordinary life are lived.

The second shore is the near one, on which the experience of loss in the flow of everyday life makes the voices of women "public" in the process of mourning. In the genre of lamentation, women have control both through their bodies and through their language—grief is articulated through the body, for instance, by infliction of grievous hurt on oneself, "objectifying" and making present the inner state,[7] and is finally given a home in language. Thus the transactions between body and language lead to an articulation of the world in which the strangeness of the world revealed by death, by its non-inhabitability, can be transformed into a world in which one can dwell again, in full awareness of a life that has to be lived in loss. This is one path towards healing—women call such healing simply the power to endure.

And now we see the two shores together within a single frame. Was it possible for women and men to take this image of healing and recreate that which died when the desire for nationalism and autonomy from colonial subjugation became metamorphosed into sexual violation?[8] Could that which died be named, acknowledged, and mourned? Or would one be condemned to dwell alone and nameless in the ruins of memory, as Lawrence Langer calls them?[9]

Some realities need to be fictionalized before they can be apprehended. This is apparent in the weight of the distinction between the three registers of the real, the symbolic, and the imaginary in the work of Lacan, and in Castoriadis's formulation of the necessity of working on the register of the imaginary for the conceptualization of society itself.[10] I shall allow myself three scenes, or phantasms, that provide a theoretical scaffolding to the issues I address. In these three scenes I call upon the words of the philosopher Wittgenstein, the poet-novelist-essayist Tagore, and the short story writer Sadat Hasan Manto, as persons who responded to the call of the world in the register of the imaginary. Tagore and Manto are important to me for they answered in the sounds and senses of the Indian languages to the scenes of devastation; Wittgenstein because he showed the possibilities of imagination of pain within a rigorous philosophical grammar. In placing their texts within mine, I can simultaneously be there and not be there. I hope I shall be evoking these texts not in the manner of a thief who has stolen another voice but in the manner of one who pawns herself to the words of this other.[11]

I

The first scene is from Wittgenstein's *The Blue and Brown Books* on the question of how my pain may reside in another body:

> In order to see that it is conceivable that one person should have pain in another person's body, one must examine what sorts of facts we call criteria for a pain being in a certain place. . . .Suppose I feel

a pain which on the evidence of the pain alone, e.g. with closed eyes, I should call a pain in my left hand. Someone asks me to touch the painful spot with my right hand. I do so and looking around perceive that I am touching my neighbor's hand....This would be pain *felt* in another's body.[12]

In this movement between bodies, the sentence "I am in pain" becomes the conduit through which I may move out of an inexpressible privacy and suffocation of my pain. This does not mean that I am understood. Wittgenstein uses the route of a philosophical grammar to say that this is not an indicative statement, although it may have the formal appearance of one. It is the beginning of a language game. Pain, in this rendering, is not that inexpressible something that destroys communication or marks an exit from one's existence in language. Instead, it makes a claim asking for acknowledgment, which may be given or denied. In either case, it is not a referential statement that is simply pointing to an inner object.

What is fascinating for me is that in drawing the scene of the pathos of pain, Wittgenstein creates language as the bodying forth of words. Where is my pain—in touching you to point out the location of that pain—has my pointing finger—there it is—found your body, which my pain (our pain) can inhabit, at least for that moment when I close my eyes and touch your hand? And if the language for the inexpressibility of pain is always falling short of my need for its plenitude, then is this not the sense of disappointment that human beings have with themselves and the language that is given to them? But also, does the whole task of becoming human, even of becoming perversely human, not involve a response (even if this is rage) to the sense of loss when language seems to fail? Wittgenstein's example of my pain inhabiting your body seems to me to suggest either the institution that the representation of shared pain exists in imagination but is not experienced, in which case one would say that language is hooked rather inadequately to the world of pain. Or, alternately, that the experience of pain cries out for this response of the possibility that my pain could reside in your body and that the philosophical grammar of pain is an answer to that call.

II

The second scene is from Rabindranath Tagore. A prefiguration of the investment of sexuality into the project of nationalism is found in three important novels—*Gora, Ghore Baire,* and *Char Adhyaya.* Here I want to simply draw out certain passages from *Ghore Baire* (Home and the World)—a novel that is set in the context of the *Swadeshi* movement against the British Raj. The struggle is to free the self that has become frozen in language. It is this frozen self that reads itself as if it were a script. It produces a magnification of the images of both nation and sexuality, and in Tagore's reading it is the pursuit of such magnified images that can make one blind towards the unique concreteness of being and hence to the experience of suffering.

The story of *Ghore Baire* is well known. The narrative device is to relate the story through interspersed accounts of the three main characters: Nikhil, the local *zamindar* who is bound to his *praja* (subjects who include both Hindus and Muslims) by ties of patronage and love; his wife Bimala whose desire moves from Nikhil to Sandip and then returns to Nikhil; and his friend Sandip, the fiery nationalist revolutionary. I shall reproduce only some root metaphors from each character.

Bimala

When inspired by Sandip's passionate speech in favor of the *Swadeshi* movement, which she has heard with other women from behind the curtains, Bimala tells her husband that she wishes to serve food to Sandip with her own hands (i.e., not through the mediation of a servant). Serving food by a woman to a man can be a very sensuous gesture, hovering between the maternal and the sexual in Bengali imagery. This is the first time Bimala will enter any male presence except that of her husband, for according to convention, women of the feudal household do not step outside the women's arena.

> I shall speak the truth. That day I felt—why has not God made me unbelievably beautiful....Today as this great day dawns, let the men of the nation see in its women—the form of the goddess Jagaddhatri (the one who holds the earth)....Will Sandip be able to see that awakened power of the country in me? Or will he think that

I am an ordinary woman, merely the wife who lives in his friend's house?

Sandip

The magnification of her image in Sandip's eyes that Bimala desires will find an answering chord. But before I describe that, it is important to ask how Sandip constructs himself. The opening line, when the reader first hears the voice of Sandip, is enlightening:

> When I read my own account, I reflect, is that Sandip? Am I simply constructed in language? Am I just a book constructed of flesh and blood?

And then responding to the desire for the magnification of the image of Bimala that would merge with the image of the nation—a desire, however, which is read as a need—Sandip continues:

> Unless they can behold the nation with their own eyes, our people will not awaken. The nation needs the icon of a goddess. . . .It will not do if *we* construct the icon. It is the icons that have been transmitted by tradition that will have to be transformed into the icons of our nation. The path of worship is deeply transcribed in our country—traversing that path we shall have to direct the devotional stream towards the nation.
>
> When I saw Bimala, I said *that* god(dess) for whose worship I have come to the earth after a hundred thousand *yugas*, till s(he) revealed her form to me, till then could I have believed in her with all my body and soul? If I had not been able to behold you, then I could not have seen the whole country as one, this I have told you many times. I do not know if you understand this. It is very difficult to explain that the gods in their heaven remain invisible, only in the world of death do they show themselves.

And as reported speech in Bimala's story:

> Sandip got up and said, man reaches such a state when the whole world comes to be concentrated in one small place.[13] Here in your salon I have seen my world revealed. . . .I worship you. . . .After seeing you my *mantra* (sacred formula) has changed. Not *vande matram* (I worship the nation as mother) but *vande priyam* (I worship the nation as beloved), *vande mohinim* (I worship the nation as the enticing one). The mother protects us. . .the beloved destroys us. Beautiful is that destruction. You hear the tinkling of the bells of

that dance of death. This delicate, luminous, fruit bearing, the one cooled by the Malay mountains[14]—this earth of Bengal—you have altered its image in the eyes of your devotee in the fraction of a second [lit. in the blinking of an eye]. You, oh Mohini (the enticing one, a female form that god Vishnu took to entice the demons to drink poison)—you have come with your vessel of poison—I shall either die after drinking this poison or shall become the one who has conquered death.

Nikhil

In an argument with Sandip:

> I am willing to serve my country but not to worship it. To offer worship to anyone else except that which should be worshipped is to destroy it.

In an argument with Sandip on the nation as an icon (as reported speech in Sandip's voice):

> But all this is very difficult to explain to Nikhil. Truth is now like a prejudice in his mind. As if there is a special substance called truth. I have said to him often that where falsity is truth there falsehood *alone* is truth. That falsehood shall be superior to truth. Those who can think of the icon of the nation as a truth, that icon will do the work of truth. We as a people cannot visualize the idea of a nation with ease but we can see the icon as the nation easily. When all this is well known then those who want to accomplish the project of nationalism, will have to work with this understanding.
>
> Nikhil suddenly got very agitated and said, you have lost the power to serve the truth, therefore you want a sacred formula to drop from the skies. This is why when for hundreds of years the work of the nation has remained undone, you now want to make the nation into a god so that you can stretch your palms in supplication and receive a blessing as if by magic.

And finally in accepting his defeat in that his wife and beloved Bimala saw him as a diminished human being in comparison to Sandip, but refusing to accept this as the extinguishing of the self:

> Today I shall have to see myself and Bimala completely from the outside. I am greedy. I wanted to enjoy that Tilottama (a mythic woman created by the gods so that every particle of her being was perfect) as my mental creation. The Bimala who had an external

existence had become a pretext for that. But Bimala is what she is—she does not have to become Tilottama for me—there is no reason for that.

Today I have understood this clearly—I am just a contingency in Bimala's life. That person with whom Bimala's whole being can merge, that person is Sandip. But it would be a great lie if I were to say that it means I am nothing for my manhood was not simply a means to capture the women of the interior.

An Interlude

The movements that run through these three voices may be brought together at this moment for a tentative weaving together. Each of the two men have found their destruction in Bimala, but in different ways. Sandip began his account by voicing the idea that he was just a script—someone who had no existence outside of language. In the only moment of authenticity that is permitted to him, which comes when Bimala has turned away from him, she responds to a passionate plea by saying "Sandip Babu, have you got several speeches written in your exercise book—so you can produce an appropriate one for each occasion?" Sandip's own fear is finally confirmed in the reflection in Bimala's speech—he exists only in language. His words do not falsify an inner life or draw a veil over it—they are indeed functioning to hide the fact that there is no inner life to hide. His search for the nation is a search for an icon, his desire for the other is for a magnification of image in which the lack of individual self may be hidden by a collectivization of desire. I would have been tempted to draw an analogy with the idea of certain kinds of ghosts in folklore, whose identities are revealed in a mirror by the fact that they cast no reflection. But Rabindranath himself, who appears in the voice of a schoolmaster, compares him to the new moon (*amavasyar chand*)—simply an absence.

As distinctions dissolve and the nation becomes a magnified image of beloved worshipped in the abstract, it becomes possible to inflict all kinds of violence on all those who resist this or who create counter images, equally enlarged. The desire for icons allows the nation as an absent object to be made magically visible through an investment in this magnified sexuality. The potential for violence is written in this construction. The story ends with a communal carnage that the reader does not gaze at directly but that is happening outside the immediate frame, waiting as it were, as the double of the nationalist ideology that has been propounded.

Nikhil may seem to have won since Bimala returns to him. But in their last exchange of intimacies, Bimala falls on his feet and begs him to let her worship him. Is this traditional slippage between husband and god not what he has tried to resist in their relationship all along? He does not try to stop her from this disastrous identification any more: "Who am I to stop her—after all it is not I who am the recipient of this worship." Nikhil's defeat is the realization that the everyday life embodied in tradition lives as much in the worship of icons (the husband as god) as the new transformations that Sandip is trying to bring (nation as god). We see Nikhil riding away from us into the heart of the carnage, offering himself either as a sacrificial victim or as a martyr (but never being named as such)—the very magnification of the image of nation and the investment of sexual desire in it has made it into a monster. We only know, as the voice of the schoolteacher tells us, that it will not do for him not to go there, for what is being done to the women is unspeakable. Towards the end he is brought back, injured, in a carriage. The news, says the person who has rescued him, is not good. We do not know if he will live or die.

Tagore does not permit himself a closure. Nikhil is the truth seeker who can find comfort neither in the psychological clichés of tradition (husband is god), nor of modernity (nation is god). He sees the potential of violence in both. Tradition is what diminishes women and permits a subtle everyday violence to be perpetrated upon them. Thus, when Bimala once comments that women's hearts are ungenerous, small, Nikhil replies, "yes, like the feet of Chinese women that are tied and never allowed to grow." In the modern project of building a nation the image is not diminished, but enlarged. Its dramatization means that bodies of women are violently appropriated for the cause as nationalism gives birth to its double—communalism. If one deified women so that the nation could be imagined as the beloved, the other makes visible the dark side of this project by making the bodies of women the surfaces on which their text of the nation is written.[15]

Body and language both function here as simulacrums in which collective desire and collective death meet. Nikhil, the truth seeker, prefigures the image of the martyr who must offer himself in an unheroic mode so that the magnified images of gods and demons have a chance to be humanized again. I think this is the task Tagore sets his reader—to hear the unfinished nature of this story, the transformations of the projects of tradition and modernity.

III

The third phantasm I want to evoke is from a story by Sadat Hassan Manto entitled "Khol Do," which I first analyzed in 1986.[16] The setting is the Partition of India and the riots, though we never gaze at the violence directly. An aged father and his daughter take a journey from one side of the border to the other. On reaching his destination, the father cannot find his daughter. He goes berserk searching for her. He comes across some young men who are acting as volunteers to help trace lost relatives. He tells them about his daughter and urges them to find her. They promise to help.

The young men find Sakina, the daughter, hiding in a forest half crazed with fear. They reassure her by telling her how they had met her father. She climbs into the jeep with them. One of them, seeing how embarrassed she is because she does not have her *duppata* (veil), gives her his jacket so that she can cover her breasts.

We next see a clinic. A near dead body is being brought on a stretcher. The father, Sarajjudin, recognizes the corpse. It is his daughter. Numbly he follows the stretcher to the doctor's chamber. Reacting to the stifling heat in the room, the doctor points to the window and says *"khol do"* ("open it").

There is a movement in the dead body. The hands move towards the tape of the *salwar* (trouser) and fumble to unloosen (lit. open) it. Old Sarajjudin shouts in joy "my daughter is alive—my daughter is alive." The doctor is drenched in sweat.

As I understood this story in 1986, I saw Sakina condemned to a living death. The normality of language has been destroyed, as Sakina can hear words conveying only the "other" command. Such a fractured relation to language has been documented for many survivors of prolonged violence, for whom it is the ordinariness of language that divides them from the rest of the world. I noted that even Sakina's father cannot comprehend the non-world into which she has been plunged, for he mistakes the movement in the body as a sign of life whereas in truth it is the sign of her living death. Only the doctor as the off-the-center character in the story can register the true horror.

On deeper meditation, I think there is one last movement that I did not then comprehend. In giving the shout of joy and saying "my daughter is alive," the father does not speak here in personalized voices of tradition. In the societal context of this period, when ideas of purity and honor densely populated the literary narratives, as well as family and political narratives, so that fathers willed their daughters to die for family honor rather than live with bodies that had been violated by other men, *this father wills his daughter to live even as parts of her body can do nothing else but proclaim her brutal violation.*

In the terms set by the example from *The Blue and Brown Books,* one may ask if the pain of the female body so violated can live in a male body. One can read in Manto a transaction between death and life, body and speech, in the figures of the daughter and the father. In the speech of the father, at least, the daughter is alive, and though she may find an existence only in his utterance, he creates through his utterance a home for her mutilated and violated self. Compare this with hundreds of accounts purporting to be based on direct experience in which the archetypal motif was of a girl finding her way to her parents' home after having been subjected to rape and plunder, and being told, "why are you here—it would have been better if you were dead." As I have argued elsewhere, such rejections may not have occurred as often as they were alleged to have happened in narratives. But the widespread belief in such narrative truths of sacrificing the daughter to maintain the unsullied purity and honor of the family attests to the power of this myth. To be masculine when death was all around was to be able to hand death to your violated daughter without flinching—to obliterate any desire for the concreteness and uniqueness of this human being who once played in your family yard.[17] In the background of such stories, a single sentence of joy uttered by old Sarajjudin transforms the meaning of being a father.

In Tagore's reading of Sandip, he was capable of constituting himself as a linguistic cliché. In Manto, the sentence, "my daughter is alive," is like Wittgenstein's, "I am in pain." Although it has the formal appearance of an indicative statement, it is to beseech the daughter to find a way to live in the speech of the father. And it happens not at the moment when her dishonor is hidden from the eyes of the world but at the moment when her body proclaims it. This sentence is the beginning of a relationship, not its end.

At this moment I want to present the glimpse of a later argument. I have written elsewhere that in the gendered division of labor in the work of mourning, it is the task of men to ritually create a body for the dead person and to find a place in the cosmos for the dead. This task, which is always a very difficult one for the mourner, may even become repulsive, as when members of the Aghori sect, who live on cremation grounds, state that in the cases when someone has died an unnatural or violent death, they have to consume parts of the dead body so as to free the dead person from living the fate of a homeless ghost. I wonder if Sarajjudin performed this terrifying task of accepting the tortured relationship with the daughter whom other fathers may have simply cast away as socially dead. And instead of the simplified images of healing that assume that reliving a trauma or decathecting desire from the lost object and reinvesting it elsewhere, we need to think of healing as a kind of relationship with death.

IV

Nadia Serematakis has recently used the idea of the ethics of antiphony to describe the structure of Greek mourning rituals. She shows how the interaction between acoustic, linguistic, and corporeal orientations gives a public definition to a "good death" and distinguishes it from a "bad death": "The acoustics of death embodied in 'screaming' and lamenting and the presence or 'appearance' (*fanerosi*) of kin construct the 'good death.' The silent death is the asocial 'bad death' without kin support. Silence here connotes the absence of witness."[18] Thus, it is the special role of women to "witness" death and to convert silence into speech.[19] In the rendering of this issue by Serematakis, death is always seen as physical death. What happens to the work of mourning when women have been abducted, raped, and condemned to a social death? The classic ritualistic solution in this case is for the social body to cut itself completely off from the polluted individual. This is objectified and made present by the performance of symbolic mourning for the "dead" person, by such ritualistic devices as the breaking of a pot that comes to stand for the person who has socially died but is physically alive. This is the sentiment underlying the stories I described earlier of kinsmen refusing to accept women who had been abducted or violated; or of men construing their kinship obligations in terms of the obligation to kill a beloved sister or wife rather than let her fall into the hands of men of the other community. Such women who were violated and rejected may be said to be occupying a zone between two deaths, rather than between life and death. Let us take a step backwards towards mourning in everyday life as it occurs in the case of "normal" deaths and ask whether it was possible to deploy the cultural codes to represent the kind of social death that I have described. It does not seem an easy matter to transform these "bad deaths" into "good deaths."

In an earlier paper, I described the division of labor between women and men, between professional mourners and close relatives, and between kin and affines in giving structure to the work of mourning in Punjabi families.[20] It is through the ritual work performed by the professional mourners (usually women of the Barber caste who have very specialized roles in the death rituals) that grief was objectified in the form of a portrait. We can glean from descriptions given in several accounts that women would form a circle around the dead body and move in circular forms, all the time beating their breasts and inflicting injuries upon their own bodies. In the frenzy of this "grief" they would tear at their clothes and their hair, improvising various mourning laments to make the loss that has occurred public and utterable. They would give the lead in the mourning laments to the women who were closely related to the dead person. The laments would articulate what the loss has meant for each person, now bereaved. The address was to the dead person, to the living, and to their own bodies, as well as to the gods. I give a brief example of each kind of address:

(To the dead son)—Open your eyes just once my beloved jewel (*mere lal*)—you have never stalled any request I made of you.

(To the men who are going to take the dead body of her husband to the cremation ground)—Do not let the fire touch him—I fold my hands before you—he could never bear the heat.

(To one's own body)—Are you made of stone that you do not break when you see this calamity?

(To the family goddess, referring to the fact that the goddess is a virgin—address is by the mother of a dead son)—You call yourself a goddess—you were just jealous of the good fortune of my *bahu*—son's wife—you had to make her a widow because you have yourself never found a husband—you call yourself a goddess—you are a demoness.

I could give extensive examples of blasphemy in the laments, on how women rage against the idea that gods are *just* beings, rather than callous, small-minded beings who play with the happiness of mortals. They rage against their bodies that have to bear pain within, rather than just disintegrate in the face of such tragedy. But since the mourning laments also have a dialogical element, soon other women begin to punctuate this by the counsel to get on with the work of living and by assurances to the most deeply affected mourners that the support of the community is with them. It is not that grief is seen as something that shall pass. Indeed, the representation of grief is that it is metonymically experienced as bodily pain and the female body as one that will carry this pain within forever. A mimesis is certainly established between body and language but it is through the work of the collectivity that this happens rather than at the level of individual symptom. A mourning lament from rural Greece recorded by Loring Danforth bears the same grammar as the mourning laments in Punjabi families:[21]

> My child, where can I put the *ponos* I feel for you?
> If I toss it by the road side, those who pass will take it.
> If I throw it in a tree, the little birds will take it.
> I will take it in my heart so that it will take root there
> So that it will cause me *ponos* while I walk.
> So that it will kill me as I stand.

So, in a sense, it is the objectification of grief on the body taken both as surface and as depth, as well as in language, that bears witness to the loss that death has inflicted. According to Serematakis, it is this witnessing that can make the performance of death public and even convert a bad death into a good death. In my own experience, the question of how good death and bad death is to be defined by the act of witnessing is a more complicated one, and I shall return to it later.

The excess of speech in the mourning laments and the theatrical infliction of harm on the body by the women stands in stark contrast to the behavior of men. In the course of everyday life men dominate the public domain in terms of the control over speech, but in the case of death they become mute. While the corpse is in the house, all the preparations, including the bathing and dressing of the dead body, are performed by the women. Women cling to the corpse imploring the dead person not to leave them. It is the men who have to disengage the dead body from the weeping and wailing women, to carry it on their shoulders to the cremation *ghats,* and to give the sacred fire to the dead person. It is they who gather the bones on the fourth day and perform the ritual of immersing these into the sacred river. For a period ranging from ten to thirteen days, the dead person hovers between the living and the dead in the form of a ghost, and it is through the gift of a body ritually created for him or her by the chief mourner (usually the husband or son) that the ghost finally becomes an ancestor. Thus, if women perform the task of bearing witness to the grief and the loss that death has inflicted (otherwise people will say was it a dog or cat that died, one woman told me), it is men who must ritually create all the conditions so that the dead can find a home.[22]

But if the good death is defined by the bearing of witness on the part of women so that grief can move between the body and speech that can be publicly articulated, as well as the performance of rituals for the dead so that they do not have to wander in the world of the living as ghosts, how is bad death to be represented?

In a sense, every death, except that of a very old person, introduces disorder in personal and social life. But in the flow of everyday life this is understood to be caused by events beyond the control of the living community. Indeed, one of the underlying tensions of mourning rituals is to absolve the living of responsibility for the death that has occurred. A common refrain in mourning laments is to say that the ostensible cause of the death (for instance a particular disease) is only the pretext for death to do its appointed job. Of course, when death is seen to be caused by the willful action of others, then a great tension prevails as to what definition of the situation will come to prevail through the control of mourning laments.

All this is reversed when the normal flow of life is seen as disrupted by the violence of men. In that case women bear witness to this disorder by a new construction of speech and silence. A woman recalled to me a mourning lament that witnessed the defeat of the Sikhs at the hands of the British troops in the Anglo Sikh wars:

> The crowns on the heads of the young wives—
> The flowing laps of the mothers—
> The swagger of sisters protected by brothers—
> Wiped out in a moment—
> Oh, from seven seas across came the white man to fight.

She went on to say that although everything was wiped out it was possible for the women to wail since their men had died heroically in war. The men had died as husbands, sons, and brothers. But in the case of all that died in the Partition, there was nothing but silence—for the men who inflicted such violence on women were not only strange men but also men known and deeply loved.[23] It is to an elaboration of this statement that the next section is devoted. It is an amplification that I have constructed—for it was never possible for me to get an exegesis of such statements from the women themselves.

V

In the literary imagination in India, the violence of the Partition was about inscribing desire on the bodies of women in a manner that we have not yet understood. In the mythic imagination in India, victory or defeat in war was ultimately inscribed on the bodies of women. The texts on the *vilap* (mourning laments of Gandhari in the *Mahabharata* or of Mandodari in the *Ramayana,* all whose kin were slain in the epic battles) are literary classics. This is a metaphoric transformation of the role of witnessing death in everyday life. Yet, the violence of the Partition was unique in the metamorphosis it achieved between the idea of appropriating a territory as nation and appropriating the body of the women as territory. As we saw earlier, a prefiguration of this is found in Tagore's rendering of the idea of the magnification of the image of nation, which draws its energy from the image of magnified sexuality. However, this image of sexuality and its intimate connection with the project of nationalism has not only a genealogy in the Indian imagination, but it was also an important narrative trope in the representation of the violation of the project of the Empire. The image of the innocent white woman who was brutally raped by the barbaric sepoys was an important narrative trope for establishing the barbaric character of the natives in 1857, when the first large-scale rebellion against the British took place. Jenny Sharpe has analyzed the image of helpless women and children being cut to pieces by leering sepoys as establishing the "truth" of the "mutiny."[24] As she says, "Commissioners and magistrates entrusted with investigating the rumors could find no evidence of systematic rape, mutilation and torture at Cawnpore or anyplace else. The official reports, however, came too late, as the sensational stories had already done their work. Rebels were seen as sadistic fiends, and Nana Sahib was especially vilified for the unforgivable crime of desecrating English womanhood. Barr exhibits a predictable understanding of the Cawnpore massacre when she writes that 'one of the most revered of Victorian institutions, the English lady, was slaughtered, defiled and brought low.' When the massacre of women is reported as the destruction of an institution, we know that the sacred image of English womanhood has outlived the story of women's lives."[25]

Thus, we have the interweaving of two strands. First, the idea that women must bear witness to death, which is found in the classical Indian literature and the everyday life, gets transformed into the notion that the woman's body must be made to bear the signs of its possession by the enemy. The second strand seems to come from a narrative trope established at the time of the mutiny that equates the violation of the nation with the violation of its women. It is not clear whether during the riots nationalist slogans were physically imprinted on women, although the most horrific stories about such violations are commonly believed.[26] What is clear is that at least one hundred thousand women from both sides of the border were forcibly abducted and raped. The figures given in the Legislative Assembly during the Constituent Assembly debates in 1949 confirm this. It also affirmed that processions of women who were stripped naked were organized with the accompaniment of jeering crowds in cities like Amritsar and Lahore.[27] Family narratives abound on men who were compelled to kill their women to save their honor. Such sacrificial deaths are beatified in family narratives, while women who were recovered from their abductors and returned to their families or who converted to the other religion and made new lives in the homes of their abductors hardly ever find a place in these narratives, although they occur frequently in the literary representations.

When women's bodies were made the passive witnesses of the disorder of the Partition in this manner, how did women mourn the loss of self and the world? It is in considering this question that we find startling reversals in the transactions between body and language. In the normal process of mourning, grievous harm is inflicted by women on their own bodies, while the acoustic and linguistic codes make the loss public by the mourning laments. When asking women to narrate their experiences of the Partition I found a zone of silence around the event. This silence was achieved either by the use of language that was general and metaphoric but that evaded specific description of any events so as to capture the particularity of their experience, or by describing the surrounding events but leaving the actual experience of abduction and rape unstated. It was common to describe the violence of the Partition in such terms as rivers of blood flowing and the earth covered with white shrouds right unto the horizon. Sometimes a woman would remember images of fleeing, but as one woman warned me, it was dangerous to remember. These memories were sometimes compared to poison that makes the inside of the woman dissolve, as a solid is dissolved in a powerful liquid (*andar hi andar ghul ja rahi hai*). At other times a woman would say that she is like a discarded exercise book in which the accounts of past relationships were kept—the body, a parchment of losses. At any rate, none of the metaphors used to describe the self that had become the repository of poisonous knowledge emphasized the need to give expression to this hidden knowledge.

This code of silence protected women who had been brought back to their families through the efforts of the military evacuation authorities after they were recovered from the homes of their abductors, or who had been married by stretching norms of kinship and affinity since the violation of their bodies was never made public. Rather than bearing witness to the disorder that they had been subjected to, the metaphor that they used was of a woman drinking the poison and keeping it within her: "Just as a woman's body is made so that she can hide the faults of her husband deep within her, so she can drink all pain—take the stance of silence." And as one woman told Ritu Menon and Kamla Bhasin (cited earlier), "what is a woman—she is always used?" Or, as was told to me, "what is there to be proud in a woman's body—everyday it is polluted by being consumed." The sliding of the representations of the female body between everyday life into the body that had become the container of the poisonous knowledge of the events of the Partition perhaps helped women to assimilate their experiences into their everyday lives.

Just as the relation between speech and silence is reversed in the act of witnessing here, so is the relation between the surface and depth of the body. In the fantasy of men, the inscription of nationalist slogans on the bodies of women (Victory to India, Long live Pakistan), or proclaiming possession of their bodies (This thing, this loot—*ye mal*—is ours), would create a future memory by which men of the other community would never be able to forget that the women as territory had already been claimed and occupied by other men. The bodies of the women were surfaces on which texts were to be written and read—icons of the new nations. But women converted this passivity into agency by using metaphors of pregnancy—hiding pain, giving it a home just as a child is given a home in the woman's body. Kriesteva's description of pregnancy—it happens but I am not there—may also be used to describe such violence. But the subsequent act of remembering only through the body makes the woman's own experience displace being from the surface to the depth of the body. The only difference is that unlike the child, which the woman will be able to offer to the husband, this holding of the pain inside must never be allowed to be born. This movement from surface to depth also transforms passivity into agency.

It was again Sadat Hasan Manto who was able to give literary expression to this. In his story *Fundanen* (Pompoms), a woman is sitting in front of a mirror. Her speech is completely incoherent, but like many strings of nonsense used in rhymes or musical compositions, its phonetic properties are like theatrical or musical representations. Interspersed between the strings of nonsense syllables are meaningful sentences with precise information such as the bus number that brought her from one side of the border to the other. The woman is drawing grotesque designs on her body, registering these only in the mirror. She says she is designing a body that is appropriate for the time, for in those days, she says, women had to grow two stomachs—one was the normal one and the second was for them to be able to bear the fruits of violence within themselves. The distortion of speech and the distortion of body seems to make deep sense. The language of pain could only be a kind of hysteria—the surface of the body becomes a carnival of images and the depth becomes the site for hysterical pregnancies—the language having all the phonetic excess of hysteria that destroys apparent meanings. When Tagore's Bimala said that she wondered if Sandip could see the power of the nation in her, she seems to have prefigured Manto's women in whom one could see the completion of that project of making the nation visible by a surrealist juxtaposition of images.

So, if men emerged from colonial subjugation as autonomous citizens of an independent nation, then they emerged simultaneously as monsters. What kind of death rituals could have been performed for these wandering ghosts to be given a place in the cosmos? We have to again turn to the register of the imaginary. Intizar Hussain described this in his story "The City of Sorrow," in which three nameless men are having a conversation. The story opens with the first man saying, "I have nothing to say. I am dead." The story then moves in the form of a dialogue on the manner of his dying. One of his companions asks how he actually died. Did he die when he forced a man on the point of his sword to strip his sister naked? No, he remained alive. Then perhaps when he saw the same man forcing another old man to strip his wife naked? No, he remained alive. Then, when he was himself forced to strip his own sister naked? Then too he remained alive. It was only when his father gazed at his face and died that he heard in his wife's voice the question, "don't you know it is you who are dead?" and he realized that he had died. But he was condemned to carry his own corpse with him wherever he went.

It appears to me that just as women drank the pain so that life could continue, so men longed for an unheroic martyrdom by which they could invite the evil back upon themselves and humanize the enormous looming images of nation and sexuality. But it was not through the political discourse that this was achieved. The debates in the Constituent Assembly on the issue of abducted women were full of the imagery of restoring national honor by recovering the women who had been abducted from the other side and returning "their" women back to the Muslims. Mahatma Gandhi, writing about the exchange of women and the exchange of prisoners on the same page of his Delhi diary, said that it had pained him to learn that many Hindu men were reluctant to return the Muslim women. He urged them to do so as a form of repentance. Jawaharlal Nehru urged Hindu men to accept the women who were recovered and to not punish them for the sins of their abductors. In this entire discourse of exchange of women from both sides, it was assumed that once the nation had claimed back its women, its honor would have been restored. It was as if you could wipe the slate clean and leave the horrendous events behind.

VI

It was on the register of the imaginary that the question of what could constitute the passion of those who occupied this unspeakable and unhearable zone was given shape. The zone between the two deaths that the women had to occupy did not permit of any speech, for what "right" words could be spoken against the wrong that had been done them. Hence, Manto's Sakina can only proclaim the terrible truth of this society by a mute repetition—*murde main kuch jumbish hui* (there was a movement in the corpse). The task of mourning for the men was to hear this silence, to mold it by their presence. Hence the joyful cry of the father that his daughter was alive. This being alive in the zone of the two deaths, and this witnessing of the truth of the women's violation, is how mourning in this zone could be defined. Here the issue is not that of an Antigone, mourning for her dead brother in defiance of the law of Creon, proclaiming that the register of someone who has been named must be preserved, as Lacan makes us witness it in his interpretation of Antigone's famous passage that she would not have died for a husband or a child but that this concerned her brother, born of the same father and the same mother (the product of criminal desire and criminal knowledge).[28] Here it is the issue of the women drinking poisonous knowledge and men molding the silences of the women with their words. Truth does not need here the envelope of beauty as Lacan would have it, but rather a renouncing of it as Tagore's Nikhil came to state it.

It is often considered the task of historiography to break the silences that announce the zones of taboo. There is even something heroic in the image of empowering women to speak and to give voice to the voiceless. I have myself found this a very complicated task, for when we use such imagery as breaking the silence, we may end by using our capacity to "unearth" hidden facts as a weapon. Even the idea that we should recover the narratives of violence becomes problematic when we realize that such narratives cannot be told unless we see the relation between pain and language that a culture has evolved. I have found it important to think of the division of labor between men and women in the work of mourning as a model on which the further work of transforming could be done in thinking about the relation between pain, language, and the body. Following Wittgenstein, this manner of conceptualizing the puzzle of pain frees us from thinking that statements about pain are in the nature of questions about certainty or doubt over our own pain or that of others. Instead, we begin to think of pain as asking for acknowledgment and recognition; denial of the other's pain is not about the failings of the intellect but the failings of the spirit. In the register of the imaginary, the pain of the other not only asks for a home in language but also seeks a home in the body.

It is not that there is a seamless continuity between the distant shore and the everyday shore, between the registers of the imaginary and the real, but one can only understand the subtle transformations that go on as we move from one shore to the other, if one keeps in mind the complex relation between speaking and hearing, between building a world that the living can inhabit with their loss and building a world in which the dead can find a home. It worries me that I have been unable to name that which died when autonomous citizens of India were simultaneously born as monsters. But then I have to remind myself and others that those who tried to name it, such as Manto, themselves touched madness and died in fierce regret for the loss of the radical dream of transforming India, while those who found speech easily, as in the political debates on abducted women in the Constituent Assembly, continue to talk about national honor when dealing with the violence that women have had to endure in every communal riot since the Partition.

ENDNOTES

[1]In thinking through some of the issues raised in this paper, I was greatly helped by an idyllic three day retreat at Kasauli. I thank Geeta Kapur and Vivan Sundaram for their warm hospitality and the marvelous conversations. Kumar Shahani helped with some of the most difficult passages for which I offer my gratitude. Without Sanmay, though, I would never have had the courage to write.

[2]G. D. Khosla, *Stern Reckoning* (Delhi: Oxford University Press, 1989; first published in 1951), 3.

[3]Veena Das, "Composition of the Personal Voice: Violence and Migration," *Studies in History* 7 (1) (1991): 65–77; and Veena Das, *Critical Events: An Anthropological Perspective on Contemporary India* (Delhi: Oxford University Press, 1995).

[4]Stanley Cavell, *Philosophical Passages: Wittgenstein, Emerson, Austin, Derrida* (Oxford: Basil Blackwell, 1995).

[5]See especially Veena Das and Ashis Nandy, "Violence, Victimhood and the Language of Silence," in *The Word and the World: Fantasy, Symbol and Record* (Delhi: Sage Publications, 1986); Das, "Composition of the Personal Voice"; and Das, *Critical Events: An Anthropological Perspective on Contemporary India.*

[6]See Stanley Cavell, *A Pitch of Philosophy: Autobiographical Exercises* (Cambridge, Mass.: Harvard University Press, 1994) and Stanley Cavell, "Philosophy and Modernity: The Case of Wittgenstein's *Philosophical Investigations,*" paper presented to the seminar on Modernity Reconsidered at the Swedish Collegium of Advanced Study in the Social Sciences, 26–29 April 1994. Cavell, elsewhere, describes the later thought of Wittgenstein as "...providing a theory of the drive to metaphysics and the possibility and necessity of skepticism—as much a philosophy of metaphysics as it is a philosophy of the ordinary." Cavell, *Philosophical Passages: Wittgenstein, Emerson, Austin, Derrida,* 78.

[7]In the felicitous expression of Robert R. Desjerlais, *Body and Emotion* (Philadelphia, Pa.: University of Pennsylvania Press, 1992), grief is transformed into pain that clings to the body.

[8] I have to refer back to the haunting images that Khwja Ahmad Abbas, the Urdu writer, used to refer to the atrocities on women. "Did the English whisper in our ears that you may chop off the head of whichever Hindu you find, or that you must plunge a knife in the stomach of whichever Muslim you find? Did the English also educate us into the art of committing atrocities with women of other religions right in the marketplace? Did they teach us to tattoo Pakistan and Jai Hind on the breasts and secret organs of women?" Khwja Ahmed Abbas, "Prastavna," in Ramananda Sagar, *Aur insan mar gaya* (Delhi: Rakjamal Prakashan, 1977, in Hindi). See also Das, *Critical Events: An Anthropological Perspective on Contemporary India*, 184.

[9] Lawrence Langer, *Holocaust Testimonies: The Ruins of Memory* (New Haven, Conn.: Yale University Press, 1991).

[10] C. Castoriadis, *The Imaginary Institution of Society* (Cambridge: Polity Press, 1987).

[11] On the concept of pawning of voice, see Cavell, *A Pitch of Philosophy*.

[12] Ludwig Wittgenstein, *The Blue and Brown Books* (London: Basil Blackwell, 1958).

[13] If Sandip sounds like a textbook, this is precisely what is intended. This point was completely missed by the many critics of Tagore.

[14] All these adjectives describe the goddess and were given a different life by Bankimchandra to describe the nation.

[15] It would be obvious that my interpretation of this text differs considerably from the interpretation offered by Ashis Nandy, *The Illegitimacy of Nationalism* (Delhi: Oxford University Press, 1994), who argues that Tagore's women stand for an authentic, unencumbered relation to tradition and hence are the defense which the culture puts up in response to both colonialism and an illegitimate nationalism that is modeled on the colonial image. Clearly Tagore has a more complex relation to tradition as evident in Nikhil's sense of defeat when Bimala insists on offering him her worship. Similarly, I cannot agree with Partha Chatterji, *Nationalism: A Derivative Discourse?* (Delhi: Oxford University Press, 1990), that Tagore's nationalism is simply a derived discourse.

[16] This story is included in an anthology of stories on the Partition translated by Alok Bhalla, ed., *Stories about the Partition of India*, vols. I, II, III (Delhi: Indus Publications, 1994), but there are many problems with the translation as I have pointed out elsewhere. See Veena Das, *Review of Stories about the Partition of India*, vols. I, II, and III, ed. Alok Bhalla (Delhi: Indus Publications, 1994).

[17] Das, *Critical Events: An Anthropological Perspective on Contemporary India*. See my account of the narration by a man on how he had felt compelled to kill his favorite sister because the other modes of dying were too painful for her.

[18] Nadia C. Serematakis, *The Last Word: Women, Death and Divination in Inner Mani* (Chicago, Ill.: University of Chicago Press, 1991), 101.

[19] See also Charles L. Briggs, "Personal Sentiments and Polyphonic Voices in Warao Women's Ritual Wailing: Music and Poetics in a Collective Discourse," *American Anthropologist* 95 (4) (1993): 929–57.

[20]Veena Das, "The Work of Mourning: Death in a Punjabi Family," in Merry I. White and Susan Pollock, eds., *The Cultural Transition: Human Experience and Social Transformation in the Third World* (London: Routledge, 1986), 179–210.

[21]Loring Danforth, *The Death Rituals of Rural Greece* (Princeton, N.J.: Princeton University Press, 1982). This is not to suggest any underlying similarity between the theoretical frames used by Danforth and Serematakis. See also Margaret Allexiou, "Reappropriating Greek Sacrifice," *Journal of Modern Greek Studies* 8 (1990): 97–123.

[22]For a detailed discussion of the structure of these rituals and the manner in which caste and kinship categories are utilized, see Veena Das, *Structure and Cognition: Aspects of Hindu Caste and Ritual* (Delhi: Oxford University Press, 1977), chap. 5.

[23]Das, "Composition of the Personal Voice."

[24]Jenny Sharpe, *Allegories of Empire: The Figure of Woman in the Colonial Text* (Minneapolis, Minn.: University of Minnesota Press, 1993).

[25]Ibid., 64.

[26]Abbas, "Prastavna"; and Das, *Critical Events: An Anthropological Perspective on Contemporary India.*

[27]Das, *Critical Events: An Anthropological Perspective on Contemporary India;* Uruashi Butalia, "Community, State and Gender: On Women's Agency during Partition," *Economic and Political Weekly* 17 (1993): WS12–WS24; Ritu Menon and Kamla Bhasin, "Surviving Violence: Some Reflections on Women's Experience of Partition," paper presented at IV Conference of the Indian Association of Women Studies, 1990; and Ritu Menon and Kamla Bhasin, "Recovery, Rupture, Resistance. Indian State and Abduction of Women during Partition," *Economic and Political Weekly* 17 (1993): WS2–WS12.

[28]J. Lacan, "The Essence of Tragedy," in J. A. Miller, ed., *The Seminar of Jacques Lacan, Book VII,* trans. Dennis Porter (London: Norton & Co, 1992).

Cosmologies of the powerless hold the capriciousness of gods and the sheer contingency of events responsible for the disorder of their lives; this, at the very least, has the potential of freeing those who suffer from having to take personal responsibility for their fate. . . .But in the cosmologies of the powerful, conversely, there is no place for chaos. For, if the contingent and chaotic nature of the world were acknowledged in these, it would have the potential to dismantle the structures of legitimacy through which suffering is imposed on the powerless. Clothed in the language of responsibility, the discourse of power ends up with the equation that pain is equal to punishment and that the injustice of life, testified to by suffering, can only be redeemed by further suffering.

Veena Das

From *Critical Events: An Anthropological Perspective on Contemporary India*

Delhi: Oxford University Press, 1995

Stanley Cavell

Comments on Veena Das's Essay "Language and Body: Transactions in the Construction of Pain"

T HIS ESSAY LEAVES ME WITH A SENSE not only of achieved depth but of inexhaustible tact, of simplicity and attention in the face of unencompassable devastations of spirit. With no thought of doing it justice, I will trace a line or two of Veena Das's more elusive thoughts, which readers of her essay may be having some difficulty with.

The first sentence of her essay ends by confessing that she finds that the languages of pain "often elude me." In what follows I will be guided by the thought that to understand her perplexity is the surest route to understanding her readers' perplexity.

Veena Das's topic is pain, in a historical instance in which its "enormity. . .is not in question." Her problem presents itself to her as the lack of "languages of pain through which social sciences could gaze at, touch or become textual bodies on which this pain is written." This opening sentence fairly obviously enacts, in its open tolerance of obscurity, the absence of such standing or given languages for such pain. If the scientific intellect is silent on the issue, she who speaks scientifically—committed to making herself intelligible to others similarly committed—is going to have to beg, borrow, steal, and invent words and tones of words with which to break this silence.

Her entire essay can be taken, thereafter, as providing an understanding of why this is a reasonable, sometimes necessary, way for an investigation of pain to begin, since, evidently, agreement about

Stanley Cavell is Walter M. Cabot Professor of Aesthetics and the General Theory of Value at Harvard University.

93

this is no more to be taken for granted than is agreement upon a language of pain. Das is exactly, I believe, in this beginning, being faithful to the concept of pain. She epitomizes this concept, in effect, in the last paragraphs of the essay in remarking that "denial of the other's pain is not about the failings of the intellect but the failings of the spirit." She accounts for this quality of failure early, in response to the passage she quotes from Wittgenstein (from *The Blue and Brown Books*), by noting that the utterance "I am in pain" is one that "makes a claim asking for acknowledgement which may be given or denied. In either case it is not a referential statement that is simply pointing to an inner object." In a text of mine to which Veena Das calls attention, I note that the utterance "I am in pain" is not simply a statement of fact (a point the logical positivists had their reasons for emphasizing) but is (as well) an expression of the fact it states; it is at the same time an utterance whose expression by me constitutes my acknowledgment of the fact it expresses (a point the positivists had no use for emphasizing, and that even J. L. Austin, in his critique of positivism's theory of expressive language, missed). One might even say that my acknowledgment is my presentation, or handling, of pain. You are accordingly not at liberty to believe or to disbelieve what it says— that is, the one who says it—at your leisure. You are forced to respond, either to acknowledge it in return or to avoid it; the future between us is at stake. Two implications follow: *1)* Not to respond to such a claim, when it is you to whom it is addressed, is to deny its existence, and hence is an act of violence (however momentary, mostly unnoticeable); as it were, the lack of response is a silence that perpetuates the violence of pain itself. *2)* If the study of a society requires a study of its pain, then so far as there is an absence of languages of pain in the social sciences—which is, after Veena Das's text, to say, languages in which pain is acknowledged, in which its existence is known ("witnessed" is the term she offers us, correctly and threateningly)—social science participates in the silence, and so it extends the violence it studies.

This is not exactly a "fault" of science. It happens, given what pain is, that its demand for acknowledgment is bound to be questionable in the everyday life of a society—with respect both to the justice of the demand for acknowledgment and to the degree to which that demand has been answered. (This may be taken to be what Rawls's "conversation of justice," as I have named it, is meant to take up; unsuccessfully in my view.) So, I understand Veena Das's more or less implicit claim to be a double one, namely that the study of social suffering must contain a study of a society's silence toward it (or, say, the degree of its incapacity to acknowledge it), and that the study of that suffering and that silence must contain an awareness of its own dangers in mimicking the social silence that perpetuates the suffering. (Why "dangers"? One might say that a society must be allowed some degree of unconsciousness of itself, to disguise itself from itself. But a science can make no allowance for itself of such a kind. To recognize what it does not know is part of its mission of knowledge.)

But does not such a claim as I am making on Veena Das's part make a drastic, unwarranted general assumption about the relation of social science to its object of study? The assumption, as I have put it, is that the social suffering it may have to study is in fact "addressed" to the practitioner of the science, that science owes its subject a response of acknowledgment. The wish to speak of what science "owes" its subject is, I think, quite similar to the way Veena Das's writing elicits the question that dominated the thoughts of contemporaries of mine in graduate school who were engaged in social scientific fieldwork, namely whether the claim to objectivity in the description of a culture must come from a stance inside or outside the culture.

I understand her writing to seek to put such a distinction into question. It is here that the point of her citation of Wittgenstein on pain is most precise. *Philosophical Investigations* is the great work of philosophy of this century whose central topic may be said to be pain, and one of its principal discoveries is that we will never become clear about the relation of attributions of the concept of pain, nor any of the concepts of consciousness, nor, hence, of unconsciousness—neither of my attribution of pain to myself nor of my attribution of pain to others—without bringing into question the apparently endless pictures we have in store that prejudicially distinguish what is internal or private to creatures (especially ones with language, humans) from what is external or public for them.

And I take it that no escape from Veena Das's prose will be provided by hurrying to suppose that she feels addressed by her subject because it is hers by birth, that she is an Indian woman, so naturally she is concerned about the fate of Indian women. As Austin used to ask about hurried assertions, "How many things are wrong with that statement?" One thing that is wrong with that statement is that her being an Indian woman seems to have more to do with her dissatisfaction with what she has said than with her motivation to say it. Something else that is wrong is the neglect of her claim that Indian women and Indian men have said plenty about the suffering she is trying to name, but that they have spoken out of frozen positions (from different idolatries, of women, of men, of nation, of God), not freely, not humanly. Something that is further wrong is the neglect of her claim (again in her final paragraph) that she has herself failed to say something specific, perhaps essential: "I have been unable to name that which died when autonomous citizens of India were simultaneously born as monsters." She goes on to remind us that one who tried to name it, whom she quotes, himself touched madness. The overarching neglect in that imagined attribution of her desire for speech and her doubts of speech about her scene of suffering is of her identifying herself, as well as being an Indian woman, as being a social scientist. It is for science that she (also) speaks, and on behalf of which she is disappointed. She does not give up on the idea that the unknown language of mourning and of healing that she seeks to name might take the form of a tone we may recognize as knowledge, as science.

But what she says, or implies, of that tone as it stands is that neither a standing idea of participation nor of observation will suffice to achieve reason in the present case. Participation is doubtful (does a society have available in every case the means to participate in its suffering, and when it does might not any given member or group of members decline to participate?), and observation is complicitous (the official response to the women's suffering precisely avoids the experience of it). I put this point earlier by suggesting that science as it stands in this case mimics its topic. This is one way in which Veena Das's idea of pain entering the body of a text realizes itself (but negatively, uncreatively): not to experience the death of these women, alive or dead, is to avoid the experience, deny it, refuse its acknowledgment; and that is either to incorporate a woman's private, unshareable, unspeakable knowledge of her death, and of the monstrousness that caused it, or to incorporate the men's public, civilized ignorance of that death and of that cause.

Let me offer a speculation in conclusion. The difference between natural and social science is not that one is interpretative and the other is not, but that in the one case conviction in its objectivity is continuous (except in intellectual crises), and that in the other conviction may have to be won afresh in each project (as if there are nothing but crises). But is there not something else? Has not Veena Das begged the question, proving only what she already assumes—that pain is a spiritual as well as an intellectual problem, that to fail to know the pain of others is to deny it, to annihilate the existence of the one who suffers? If there is a circle here, it means that something is ungrounded, at least in a sense in which we had expected grounding. But perhaps the ground is already under our feet.

This seems to me a place Veena Das finds company in work of mine, especially that on Wittgenstein. So, I will testify to my conviction in two moments in which she finds her ground: first, in her appeal to her own experience (e.g., "In my own experience the question of how good death and bad death is to be defined by the act of witnessing is a more complicated one"), an appeal in her writing that I unfailingly place confidence in and am grateful for; second, in her use of Wittgenstein's example of "feeling pain in the body of another," a passage that no one, to my knowledge, has put to more creative, nor sounder, use. I take Wittgenstein's fantasy in that passage as a working out of Descartes's sense that my soul and my body, while necessarily distinct, are not merely contingently connected. I am necessarily the owner of my pain, yet the fact that it is always located in my body is not necessary. This is what Wittgenstein wishes to show—that it is conceivable that I locate it in another's body. That this does not in fact, or literally, happen in our lives means that the fact of our separateness is something that I have to conceive, a task of imagination—that for me to know your pain, I cannot locate it as I locate mine, but I must let it happen to me. My knowledge of you marks me; it is something that I experience, yet I am not present to it, as in the experience (as Veena Das cites from Julia Kristeva) of giving birth. (I think in this connection of a remark of Catherine Clément's near the end of her book on opera: "The uterus. . .is an organ where the thought of beings is conceived." If such a thought marks an essential route toward overcoming skepticism with respect to the existence of oneself and others, and if skepticism with respect to others is one tacit, if blurred, model for skepticism with respect to the so-called external world, then it is perhaps no wonder that philosophers have characteristically failed either to defeat skepticism or to ignore it.) Wittgenstein had asked, "What gives us *so much as the idea* that living beings, things, can feel?"[1] This idea of the knowledge of the existence of others more or less reverses Kant's insistence that knowing is an active process, and that sensing is a passive one. My knowledge of myself is something I find, as on a successful quest; my knowledge of others, of their separateness from me, is something that finds me. I might say that I must let it make an impression upon me, as the empiricists almost used to say. (Whether that is sufficient empiricism to establish some part of a scientific discourse is perhaps a question worth trying to articulate.) And it seems reasonable to me, and illuminating, to speak of that reception of impression as my lending my body to the other's experience. The plainest manifestation of this responsiveness may be taken to be its effect on a body of writing. Whether this is ever true of one's own writing one is oneself not in a position to say. But I am sure it is true of the work of Veena Das now before us.

ENDNOTE

[1]Ludwig Wittgenstein, *Philosophical Investigations* (Oxford: Blackwell, 1958), section 283.

Mamphela Ramphele

Political Widowhood in South Africa: The Embodiment of Ambiguity

WIDOWHOOD SWEEPS WOMEN into a liminal phase in which the woman's tie to the departed spouse is publicly reenacted: "The widow in mourning having lost her spouse and yet still considered married is in a special kind of ambiguous, transitional state typically involving pollution and related beliefs."[1] The widow becomes the embodiment of loss and pain occasioned by the sting of death, and her body is turned into a focus of attention, as both subject and object of mourning rituals. The individual suffering of a widow is made social, and her body becomes a metaphor for suffering.

This essay will examine the transposition of the widow from the role of enacting and embodying personal loss to that of incorporating public loss. The shifting of the focus and locus of grief from the personal to the political adds important dimensions to the ambiguity of widowhood, the ritual dangers represented by her body, and the power that emanates from the very ritual dangers she signifies. Political widowhood raises questions of importance about pain and suffering as social phenomena, and the extent to which social space is created or denied for the public expression of pain, loss, and suffering of individual social actors.

THE POWER OF NAMING

Widowhood in South Africa is not simply about the loss of a spouse. It stands apart from widowerhood, which is, on the whole,

Mamphela Ramphele is Deputy Vice Chancellor of the University of Cape Town in South Africa.

a transient phase when the loss of a wife is registered, grieved, mourned, and bracketed. A widower is encouraged to take on the challenge of picking up the pieces and to face life again. He is reminded that he must be strong and swallow his pain. His body is not marked in any significant way except to have his head shaved, as is the custom in most African communities. He also is required to wear a black button or arm band. The period of mourning for widowers is generally six months, compared to at least one year for widows. The widower's status is the ultimate recognition that a man's identity in most patriarchal societies is perceived and presented as complete in itself, independent from the women in his life, including his wife.

The widower's movements and social contacts are not monitored, nor does he have to stay out of the public arena, a behavior that is expected of widows. He belongs to the public arena by virtue of his manhood. The only exception to this lax treatment of widowers compared to widows in African customary practice is reported by John Rankie Goody amongst the LoDaaga in Côte d'Ivoire, a matrilineal community that monitors widowers more stringently than widows.[2] The rationale for this practice is that a widower may be so distraught by the loss of a nurturer that he may contemplate harming himself.

The fear of the ritual danger embodied in widows is expressed in terms of "heat," "darkness," and "dirt." But it is the sexuality of the widow that is singled out as the ultimate reservoir of extreme danger to herself, any partner she may encounter, and the community she lives in. In certain communities, a special ritual is undertaken to make this danger even more potent by symbolically hitting her over the head with the hoof of the cow slaughtered for her husband's funeral rites.[3] Her body is marked in different communities by some or all of the following practices: shaving her head, smearing a mixture of herbs and ground charcoal on her body, wearing black clothes made from an inexpensive material, and covering her face with a black veil and her shoulders with a black shawl.

A widow expresses her liminal status in a variety of ways depending on local custom: these may include eating with her left hand, wearing clothes inside out, wearing one shoe, or eating out of a lid instead of a plate.[4] The proscription of social intercourse finds expression in widows being bound to stay at home, except for essential business trips, for which they would have to be accompanied and precautions taken to prevent them from polluting the unwary. Widows are prohibited from participation in public ceremonies and celebrations. Amongst the Warlpiri, Dussart describes how silence is also a marker of grief and mourning. Widows use sign language throughout their period of mourning, and the return to verbal speech becomes a symbolic mark of the end of mourning.[5]

Political widowhood incorporates, elevates, and transforms some of the elements of the ritual dangers embodied in personal widowhood. Individual pain and loss is claimed and given a public voice. Thus, ritual danger is contained and transformed into ritual power. By sharing the pain with the widow and her family, the circle is widened to incorporate "the political family," represented by the political formation to which the deceased belonged. The enlarged family circle brings with it resources and corresponding responsibilities and obligations.

Veena Das makes an important point that "pain is the medium through which society establishes its ownership of individuals."[6] The acknowledgment of the pain and loss of social actors is a profoundly political act. Not all widows are acknowledged as political widows, nor are all political widows "widows." The term "political widowhood" reflects the appropriation of certain women's bodies as part of the symbolic armor mobilized by political movements in the contest for moral space following the fall of heroes in the struggle for power. The claims political formations make or fail to make on the dead, and consequently on their widows, have significantly influenced the trajectories of women's lives in South Africa.

But the symbolism of political widows extends beyond those whose partners/spouses have died in a struggle. It also includes many women who lived as "widows" during the long periods of their spouses' imprisonment. The inclusion of this second category of political widow is deliberate and intended to show the complexities of the processes of negotiation of the personal and political by women who were drawn by choice or force of circumstance into the struggle for liberation in South Africa. Political widowhood is a particularly ambiguous status. It is both an acknowledgment and a denial of women as social and political actors in their own right. An understanding of the impact of the processes of negotiation of gender relations in a body politic that vacillates between accepting and not accepting women as codeterminants of history is important in the unfolding reality of South Africa.

My personal interest/involvement in this exploration is as one who is "a political widow who could never be,"[7] but is nevertheless pursued by interested parties as someone who should be socially classified as a widow. Through being personally implicated in the subject of my inquiry, I bring another perspective to Veena Das's comment on the mode by which knowledge is produced in anthropology as being "the mode of intimacy" in the "here" and "now."[8] My analysis is based on personal narratives, newspaper reports, interviews with fellow travelers, and is then placed within a review of the *general* relevant literature. However, as Das emphasized,[9] it is by articulating the lived experience of political widowhood that I show how political movements fold into personal biographies.

AMBIGUITY ENACTED

The ambiguous status of a political widow goes beyond the perceived ritual danger inevitably embodied in South African women based simply on gender distinctions. The widow embodies a desired social memory about the fallen hero and the nobility of the commitment he made to the struggle. A widow must demonstrate a worthiness to personify that social memory for the benefit of society. Nobility, heroism, and the ultimate sacrifice of death, which, both collectively and individually, represent the highest ideals of public service, are not easily associated with a woman's body. Culturally conditioned oppositions create boundaries that the body politic jealously guards: male/female, sacred/profane, private/public, and personal/political. It is thus not surprising that the incorporation of a woman's body, associated with pollution and the private domain, as a social memory for public service and heroism, has to be highly ritualized to disguise the conflicts the female body inevitably suggests.

MALE/FEMALE

The body politic depicts and treats the female body as incomplete and inadequate to the task of representing nobility, heroism, and public office. The female body usually requires a male body to render it whole and acceptable, and yet when the man's body, having lost its vitality, lies helplessly without form, its helplessness and lifelessness acquire meaning from the proximity of the relatively frail body of the widow.

The importance of the body of the woman in funeral rites is symbolized in many different ways among different cultures and changes over time within cultural groups. For example, in some Shangaan communities in the Eastern Transvaal, the widow (or widows in the case of polygamous marriages) spends the night in the same room with her husband's corpse in the company of selected older women belonging to her husband's kinship group. At some point during the course of the night, the widow is made to carry the corpse on her back to signify their ties beyond death and her strength and bravery in being able to substitute for her deceased husband when necessary. Despite the cross-cultural variations, Maurice Bloch suggests that we can construct an ideal type in which the polluting aspect of the corpse is associated with women, who also bear the responsibility of becoming the channel for the expulsion of the polluting elements through mourning.[10]

There is a sense in which *sati*—a practice prevalent in some communities, such as the Rajputs in Milia, in which widows join their dead husbands on the funeral pyre—could be seen as the ultimate incorporation of the male body into the female body. The widow, in choosing or being made to choose to join her husband on the funeral pyre, is symbolically interposing her body between the triumph of death and the man's helpless body. In this practice, the woman is seen by some as a helpless victim and by others as protecting the husband's lineage and its honor.[11] Traditionally, before a woman left the home with the intention to commit *sati*, she made imprints of her hands on the wall of the threshold among the martial communities. Men were customarily enjoined to worship these imprints before they left for war to evoke the protection given by the *sati*: the woman's body and its memory stood between a man and the dangers he faced in war.[12] If a man were to die heroically in the war, then his wife was expected to commit *sati,* so that the heroic sacrifice was replicated by the sacrifice of her body.

In political funerals in South Africa, particularly those involving senior political actors during the political struggle, the ritual of handing over the man's military paraphernalia to his widow amid measured salutes from his comrades dramatizes the acceptance of the female body into the holy of holies, from which she would ordinarily have been excluded. She then becomes the custodian of the symbols of his heroism. Clearly, the symbolism of gender in relation to heroic sacrifice can take different social forms.

SACRED/PROFANE

The female body is perceived in many cultures as the embodiment of the profane or unclean.[13] This profanity is particularly concentrated in a woman's sexual organs. A woman who is menstruating is perceived as posing a particular ritual danger to regenerative and reproductive activities in a community, as well as the safety of those engaged in preparation for war. A widow assumes even greater potential for ritual danger, and would thus be prohibited from going near newborn babies, growing crops, and battlefields.

Political formations across the globe have learned to harness the power of the ritual danger incorporated in widows. By selectively presenting political widows in battle against their foes, politicians create an inaccessible and ultimately unassailable political space. Thus, by exploiting the very fear that they have themselves mastered, they put their enemies in a relatively more vulnerable position.

During the time that the African National Congress (ANC) was banned, its memorabilia were prohibited—one could not wear their T-shirts, fly their flags, nor display their green, gold, and black colors without inviting serious repercussions. Yet, Winnie Mandela could defy these prohibitions by invoking her role as the political widow of the most celebrated political prisoner. In that role, she was not readily accessible to the security police, and this served the cause of the ANC very well. Winnie Mandela could also quote Nelson Mandela in public speeches, in spite of the strict illegality of such an action, without any direct reaction from the security system.

PERSONAL/POLITICAL

The loss of one's partner and spouse is profoundly personal. It remains deeply etched in one's psyche and soul, defying attempts to give it an escape route through the sound of wailing or words of grief. The pain of the loss of a life partner becomes incorporated in the body of the surviving spouse, sometimes becoming inaccessible even to the sufferer.

The very nature of mourning rituals makes for little personal space, as family and friends rally around to lend support and share the pain and grief. Such support is a source of great strength for the affected person.[14] Philippe Ariès has lucidly explicated the importance of mourning as a social phenomenon and the vital role of the support offered by others in acknowledgment of one's loss. But he also points to the fact that helping the survivor was neither the sole nor primary purpose of mourning: "Mourning expressed the anguish of a community that had been visited by death, contaminated by its presence, weakened by the loss of one of its members."[15]

Thus, the meaning behind the communal support bereaved families receive is ambiguous. In focusing on the woundedness of the community, the bereaved individual may become simply part of the "ritual exercises, totally devoid of spontaneity."[16] Thus, the individual would have little space to come to terms with her personal loss, and the process of healing would be delayed.

Anthropologists have traditionally focused on the collective rather than the individual, and the individual is often subsumed as a result. James Clifford's critique of anthropology refers to the devices ethnographers have used to cope with the doubts they have had about "inhabiting indigenous minds": "Ethnographers have generally refrained from ascribing beliefs, feelings, and thoughts to individuals. They have not however hesitated to ascribe subjective states to cultures, e.g., 'the Nuer think' or 'the Zulu believe.'"[17]

Mourning rituals are, by their very nature, collective processes and have understandably received elaborate attention by anthropologists, whereas the individual's struggle with grief has not. It is my contention that the lack of attention to the space required by individuals to grieve properly has impoverished our understanding of how individuals, or categories of individuals, such as children and women, within the collectives we study come to terms, if at all, with the personal loss of loved ones.

The enlargement of the circle of mourners to incorporate the body politic to which the deceased also belonged brings both added support and tension. Political formations naturally want to make as much political capital as possible out of the death of a comrade. The funeral becomes a form of political theater that has to be managed to achieve the desired outcomes for the political formation involved. Inevitably, problems arise in balancing the wishes of the family and the desires of the politicians.

The profile desired by politicians may create tensions for the family. For example, during the height of the civil war in the mid-1980s in South Africa, many families were dragged into mass political funerals against their will. They wanted to put their dead to rest without further pain, given the violent and shocking nature of the deaths of their loved ones. They also feared being caught in the cross fire between "the comrades"[18] and the Apartheid security forces, which often ensured that mourners ended up having to run for their lives without completing the final rites for their loved ones. On the other hand, mourners feared displeasing or defying "the comrades," who felt that it was the duty of the mourners to use every available means to advance the struggle and did not approve of any retreat from such awesome tasks. The staging of mass political funerals assumed enormous significance as opportunities to put the evil and brutality of the state in full public view. The more coffins one could line up, the stronger the message that could be communicated in this regard:

> I participated in one mass political funeral in Guguletu in 1985 during which there were ten identical coffins which finally arrived at the local soccer stadium at about 11.30 am for a funeral service which had been scheduled to start at 10 am. A turf battle between the security forces and the organisers of the mass funeral preceded, and delayed the service. The police wanted to prevent the mass funeral service going ahead given the political capital they knew "the comrades" would derive out of it. This police interference merely strengthened the resolve of the comrades to go ahead.

The turf battle was only put on hold by the intervention of the priests who were to conduct the service who promised to keep the peace in exchange for the police keeping a low profile throughout the service. The funeral service was largely conducted in English, in a township where literacy levels are low (60%) and the level of competence in the English language minimal, this included the families and widows of the dead. The political theatre of mass funerals was not primarily intended for the audience in physical attendance, but for national and international audiences. The latter audience assumed greater importance in the message being communicated, because of the potential action they could mobilise in support of the cause.

The bereaved families became an incidental part of the audience to this political theatre. Their personal pain and loss had little space for expression as they sat huddled together, some as strangers to one another, but united by their common pain and grief. It was a hot day, and they were sitting with little shelter or refreshments in this rudimentary soccer stadium. They cut tragic figures. It was not until 4 pm that the funeral procession left for the graveyard, and only around 5.30 pm that they finally could retreat into the personal family space to claim their loss and suffering in its full personal sense.[19]

The political theater enacted in funeral rites of a fallen hero also becomes an occasion to make a statement about his position in history, the invincibility of "the struggle" in spite of losses along the way, which suggests the dispensability of individuals, and the inevitability of the ultimate price that has to be paid for freedom. Personal pain and loss become depersonalized into one more death along the path of freedom, one more container of blood emptied to water the tree of freedom, one more statistic in the long saga of the nation's losses.

History is often reinterpreted, reenacted, and represented in a manner that is intended to shape social memory in the political speeches and other ceremonial acts that are part of political funerals.[20] Symbols in the form of flags, T-shirts, and other memorabilia find space for defiant display. One of the political widows of the mid-1980s recalls how she was shocked to find her husband's coffin wrapped in the flag of the South African Communist Party (SACP), when she had known him to have been a member of the ANC.

The claim that was made by the SACP stands unchallenged in history, because neither the dead man nor his widow could take back the powerful symbolic statement made by the wrapping of that flag. The claim on the dead man had a finality to it. But more importantly, it was a sign of the SACP's claim on the widow's body. This woman chose to exercise her own rights, strengthened by her intimate knowledge of her husband's political commitment, but she could have been put in a more vulnerable position if she had not had the personal resources to resist this pressure.

Tensions also surface around broader logistical questions regarding the choices of the location of the funeral and speakers from the family versus those from the party. Tensions related to the extent to which one gives free reign to one's sense of personal loss are no less important. On one hand, one could give free reign to one's feelings, thereby running the risk of rewarding the killers with a sense of satisfaction that they have succeeded in inflicting a mortal wound not only to the dead man, but also to those around him by leaving them helpless. On the other hand, the brave face often presented by political widows contrasts so starkly with the reality of the moment that it borders on the theatrical. Dimpho Hani's case comes to mind:

The brutality of the assassination of Chris Hani, a prominent leader of the South African Communist Party, shocked South Africa and the world in its boldness in April 1993, just before the dawn of the liberation he fought so hard for as a senior ANC guerrilla, surviving many near deaths at the hands of the South African security forces. The right-wing assassins succeeded where their comrades in the Apartheid security forces had failed.

Dimpho's grief as a widow and mother of children suddenly robbed of a loving father must have been unbearable. But she steeled her nerves and went through the pre-funeral arrangements, funeral ceremony, and post-funeral formalities with little show of emotion. She was only able to find sufficient personal space to express her grief and to take leave of her beloved during her lone daily visits to his grave in the weeks following the funeral.

She was then able to restore her own internal equilibrium, and claim ownership of the pain and suffering occasioned by her husband's death. It is on the solid foundations of this personal space that she could confront the killer of her husband when he appeared in the

Johannesburg Supreme Court a few months later, not as a political operative, but as one personally wronged.[21]

Court cases following political deaths, be they inquests or, more rarely, criminal cases,[22] reenact the political drama of the death in its horrid details. The desire for the truth to be aired is in conflict with the pain it causes.

> Nyameka Goniwe, one of the widows of the Cradock four, speaks of the dilemma of wanting to know the truth, but also of the torture of the long-drawn process of getting to the bottom of what actually happened. Her husband, Matthew Goniwe, was one of four community leaders in Cradock, a small Eastern Cape Town, during the heady days of civil strife in the mid-eighties. Their effectiveness as civic leaders led to an instruction from senior police officials, sent via a top secret signal to the local security police, to have them "permanently removed from society." They were way-laid by security police at a road block on their journey home between Port Elizabeth and Cradock. Their charred bodies were found days later in a burnt out car.
>
> In a cruel twist of irony, she found herself on American National Public Radio in the run-up to the April 1994 elections in South Africa, on the same side with Dirk Coetzee a former policeman, and self-confessed murderer of political opponents, including a famous Durban lawyer, Griffith Mxenge, who is now a repentant member of the ANC. Her wish was to have the proceedings come to a close "so that I can then be able to learn to live with my pain."[23]

Full knowledge of the source of one's pain does make the suffering bearable. It puts one in a position to exercise one's right to make claims for historical wrongs done. These claims need not be exclusively material; they are, more importantly, claims for the acknowledgment of one's pain, and thus for its transformation into the arena of suffering worthy of social attention. Exposing one's wounds and having them acknowledged creates the possibility for the healing process to start from the base.

PRIVATE/PUBLIC

Death is by its very nature a public affair. The death of a person can only be registered as a memory by another. Even where the personhood of the departed is not acknowledged or recognized, as in a case of infanticide, or "the disappeared" in Guatemala, where widows of political activists were prohibited by the repressive regime from wearing mourning clothes, memories of deaths are carried as secret histories by families, ready for public release at more appropriate times. There is no such thing as a private death. Death attracts the public as both witness and participant. News of a death spreads very rapidly. Thus, a wider public is incorporated into the death rituals—an affirmation of the unification of humanity in a common destiny.

The desire for privacy by the bereaved often goes unheeded; if anything, it invites even greater attention because of the fear that, if left alone, the bereaved may become more vulnerable to contemplating undesirable and desperate actions (i.e., suicide). It is not uncommon for those sharing grief with the widow in South Africa to engage in endless chatter intended to make light of the moment and to temporarily take her mind off graver thoughts.

The political funeral ceremony signals a widow's entry into the public arena. Gender boundaries that the body politic polices so actively under other circumstances are lowered. The desired public profile of the widow is carefully nurtured and managed. This management includes her mourning clothes, which, while communicating grief, must also communicate dignity. The political widow, unlike other widows, does not wear the symbols of ambiguity in the form of cheap clothes worn inside out, or one shoe; the shaven head is replaced by carefully groomed hair and an appropriate hat.

The negotiation of the public space after the funeral involves a number of issues. The label of "political" widow carries with it public ownership of the person of the widow. She becomes a valuable resource for the political organization to which her husband and/or herself were affiliated. She embodies the social memory that has to be cultivated and kept alive to further the goals of the struggle, and hopefully to also act as a deterrent against further losses such as hers. She also becomes the embodiment of the brutality of the state, which leaves women like her in a vulnerable, liminal state.

Political widows are chosen, and targeted for special tasks. The label of political widow is not automatically bestowed on all women whose husbands have fallen in the struggle. The majority of women languish in obscurity because their husbands were not appropriate symbols for the limelight or because they were themselves not perceived to be appropriate candidates for the role of political widowhood. The pain of these widows is exacerbated by the failure of society to acknowledge their pain, and thus to help them make sense of their losses.

> Nohle Mohapi was barely in her mid-twenties in 1976 August when her husband Mapetha Mohapi was reported by the security police to have hung himself with his own jeans on a prison door grill after only a few weeks in solitary confinement. He had joined the long list of deaths in the detention.
>
> The suicide label was one used with great creativity by the security police at the height of the repressive period. Detainees slipped on pieces of soap in showers and died, they jumped through barricaded windows whilst under constant guard, some were supposed to have starved themselves to death, whilst shaming brain damage from mysteriously sustained head injuries.
>
> But women like Nohle have also been denied a place in the social memory of South Africa because their husbands were activists who laid the foundations on which others built the visible segments of the victorious struggle being celebrated by South Africans now. Society has forgotten most of the leaders of the Black Consciousness Movement such as the Mohapi's of yesterday, and thus also forgotten their widows. Their pain is a private one. Their claims are yet to be made, let alone acknowledged.[24]

The "suicide" label is a particularly troublesome one for bereaved families to deal with. Suicide is regarded by most people in the black community as a cowardly way out of life. Heroes do not commit suicide. They are supposed to confront hardship, torture, and the tribulations of war with courage. Hence, those women whose husbands were killed by the security police but were made to appear as having committed suicide bear an added burden.

The status of "political widows" who do not officially qualify as political widows is even more ambiguous. The eagerness to label such women as political widows signals society's anxiety to reestablish its own equilibrium by symbolically removing transgressives from the liminal unknown to the liminal known where social tools exist to deal with them.

It is remarkable the extent to which my public persona is often given "respectability" by summoning Steve Biko from the grave to accompany me and clothe my nakedness, a nakedness that is intensely troubling to the patriarchal society I find myself in. In summoning him to my side as a "political widow who could never be," society chooses to forget the relationship I had with him as a colleague and fellow activist, but only dwells on the aspect of our relationship that presents me as an instrument of his nurture and the bearer of his son. This phenomenon extends beyond South Africa. This is not to deny the important role Steve Biko played in my personal life and development, but rather to pose the question about the extent to which that relationship has become a marker on my body that enables the body politic to relate to me. The transgressive nature of our intense relationship is simplified and normalized by the patriarchal society, thus enabling society to deal with it as well as with myself as the embodiment of that transgression. I am unwilling to have my historical agency silenced by such simplifications.

The public role of the political widow derives from her relationship with her husband; she is not seen as a woman but as someone standing in for a fallen man. She becomes the ultimate honorary man. Her relationships are shaped by her late husband's relationships: his friends and comrades become her friends; his enemies become her enemies. Her agency is not completely eliminated, but constrained. To the extent that she can renegotiate the terms of her engagement, she is able to enlarge her sociopolitical space as a public figure. It is a tough balancing act fraught with danger.

The agency of the political widow is, by definition, constrained by those sponsoring her role. To the extent that there is congruence between their goals, strategies, and tactics and her own, a political widow continues to enjoy the patronage that comes with the role. Any major divergence, particularly if it takes on a public nature, poses major threats not only to the relationships but to her public status.

Winnie Mandela is a celebrated case of a political widow who was privileged above all other widows in similar, and in some cases worse position. Mrs. Albertina Sisulu, her contemporary in this regard, had to earn her keep, and struggle to get enough money to pay her aeroplane fare, and had to use the train to Cape Town to visit her husband, Walter Sisulu, Mandela's contemporary.[25] Both the ANC and the international anti-Apartheid movement differentially supported Winnie Mandela during her many trials and harassment by the security police who both feared and hated her.

Winnie Mandela's privileged position was in part due to her status as the widow of the celebrated Mandela. But it was also because she was a suitable candidate for a visible public role: her physical beauty, her regal deportment and her flair for the right attire for each occasion, her capacity to communicate and articulate her own, and other people's pain, all stood her in good stead.

Her personality enabled her to transform herself from a victim of oppression, into a symbol of resistance and defiance. She was denied married life in the prime of her life—she was only able to live with her husband intermittently for a total period of 6 months before he was imprisoned for 27 years; detained in solitary confinement; and finally banished to a small Orange Free State town of Brandfort, she concluded that, "In my case there is no longer anything I can fear. There is nothing the government has not done to me. There isn't any pain I haven't known."[26]

She took many risks and in so doing earned the respect of all those opposed to Apartheid. The transformation of Winnie the person and woman into a symbol took many dimensions. She became "Mother of the Nation" with all the rights attached to that. But her defiance did not exclude those who were her original sponsors. She became an agent of history in her own right, and her own person in every way. It is in the interpretation of her rights and responsibility as "Mother of the Nation" that her fortunes began to decline. The "Mother of the Nation" was implicated and finally convicted of complicity in unmotherly activities of kidnapping which led to murder of a child political activist. Her highly publicised fall from grace in the ANC did not seem to dampen her spirits.

Winnie Mandela's tenacity is legendary. She has thrived on her political widowhood status, but ultimately transcended it. She is now a free agent with enough of a power base to compel her former sponsors to continue to pay their respects to her. She is the ultimate outsider-insider. She is done with the business of being a woman, and has become a powerful agent for better or worse.[27]

Winnie Mandela's case also raises further ambiguities: she belongs to a category of political widows whose husbands are not dead but imprisoned. The rhetoric of liberation, while keeping hope alive for the release of political prisoners, was particularly focused on Mandela's release, and yet the process by which one so publicly visible as Winnie Mandela could be made to retreat back into the private space reserved for women was not thought through.

There was no properly elaborated ritual for her return to the private sphere as there had been for her emergence into the public sphere twenty-seven years before. The public space became contested territory between the hero and his erstwhile stand-in. It is difficult to imagine how one so publicly visible as Winnie Mandela could acquiesce to the demands to retreat into the invisibility of the private sphere.

CONCLUSION

The leaders of the new South Africa are correctly stressing reconciliation after all the years of civil war. The personal pain of Mr. Mandela as a political prisoner and his transcendence of it to become the first black leader of South Africa are offered as reasons for others to heed his call to "let bygones be bygones."

To "let bygones be bygones" presumes an acceptance of pain and the acknowledgment of that pain by one's fellow human beings, particularly those who are contextually linked to the pain: the perpetrators, the witnesses, and the companions in the post-traumatic period. Personal pain is a degrading and dehumanizing experience unless meaning is vested in it. The investment of personal pain with meaning transforms it into suffering, which then becomes a social process. The individual derives dignity out of the acknowledgment of her pain and is thus in a better position to feel worthy of the suffering, and available to the possibilities for healing.

There are too many individuals, families, and communities whose pain remains unacknowledged. The definition of "the political" as opposed to "the personal" is in itself a political question. Political widows who are victims of forced removals, random killings, or industrial accidents are as deserving as any other of making claims for historical wrongs done to them. Their private suffering needs to be made visible as social suffering, enabling them to stake their historical claims and thereby restore their dignity.

But as long as women have to resort to "widowhood" to be able to make claims on a society that does not recognize the wounds it inflicts, the dream of full citizenship for women will remain unattainable. The retreat by women into nonthreatening, traditional roles may offer benefits, but they come at a price.

Druze war widows are a case in point: these women find themselves in the position of receiving generous public support, but in exchange they are expected to maintain a low public profile prescribed for all widows.[28] The "generosity" of the Israeli government is justified as payment for "a sacred debt." Druze war widows' claims of their own pain is subsumed in this rhetoric of "the sacred," which does not tolerate any "profanity." Transgressive widows, political or otherwise, reintroduce the profanity that ritualized control is intended to cleanse from their bodies.

The discourse of women as victims has been valuable to early feminism, but it has, over the years, been replaced by the reassertion of women's agency in history.[29] The theoretical formulation of human agency in history is not yet satisfactorily developed. We still cannot adequately explain why, and under what circumstances, some people act as agents of change and others do not. Women's agency is a particularly difficult area of such inquiry given the many layers of interconnectedness, negotiated meanings, and social spaces that women traverse in their daily lives.

There is one constant entity in this complex web of connectedness that may hold the key to some of the critical questions that need to be formulated towards a greater understanding of women's agency in history. A woman's body, as the embodiment of the generative and reproductive power that knits generations together, holds the secret of her ability to concomitantly embody ritual danger and ritual power. The woman is a victim to the extent that she internalizes and acknowledges only the perceived ritual danger of her body. The extent to which she also has the ritual power of her body acknowledged determines the extent to which she will be able to transform personal pain into social suffering—not on her behalf, but for the sake of the society she lives in.

ENDNOTES

[1]B. A. Pauw, "Widows and Ritual Danger in Sotho and Tswana Communities," *African Studies* 49 (2) (1990): 85.

[2]John Rankie Goody, *Death, Property and Ancestors* (London: Tavistock, 1962).

[3]Pauw, "Widows and Ritual Danger in Sotho and Tswana Communities," 80.

[4]Ibid., 85.

[5]F. Dussart, "The Politics of Female Identity: Warlpiri Widows at Yuendumu," *Ethnology* 31 (4) (1992): 337–50.

[6]Veena Das, *Critical Events: An Anthropological Perspective on Contemporary India* (Delhi: Oxford University Press, 1995).

[7]I am referring here to the fact that if one is not formally married to a man, one cannot technically be called his widow. But for a variety of reasons, some women, who have shared special, intimate relationships with men of prominence, become associated with them in almost the same way that widows are associated with their deceased husbands.

[8]Das, *Critical Events: An Anthropological Perspective on Contemporary India.*

[9]Ibid.

[10]See Maurice Bloch, "Death, Women, and Power," in Maurice Bloch and Jonathan Parry, eds., *Death and the Regeneration of Life* (Cambridge: Cambridge University Press, 1982), 226.

[11]See Veena Das, "Gender Studies, Cross-Cultural Comparison and the Colonial Organization of Knowledge," *Berkshire Review* 91 (1986): 58–76; Vasudha Dhagamwar, "Saint, Victim or Criminal," *Sominar* 342 (1988): 34–39; Ashis Nandy, "A Nineteenth Century Tale of Women, Violence, and Protest," in V. C. Joshi, ed., *Rammohun Roy and the Process of Modernization in India* (Delhi: Vikas Publishing House, 1975); and L. Mani, "Multiple Meditations: Feminist Scholarship in the Age of Multinational Reception," in James Clifford and Vivek Dhareshwar, eds., *Traveling Theories, Traveling Theorists* (Santa Cruz, Calif.: University of California at Santa Cruz, Center for Cultural Studies, 1989).

[12]Rajeswari Sunder-Rajan, "Representing *Sati*: Continuities and Discontinuities," in Rajeswari Sunder-Rajan, *Real and Imagined Women: Gender, Culture, and Postcolonialism* (London: Routledge, 1993).

[13]Carol P. MacCormack and Marilyn Strathern, *Nature, Culture and Gender* (Cambridge: Cambridge University Press, 1980).

[14]See for example Philippe Ariès, *The Hour of Our Death* (New York: Knoff, 1981).

[15]Ibid., 582.

[16]Ibid.

[17]James Clifford, *The Predicament of Culture: Twentieth-Century Ethnography, Literature and Art* (Cambridge, Mass.: Harvard University Press, 1988), 47.

[18]Comrade is a term that gained currency in South African liberation circles in the 1980s to denote solidarity among political activists.

[19]See *Argus Newspaper* archives, 1976–1990.

[20]See Paul Connerton, *How Societies Remember* (Cambridge: Cambridge University Press, 1989).

[21]Dimpho Hani is the widow of Chris Hani, the South African Communist Party Secretary General who was assassinated in 1993 by right-wing elements in South Africa. Dimpho is currently a Member of Parliament in South Africa. See *Weekly Mail and Guardian* archives, 1993–1994.

[22]Very few criminal cases for the many political murders committed against enemies of the Apartheid state were ever brought to court because of the close relationship between the perpetrators of these crimes and the law enforcement agencies.

[23]National Public Radio live broadcast, April 1994, USA.

[24]Nohle Mohapi is the widow of Mapetha Mohapi. See *Daily Dispatch* archives, 1976–1978.

[25]See Charles Villa-Vicencio, *The Spirit of Hope: Conversations on Religion, Politics, and Values* (Braamfontein, South Africa: Skotaville Publishers, 1994).

[26]Diana E. H. Russell, *Lives of Courage: Women for A New South Africa* (New York: Basic Books, 1989), 107.

[27]Carolyn G. Heilbrun, *Writing a Woman's Life* (New York: Norton, 1988).

[28]R. Katz, "Widowhood in a Traditional Segment of Israeli Society: The Case of the Druze War Widow," *Plural Societies* 20 (1) (1990): 22.

[29]Linda Alcoff and Elizabeth Potter, *Feminist Epistemologies* (New York: Routledge, 1993); and Sylvia Yanagisako and Carol Delaney, *Naturalizing Power: Essays in Feminist Cultural Analysis* (New York: Routledge, 1995).

The world's most ruthless killer and the greatest cause of suffering on earth is. . .extreme poverty.

Poverty is the main reason why babies are not vaccinated, clean water and sanitation are not provided, and curative drugs and other treatments are unavailable and why mothers die in childbirth. Poverty is the main cause of reduced life expectancy, of handicap and disability, and of starvation. Poverty is a major contributor to mental illness, stress, suicide, family disintegration and substance abuse.

Poverty wields its destructive influence at every stage of human life from the moment of conception to the grave. It conspires with the most deadly and painful diseases to bring a wretched existence to all who suffer from it. During the second half of the 1980s, the number of people in the world living in extreme poverty increased, and was estimated at over 1.1 billion in 1990—more than one-fifth of humanity.

World Health Organization

From *The World Health Report 1995: Bridging the Gaps*

Geneva: World Health Organization, 1995
Reprinted by permission of the World Health Organization.

Vera Schwarcz

The Pane of Sorrow: Public Uses of Personal Grief in Modern China

All those who trade on sorrow
Must
Join together like cabbages
Must find the only possible way
To spin the pyramid around
So all four sides will be bathed by sunlight

—Gu Cheng
"Bulin's Last Will and Testament"

T O SPEAK TOO MUCH OF GRIEF is to blunt its edge. It might even make us deaf to the cry that sparked discourse about suffering in the first place. A cold, calculating intelligence cannot grasp the rough contours of grief. Diagnostic techniques, whether in the hands of medical professionals or political authorities, frequently maul its fragile core. To preserve the significance of personal suffering in public life we need a more indirect approach; one that accepts and, indeed, nourishes ambiguity. This, in the words of Cynthia Ozick, is the discrete province of metaphor, "the reciprocal agent, the universalizing force that makes it possible to envision the stranger's heart."[1] In order to fathom the hearts of strangers in pain, we must accept the fractured vision (and versions) of those who have known social suffering firsthand. Fragments of experience must suffice in place of encompassing theories about the nature of pain.

Vera Schwarcz is Professor of History and Mansfield Freeman Professor of East Asian Studies at Wesleyan University.

119

The aim of this essay about the Chinese experience of sorrow is to peel away the encrustations of bureaucratic and theoretical talk that have muffled the voice of individuals in pain. At its best, history works like poetry: it cuts through worn generalizations with the aid of discrete detail. The historical and cultural details of grief, in turn, help us avoid the predicament that Veena Das warns about when she describes the Indian victims of the 1984 gas poisoning in Bhopal: "The more suffering was talked about, the more it was to extinguish the sufferer."[2] Conversely, absence of talk—or, rather, modest use of metaphorical discourse—serves us better in the presence of massive grief.

Half a decade before the Bhopal disaster, a young Chinese poet, Gu Cheng, joined the struggle against the obliteration of the voices of sorrow in his native land. Gu Cheng was born in 1957, the year in which Mao Zedong first invited voices of criticism to flourish in Chinese society and then proceeded to silence those who had dared to speak the truth. This rhythm of hope and despair repeated itself in Gu Cheng's adolescent years as he became swept up in the Cultural Revolution of 1966–1976. Coming out of the nightmare that claimed the lives of dozens of his schoolmates and extinguished the dreams of many more, Gu penned the following brief poem in 1980, titled simply "A Generation":

> The night has given me dark eyes
> But I use them to look for light.[3]

The search for "light" with eyes trained by the darkness of pain led Gu Cheng into direct confrontation with the authorities that denied the burden of his generation's grief.

The battle over who can speak about sorrow is invariably a battle about words. The battle in 1980, as now, is fought with words. Policymakers in the Chinese Communist Party, like legal experts in India, have used language to cover up grief. They prefer to talk about the "pathology of modernity," the "diseases of Western civilization," and even "the spiritual pollution of bourgeois culture" in order to dim the very light by which the poet seeks to illuminate the specific sufferings of his generation.[4] Gu Cheng had tried to cut through this fog of generalizations with murky metaphors about those "who trade on sorrow."[5] To hear the cry of Gu Cheng, scholars of social suffering must first humanize their subject. In the words of Arthur Kleinman, we must leave behind the medicalized discourse of disease and listen to the illness narrative of individuals in pain.[6] In this essay I use "sorrow" and "grief" more often than "suffering" because these shorter, simpler words muffle less of the ache that colors Chinese history in our time.

The Chinese ideogram for "sorrow," *ku,* is comprised of the word for "ancient" and the radical for "grass." It captures vividly the notion of old hurt grown terribly sour over time. In fact, the same character, *ku,* can mean both "sorrow" (as in *kuhai,* a "sea of suffering") and "bitter" (as in *kugua,* the "bitter melon" grown in Mongolia). This appreciation for the bitterness at the heart of suffering is key to all Chinese expressions of grief.[7] Only those who have crossed the sea of suffering, who have tasted the sourness of sorrow, can express it in a truly convincing fashion. This intimacy with grief comes through in one of the most famous poems by Li Yu, the last ruler of the Southern Tang dynasty (A.D. 937–978). Taken into captivity, this fallen Son of Heaven wrote about his lost homeland with the bitterness of one who might have saved it. Li Yu's personal sorrow became, over time, a communal lament about the powerlessness of memory in the face of a once glorious past:

> Spring bursts, autumn wanes,
> but I have lost the scent of time.
>
> Memory—
> a merciless hound. . . .
>
> My homeland, I cannot bear
> to think of you in dead of night.
>
> Lustrous stones are rooted there still
> while my sap's gone dry.
>
> You ask, my friend,
> How deep this grief?
>
> Simply a spring swelled river
> too eager to embrace the sea.[8]

When the last ruler of the Southern Tang dynasty tried to take the measure of grief, he came up against his culture's reticence about this subject. Not surprisingly, Li Yu resorted to a metaphor of nature, to a "spring swelled river" rushing into the oblivion of the sea, when he wanted to give an approximation of his pain. Long before Communist Party commissars tried to silence the voices of writers like Gu Cheng, Confucian culture itself sought to mute, or at least to moderate, the public expression of personal sorrow.

THE "TIDAL FLOOD OF HEART'S BLOOD"

Ancient psychology insisted that human nature is ordinarily in a tranquil state, like a body of still water. Emotions, especially strong feelings such as grief and sorrow, were the manifestation of harmony disturbed. When a person lost calm and balance, the "tidal flow of heart's blood" (*xin xue lai chao*) would be unleashed—not infrequently in very powerful and moving poems. The Tang dynasty poet and essayist Han Yu (764–824) described this outpouring of imbalance: "Whatsoever thing loses its calm and balance, is bound to make a noise. . . .The human voice, condensed and purified, becomes language, and literature is language further condensed and purified."[9] Han Yu himself was a master "noise" maker. A disgruntled conservative in matters of aesthetic taste, he poured his suffering into memorable poems and essays. Yet even his own creative output did not prevent Han Yu from longing for a state of undisturbed harmony, before the billows of sorrow stir up the waters of the emotionless self. In this, Han Yu partakes of the fatalism embedded in traditional Chinese psychology—a sense that strong feelings, especially of pain and suffering, accomplish little more than the uncovering of the bitterness of rancor.

This inclination toward reticence in matters of grief is given even more encompassing significance in the Taoist classic, *Jin Shu*. Lest we mistakenly blame Confucianism for keeping the lid on turbulent emotions, this third-century work reminds us simply that *qing you yi sheng, bu yi ze wu qing*: "Feelings arise out of memory. If there is no memory, feelings will dissolve as well."[10] The warning here concerns not only sorrow but all excitable life that is rooted in memory. To keep or to restore one's natural equanimity, the remembering self has to be extinguished first.

Yet this is precisely what the cantankerous conservative Han Yu was unwilling to do. This is what the captive emperor Li Yu could not fathom though he was cut off from the homeland of his memories. The inability to forget sorrow is what got Gu Cheng in trouble with the Communist authorities when he insisted on seeking "light" with the night-trained eyes of his generation. To be sure, it was easier for Gu to write about grief than it had been for his illustrious predecessors. By the time of the Cultural Revolution, China's traditional reticence about personal sorrow had been under assault for almost one hundred years.

Traditional Chinese fatalism started to erode at the turn of the twentieth century, along with the imperial system. Social Darwinism, which became popular among China's reformers, sanctioned a more aggressive attitude toward both individual and collective destiny. A civilization once eloquently indirect about disturbing emotions learned how to shout, polemicize, and artfully craft individual suffering into something publicly useful. Six decades after British gunboats challenged China's imperial order during the Opium War of 1840, Chinese radicals themselves launched an attack on Confucian tradition. By the time of the New Culture Movement (1917–1921), the Chinese imperial system had been overthrown. The Republican Revolution of 1911 had deteriorated into political wrangling among different warlords. This climate of disillusionment with political change led Chen Duxiu, who became one of the founders of the Chinese Communist Party in 1920, to call for China's first "Cultural Revolution."[11] One year before the May Fourth Movement of 1919 (the first massive student movement for science and democracy in Tiananmen Square) this Peking University professor pleaded with the young people: "If you want blessings, don't fear sufferings. The sorrows of individuals today often become the blessings of the future....The individual should leave behind a society that future individuals can enjoy as well."[12]

Chen Duxiu's own world view was deeply colored by concern with the "survival of the fittest." Individual suffering was useful because it had a distinctive social purpose: it could improve the lives of future individuals. Han Yu's reluctance about making "noise" out of one's grief gave way to an almost exhibitionist infatuation with sorrow. To suffer was, almost by itself, to contribute to the social revolution at hand. This notion, limited to educated youths during the May Fourth Movement of 1919, spread out to encompass the masses during the Maoist Revolution.

Chen Duxiu was the shrillest, often the most dogmatic of the iconoclastic intellectuals who broke the sound barrier surrounding suffering in twentieth-century China. But there were others, too, far more subtle, like the writer Lu Xun. He joined Chen Duxiu's call for a "Cultural Revolution" but with a burden of grief all his own. Having witnessed his father's death at the hands of traditional medical practitioners, Lu Xun became a bitter critic of slavish adherence to any inherited wisdom. Before the Republican Revolution of 1911, Lu Xun went to Japan to study modern medicine. Once there, however, he changed his calling. He turned to literature because he deemed it a more effective scalpel with which to dig out the sources of China's suffering. In the preface to *Nahan* ("Call to Arms," his first collection of short stories published in 1921) Lu Xun described his change of heart:

> I felt that medicine was not so important after all. The people of a weak and backward country, however strong and healthy they may be, can only serve to be made examples of. . .and it doesn't matter how many of them die of illness. The most important thing, therefore, was to change their spirits, and since at that time I felt that it was the best means to this end, I determined to promote a literary movement.[13]

The literary movement launched by Lu Xun and Chen Duxiu in 1918 continued apace with the social revolution that unfolded in the 1920s and 1930s. Its lofty ambition to promote a change of spirit was coarsened during the decades that followed. The White Terror of the late 1920s and the Anti-Japanese War of 1937–1945 brought violence close to the lives of Chinese people in all walks of life. A landscape long marked by natural disasters was now ravaged by politically manufactured chaos as well. First, the Nationalist Party tried to persecute the Communists into oblivion. Then the Japanese armies raided and looted much of North China. When Chen Duxiu had urged youths not to fear their sufferings, he had spoken metaphorically about how future generations would benefit from present sacrifice. Lu Xun, too, had envisaged his "Call to Arms" as a war of words. By the 1930s, however, violence had reached his own life. After the murder of one of his young leftist friends by the Nationalist police, Lu Xun cried out in bitterness. Like Han Yu, he wished he could have kept quiet. Lu Xun longed for the muted cadence of suppressed grief, but memory would not leave him alone: "I have some memories, but fragmentary in the extreme. They remind me of fish scales scraped off by a knife, some of which stick to the fish while others fall into the water. When the water is stirred up, a few scales may swirl up, glimmering, but they are streaked with blood."[14]

This bloodying of Chinese society and of Chinese memories continued during the Communist revolution. Lu Xun himself was canonized by Mao Zedong after his death in 1936. Yet, his followers, the critically-minded intellectuals who sought to speak about the endurance of social suffering even in the "liberated areas," were ruthlessly suppressed. While he silenced the voices of those who tried to stir the bloody fish scales of memory, Mao Zedong encouraged (indeed required) the public recitation of personal grief in "speak bitterness" sessions. This stylized recollection of class-induced sorrows developed into a performance art that enabled poor peasants, daughters-in-law, and coolies to translate individual suffering into a public commodity. "Speak bitterness" sessions became dramatic events in which a member of the oppressed masses was expected to dig into his or her heart and spew out in public the sour mixture of *ku*—a personal history both bitter and sad.

The American journalist Jack Belden observed such a performance in the Communist areas before 1949. The heroine was Gold Flower, a young girl married into a miser's household. Urged, then forced by fellow women activists to speak out, the girl spat her grief onto the face of her father-in-law: "I married into your family—yes! But there's been no millet for me to eat. No clothes in the winter. Are these not facts? Do you remember how badly you have treated me in these past five years? Have you forgotten my mother was sick and you made me kneel in the courtyard for half a day? In the past I suffered from you. But I shall never suffer again."[15] Having gotten the bitter words out of her long-silenced throat, Gold Flower was pushed further. One of the other girls found it easier than the "heroine" herself to draw back her lips and launch a ball of saliva right between the eyes of the old man.

After this first shot, others darted in, spat in his face, and darted away again. "The roar of voices grew louder. The old man remained standing with his face red and his beard matted with saliva. His knees were trembling and he looked like such a poor object that the women laughed and their grumbling and groaning grew quieter."[16]

This abusive spillover of *ku hai*, of "the sea of bitterness" that lay buried in so many hearts, was but one manifestation of the public uses of personal grief in the Chinese revolution. During the long era of Mao Zedong, from 1949 to 1976, official appropriations of individual suffering became further ritualized. *Yiku sitian* (recalling the suffering of old life while meditating on the new) became a way to enforce amnesia about unspeakable portions of one's own history. Happy, often falsified memories were inserted in the new, Communist era while the personal past remained shrouded in a mandatory condemnation of its bitterness. According to Ci Jiwei, this memory-manipulation process promoted indebtedness to the Party:

> Each reading of history or participation in *yiku sitian* is expected to redouble the memory of debts and the readiness to act as debtors. The debts are to be paid with the currency of loyalty and obedience. But the debts are piling up with each passing day, for the party never stopped doing good deeds for the People, who can only hope to repay a fraction of those debts and must pass the remainder, and a fitting sense of indebtedness, to the next generation. In this way political obligation takes on the tangible and sentimental character of interpersonal debts.[17]

In spite of all of these public manipulations of sorrow, there was one concrete consequence of the thought revolution launched by Chen Duxiu and Lu Xun in the late 1910s: suffering was no longer a worthless, personal burden. It now had a didactic value in communal life. The sour taste of *ku* became a source of positive insight. And thus, modern Chinese became spiritual kin to Jews, who also had to learn to extract lessons from suffering. In Hebrew, the very word for suffering, *tzara*, embodies this possibility. As Rabbi Benjamin Blech points out in a recent work, "Rearrange the letters of *tzara* and you have the word *tzohar*, a window. Through pain one can see further, through grief one can gain remarkable vision. The pain of suffering can be turned into the pane of insight."[18]

The Jewish view of suffering insists that pain can teach us something in proportion to our willingness to question the limits of human knowledge itself. Simply put, suffering both humbles us and clarifies our minds. This is quite different from the Christian notion that pain ennobles us, that we become somehow saintly through the very act of suffering. Yet, Christian notions of pain have been projected upon Jewish suffering from Job through the Holocaust. Even such an eminently sympathetic writer as the Polish intellectual Adolf Rudnicki falls into this pattern when he states, "No other nation has so many synonyms for suffering as have the Jews. . . .Everybody knows what the Germans did during the Second World War has no equivalent in history, yet it was all contained in the Jews' ancient vocabulary."[19]

Classical Chinese, like Old English or Old French, has at least as many synonyms for suffering as the Biblical Hebrew of the Book of Job. Nonetheless, Jews and their words are seen as particularly ample for the burden of historical pain. To counter this misinterpretation, it is important to return to an essentially Jewish understanding of suffering as a challenge to human knowledge.[20] A pane of insight emerges, as Rabbi Blech points out, precisely where and when pain cannot be reduced to words. A Jewish reading of the Book of Job emphasizes this test of our linguistic and conceptual arrogance (as opposed to the Christian view that suffering is a "gift whereby character is deepened, strengthened, purified and lifted Godwards"[21]). Moses Maimonides, the great medieval scholar, insisted that the message of Job is to pay attention "to the inference to be drawn from natural matters, so that you should not fall into error and seek to affirm in your imagination that His knowledge is like our knowledge or that His purpose and His providence and His governance are like our purpose and our providence and our governance."[22]

A pane of insight opens, according to Maimonides, whenever human words and human knowing are stretched to their outer limits. The contemporary poet David Rosenberg takes this one step further when he gives Job a voice that continues to challenge our conventional ways of dealing with suffering:

you are all plasterers
you think you are doctors
but it's only broken walls before you

you smear them over
with a whiteness of lies
a color you take for truth itself

you should shut up before them
and your silence becomes
a road to wisdom.[23]

Survivors of the Bhopal disaster might have cried out in similar anguish. They, like Job, point toward a silence-studded road to wisdom. This is a path familiar to Han Yu, who spilled out his heart's "tidal blood" only when he could no longer contain it, and then in only the most restrained of words. Job's voice is also familiar to eccentrics and "madmen" from the time of Confucius to that of Gu Cheng. All of them seek light with night-trained eyes.

"I AM A CHILD OF SORROW"

To suffer is to be shut in, to be locked up by grief in a world without light. A pane opens when sorrow is somehow voiced, shared, spewn out of the closed world of the individual in pain. When others respond to the voice of the sufferer—not with "a whiteness of lies," nor with the platitudes of plasterers pretending to be healers, but with truthful attentiveness—the window of insight becomes broader still. The echo of genuine responsiveness gives meaning to personal grief, heartens one to say more, to probe further a wound that might have festered in silence otherwise.

In Chinese tradition, the madman and the rustic were granted the possibility of sorrowful insight. In the twentieth century, that possibility became accentuated by an almost endless series of wars and revolutions. Starting with the "Diary of a Madman" (the first short story written in vernacular Chinese by Lu Xun in 1918), public uses of grief became not only acceptable, but a powerful weapon in the struggle for enlightenment. Unlike Foucault's reading of the discourse of madness, Chinese radicals were not immobilized but empowered by talking "crazy." Such talk broke through the reserve of tradition as well as Maoist dogmatism. It allowed the light of dissent into the otherwise claustrophobic chamber of Chinese political life.[24]

This glimmer of light has enabled China to withstand the pressure toward "cleansing" personal and social history. In Eastern Europe, by contrast, we witness a veritable frenzy of mutual blame by former Communist Party officials and secret police agents. To be sure, China cannot undertake such cleansings because the Party is still in power in Beijing. The brutal crushing of the Tiananmen demonstrations in June 1989 proved that the state can still plaster over the truth about who killed whom. Yet, the reason for China's restraint in the rush toward what Václav Havel called "lustration" may also be found in the fact that some sunlight has already been pouring over the subject of social suffering in the works of young artists like Gu Cheng. For almost a century, Chinese poets, historians, literary critics, and even Party officials have found ways to express the burden of grief in a publicly useful idiom. If we can understand this distinctly Chinese idiom, we may be able to enrich our strategies for coping with social suffering.

Yet, the idiom is obscure, forcibly opaque so as to avoid the ire of powers to be. Those long isolated from power cannot afford to speak directly. They must veil their voices. Gu Cheng took on the mantle of the rustic who speaks in obscure words. In a poem titled "Resume," he evokes the loneliness of sorrow as a hope for understanding:

> I am a child of sorrow
> from cradle to the grave undergrown
> from the northern grasslands I walked out...
> wrapped in indifferent smoke
> I still tell my green tales[25]

At one level, this poem is simply a description of Gu Cheng's generation—a generation of intellectual youths sent into the northern grasslands to carry out the message of Chairman Mao. There, they labored and suffered deprivations and humiliations (including starvation and rape). Having gone into the countryside as idealists, they were left to contend with the indifference that engulfed all of China in the 1970s. According to Gu Cheng's father, the Army-trained professional writer Gu Gong, this is a generation that cannot but baffle and trouble its elders. Some may be tempted to dismiss the outcry of these youths as an imitation of Western modernism or slavish mimicking of the May Fourth tradition. But Gu Gong insists that his son crafted a whole new aesthetic out of the bleakness of his distinctive suffering:

> How can we understand, how can we penetrate the heart of the new generation, the pursuits of the new generation, the poetry of the new generation? What has formed Gu Cheng's thoughts, sounds, sense of beauty and ugliness?...Are they inherited from the new beauty and ugliness?...Are they inherited from the new schools of thought that arose after "May Fourth"? Have they been influenced by modern schools from the West? No, no, Gu Cheng has grown up in a cultural desert, in an archaic age in the arts. . . .These poems are the spring and oasis his generation has found in the wasteland.[26]

It is in this wasteland that the "child of sorrow" found his voice. It is neither sonorous nor artful, but it does cry out with an indictment and a plea. By calling himself "undergrown" from cradle to grave, Gu Cheng is accusing the revolution of dwarfing its supporters. By persisting in the telling of "green tales," he asks others to draw sustenance from the sorrows of his generation.

A green tale is one that has the seeds of growth buried within. It is often a parable. This is the kind of tale we read about in the *Analects* when Confucius meets the madman of Qu. In Book 8, the story is told of how the recently dismissed adviser to kings, the uncrowned Sage, is accosted by the song of a seemingly deranged wanderer:

> Oh phoenix, phoenix
> How dwindled is your power!
> As to the past reproof is idle,
> But the future may be remedied.
> Desist, desist!
> Great in these days is the peril of those
> Who fill office.[27]

Confucius dismounts, eager to learn from the passing madman. But he hastens away before his message can be decoded. The unconsummated encounter ensures that the "crazy" song is heard over and over again. Unexplained, the warning grows in significance over time. Confucius, like Gu Cheng, knows that politics is a soiling affair. But the story of the Madman of Qu, like the poem

"Resume," tells us something else: the bitterness of the past can only be assuaged by a nuanced retelling of grief in the present. The very obscurity of the madman's song, like the young poet's murky metaphors, ensures that no one meaning will exhaust the tale of sorrow.

By remaining obscure, the "madman" also gains a measure of protection from the oppressive state. Rubie Watson, in her recent book *Memory, History and Opposition,* underscores the importance of indirect speech-acts for those who, like Gu Cheng, want "to talk back" to regimes that do not usually countenance any expression of social suffering: "The photos and personal documents of Stalin's 'disappeared' posted on a Moscow street; the creation of an unauthorized cemetery in a Soviet gulag...the unsanctioned mourning of Zhou Enlai in January 1976...were both simple and silent...inherently ambiguous, managing to appear individual and collective, silent and noisy at the same time."[28]

This terribly narrow ground between silence and speech, between individual grief and its indirect expression in the public domain had been explored in China for many centuries before the repressive Maoist regime. Qu Yuan, the disheartened official of the fourth century B.C., offers us an even more powerful example of the alchemy of grief than even the madman of Qu. Banished for his political opinions (not unlike former Red Guards, though they were banished for the more positive-seeming purpose of spreading the Great Helmsman's opinions), Qu Yuan decided to commit suicide, but not before pouring out his suffering in a long poem titled "*Li Sao*" ("Encountering Sorrow"). The disillusioned official met his grief head on. He did not hide from the burden of his rancorous feelings, nor did he simply cast them, along with himself, into the waters of the Milo River. Rather, according to the many layered mythology that grew up around Qu Yuan, he chose to leave behind a testament of his sorrow. That testament, like the song of the madman of Qu, echoes on in time. One man's skillfully conveyed suffering becomes a map on which others can locate their disillusionment as well:

> The age is disordered in a tumult of changing:
> How can I tarry much longer among them:
> Orchids and iris have lost all their fragrance;

Flag and melilotus have changed to straw.
Enough! There are no true men in the state:
no one to understand me.[29]

On the surface, Qu Yuan's "Encountering Sorrow" is cluttered by images of a lover (the official) fruitlessly seeking the affections of his beloved (the king) and by flowers symbolizing the hopes of a pure-minded social servant. But underneath all the talk of despoiled orchids and iris, around the evocations of desiccated straw, is the sufferer's own diagnosis of grief: a lack of understanding in the community. This diagnosis resounds through the ages. When sorrow closes in like a vise upon the heart, the need to be heard is ever greater. Wars and revolutions bring about deafening noises of their own. It becomes more and more difficult to listen for the soft-spoken voice of grief, and all the more necessary as well.

The modern historian Gu Jiegang was on intimate terms with both the noise of revolution and the muffled cry of personal sorrow. Born in 1895, Gu was part of the May Fourth generation—the students to whom Chen Duxiu addressed his plea for suffering in 1918. This is also the generation of Mao Zedong (born in 1893), who led the social revolution that eventually engulfed and almost drowned out the voices of intellectuals like Gu Jiegang. In 1926, long before the anti-intellectual campaigns of the 1950s and 1960s, Gu Jiegang wrote an autobiographical essay for a symposium on ancient Chinese history. Already, the dread of despair could be heard.

The memory of the May Fourth Movement was still fresh in 1926. Less troubled times might have nourished more optimism among the young radicals who had begun to quarrel with tradition in the late 1910s. Gu Jiegang had been one of the most prominent participants in the May Fourth debates about new culture. He was the star pupil of such arch critics of historical scholarship as Qian Xuantong and Hu Shi. The teachers were the first to attack China's inherited values head on. They were the bitter iconoclasts who called themselves "doubters of antiquity."[30] Their students were expected to deepen the critique. Gu did this, but more thoughtfully and with more anxiety than his teachers might have imagined.

Historical criticism was not just a political program or professional interest for Gu Jiegang. Uncovering forgeries, exposing layers of mythology at the core of China's classical legacy was painful and very slow work. The increasing pace of social change in the 1920s left no time and little tolerance for the scholarly passions of Gu Jiegang. His 1926 autobiography was fashioned as a boulder in the midst of a tidal river. It could not arrest the flow, but it could mark a place. Not unlike Qu Yuan's "Encountering Sorrow" or Gu Cheng's "Resume," Gu Jiegang's essay was intended to use publicly the pain of personal grief. In the Chinese tradition of the *zi xu*, his autobiographical preface was objective and subjective at once. According to Arthur Hummel, the translator of Gu's 1926 essay, this was an "intimate, unaffected…objective self-revelation…without evident self-consciousness."[31]

His family background bred into Gu Jiegang all the characteristics of a race horse. Generations of scholars before him made it possible to be brilliantly literate at an early age. He read novels and drama by the age of six and was making critical commentaries on the classics three years later. Yet, intellectual precocity left Gu Jiegang highly vulnerable as well. Physically inactive, sickly, his sufferings increased along with prodigious intellectual work. The 1926 autobiographical essay chronicles his personal sorrow along with his growing explorations of historical criticism. In 1900, when he was seven years old, he wrote his first essay on ancient history: "I placed it in my mother's vanity-box.…Unhappily my mother never recovered from that illness and [in the distraction] the little history was lost."[32]

The simultaneity of a mother's death and the loss of a historical essay are meant to shed mutual light on each other. The pain of being orphaned becomes a pane of insight for the older scholar who looks back over ancient classics and personal sorrow at the same time. This confluence of sadness and understanding continues in Gu Jiegang's *zi xu* when he records the death of his first wife in 1917 alongside the birth of his interests in folklore and, later, the paralysis of his beloved grandmother in 1921 alongside the beginning of his critical studies of China's most famous novel, *The Dream of the Red Chamber*. Throughout this chronicle of suffering and the emergence of critical thought, one hears the breathless cadence of tumultuous times. Like Qu Yuan, Gu Jiegang feels increasingly assaulted by society. Like Gu Cheng, he suffers from its ruthlessly "indifferent" demands. In one particularly poignant passage Gu Jiegang describes himself as a mule driven to death by a merciless master:

> Society...insists on my being a producer and not a consumer; to speak very frankly, it does not really love me, it wants to merely use me....When a mule is fully grown he is expected to recompense his owner by pulling a heavy cart, loaded with coal, rice, bricks, stones until the load becomes utterly intolerable. When the beast can no longer draw it, the lash is applied until his hide is laid open and blood flows forth. But of all of this the owner is entirely oblivious— only when the breath is exhausted and he falls dead in his tracks, can his work be said to be finished.[33]

In 1926, the mule beaten to death was only a metaphor—an extreme one, as Gu Jiegang himself hastens to add. Forty years later, however, it took on horrific reality for intellectuals of Gu's generation. During the early years of the Cultural Revolution, professors were herded into *niu-peng*, "ox pens," by their students, now turned into fierce Red Guards. They were forced to pull carts loaded with coal and bricks. At Peking University, senior professors built the very prisons that housed them from 1967 to 1968. There, they lived twenty to one room, sleeping on straw mattresses, waiting for the daily call of interrogation and beatings.

Among those incarcerated in Peking University's "ox pen" was Zhu Guanqian, China's foremost philosopher of aesthetics and Gu Jiegang's fellow activist in the New Culture Movement. Born in 1897, Zhu completed his education at Edinburgh University where he had written a masterful thesis on the psychology of tragedy. He revised this work for publication in 1933, less than four decades before he was to taste the meaning of tragedy on his own skin. An inquiry into classical Greek drama as well as modern Freudian theory, Zhu Guanqian's book may be read as a brilliant foreshadowing of the pain that befell its author, or as a parable about the inner spiritual resources that enabled him to survive suffering with dignity:

> To contemplate a great tragedy is like watching a great storm. We first feel the thrill of fear before some overwhelming power; then we are somehow uplifted by that fear-inspiring power to a level of vitality which we seldom reach in actual life. In a word, the tragic uplifts us after it has overwhelmed or threatened us. In the tragic

experience a rush of self-expansion follows a sense of humiliation, a feeling of wonder and admiration follows a thrill of fear.[34]

Here, individual grief is lifted out of the prison of personal experience. A truly "tragic" event, according to Zhu, is one that takes us out of the self, energized by terror and the sense of wonder that often follows in its wake.

THE WORLD'S COARSE THUMB

Zhu Guanqian had been part of a generation for whom the Cultural Revolution *could* have had tragic significance. He not only suffered its grief on his own skin, but he also had enough spiritual resources to confront the storm with vitality. The long decades of Zhu's formative development were behind him by the 1960s. He, like Gu Jiegang, had witnessed and been part of many social upheavals—some of the historical "storms" had been engineered by intellectuals (like the May Fourth Movement of 1919), some were endured by them (like the Anti-Japanese War of 1937–1945), some left a bitter taste (like the Anti-Rightist Campaign of 1957–1958). By the time of the "ox pens," Zhu Guanqian was an old man capable of what he had earlier called "reserve." The dignity that he foresaw as part of the tragic experience manifested itself through a capacity for holding back.

Older intellectuals, the most abused victims of the Cultural Revolution, had been, ironically, less depleted by its ravage than the younger Red Guards. They suffered from history, but were not overwhelmed by it. The Maoist youth, by contrast, had less spiritual terrain to build upon before the storm. Its painful decade was synonymous with their formative years. The Cultural Revolution became their whole life. And it continues to be the hole through which they view subsequent history. Their wounds have yet to be fully converted into a source of insight.

When I met Zhu Guanqian on April 2, 1980, I was not prepared for the vitality of this aged survivor. I had heard that he was one of the senior professors most severely beaten in the *niu-peng*. The bent, slowly shuffling walk of the octogenarian who greeted me in the offices of the Beijing University Philosophy Department confirmed my image of the pathetic victim. Then, I noticed his eyes.

Though weak, they shone with excitement as he spoke about his current work—a translation and critical study of Vico's "New Science."[35] We did not talk about the "ox pens" since the subject was too raw in the first few years after the death of Mao. But it was clear that Zhu Guangian was trying to rethink history on his own terms. The aesthetician who began his distinguished career with the psychology of tragedy, with the study of Freud and Croce, was now breaking new ground through his scrupulous historical studies. His thought had been affected, even deflected by the Cultural Revolution. But it had not been overwhelmed.

Zhu remained a vital thinker in spite of the beatings he endured. In his animated conversation about the historical significance of tragedy, I glimpsed the writer of the 1930s who had inspired several generations of Chinese intellectuals with his "Letters to Youth." The same old man who was approaching the tough text of Vico with fresh insight in 1980 had been admonishing youth to take their historical experiences seriously since the May Fourth Movement of 1919. In simple yet artful words, he had spoken to them about beauty, sex, and truth, about Goethe and Leonardo da Vinci.

In one of his "Letters to Youth," Zhu Guanqian describes his own feelings upon seeing the Mona Lisa in Paris and concludes with advice about building up inside oneself enough reserves of beauty and spirituality to withstand "the world's coarse thumb." This phrase comes from Browning's poem "Rabbi Ben Ezra," which Zhu quotes admiringly:

> But all the world's coarse thumb
> And finger failed to plumb. . .
> Thoughts hardly to be packed
> Into a narrow act,
> Faces that broke through thoughts and escaped,
> All I could never be,
> All, men ignored in me,
> This I was worth to God, whose wheel the pitcher shaped.[36]

Four decades after this letter, Ji Xianlin—one of the "youth" who most admired its author—became Zhu Guanqian's "pen-mate" at Beijing University. By 1967, Ji himself had become a distinguished professor of Sanskrit and Indian religions. Born in

1911 (the year of the abortive Republican Revolution), Ji Xianlin spent the years of World War II in Göttingen, one of the very few Chinese intellectuals who was able to witness and comment on the rise and fall of Nazism firsthand. That historical experience would stand Ji Xianlin in good stead during the Chinese Cultural Revolution. It strengthened him and gave him perspective—precisely what Zhu had advised much earlier. The "world's coarse thumb" was merely a poetic phrase in the early 1930s but it became an intrusive reality in the "ox pens." There, the older professors were packed in; there they labored in terror; there they had to find ways to safeguard a little bit of thought and fancy from the persistent interrogations of ideology-crazed youth.

During the Cultural Revolution, the wheel of history seemed to crush, or at least permanently alter, the consciousness of so-called "class enemies" like Zhu Guanqian and Ji Xianlin. Yet, in the end, as Zhu foresaw in the 1930s, the pitcher shaped the wheel. By 1986, the year of Zhu Guanqian's death, Ji Xianlin commemorated his teacher-friend in words that made his moral victory amply apparent. Sorrow had acquired meaning through the very dignity that the sufferer had managed to maintain during the worst abuses of the Cultural Revolution. Whereas Zhu had been eloquently reticent about his own grief during our meeting in 1980, Ji Xianlin—a similarly vital and thoughtful old man—could afford to recall the failure of total humiliation that took place in the "ox pens:"

> In the thirty years [since the founding of the People's Republic in 1949] storms raged, and some of the older intellectuals who bore them were refined by the process. The most telling example of this is the catastrophe of the decade [of the Cultural Revolution, 1966–1976]. Mr. Meng Shi [Zhu Guanqian's given name] was incarcerated in the ox-pens....My former teacher would now become my pen-mate. Life in the ox-pens cannot be easily described. Perhaps it is best omitted here. But there is a small incident about Mr. Meng Shi in the ox-pen that I will never forget. His short stature always made it hard for him to move, made him grow stiff easily. Yet in the most inhospitable environment of those times, he insisted on physical and spiritual exercise. I was most shocked by this, and also fearful for him. At night, after the lights were turned off, he tossed and turned in his bed studying some famous pavilion. In morning,

he would run to a corner and practice *tai ji quan.* One time, he was discovered by the so-called "staff to promote reform." They beat him fiercely. In the eyes of these young "lords," our bodies and souls had committed grave sins. This incident might seem small, yet its significance is not. . . .Mr. Meng Shi did not despair about our calling. He would never raise his hand to take his own life. In other words, he was rather different from our other brothers in misery who were overwhelmed by the humiliation. I never spoke to him about this, but it is vividly engraved in my heart.[37]

Reticence still prevails in this account of humiliation. Ji Xianlin details only one fragment of life in the ox pens. His teacher's death licenses painful recollection as well as a play on words. Zhu Guanqian, noted aesthetician, and Ji, the famed Sanskritist, had been *peng you*—an expression that can mean both "friends" and "pen-mates."[38] The awful decade endured with quiet dignity was not a subject of conversation between them. Death loosened, only somewhat, the tongue of the younger survivor. Yet, the significance of this memory is not to be missed: it aims to prove the limited dominion that the "world's coarse thumb" has even in the darkest hours.

Suffering, as Veena Das aptly put it, "poses an existential and cognitive problem of loss of meaning."[39] This is also the challenge to our knowledge categories that Moses Maimonides saw at the core of the Book of Job. Religion can help us face this epistemological challenge and so can memory, with its conscious attachment to cultural tradition. Zhu Guanqian managed to hold back part of himself from the brutally intrusive Red Guards by practicing *tai ji quan* and by meditating on an old pavilion glimpsed from the window of the "ox pen." His former student Ji Xianlin, though given to deeper despair about the shared calling of intellectuals, insists that he was the author of his own fate. Recalling the painful times of the Cultural Revolution allows this sufferer to reclaim some freedom and dignity in the face of history.[40]

Gu Jiegang, the pain-ridden historian, also sought such solace in the writing of his autobiography in 1926. Although the image of a mule beaten to death was only a metaphor, he knew the coarseness of the world on his own skin. In addition to the chronicle of sorrow (the death of his mother, wife, and grandmother) that accompanied the evolution of his critical faculties, he takes note of the intrusion of history on the work of the historian. During the very months that he was working on the autobiography, a war between warlords had broken out in Beijing:

> The aeroplanes made their daily round, the populace had visions that demons of death were circling over the city. Members of my household were so frightened that the mere clanking of covers on water-jars or the slamming of doors in the court-yard created illusions of hissing bombs and cannon's roar.[41]

For an ill man with nerves made taut by prolonged insomnia, this was sheer torture. To make matters worse, Beijing University, Gu Jiegang's employer during those months, issued only 15 percent of the faculty salaries. The pressure to provide for his family, to write the autobiography, and to keep on with research almost crushed Gu Jiegang. Yet, as the pain-drenched essay makes amply clear, he persisted—feeling soiled as well as inspired by history:

> I feel as though I were in the position of a sorter of old rags and paper in a paper-factory, where materials are unending, offensive, unclean and disorderly. Being without suitable tools, the worker is reduced to sorting with his own bare hands. Yet I cannot say that I am disgusted with my task or ever lose heart—I simply follow the program I laid down, and in that way manage to make moderate progress.[42]

This determination to proceed with sorting out "old rags" recalls the magnificent modesty of Camus's plague. But Gu Jiegang gives himself no heroic airs. He does not magnify the existential significance of historical research. He is simply reclaiming a small corner of his own mind from the all-intrusive pressure of society. It is this gesture that was reenacted by Zhu Guanqian in the "ox pens" and that was impossible for the younger Red Guards, who were consumed by the ritual obligations of the Cultural Revolution. The students were the "staff" promoting "thorough reform" in the "ox pens." Yet they were deeply victimized by the suffering perpetuated upon their elders. Their whole youth was consumed by acting according to an absolute faith in Chairman Mao. When that faith snapped, they remained trapped in a net of emptiness, burdened by their own wounds.[43]

After the death of Mao in 1976, with great difficulty, the younger generation started to reappropriate the tradition of the Madman of Qu. Having become rusticated because of dogmatic idealism, they returned to the cities with a howl of remonstrance. They showed off their wounds; they wrote elusive poems like those of Gu Cheng; they tried to warn subsequent generations of students about the entanglement of politics. Like the itinerant singer who accosted Confucius, they sought to disturb the consciences of those who had not suffered, or those who took suffering too lightly. Although Gu Cheng's generation of former Red Guards did not succeed in averting subsequent disasters (to wit—the terrible persecution of youth during the 1989 crackdown in Tiananmen Square), they have revived public appreciation for the voice of personal sorrow.

THE VOICE OF THE UNDISTURBED IS THIN AND LIGHT

In 1980, a seventy year old Chinese intellectual arrived in Japan to talk about the poetry of grief. Qian Zhongshu was no ordinary scholar. He was part of Ji Xianlian's superbly literate and much persecuted generation. Famous as both a novelist and a literary critic, Qian Zhongshu did not go to Japan wearing suffering on his sleeve. Rather, in the muted tone that is his distinctive hallmark, he spoke about himself as a "country bumpkin," as someone who "can't find a house with eaves to shelter you from rain."[44] Only those intimately familiar with the deprivations and humiliations endured by Chinese intellectuals in the Mao era might decode this metaphor. Yet, even unexplained, it serves as an appropriate springboard for Qian's meditations on the poetry of grief.

Qian Zhongshu did not go to Japan to lament his own sorrow, but rather to speak about the depths achieved by other Chinese who suffered from history. *"Shi ke yuan"* ("Poetry may be used to grieve"), the title of Qian's public address in Kyoto, is drawn from the Confucian *Analects*. There, the ancient Sage suggested that poetry has several functions, one of them being to convey grief. The word *yuan,* however, does not connote merely "grief" and "sorrow" but has the added edge of "rancor" and "grudge." Qian Zhongshu, the man who refused to be rancorous in public about his own suffering during the Cultural Revolution (even in a preface to his wife's memoir about their years of persecution in the countryside[45]), managed nonetheless to evoke the complex mindset of those racked by pain.

Away from his native land, through the roundabout discourse of literary criticism, a victim of persecution translated his own sorrow into a pane of insight. Indirectly, Qian Zhongshu makes use of his own experience with the disturbances of history to clarify the grief of others who were ensnared by their times. Foremost among the predecessors thus illuminated are Si Ma Qian, the historian-eunuch of the Han dynasty, and Han Yu, the Tang dynasty poet-official-essayist who wrote about the "noise" of disturbing emotions. By situating himself in a lineage of men literally and figuratively deformed by history, Qian Zhongshu shows how grief need not become a rancorous sore. Instead, through the alchemy of poetry, it becomes something meaningful as well as beautiful—in the manner of an oyster whose sickness breeds pearls and of the cedar whose drooping develops its much-praised knobs.

Qian Zhongshu himself is like a knobby cedar. A cosmopolitan intellectual trained abroad, he returned to China to witness the war against Japan and the repeated cycles of revolutionary mobilization that eventually cannibalized his own life during the Cultural Revolution. Yet, all this experience with the ravage of history did not leave Qian rancorous but, rather, full of grief. His words of appreciation for the voices of past victims of historical suffering may be used to describe his own powerful writing: "The voice of the undisturbed is thin and light, that of the sorrowful refined."[46]

These words may be read to praise suffering as the royal path to good writing. But Qian Zhangshu is too sober a sufferer to go that far. He is intimately familiar with the wide variety of faked sorrow that was cultivated by Chinese literati who sought to give their writing the added depth of grief:

> Some young fellow moans about the inconveniences of age; some fat cat wallowing in lucre bewails the trials and tribulations of poverty; an ordinary person experiencing a nice, ordinary day waxes lyrical on the subject of "strong sorrow" or the "melancholy of autumn."[47]

Low-cost sorrow does not give us depth of understanding, regardless of the writer's literary ambitions. If we are moved by the voices of pain, it is because they bear the imprint of genuine history. Qian Zhongshu's caution must be heard: suffering cannot be sought or manufactured. Once encountered, however, it may be used to illuminate corners of human experience too dark to even imagine before.

This is Job's message to our time as well: not to wallow in the grandeur of our imagined or real pain, but rather to push language and the categories of our knowing to the edge. Job, like Han Yu and Qian Zhongshu, is left with bitter fragments of speech in his mouth. It is these fragments that the poet David Rosenberg reassembles to show Job's quest for a new way of living *with* suffering:

> O earth, cover not over my blood!
> don't be a tomb a museum
> for my miserable poem
>
> my cry against this sinking
> leave my voice uncovered
> a little scar on your face. . .
>
> because he brought me out here
> into the darkness
> where I must continue speaking. . .
>
> my voice goes out of me
> a wounded bird.[48]

To say that pain has no music is to know that those who suffer are in a hell without song. Broken speech and scars are metaphors that cannot be laced with romantic meaning. Yet, in the very hell of grief, a rope is flung or created. This is what David Rosenberg does through Job's confession: "I must continue speaking." This, too, is Qian Zhongshu's point when he calls poetry a vehicle of grief. And also what the former Red Guard Gu Cheng creates in a poem called "Feeling." This work continues the theme of "Resume" by mirroring the poet's deformities:

> My shadow
> Is twisted.
> I am trapped in a landmass.
> My voice is covered with
> Glacial scars,
> Only the line of my gaze
> Is free to stretch.[49]

Gu Cheng's poem is not the outcry of some young fellow who moans about the inconveniences of the age. He endured its ravages on his own skin. When he talks about a twisted shadow, it is to evoke the real misshapenness of his generation of forcibly exiled youth. Like David Rosenberg's Job, Gu Cheng is a poet both wounded and wounding. Having suffered "glacial scars," he goes on to stretch and push language past its breaking point. In his poem "Feeling," the violence of the poet is cast in a passive voice. Only his twisted shadow bespeaks a deformation that goes beyond the sufferings of his generation.

The full extent of Gu Cheng's trauma did not become apparent until years later, after he left the "trapped landmass" of his motherland. Far from China's shores on an island in New Zealand, Gu Cheng spent years dissecting his mother tongue, pushing closer and closer to the broken sound of birds.[50] Then, on October 8, 1993 he murdered his wife and himself in an act of supposed revenge. Xie Ye, the bride of his youth, a woman who had also been through the deforming experience of the Cultural Revolution, seemed on the verge of leaving him. Realizing too late that "all I ever wanted had been right at my side,"[51] Gu Cheng cut short two lives. In a letter to his son, Mu Er, he wrote, "I once thought of writing a book to let you know why I was afraid of you, wanted to leave you, love you. Your mother wants to go off with someone else, she broke up this home, at the moment when your father was on the verge of regret and return and went off with another. . . .Don't blame your father, he loved you, loved your mother, he could not live without his family. . . .I hope you will not be too much like me."[52]

Here, a convoluted version of individual grief is used to silence two lives and maim a third. The effort to find some way to translate personal sorrow into a meaningful public idiom failed for Gu Cheng. In the end, he lacked *ren* (endurance)—a word that in Chinese can also mean "pain" and "suffering." The ideograph for "endurance" is composed of a knife poised over the heart. To go on with life after sorrow, to be on intimate terms with grief is to accept the ever-present possibility of violence, emotional as well as physical. Those who manage to survive the brutalities of history must also learn to live with the threat of humiliation even as they craft literary works. Gu Cheng in New Zealand was incapable of *ren*. Gu Jiegang, Zhu Guangian, Ji Xianlin, and Qian Zhongshu, on the other hand, outwitted the bitterness of their history. Being older than Gu Cheng, these intellectuals had more inner resources to give suffering meaning. As part of the pre-1949 generation, they had full access to China's cultural inheritance. They had not grown up in a "wasteland" like Gu Cheng. They knew and could build upon the tradition of Confucius's madman and that of Qu Yuan and Han Yu. Broken spirited and broken tongued, these twenti-eth-century survivors of war and revolution managed nonetheless to craft works of hope. Their hope was neither grandiose nor eloquent. Rather, in the words of Lu Xun, they doggedly stayed on the path, even where there was none: "Hope can be neither af-firmed nor denied. Hope is like a path in the countryside: origi-nally there was no path—yet, as people are walking all the time in the same spot, a way appears."[53]

This is what we must do as well. Those of us who seek to understand and to rethink the meaning of social suffering cannot but stay on the path that is no path at all. Broken words, frag-ments of metaphors, snippets of survivor testimony are all we have to guide us. But this may prove enough. By examining and reex-amining the way in which communal and individual sorrows shade into each other, a way may yet appear.

ENDNOTES

[1]Cynthia Ozick, *Memory and Metaphor: Essays* (New York: Alfred A. Knopf, 1989), 279.

[2]Veena Das, "Moral Orientations to Suffering: Legitimation, Power and Healing," in Lincoln C. Chen, Arthur Kleinman, and Norma C. Ware, eds., *Health and Social Change in International Perspective* (Cambridge, Mass.: Harvard Series on Population and International Health, 1994), 163.

[3]Helen F. Siu and Zelda Stern, eds., *Mao's Harvest* (New York: Oxford University Press, 1983), 16. For a fuller discussion of Gu Cheng's generation of poets—the so-called "wounded" generation that came to public attention in the late 1970s—see Vera Schwarcz, "In the Shadow of the Red Sun: A New Generation of Chinese Writers," *Asian Review* (Fall 1989): 4–16.

[4]It is interesting to note that many of the same terms that are used to dull the edge of suffering in China are also used in Japan. See Margaret Lock's discussion of *bunmeibo* ("diseases of civilization") in Margaret Lock, "Flawed Jewels and

ps, ```
```

National Dis/Order: Narratives on Adolescent Dissent in Japan," *The Journal of Psychohistory* 18 (4) (Spring 1991): 511–17.

⁵Gu Cheng, *Bulin's Last Will* (Hong Kong: Nineties Press, 1989).

⁶Arthur Kleinman, *The Illness Narrative* (New York: Basic Books, 1988).

⁷For a fuller discussion of the way in which Chinese theories of language can affect (and change) Western thought, see Chad Hansen, "Chinese Ideographs and Western Ideas," *The Journal of Asian Studies* 52 (2) (May 1933): 373–99.

⁸My translation of Li Yu's "Yu Mei Ren," in *Kuei Yeh Chi*, ed. Wu-chih Liu and Irving Yuching Lo (Sunflower Splendor) (Bloomington, Ind.: Indiana University Press, 1976), 133.

⁹Han Yu, "Song Meng Dongye Xu" (A dedication in honor of Meng Dongye), quoted in Qian Zhongshu, "Poetry as a Vehicle of Grief," *Renditions* (Spring & Autumn 1984): 29.

¹⁰I am indebted to Professor Yü Ying-shih of Princeton University for extended conversations about the sources of personal and public memory in traditional China. It was Professor Yü who first drew my attention to the late third-century Taoist classic *Jin Shu*. The Taoist injunction against memory as the focus of disturbing emotion is also echoed in Confucian admonitions on filial piety that require one to maintain mental well-being—if not for one's own sake, at least for one's parents'. According to Han Confucians, as well as Taoists, to dwell on the painful past is to arouse distressing, dangerous, and—in the long run—unfilial emotions.

¹¹For a fuller discussion of the term "Wen hua geming" during the late 1910s, see Vera Schwarcz, *The Chinese Enlightenment* (Berkeley, Calif.: University of California Press, 1986), 94–144.

¹²Chen Duxiu, "Rensheng wenti faduan" (The origins of the question of human existence), *Xin qingnian* (New Youth) (February 1918): 101.

¹³Lu Xun, *Quan Ji* (The Collected Works of Lu Xun) (Beijing: Renmin wenxue chuban she, 1982), vol. I, 416–17.

¹⁴Lu Xun, "Dao nian Wei Suyuan," in Ibid., vol IV, 67.

¹⁵Jack Belden, *China Shakes the World* (New York: Pelican Books, 1973), 389.

¹⁶Ibid., 390.

¹⁷Jiwei Ci, *Dialectic of the Chinese Revolution: From Utopianism to Hedonism* (Stanford, Calif.: Stanford University Press, 1994), 82–83.

¹⁸Benjamin Blech, *The Secret of Hebrew Words* (Northvale, N.J.: Jason Aronson Inc., 1991), 90.

¹⁹Adolph Rudnicki, *Ascent to Heaven*, trans. H. C. Stevens (London: Dennis Dobson, Ltd., 1951), 23. This story and its assumptions about Jewish memory are discussed further by Sidra Ezrahi in "The Holocaust Writer and the Lamentation Tradition," *Confronting the Holocaust*, ed. Alvin H. Rosenfeld (Bloomington, Ind.: Indiana University Press, 1978), 134–39.

[20]I am greatly indebted to Professor Stewart Miller from the University of Connecticut for drawing my attention to distinctively Jewish conceptualizations of suffering, especially in Louis Jacobs, "The Beraita On Sufferings in B. Berakhot 5a b," *Studies in Aggadah, Targum and Jewish Liturgy* (Jerusalem: Magnes Press, 1981).

[21]John Edgar McFayden, *The Problem of Pain: A Study in the Book of Job* (London: Jame, Clarke & Co., 1909), 259.

[22]Moses Maimonides, *The Guide of the Perplexed,* trans. Shlomo Pines (Chicago, Ill.: University of Chicago Press, 1963), 497.

[23]David Rosenberg, *Job Speaks* (New York: Harper & Row Publishers, 1977), 25.

[24]In contrast to China, with its waves of war and revolution and often *forcible* expressions of private grief in the public domain, Japan has maintained its reticence about suffering. Even with the rich Buddhist vocabulary available to talk about the problem of pain (both individual and social), people in Japan, according to Margaret Lock, "do not share suffering by speaking about it or spewing it out—on the contrary one swallows it down. But, one can relive it in memory by reading and reflecting on the sorrowful writings of others, on poetry and reconstructed historical accounts all of which individuals can draw from *privately* to help them swallow the pain." Personal communication, 29 August 1994.

[25]Gu Cheng, "Ziwo jieshao" (Resume), translated in *Seeds of Fire: Chinese Voices of Conscience,* ed. G. Barme and J. Minford (New York: Hill and Wang, 1988), 238.

[26]Gu Gong "The Two Generations," in Siu and Stern, eds., *Mao's Harvest,* 14.

[27]This passage from Book VIII of the *Analects* is translated and discussed at length in Lawrence Schneider, *The Madman of Ch'u* (Berkeley, Calif.: University of California Press, 1986), 17–21.

[28]Rubie Watson, ed., *Memory, History and Opposition* (Santa Fe, N.Mex.: New Mexico School of American Research Press, 1994), 7.

[29]This specific translation of Qu Yuan's much studied *Li Sao* comes from Lyman P. Van Slyke, *Yangtze: Nature, History and the River* (Reading, Mass.: Addison-Wesley Publishing Company Inc., 1988), 135.

[30]For a further discussion of Qian Xuanton's self-appellation *yigu* ("doubter of antiquity") as well as the entire New Culture Movement see Schwarcz, *The Chinese Enlightenment,* 25–35.

[31]Arthur Hummel, "Introduction," in *The Autobiography of a Chinese Historian* (Leyden: E. J. Brill Ltd., 1931), vii. In this introduction, Hummel suggests that the closest parallel in modern Western writing to the Chinese tradition of objective autobiography may be found in Thoreau's "Walden."

[32]Ibid., 8.

[33]Ibid., 174.

[34]Zhu Guanqian, *Beiju xinli xue* (The psychology of tragedy) (Anhui: Jiaoyu chuban she, 1989), 433–34.

[35]This encounter with Zhu Guanqian is described in Vera Schwarcz, *Long Road Home: A China Journal* (New Haven, Conn.: Yale University Press, 1984), 242–44.

[36]Zhu Guanqian, "Gei qingnian de shier fengxin" (Twelve letters to youth), *Zhu Guanqian quanji* (Complete Works of Zhu Guanqian) (Anhui: Jiaoyu chuban she, 1987), vol. I, 55.

[37]Ji Xianlin, "Ta shixian le shengming de jiazhi" (He realized the value of life), *Zhu Guanqian jinian ji* (Commemorating Zhu Guanqian) (Anhui: Jiaoyu chuban she, 1987), 28–29.

[38]This wordplay came up several times during my interview with Professor Ji Xianlin on 2 November 1993 at his home on the campus of Beijing University.

[39]Das, "Moral Orientations to Suffering," 139.

[40]Interview with Ji Xianlin, 2 November 1993.

[41]Hummel, *The Autobiography of a Chinese Historian,* 183.

[42]Ibid., 177.

[43]This image of social life as a suffocating "net" appears in much of the writing of the "wounded" generation of former Red Guards and is discussed in Jonathan Spence, *The Gate of Heavenly Peace* (New York: The Viking Press, 1981), 370.

[44]Qian, "Poetry as a Vehicle of Grief," 21.

[45]Qian Zhongshu, "Preface" to Yang Jiang, *A Cadre School Life* (Hong Kong: Joint Publishing Co., 1982).

[46]Qian, "Poetry as Vehicle for Grief," 32.

[47]Ibid., 35.

[48]Rosenberg, *Job Speaks,* 39, 61, 78. Job's insight into difficulties of broken speech are also mirrored in a poem by Ellen Bryant Voight. As an American writer, her voice is not scarred by the Jewish poet's religious outrage nor by the historical burdens of Qian Zhongshu. Yet Voight comes to the same conclusion: we must not confuse real suffering with the beauty and depth it imparts to the voice of those who endured its humiliations:

> This wasn't the music of pain. Pain has no music,
> pain is a story: it starts,
> Eurydice was taken from the fields.
> She did not sing—you cannot sing in hell—
> but in that viscous dark she heard the song
> flung like a rope into the crater of hell.

Ellen Bryant Voight, "Song and Story," *The Best American Poetry 1993* (New York: Collier Book, 1993), 212.

[49]Gu Cheng, "Ganjue" (Feeling), translated in Siu and Stern, eds., *Mao's Harvest,* 40.

[50]Gu Cheng talked to me about his life and writing in New Zealand during a 1985 symposium on poetry held at Asia Society in New York. See Schwarcz, "In the Shadow of the Red Sun," 4–5.

148   *Vera Schwarcz*

⁵¹Gu Xiang, "Gu Cheng, Xie Ye zuihou de rizi" (The last days of Gu Cheng and Xie Ye), *Jiushi niandai* (The Nineties) (May 1994): 80. I am very grateful to Professor Kim-Ya Tam of Trinity College for drawing to my attention these three essays by Gu Cheng's older sister.

⁵²*Jiushi niandai* (July 1994): 103.

⁵³Simon Leys, *The Burning Forest* (New York: Holt, Rineholdt and Winston, 1984), 223.

Tu Wei-ming

Destructive Will and Ideological Holocaust: Maoism as a Source of Social Suffering in China

C HINA HAS WITNESSED MASSIVE SUFFERING in her modern transformation. Without exaggeration or a stretch of the imagination, an examination of the frequency and magnitude of
destructiveness in China since the mid-nineteenth century may
reveal it to have been one of the most violent countries in human
history. A chronology of China's man-made disasters, generated
by domestic conflicts as well as outside aggression, in the last 150
years makes it blatantly clear that a defining characteristic of
modern Chinese history is the destruction of lives, property, institutions, and values. The poignant question, "Why does a culture
that condemns violence, that plays down the glory of military
exploits, that awards its highest prestige to literary rather than
martial figures, and seeks harmony over all other values, in fact
display such frequency and variety of violent behavior, that is of
the use of physical force against persons?"[1] needs to be addressed.
By examining the political, moral, and cultural nexus that has
generated so much human misery, we can understand both the
social sources of that suffering and the historical shape that much
of the collective experience of brutal trauma has taken on the
contemporary Chinese social landscape.

It is convenient to single out imperialism as the major cause of
China's disorder in modern times. After all, the Taiping Rebellion,
which displaced more than ten million people, the unequal treaties
that significantly undermined the political authority of the Chinese

*Tu Wei-ming is Professor of Chinese History and Philosophy at Harvard University and,
effective January 1, 1996, Director of the Harvard-Yenching Institute.*

149

state and carved China into foreign spheres of influence, the disintegration of the Manchu empire, Japanese aggression, the internecine
warfare among the warlords, and the showdown between the
Nationalists and the Communists, which contributed to an inestimable loss of lives, property, institutions, and values, are all easily
attributable to the coming of the West as an engine of destruction.

Yet, the most devastating period of social suffering in China has
occurred during the last forty years, after Mao Zedong proudly
announced at the founding of the People's Republic the removal of
feudalism and imperialism, the two great mountains blocking China's
modernization. Imperialism was historically responsible for initi-
ating a process of fundamental restructuring of society that eventually led to the establishment of the Communist leadership in
China. But the style of political control that was instrumental in
inflicting unprecedented suffering among the Chinese people was a
mixture of several factors that are largely independent of the
damage caused by the imperialists. Indigenous Maoist ideological
assaults must be held accountable for much of the collective suffering in socialist China. To be sure, Marxist-Leninist and Stalinist
policies were inseparable from the imperialist discourse. China's
domestic policies were often responses to geopolitical conditions
abroad, shaped predominantly by the Americans and the Russians.
From the Chinese perspective, the Korean War and the war in
Vietnam incited much of the anti-American sentiment that, in
turn, profoundly influenced the modus operandi of China's economy
and polity. Nevertheless, it was Mao's destructive political-moral
will and the ensuing radical ideology that created the havoc of
China's peculiarly violent twentieth-century society.

The peculiarity of this modern Chinese version of social violence
and its traumatic aftermath in prolonged social suffering is complex and elusive. Not only the available methods of analysis but
also the familiar conceptual apparatuses are inadequate to come to
terms with this historical complex. A new orientation is needed.
Ordinarily, violence can be portioned into victims and victimizers;
even though victims may be implicated sometimes as active contributors or instigators of violent acts and thus partly responsible
for their suffering, the victimizers are held accountable as the
agents who have inflicted physical injury or psychological pain. In
the Chinese case, millions suffered, including those who occupied

the most powerful and influential positions, yet the victimizers could not be easily identified, and the victims, by and large, felt profoundly guilty without being able to specify the causes for their suffering. The pervasive destruction affected millions, yet the real culprit behind the scenes of death and desperation was unnamed. Such was the sinister force of this ideological holocaust!

However, it is important to resist the temptation to present the history of Chinese communism in purely negative terms. China emerged from a semicolonial country, a mere geographic expression, to become a unified, independent, modern civilization-state: production and services increased at a steady rate for more than four decades; the infrastructure of the country (e.g., irrigation, sanitation, transportation, and communication) improved significantly; the quality and spread of public health virtually doubled the average peasant life expectancy; and Chinese workers, farmers, and soldiers have maintained a respectable living standard among developing nations. All of these improvements happened during the Communist rule. It is also important not to blame Mao as solely responsible for the ideological holocaust. We learn from historians, such as R. MacFarquhar, that Mao was not particularly active in the infamous Anti-Rightist Campaign (Deng Xiaoping was much more involved in destroying the livelihood of the liberal-minded intellectuals) and from journalists, such as E. Snow, that Mao deeply regretted the violence and the destruction of precious artifacts during the Cultural Revolution. Yet, Maoism[2] as a revolutionary creed of a newly established moral community was instrumental in creating an ethos in which collective violence was not only tacitly condoned but openly, explicitly, and vigorously encouraged.

MAOISM: MORAL COMMUNITY AND COLLECTIVE VIOLENCE

Despite a spate of books on Maoism, few attempts have been made to link its socio-logic to the tragic events that wove a complex and dreadful texture into the history of communism in China: the Anti-Rightist Campaign that brutally destroyed the intelligentsia by sending millions to the countryside, rendering the majority of the intellectuals déclassé for two decades; the "three hardship years" following the disastrous policy of the Great Leap Forward, which claimed as many as forty-three million lives, mainly due to starvation;[3] and the Cultural Revolution, which not only severely damaged the body politic but destroyed inestimable national cultural treasures in art, literature, and religion.[4] Among scholars of contemporary China, there is consensus that Mao himself was the single most important motivating force behind these events. The historical record (even the official account of the Chinese Communist Party) clearly shows that Mao personally initiated the "freedom of speech" campaign under the slogan "let one hundred schools bloom" in 1956, that he tenaciously mobilized the national effort to industrialize through the rapid increase of steel production in 1958, and that, against overwhelming odds, he incited the Red Guards to rebel against all authority. However, there is no serious effort to suggest that Mao's ability to exercise seemingly unlimited dictatorial power might have been, in a significant way, rooted in the persuasive power of the ideology itself.

David Apter and Tony Saich recently studied the Yan'an legacy by employing social theory constructs of discourse community, exegetical bonding, symbolic capital, and inversionary ideology. In their cultural critique, Mao is a master storyteller who ingeniously transforms himself from the narrator to the pivotal figure in modern China's collective narrative and thus defines the rules of the discourse, the terms for the exegesis, the parameters of the symbolic resources, and the main thrust of the ideology. They identified the critical period for the formation of Maoism to be from 1937 to 1942.[5] The story of Mao's rise to prominence in the Chinese Communist Party (CCP) is well known. Party historians have generally singled out the Zunyi Conference (1935) during the Long March as the critical event in Mao's emergence as the indisputable leader of the CCP, but it was in the loess caves of Yan'an that Mao built a stronghold where he could transform political leadership into ideological authority. How this nexus of political, moral, and cultural authority became a demonic force of destruction demands further explanation.

The well-documented and careful archival works by a coterie of conscientious scholars and journalists, notably Benjamin Schwartz, Liao Gailong, Stuart Schram, Li Rui, and Edgar Snow, have convincingly demonstrated that Mao's leadership was established by his ingenuity as a military strategist, fearlessness as a revolutionary, vision as a theoretician, persuasion as an ideologist, rapport with the peasant community, and charisma. His ability to win the support of an experienced general like Zhu De, outmaneuver a shrewd competitor like Zhang Guotao, and gain the loyalty of a seasoned intellectual like Zhou Enlai clearly indicates that Mao's ascendancy in the Chinese Communist movement was the result of many factors. This manifold assessment of Mao's strength provides a necessary background for an in-depth analysis of the sources of his authority, specifically his appeal to and manipulation of the intellectual community. Never in Chinese history have we observed such a combination of the ingenious use of symbolic power and outright anti-intellectualism. Mao's obsession with and contempt for the literati made him a nihilist with literary flair. The task of understanding his destructive power lies not only in a depiction of who he was and why he behaved as he did but also in an appreciation of what he symbolized, the people to whom he appealed for support, and the way he was able to have such a damaging effect.

It is difficult to ascertain how self-conscious Mao was that he was building a discourse community as the basis for his authority. His conscientious effort to make his own writings the core curriculum for the revolutionary movement seems to indicate that he had a great appreciation of the power of the pen. The essays "On Protracted War," "On Practice," and "On Contradiction" not only constituted the basic texts for the CCP, around which a host of exegetical readings derived their inspiration, but also justified the CCP's role as the embodiment of a sacred mission to "save the nation" (*jiuguo*). On the surface, the narrative was simple. The CCP, rather than the Nationalist government, had a comprehensive and practical strategy to deal with the Japanese aggression. By arousing the patriotic sentiments of the peasantry, who constituted 80 percent of the Chinese population, and organizing the Red Army into effective guerrilla fighters, Mao would render China militarily prepared to endure the protracted warfare necessitated by Japan's invasion.

The Long Marchers, having survived the most trying ordeal, were ready to save the nation. Underlying the narrative, the theme of violence looms large. Those who had endured the most devastating ordeal embodied the will to face up to the demonic force from abroad. Those who could mobilize the property-less peasantry in a fierce struggle against the landlord class, furthermore, would reinvigorate the revolutionary power of the seemingly enfeebled Communists, enabling them eventually to prevail over the Nationalists. In Mao's mind, this message of violent struggle was encoded in nature as well:

> Mountains!
> Like great waves surging in a crashing sea,
> Like a thousand stallions
> In full gallop in the heat of battle.
>
> Mountains!
> Piercing the blue of heaven, your barbs unblunted!
> The skies would fall
> But for your strength supporting.[6]

Mao's appeal to the will of the Chinese people to overcome foreign belligerence and domestic incompetence resonated with the concern of intellectuals throughout China, including those in the base areas of the Nationalists. For the Nationalists in 1945, who had been besieged by Japanese forces and demoralized by protracted warfare for eight long years, the euphoria of victory was soon overshadowed by anxiety over inflation and military confrontation with the Communists. Mao's poem, a sort of self-identity, caused a stir in Chongqing literary circles when it was unofficially published upon completion of his negotiations with Chiang Kai-shek and after his departure from the Nationalist wartime capital:

> But alas! Qin Shihuang and Han Wudi
> Were lacking in literary grace,
> And Tang Taizhong and Song Taizu
> Had little poetry in their soul;
> And Genghis Khan,
> Proud Son of Heaven for a day,
> Knew only shooting eagles, bow outstretched.
> All are past and gone!
> For truly great men
> Look to this age alone.[7]

Mao's panoramic view of the four esteemed emperors and the terrifying Mongolian ruler in the imperial era evoked sensations of

China's greatness and revealed a grandiose self-image, verging on megalomania, but the poem's distinct message was not merely personal ambition but the embodiment of China's destiny. To the literati, the key meaning inscribed in the poem was the reference to literary grace and poetic soul, a quality that Mao obviously claimed for himself but denied the founding fathers of great dynasties. For all that, there was more battle cry than aesthetic elegance in Mao's assertive voice.

Mao's deliberate attempt to establish himself as a member of the literati is well documented, but his ability to strike a sense of awe in sophisticated intellectuals through face-to-face communication and personal correspondence is yet to be fully studied. We have only begun to understand how his idiosyncratic self-assertion became deeply ingrained in the collective experience of the CCP and how it profoundly shaped the communal awareness of the Chinese intelligentsia as a whole. Mao characterized himself as beyond any belief in the evil spirits. This fearlessness must have appealed to many intellectuals who had already abandoned the life of the mind for political activism. It took decades for some of the most self-reflective of them to realize that their attraction to, if not genuine admiration for, Mao's unbridled recklessness may have significantly contributed to his charismatic power. An analysis of Mao's genre (*Mao wenti*), as an integral part of a long-term project to study Party culture (*dang wenhua*), was initiated by a group of dissident intellectuals after the Tiananmen tragedy of 1989. It is extremely difficult, especially for those who have been victimized, to think through the process by which a single individual assumed such demonic force and created such devastation; even with considerable hindsight it remains perplexing and mystifying.[8]

Paradoxically, Mao's demonic potency lay precisely in the deceptively simple vision—one person's wishful thinking disguised as the collective's prophetic insight—reflected by an ever-extending circle of Chinese:

> To Kunlun now I say,
> Neither all your height
> Nor all your snow is needed.
> Could I but draw my sword o'ertopping heaven,
> I'd cleave you in three:

One piece for Europe,
One for America,
One to keep in the East.
Peace would then reign over the world,
The same warmth and cold throughout the globe.[9]

Especially noteworthy is the fact that this poem was composed toward the end of the Long March, literally "on horseback," when "Mao had crossed twenty-four rivers and eighteen mountain ranges, in weather now tropical and now frigid. He had arrived in the loess country of the northwest with only 10 percent of the troops [his First Front Army, which made up about one-quarter of the Long Marchers, dwindled from thirty thousand to three thousand] who had left Jiangxi one year before."[10] What Mao envisioned then was China's rightful place in his perception of a just world.

It is remarkable that a man with limited formal education from remote Shaoshanchong in Hunan, who learned about Kang Youwei and Liang Qichao's reformism in his teens, and who first saw a map of the world at nineteen, felt ready to embark on a journey to save China. It is equally remarkable that this fiercely competitive and blatantly presumptuous youth, with the social experience of "struggle" and hatred, revenge and contempt, became the embodiment of a master narrative: the liberation of the Chinese people from poverty and ignorance. It is even more remarkable that this dreamer of destructive visions, imbued with a strong dose of revolutionary romanticism, has been regarded by his millions of followers, including sophisticated intellectuals trained in Western Europe and North America, as China's savior for half a century.

Referring to "the official founding of the CCP [that] occurred in late July and early August of 1921" as a "dramatic episode," David Apter, with his focus on Yan'an as Mao's "simulacrum," comments on the rise of Mao:

This episode, the spy, the water, the dangerous terrain, the trials, and tasks are conditions for Mao's own story of coming to power. It is a tale of overcoming in which not only does he defeat his enemies despite serious setbacks, he overcomes his ignorance of Marxism to triumph over those Russian-trained adepts who represented themselves as the real Marxist intellectuals. His story is also about the evolution of his thoughts.[11]

Mao's ability to condense the stories of the decline and fall of China, the conflict of the CCP with the Nationalists, and his own struggle within the Party into an "epic, drama, and passion play" helped him "to deposit much mystique in a common fund." As Apter notes,

> Each [of the three stories] offers a different resonance adding layers of symbolic intensity to Yan'an as a simulacrum. Each is received in speeches, used to illustrate texts. Running through them is a common theme, embodied and embellished by "political yearning."[12]

The emergence of Maoism as the radical ideology, the rise of Mao as the revolutionary leader, the establishment of the CCP as the institutional vanguard for the struggle, and the triumph of Marxism-Leninism as the guiding principle in China's quest for a modernizing strategy are integral parts of a master narrative that forged a discourse community. The network of moral and affective relations began with a tiny minority of peasant warriors and idealist youth in the caves of Yan'an and, in less than a decade, wore its way into the collective imagination of the Chinese people, who affirmed it as the bearer of the Mandate of Heaven leading China toward the brave new world. Official CCP historians insist that the Marxist-Leninist dialectic of historical inevitability, the Party's indigenization of the anti-imperialist struggle through the experience of the Long March, Mao's leadership by exemplary teaching, and the wisdom of Maoism as a source of inspiration are essential factors in this incredible historical transformation. Mao himself believed that the Communists' ability to concentrate on the war with the Japanese as the overriding task of the Yan'an decade earned them the right to govern China. In his view, the Long March was the authenticating cultural event for the inevitable confrontation:

> The sky is high, the clouds are pale.
> We watch the wild geese flying south till they vanish;
> If we reach not the Great Wall, we are no true men!
> Already we have come two thousand leagues.
>
> High on the crest of Liu Pan Mountains
> Our banners idly wave in the west wind.
> Today we hold the long cord in our hands;
> When shall we bind fast the gray dragon?[13]

A critical examination of China's modern transformation may reveal that Marxism-Leninism was but one of the modernizing strategies and a highly ineffective choice at that; that the Long March was a desperate escape from Chiang Kai-shek's encirclements; that the bulk of the pressures of Japanese aggression (symbolized by the "gray dragon" in Mao's poem) was borne by the Nationalists; that Mao's leadership was only a contributory factor in the success of the CCP as the challenger of the Nationalist mandate; and that Maoism was not a coherent doctrine guiding the praxis of the revolution. The confrontation between the CCP and the Nationalists (1945–1949), involving massive military maneuvers, moreover, was decided on the battlefields rather than on the ideological front. No matter. On October 1, 1949, when Mao declared the founding of the People's Republic, proclaiming that "the Chinese people have stood up," liberal-democratic intellectuals as well as his CCP colleagues perceived him as the actualization of a national dream. The dreamer had become the embodiment of China's destiny; the past had authenticated the vision for the future. Individual experience became collective experience; idiosyncratic expression became cultural representation. Now the symbolic stuff of local illusion would be catalyzed into the collective emotions of traumatic social reality.

FROM CULTURAL MOVEMENT THROUGH INVERSIONARY IDEOLOGY TO SOCIAL TERROR

In September 1989, three American centers for Chinese studies (Berkeley, Harvard, and Michigan) sponsored a conference to mark four anniversaries: the French Revolution (1789), the Opium War (1939), the May Fourth Movement (1919), and the founding of the People's Republic (1949). Although the Tiananmen massacre on June 4 of that year loomed large in the minds of the participants, the evocation of memories of the four previous events helped to put China's tragic history of modern transformation in perspective. Indeed, it was the Enlightenment mentality exemplified by the revolutionary spirit of the French, as contrasted with the skepticism and empiricism of the English Enlightenment, that dominated the intellectual discourse of the May Fourth generation. It was, however, the vortex generated by the seemingly contradictory forces of an iconoclastic attack on the Confucian tradition and an impassioned commitment to the revitalization of China as a race, a civilization, and a unified polity that overwhelmed the hearts and minds of the May Fourth Chinese intelligentsia. Virtually every youth of "blood and vital energy" was sucked into this vortex: anxiety, impatience, rebelliousness, and engagement characterized the ethos. Mao, like the "enlightened" youth of his generation, was exposed to the writings of Adam Smith, Herbert Spencer, John Stuart Mill, and Darwin through Yan Fu's masterly translations, but it was in Rousseau's critique of culture, advocacy of an intimate community, and idea of the "general will" that Mao found a kindred spirit.

The acute awareness that, in less than half a century, the proud Middle Kingdom had been brought to its knees, as a semicolonial country humiliated by unequal treaties and carved up by the spheres of influence, made all educated Chinese "nationalist" in ethnicity, culture, and polity. The sense of crisis prompted by Japan's miraculous ascendancy as a full-fledged imperialist power in less than one generation and, as a result, her grave threat to China's existence compelled intellectual forces of all persuasions to take "save the nation" as the common denominator. Understandably, the overriding concern of the May Fourth generation was the preservation of the Chinese nation and the Chinese race (*baoguo baozhong*). The extreme conservatives and the radical revolutionaries shared the same burning desire to make China stand on her own feet. There was a compelling reason why Marxism-Leninism, rather than American pragmatism, German idealism, British empiricism, or French rationalism, emerged as the ideology for China's modernization: the success of the Russian revolution in 1917 and the attraction of the subsequent China policies of the USSR. The CCP's propaganda machinery played a critical role in this ideological turn. Nevertheless, we must not underestimate the vortex mentioned above that attuned the Chinese ear to the Marxist-Leninist message: it was Western to the core, and, at the same time, it was thoroughly anti-Western imperialism. In other words, it had the potential of smashing the two mountains blocking China's path toward modernity: feudalism and imperialism.

Underlying this rhetoric was the famous slogan of May Fourth that only Mr. Sai (Science) and Mr. De (Democracy) could save China. The advocacy of science and democracy as true manifestations of the Enlightenment symbolized a broad consensus of the Chinese intelligentsia.[14] With a few notable exceptions, they strongly believed that the mobilization of all the energies of the Chinese people, based on a comprehensive vision of social reconstruction, was the necessary and most economical way to save China. The absence of other Enlightenment values, such as liberty, the dignity of the individual, private property, privacy, human rights, and due process of law, occasionally stirred the more refined scholarly minds, but most intellectuals were satisfied with the simplicity and neatness of the agenda. For eighty years, the sanctity of science and democracy has never been questioned. Neither the CCP nor its most severe critics ever raised any doubts about it. It was not an accident that the likeness of the Statue of Liberty that appeared in Tiananmen Square was rechristened the Goddess of Democracy. Party ideologists have condemned liberalization as a form of spiritual pollution and human rights as alien to Chinese tradition, but they have never criticized democracy. Understandably, Mao's doctrine of "New Democracy" had thousands of patriotic intellectuals mesmerized.

Lurking behind the scenes, however, was neither science nor democracy but scientism and populism. Strictly speaking, instrumental rationality and Jacobin-like collectivism fundamentally restructured the Chinese intellectual world in the post-May Fourth period. The rich diversity of symbolic resources, characteristic of the cultural scene at the turn of the century, was gradually stylized into a dichotomous mode of thinking: progressive/regressive, revolutionary/reactionary, proletarian/bourgeois, true/false, beautiful/ugly, and good/evil. These intellectual debates continued in the Nationalist period (1927–1949). Issues pertaining to China's modernization, centering on cultural identity, Westernization, capitalism, socialism, industrialization, and a host of other problem areas, were widely debated in academic circles. Intellectual sophistication was high and many presented thoughtful recommendations for optimizing resources available to China in her modern transformation. On the whole, however, it was revolutionary praxis, the concrete procedure by which ideas were translated into institutionalized action, that claimed the most attention.

While Hu Shi and other Western-trained scholars, under the sponsorship of the Nationalist government, turned their attention to academic pursuits in the name of "sorting out and sifting our national heritage" (*zhengli guogu*), the "progressive" intellectuals, obsessed with the belief that orthodoxy naturally leads to orthopraxy, were fully engaged in determining the nature of Chinese society, expanding the cultural capital for socialist reconstruction, appropriating symbolic resources for the revolutionary cause, and empowering an increasing number to actively participate to save the nation. By the end of 1937, specifically after the Xian incident (1936) when the CCP and the Nationalists ostensibly combined forces in a holy war against Japan, the leftist turn of the Chinese intelligentsia seemed inevitable. This significantly enhanced Mao's prestige not only as a military strategist but also as a revolutionary theorist.

Mao's contempt for Western-trained scholars and his genuine affection for the peasants made him a distinguished populist who, especially in the eyes of the intellectuals, seemed to have gained privileged access to the peasant mentality. The youthful Mao chose to stay home because he did not believe that the key to China's future lay in the West or, for that matter, in Russia. His nativism, carefully cultivated by his focused investigations into peasant conditions, served him well as a nationalist. Yet, although he harbored strong anti-imperialist sentiments, he does not seem to have been xenophobic. His admiration for Lu Xun and his companionship with the literatus Guo Moruo, both returned students from Japan, his association with Zhou Enlai and Deng Xiaoping, who had both spent considerable time in France, and his friendship with the American journalist Edgar Snow indicated that he could choose not to function in an enclosed, nativistic, symbolic universe. Although he preferred to read dynastic history, traditional novels, and classical poetry, he studied Marxism-Leninism with utter seriousness and taught himself to read English documents with the aid of a dictionary. He led a deceptively simple life; he seems to have deliberately cultivated an image of rusticity. Recent stories about his sexual appetite may have seriously tarnished his integrity as an incorruptible revolutionary, but those who were intimately familiar with his life-style saw him neither as majestic nor luxurious but down-to-earth. This, of course, does not mean that he was not excessive in squandering national resources. The maintenance of his several resorts was extremely costly and his unpredictable and frequent inspection tours by train, with a huge entourage, are only a sample of his many extravagances. Nevertheless, as a ferocious reader, a captivating poet, and an idiosyncratic calligrapher, his stature as a literatus has never been seriously questioned. How could this seemingly innocuous poet, strategist, theorist, and dreamer become an engine of destruction and the source of the most heinous atrocities in Chinese history?

According to the memoirs of several victims of the Anti-Rightist Campaign, few ever challenged the verdicts of the Party, nor did anyone voice doubts about the supreme wisdom of Mao, the Helmsman. We may easily condemn this passivity and acquiescence as political blindness or outright cowardice, but case after case suggests that guilt, self-criticism, and sacrifice were such powerful mitigating sentiments that even hatred and a sense of injustice were not allowed to surface. Are the brainwashing techniques or the mechanics of psychological totalism mainly responsible for this incredible art of silencing? The absence of a well-coordinated state machinery as a disciplinary agency, the highly decentralized method of coercion, and the pervasive voluntarism of the victims as well as the victimizers suggest that the terror that the Helmsman inflicted upon millions of intellectuals was, in Lu Xun's terminology, caused by an invisible "soft knife" that cuts so deeply that society as a whole, rather than any individual, bleeds. To put it differently, no matter how many cases we can identify, the cumulative experience of individual suffering pales by comparison with the damage done to the "collective consciousness." This was the deepest layer of social suffering. Since the primacy of the "general will" demands that, at a critical juncture in China's development, any vicious attacks on the Party, irresponsible criticisms of the government, subversive remarks about the leadership, or simply idle talk will be extremely harmful to the well-being of the people, the silencing of a tiny minority is not only justifiable but necessary.

The treatment of a tiny minority, let us say 5 percent, was a large enough quota to silence the entire Chinese intelligentsia. Mao's theory of contradiction, conveniently adapted to the contingency, turned those who, in other political contexts, could be easily accommodated as members of the loyal opposition into enemies of the people. The contradictions within the people and between the people and their enemies were interpreted as radically different forms of social tension; the former was healthy and reconcilable but the latter was destructive and irreconcilable. Mao's strategy to save the Party, its leadership, and, above all, his authority worked at the expense of an entire generation of liberal-minded (including quite a few Communist) intellectuals. There was physical coercion, public humiliation, and emotional torture. Many "rightists" survived the ordeal and were "rehabilitated" in the post-Cultural Revolution period; some of them even assumed leadership positions in the Party, government, mass media, academia, and the arts.

The institutional mechanism that enabled such a massive campaign to take place at all levels of society was the work unit system (*danwei*). Scientism and populism were clearly the rationale behind the implementation of such a system. The most efficient way for China to mobilize all of her energy for socialist construction was a comprehensively planned and fully integrated structure, significantly departing from the existing organizations. Or, alternatively, in order to ensure that the newly established infrastructure would enhance rather than impede the inevitable historical process of actualizing the Communist ideas of equality and distributive justice, all existing institutions must be thoroughly modified. Lurking behind this apparent effort at social engineering was the totalistic will to control and an intense fear that charisma, the impulse to change, to deconstruct, and to reorganize, could become routinized.

Guided by instrumental rationality, at least on the surface, although the morally authenticating experiences of the Long March and of Yan'an never ceased to animate the new style of control, Mao, as a strategist, urged his colleagues to put aside the things they knew well and to learn the institutional imperatives of running a modern bureaucracy from experienced leaders in urban centers (i.e., Beijing, Tianjin, and Shanghai). Yet, Mao time and

again deliberately and ostensibly ignored the institutional imperatives and ruthlessly undermined the rules of the game in running a
modern bureaucracy. Furthermore, the leadership of the CCP, not
to mention the authority of its core members and, by implication,
of Mao himself, was to be protected and defended at all costs. The
demand for populism, however, compelled Mao to accept, implicitly if not publicly, that performance criteria, a sort of accountabil-
ity if not transparency of governance, would have to be applied to
evaluate all cadres, himself included. The very fact that each of the
members of the CCP, including the leadership core, was incorporated in the unit system, with a permanent file that included his or
her class background, education, information about personal matters such as marital status, conduct, attitudes, beliefs, and so forth,
indicates that a process of atomization was superimposed upon
the entire society. Actually, a grave consequence of this arrange-
ment was that, in theory and practice, every member of the society
was susceptible to the disciplinary mechanism of the regime. This
level of vulnerability and the deep fear it evoked bound the society
and its various subgroups, including the cadres, together.

What Mao created, as an ingenious response to the post-1949
situation, was more a cultural "process" than a social "structure"
of control, with the specific purpose of mass mobilization for
socialist construction. It was not a Stalinist totalitarianism because
the dynamism, though initiated by directives from above, was
often fueled by enthusiastic voluntarism from below. Without the
overwhelming consensus of the "general will," the major campaigns launched in the 1950s could not have exerted such devastation over the existing social structure. China's stunning performance in the Korean War (December 1950), using over seven
hundred thousand "volunteers," including Mao's son, who died in
the conflict, barely a year after the bloody struggle with the Nationalists, testified to Mao's charismatic manipulation of the patriotic sentiments of the Chinese people. They seemed more eager
than ever to commit China on a march toward the brave new
world.

The willingness, indeed commitment, to discord, conflict, contradiction, struggle, and destruction engendered a mentality evoking, most of all, the Hegelian "negative will," a will determined to
destroy systematically and thoroughly, if only as a precondition

for reconstruction. In the perspective of the Confucian discourse, characterized by the ethos of harmony, reconciliation, negotiation, shareability, and consensus, which, in theory and practice, has been the cultural tradition of the Chinese intelligentsia, the Maoists must answer the following questions: "How much bloodshed and physical violence are they ready to accept as a price to be paid for social 'progress' and the pursuit of self-assertion (by individuals and groups)? Where does one draw the line between useful discord and destructive violence—and how can one insure that favoring the former does not inevitably entail privileging the latter?"[15] As Maoist China was continuously rent by bloody conflicts between divergent ideological groups, with profoundly devastating consequences for "organic solidarity" at all levels of society, Maoists seem to contend that there is no limit to bloodshed and, as far as destructive violence is concerned, there is no need to draw the line. As forged by a rebellious peasantry, the Marxist theory of "class struggle," and the conviction that "political power grows out of the barrel of the gun,"[16] inherent in Maoism is a fundamental propensity toward deconstruction.

Mao, in an oblique reference to Kang Youwei's failure to bring about the "Great Harmony" (*datong*) through reform, expressed confidently that the Communist utopia was attainable by his revolution led by the working class.[17] A clear demonstration of Mao's revolutionary romanticism was his "land reform" (1951–1953) program. The brutal simplicity with which a whole class of landlords was indiscriminately humiliated, coerced, and destroyed made Mao a hero, indeed a savior, among numerous newly possessed families. A similar leveling process, effectively put into practice with the cathartic "struggle sessions" in the countryside, was carried out in the urban areas, with less theatrics but no less brutality, against the capitalists and the petty bourgeoisie. By the time Mao launched the Hundred Flowers campaign, an obvious response to the liberal-democratic movements in Eastern Europe, notably Hungary, the intellectuals who voiced discontent strongly believed that they were involved in a style of internal criticism for the sake of the CCP. Given the long, bitter fate that many of them endured as a consequence, their actions might appear to be naive. But Mao's punishment was extreme, and the seeming irrationality of the violence was rooted in a sharp conflict between Mao's utopian vision and the intellectuals' liberal-democratic aspirations.

The discourse community that Mao thought he had already forged was based on his experiential understanding of protracted war, practice, and contradiction. With the end of the Korean War, which considerably enhanced his prestige in the Communist bloc, and the "success" of land reform, which made him a godlike provider, he felt totally confident in allowing the intellectuals to openly and freely express their opinions on the state of the nation. To his astonishment, their frank criticism undermined the achievements of the CCP and challenged the legitimacy of his own authority. The intellectuals, in fact, subscribed to a radically different vision of society (for instance, a multiparty democratic polity with regular elections and guarantees of rights and liberties). Their underlying value orientation, liberal-democratic in nature, stressed gradualism, negotiation, coordination, compromise, and harmony. While many of Mao's colleagues were astonished by the outburst of intellectual dynamism, the Helmsman decided to steer the state into the turbulent waters of class struggle. Fearing that his utopian vision was seriously blurred by what he would, with complete vindictiveness, call the poisonous ideas of the intellectuals, he enjoined the country to refocus its attention on the socialist path.

A logical consequence of this reorientation was the marginalization of the intelligentsia, from the status of active participants or sympathetic observers to that of spoilers, indeed "enemies of the people." Those who were labeled "rightists" were immediately marginalized, alienated not only from the masses, but from other intellectuals and from their own immediate families as well. Family members were urged, often under great pressure from relatives and friends, to draw a clear line of demarcation between themselves and the targets. Furthermore, as the campaign gathered momentum, those, including spouses and children, who showed even the slightest sympathy toward such enemies of the people would suffer severe punishment for their inability to commit themselves to the right path. Once the Rightists were condemned as the "radical other," a process of "pseudospeciation," to use Erik Erikson's term, was underway. The psychopathological condemnation of the Rightists as nonpeople not only denied them any status in society but also robbed them of any dignity or decency as fellow human beings. As a result, they were reduced to subhumans and no longer existed as members of the same species. Thus, the inversionary "speciation" that made them less ("pseudo") human justified any maltreatment of them.

Millions were victimized by this kind of "soft knife" procedure, which was perceived by the victimizers as a necessary sacrifice for maintaining the purity of the socialist spirit. Mao's own exemplary teaching was a necessary precondition for this procedure to function with the kind of voluntarism it engendered. While Confucian teaching takes, as a point of departure, the bonding affection between parent and child for moral development, Maoists purposefully drove a wedge into the sacred relationships (i.e., parent-child, husband-wife, siblings, and friends) as a litmus test for loyalty to the socialist cause. The bellicose nature of Maoist thinking lies in its determination to bear the unbearable in such a way that sympathy, defined in Confucian terms as "the inability to bear the suffering of others," was condemned as the weakness of the will. The inversion of Confucian values would simultaneously defeat individualism and undermine the moral resources available to make despair meaningful. Once basic human feelings, such as loving and caring for the closest kin, were strongly criticized as petty bourgeois sentimentalism and publicly denounced as incongruous with the revolutionary spirit, they lost their legitimacy in the court of appeal of the newly constituted discourse community. It created cultural suffering by inverting the symbolic capital of the individual experience of suffering.

Especially noteworthy is the total asymmetry between the confession of guilt by the victims and the self-righteousness of the victimizers. Not only did the intellectuals who had undeservedly suffered the most demeaning maltreatment acknowledge a sense of guilt for their failure to live up to the communal standards set up by the CCP because of their class background, socialization, education, or lack of commitment, they also willingly forgave those who were the disciplining agents of the state. By contrast, no prominent victimizer was ever brought to trial even for the slightest misdemeanor. The Party, which finally decided to "rehabilitate" the victims more than twenty years later, after Mao had died and his Red Guards had deconstructed the Party leadership, made almost no attempt to bring charges against the victimizers, with the notable exception of the so-called "Gang of Four," who can hardly be classified, by any stretch of the imagination, as victims. Mao of course never acknowledged any wrongdoing in this regard.

Is it conceivable that an important reason for the massive social suffering was the consensus of the discourse community, by choice and by default, that Maoism was self-evidently true and inherently practicable? In retrospect, it is preposterous and uncanny to retrace the steps, whether real or imagined, that eventually led to the holocaust of the Cultural Revolution in which even the victimizers were pitiful mockeries of their professed idealism and heroism. For a decade (1966–1976), intra-party conflict aside, the entire society was embroiled in a struggle crudely defined in terms of the two lines: socialist/capitalist, progressive/reactionary, leftist/rightist, native/foreign, new/old, selfless/selfish, and good/bad. While in any concrete situation neat categories are inevitably mixed, what Maoism initially symbolized to the Red Guards was, however, a clear message: the socialist path, progressive polity, leftist ideology, native method, new vision, selfless leadership, and good people; a clear break from the feudal past, bureaucratism, elitism, privilege, and corruption as practiced by the capitalist-roaders.

The special shape of social suffering as forged by Maoism is inconceivable without reference to the persuasive power of the rhetoric of the discourse community. There was no alternative intelligence anywhere to compete with the Maoist claims. There was no autonomous intelligentsia, critical mass media, or independent business community; in short, there was no civil society. Nor was there any "public discussion" similar to that conducted by the powerful and influential scholar-officials in traditional China. As the common sense of civility practiced in interpersonal relationships, so characteristic of premodern Chinese society, was gradually eroded by the new cultural movements and frontally assaulted by the revolutionary spirit, there was no defense against the linguistic violence of reducing the richly textured ritual of human interaction into a black/white struggle for survival. Despite the folk belief in human decency, which is rooted in the Mencian teaching of humanity as commiseration, the base instincts of self-preservation, aggression, jealousy, and domination overwhelmed the emotional life of the Chinese for years. The Red Guards were instinct with life and destruction; Maoism provided the rationale. It took the discourse community several decades to incubate the monster that seemed to provide the only solution to China's grave problems.

The assumptive reasons behind this are deceptively simple: *1)* At this particular juncture in Chinese history, with imperialist threats without and enemies of the people within, mass mobilization is necessary for socialist reconstruction. *2)* The Long March, the Yan'an experiment, the bitter struggle with the Japanese, and the bloody confrontation with the Nationalists may have helped China to become unified, and the Korean War may have demonstrated China's resolve as an independent nation, but China is still "poor and blank." Personal sacrifice is required for China truly to stand up to Russia, Europe, and America. *3)* The CCP, as the agency for carrying out the "general will" of the people, is always the party of the peasant, worker, and soldier. There is no presumption that the CCP can ever be incorruptible. In fact, it is openly acknowledged that routinized bureaucracy and built-in elitism have already undermined its effectiveness. The CCP has to continuously renew itself to deserve the support of the masses. *4)* The intelligentsia could become an integral part of this joint venture to bring about a truly socialist China if it were determined to free itself from the corrosive habits that make it vulnerable to the pull of feudalism and the push of capitalism. *5)* Since only through praxis do we learn to align ourselves with the objective social forces generated by the dynamism of the masses, we must take "class struggle" seriously, not only in behavior, but also in attitude and belief. *6)* We must have faith in the transformative potential of the people. Since human determination will prevail over Heaven (*rendingshengtian*), we can rely upon the activism of the masses for socialist reconstruction. *7)* Maoism, as embodied in the revolutionary experience of the Party and the supreme ideological insight of Mao himself, serves as the best guide for China's socialist transformation.

Surprisingly, the disastrous Great Leap Forward and the even more devastating Cultural Revolution followed the same deceptively simple logic: contradiction, social practice, mass line, class struggle, and continuous revolution.[18] To be sure, it was not in its abstract universalism but in its lived concreteness that Maoism exercised its sinister power. Whether or not a sophisticated intellectual could bring himself or herself to appreciate fully its philosophical elegance (there was little of this in Mao's word or deed), the force of the Maoist persuasion to conquer and subdue, if not to convince, was irresistible. Formidable minds may have tried to resist—in the case of Liang Shuming by direct confrontation and in the case of Feng Youlan by accommodation—but they were either silenced or co-opted when Mao, the thinker, assumed the role of teacher and leader. Willingness to abandon one's own philosophical stance in the face of a Maoist challenge may seem to have been an inevitable consequence of the social dynamics of a culture of terror, but, time and again, we witness a dramatic turnabout, reminiscent of religious conversion, continuously reenacted by some of the most brilliant (and betrayed) professional intellectuals. The truthfulness of the Maoist vision was complemented and supplemented by numerous acts of "exegetical bonding," a kind of hermeneutic investment in a fund of knowledge, which enhanced its persuasive power through reenacting the ritual of coordinated reading and repeating the rhetoric of assent; as a result, the story became so deeply ingrained in the communal self-awareness of the Chinese intelligentsia that to deviate from it caused a profound reflexive anxiety, moral panic.

The recent attempt to characterize Mao's nativism as no more than a reflection of his cherished dream to become an imperial Chinese emperor seriously misreads the record. However, it is undeniable that Mao jealously guarded his "imperialist" power against any competing authority and that he resisted all efforts to routinize his charisma, for fear that his infallibility would be compromised as a result. Most intimate accounts of Mao's private life convey an image of deceptive simplicity and fabricated rusticity. Mao's life as the leader of the People's Republic seems devoid of any elaborate ritual or even of any modest ceremony: he seems to have been attached to his old pajamas and worn-out blanket with a sort of infantile possessiveness; he ate plainly and led a style of life that was, by imperial standards, devoid of elegance and nicety. He was immersed in books and often conducted official business in his study, bedroom, or even in bed. He suffered from chronic insomnia and preferred to stay up late and sleep in the morning. He seemed to have had an insatiable sexual appetite, but his indulgence was neither elaborate nor debauched. He does not seem to have acquired expensive tastes. His fondness of fatty pork, his addiction to sleeping pills, his fascination with the art of the "inner chamber" (Taoist sexual practices), his aversion to bathing, and his refusal to brush his teeth (claiming that tigers do not brush their teeth either) made him special but not necessarily perverse. Even his physician, who was the source of the stories of such indulgences, describes him as a simple and rustic "peasant."[19]

THE THREE SOURCES OF MAOIST VIOLENCE

What was neither simple nor rustic was his power to terrorize, to dominate, to break people, to conjure old hatreds and animate new ones, and to destroy. Ironically, Mao's sinister power lay in his ability to combine three powers into one inseparable unity: political leadership, ideological legitimacy, and moral authority. The prophetic voice in his poem that his literary talents surpassed the four esteemed founding emperors and made the terrifying Mongolian ruler appear to be a mere hunter resonated well with his presumed self-image: a military strategist without the need to carry a gun, a political leader who transcended bureaucracy, a teacher who received little formal education, and a theorist who derived all of his ideas from practice.

Had Mao actually wanted to be an emperor, he would have inflicted less social suffering upon the Chinese people. The damage would have been confined to the political arena, no matter how broadly defined. At least the Chinese moral spirit, as it was cultivated and preserved in the collective experience of the intelligentsia, would not have been so humiliatingly injured. It was his ambition to become more than a mere emperor, fueled by a fierce arrogance that only he knew what was really good for China, that made him into something even more terrifying than the imperial dragons of China's past: a hard-hearted, self-righteous monster.

Ironically, the trinity embodied in Mao, reminiscent of the highest ideal in Confucian rulership (the sage-king), is unprecedented in Chinese history. I have only hinted at the process by which Mao assumed not only political leadership but also ideological legitimacy and moral authority. The story is complex because it involves the struggle of modern China as a race, a polity, and a civilization, the struggle of the CCP as an idea, an institution, and as the steward of a mission, and the struggle of Mao as a strategist, a dreamer, and a destroyer. Moreover, it involves the intellectuals, landlords, peasants, capitalists, workers, soldiers, cadres, and a host of other variously classified "bad elements," "counterrevolutionaries," "reactionaries," and "nonpeople."

An often neglected dimension of the narrative is the symbolic capital that Mao deliberately manipulated or unconsciously inherited that gave him inestimable purchasing power over the life of the mind. Given the economic backwardness and political impotence of modern Chinese society, the available cultural resources were essential for any mass mobilization for the revolutionary cause. In traditional China, political leadership, ideological legitimacy, and moral authority were closely intertwined but separable in theory and practice. No emperor ever managed to extend his political power fully into the ideological and moral arenas. These were the province of the scholar-officials, dictated by a set of significantly different rules of the game. The Manchu emperors, notably Kangxi, Yongzheng, and Qianlong, worked hard to achieve "sage-king" status. Kangxi's gallant effort pacified threatening Ming loyalist movements and won the tacit support of the literati class, but he basically styled himself as a devoted student of Confucian culture. Yongzheng's concerted effort to appropriate ideological legitimacy struck terror among the educated, but he was not himself a source of inspiration for the scholars. Qianlong successfully established himself as a fellow literatus and was greatly admired for his martial and literary accomplishments, but he was neither an ideologue nor an exemplar.

There were quite a few strong rulers in the dynastic history: Qin Shihuang and Han Wudi's power in shaping the polity and Tang Taizhong and Song Taizu's influence over the bureaucracy made them model emperors of "great talent and bold vision" (*xiongcaidalue*). Yet, the majority of Chinese emperors were themselves victims of an elaborate ritual system with innumerable rules and regulations to ensure a routinized and harmonized form of life. This was perhaps the reason why, contrary to popular belief, a typical profile of the Chinese emperor might very well include incompetence, weakness, youth, and lack of power. Understandably, while there were plenty of mediocre rulers surrounded by corrupt eunuchs and in-laws, there were few tyrannical despots in traditional Chinese history. Even though the symbolic system of the sage-king ideal continued to be a source of inspiration for the scholar-officials, their effort to make the king sagely was an endless task and they never confused what the emperor really was with what he ought to become. Indeed, the separation between his personality and his position enabled the scholar-officials to develop a functioning "feedback" mechanism within the bureaucracy that constituted a de facto loyal opposition not only to the powerful ministers but also to the "inner court" and the emperor himself.

Surely, the absence of the separation of church and state did not allow Chinese political culture to develop a symbolically and practically consequential priesthood, but the assumption that the Chinese emperor was, in reality, a combination of king and Pope and was therefore virtually infallible is one-sided, if not outright false. The other side of the story is that the scholar-official class, by combining the roles of cultural interpreters, transmitters, and creators with those of policy initiators, implementers, and evaluators, was much more influential than the priesthood could ever be in defining the order of things in the empire. If we broaden the category of the scholar-official class to include what was in the later imperial period often referred to as the "local gentry," as we must when we analyze Chinese society as a whole, we may very well talk about a group in actual control of ideological legitimacy and moral authority. Zeng Guofan may have been an exception in his combination of ideological legitimacy and moral authority with military might; his role as a governor, charged with the mission of suppressing the Taiping Rebellion, gave him an unusual mandate to save the dynasty, but, true to the pattern of traditional Chinese political culture before the rise of Mao, no political leader fully embodied ideological legitimacy and moral authority. Sun Yat-sen was too marginal to the cultural center to assume such a role and Chiang Kai-shek never transcended his own iron cage, "the generalissimo."

Notwithstanding Mao's early decision to cast his lot with the peasantry, it was his success in capturing the hearts and minds of the intelligentsia that bestowed upon him the charisma needed for his mass mobilization. This is not to say that in assessing the effectiveness of Maoism as a revolutionary ideology, the intelligentsia rather than the peasantry played the pivotal role. Rather, Mao's proven ability to arouse peasant nationalism and to transform many tillers of the land into guerrilla fighters and active participants in the revolutionary process through socialist education was a precondition for persuading the intelligentsia that he meant what he said and that through actual praxis his words carried a meaning that was authentic. Mao's literary talent, which was not widely known until 1946, was a happy surprise to the leftist intellectuals and became irresistible to those cultural conservatives who were seasoned in classical literature. If Mao's experience in the Long March and Yan'an alienated him from his fellow intellectuals, his immersion in traditional Chinese literary works made him a familiar face, indeed a kindred spirit. Ironically, Mao's radical otherness, especially his identification with the poor peasants, turned out to be a liberating message for the concerned intellectuals.

The Chinese intelligentsia seemed to have been well disposed to populist sentiments, having been educated in the Confucian tradition that the people are the root of politics, and agriculture is the root of the economy. If the people are not aroused, no effective political action is really possible, and if agriculture is in trouble, the economy necessarily suffers. The peasantry is the key to social stability and, by implication, to a truly revolutionary transformation of society. Underlying this glorification of the transformative potential of the Chinese people is a deep-rooted conviction that since "Heaven sees through the eyes of the people and hears through the ears of the people,"[20] the united will of the people, like the flood, cannot be stopped. The myth of Yu, the Chinese counterpart to the story of Noah, clearly shows that self-sacrifice, group discipline, hard work, patience, charismatic leadership, mass mobilization, and the right technology can channel a devastating flood into productive irrigation. Mao's favorite allegory, "The Foolish Old Man Who Moved the Mountains" (*Yugong yishan*), ingrained in the Chinese collective consciousness as the proper "modern" way of transforming China into a socialist utopia, is a simplified version of the same myth. No intellectual, individually or communally, could challenge the authenticity of this Maoist vision, for it had become an essential dimension of the whole enterprise.

It was the fusion of scientism, an aggressive anthropocentrism, and populism, the myth of the general will, that made Maoism an explosive transformative ideology. All sacred symbolic mechanisms of control—the Mandate of Heaven, the ritual of ancestral veneration, the sanctity of the land, the harmonizing patterns of the four seasons, the dignity of the religious rites in honoring spirits and ghosts, and the intrinsic values of learning—were either relegated to the background or ruthlessly secularized. Dialectic materialism, as the new orthodoxy, rendered all forms of spirituality, especially the organized religions, futile and illegitimate. Paradoxically, however, the seemingly secularized Maoism was a fertile ground for all sorts of sentiments, including highly charged ethnic, linguistic, territorial, gender, and religious emotions, to express themselves. The Maoist romantic utopianism took on millenarian and evangelical overtones during the Cultural Revolution. As the relative historical revolution became absolutized into a project of universal salvation, the messengers (the Red Guards) condemned those who failed to share their vision as "monsters and demons" (*niugui-sheshen*), a category worse than miserable sinners and hateful heathens. The deification of Mao himself provided an ironic twist to the whole process: the man who insisted that he did not believe in negative cosmic forces (*buxinxie*), and thus could never be haunted by ghosts, became the most fearful and perverse "evil spirit" in Chinese history.

THE FORMS OF SOCIAL SUFFERING FROM MAOISM

The three capital events of social suffering in the People's Republic—the Anti-Rightist Campaign, the massive starvation as a result of the Great Leap Forward, and the Cultural Revolution—were all closely connected to Mao's policies based on his utopian vision. Although they differed remarkably in terms of other causes and circumstances, the presence of Maoism (the inversionary ideology) as a key factor is undeniable.

The most obvious type of social suffering attributable to Maoism is the brutality against individuals, prompted by an ideological zealotry to be correct, pure, and totally uncompromising. The intense hatred of the enemy (landlord, capitalist, reactionary, bourgeois, nationalist agent, or imperialist spy) led to torture, murder, and even cannibalism. The psychopathology of treating those condemned to be counterrevolutionaries as subhuman, deserving no sympathy whatsoever, created an inversionary process of reducing one's closest kin to radical otherness. Among the youth with dubious class backgrounds (including virtually all members of the intelligentsia), the incredible practice of demonstrating one's commitment to the revolutionary cause by showing one's willingness to cut off primordial ties became a common occurrence. Indeed, it happened so frequently that, among the intellectuals, it was not uncommon to measure redness by the degree of alienation from parents and spouses. As a result, numerous families broke up and an immeasurable amount of guilt and frustration haunted the intellectual community for years in the aftermath.

The Maoist assault on the body politic so fundamentally shook the rigid structure of state socialism that, without the resiliency of Zhou Enlai's government apparatuses, the People's Republic might have degenerated into a lawless anarchy. The delegitimation of all forms of authority in politics and culture created a power vacuum and a dangerous occasion for violence. The main force of the Cultural Revolution was directed against hierarchy. Disappointment at those who had lost their faith in socialist idealism, hatred of those who had abused their privileges, and a desire to settle old scores blinded the fanatical leaders of the Red Guards to all other issues. Mean-spiritedness and vindictiveness soon overshadowed the appearance of distributive justice in struggle sessions. Numerous forms of humiliation, discipline, corporal punishment, and torture were invented to inflict pain and suffering upon social groups labeled as "bad elements." The effect of this unprecedented tyranny upon the intellectuals of the Party, who had hailed the Anti-Rightist campaign with enthusiasm, was profound. Many of them turned away from Mao's revolutionary romanticism in disgust. Some began to question the rationality, indeed the sanity, of Mao's vision for China.

In a deeper sense, the damages inflicted upon the value system by the Maoists were the most difficult to heal. The frontal attack not only on party politics and elite culture but also on the "habits of the heart," which had been firmly rooted in the folk traditions for generations, so thoroughly destroyed the social fabric that the post-Mao reconstruction began with the rudimentary education of etiquette. Even polite expressions such as "good morning," "excuse me," and "thank you" had to be reintroduced and relearned as legitimate utterances in social intercourse. The grammar of action, defined in terms of conflict, confrontation, contradiction, and contention—a reflection of Mao's insistence on the primacy of class struggle in social development—was, during the period of the Cultural Revolution, omnipresent in thought, literature, art, music, film, and drama. The effects of moral inversion on the social level were so extensive that kindness was mistaken for weakness, sympathy for sentimentalism, and civility for hypocrisy. The psychology of suspicion, linguistic violence, verbal aggressiveness, insensitivity in interpersonal communication, and an inability to be decent or polite in social relations would take years to overcome in ordinary practical living. A new intellectual vision, a new world view, indeed a new way of learning to be human is required to heal the wounds in the value system. "De-Maoification" is not only a political process but a social transformation and a cultural rejuvenation.

Mao occasionally acknowledged that he was responsible for some of these disasters, but there is no evidence that he ever regretted his obvious wrongdoings. The CCP, despite the bitter experience of each member of its top leadership, to this date, cannot bring itself to disown Mao, and the maltreated intelligentsia, almost two decades after the Cultural Revolution, is still mesmerized by Mao's charisma. Apparently, China has yet to free herself from the grips of anthropocentric scientism and mobilizational populism. Her attitude toward other Enlightenment values, notably human rights, liberty, and the dignity of the individual, and her treatment of minorities, especially the Tibetans, will give some indication of whether a new life orientation is in the offing.

ACKNOWLEDGMENTS

I am grateful to Arthur Kleinman and Stuart Schram of Harvard, Ying-shih Yü of Princeton, Daniel Bell of Singapore, Song Yong-bai of Seoul National University, and Viren Murthy of Honolulu who read early versions of the manuscript and offered detailed and thoughtful comments, and to Nancy Hearst and Rosanne Hall for their thorough editorial help.

ENDNOTES

[1]Stevan Harrell, "Introduction," in Jonathan N. Lipman and Stevan Harrell, eds., *Violence in China: Essays in Culture and Counterculture* (Albany, N.Y.: State of New York University Press, 1990), 1.

[2]For the sake of expediency, "Maoism," rather than the official designation, "Mao Zedong Thought" (*Mao Zedong sixiang*), will be used in this essay to refer to this ideology. The term "Maoism," specifying a coherent and independent ideology, was first used by Benjamin Schwartz in his classical study, *Chinese Communism and the Rise of Mao* (Cambridge, Mass.: Harvard University Press, 1951). I am also very much indebted to Stuart R. Schram; since his publication of *The Political Thought of Mao Tse-tung* (New York: Praeger, 1969), he has been involved in a comprehensive study of Mao Zedong Thought, enabling interested students to see its evolution in detail. It should be noted that in order to preserve the Maoist legacy, a desperate attempt has been made by the ideologists of the Chinese Communist Party to make a distinction between *Mao Zedong sixiang* (Mao Zedong Thought) and *Mao Zedong de sixiang* (Mao Zedong's thought); while the former symbolizes an official ideology that allows ideas not originated from Mao as its constitutive parts, the latter includes Mao's original ideas that must be expunged from the official party line.

[3]The figure, based on an internal CCP report of 1961, cited in Arthur and Joan Kleinman's essay in this issue, is thirty million. My figure, based on Chen Yizi's analysis, is yet to be verified. The Shanghai University journal, *Society*, in 1993 cited a figure of forty million, but that issue was immediately recalled.

[4]Perhaps the most tragic form of destruction was done by families and individuals who "voluntarily" destroyed family treasures for fear of incriminatory acts against them by ignorant Red Guards obsessed with their mission of eradicating traces of the feudal past.

[5]See David E. Apter and Tony Saich, *Revolutionary Discourse in Mao's Republic* (Cambridge, Mass.: Harvard University Press, 1994).

[6]Ross Terrill, *Mao: A Biography* (New York: Simon & Schuster, 1980), 151–52.

[7]Ibid., 165.

[8]Although no systematic studies have appeared in print on the subject, Li Tou, the literary critic, in several oral presentations, suggested that an in-depth analysis of Mao's genre and of Party culture is essential for developing a communal self-reflexivity among Chinese mainland intellectuals in exile.

[9]Terrill, *Mao: A Biography,* 152.

[10]Ibid., 159.

[11]David Apter, "Yan'an and the Narrative Reconstruction of Reality," in Tu Wei-ming, ed., *China in Transformation* (Cambridge, Mass.: Harvard University Press, 1994), 228.

[12]Ibid., 225.

[13]Ibid., 161.

[14]See Vera Schwarcz, *The Chinese Enlightenment: Intellectuals and the Legacy of the May Fourth Movement of 1919* (Berkeley, Calif.: University of California Press, 1986).

[15]Fred Dallmayr, "Tradition, Modernity, and Confucianism," *Human Studies,* vol. 16 (The Netherlands: Kluwer Academic Publishers, 1993), 208.

[16]It should be noted that this often-quoted statement was meant to convey the Maoist principle "that the party commands the gun and the gun shall never be allowed to command the party." See Ellis Joffe, *Party and Army: Professionalism and Political Control in the Chinese Officer Corps, 1949–1964* (Cambridge, Mass.: Harvard University Press, 1965), 57, as cited in Jonathan D. Spence, *The Search for Modern China* (New York: W. W. Norton, 1990), 563.

[17]Terrill, *Mao: A Biography,* 221.

[18]Tu Wei-ming, "Confucianism: Symbol and Substance in Recent Times," in Tu Wei-ming, *Humanity and Self-Cultivation: Essays in Confucian Thought* (Berkeley, Calif.: Berkeley Asian Humanities Press, 1979), 268–76.

[19]Perhaps the most damaging biography of Mao is the recently published *Mao Zedong Sirenyisheng Huiyilu* (Memoir of Mao Zedong's Private Physician) by Li Zhisui (Taipei: China Times Publishing Company, 1994). The Chinese version, based on *The Private Life of Chairman Mao* (New York: Random House Inc., 1994), has generated heated debates on Mao's personality in mainland China, Taiwan, Hong Kong, Singapore, and Chinese communities throughout the world. Endorsed by scholars, notably Andrew Nathan of Columbia University and Ying-shih Yü of Princeton University, as an eyewitness account of the carefully concealed aspects of Mao's ordinary daily life, Dr. Li's vivid description of Mao's idiosyncratic habits significantly challenges Mao's public image as an exemplar of a committed revolutionary devoted to a simple life. Ironically, however, recent surveys among college students in the People's Republic of China indicate that Mao's reputation as the most admired leader has not been tarnished. Furthermore, to the astonishment of liberal-minded Chinese intellectuals, the cult of Mao as a god and as a protector has been spreading in both peasant communities and urban centers. Mao's reemergence as a folk hero in newly constructed temples and as an amulet in taxis in major cities is not likely to be deterred by revelations of his shortcomings.

[20]The earliest reference is in the "Taishi" chapter of the *Book of Documents*; the statement in the "Gaoyaomo" chapter of the same book conveys a similar meaning. It has become well known because of Mencius's citation, in *Mencius,* 4B:5.

Quite simply, we are in the midst of a largely unheralded crisis in world mental health. Faced with a choice between reducing deficits and investing resources to address this mental health burden, poor and rich nations alike have opted to reduce deficits. Because many mental [and social] health problems, such as substance abuse, violence, suicide, and dementia, are encountered in low-income and high-income societies alike, solutions that work in one setting have potential applications in others. . . .There are many promising local experiments and demonstration projects. In fact, there is much that low-income countries can teach their wealthier neighbors, if only information is shared.

Robert Desjarlais, Leon Eisenberg, Byron Good, and
Arthur Kleinman, eds.

From Executive Summary to *World Mental Health:
Problems and Priorities in Low-Income Countries*

New York: Oxford University Press, 1995

Anne Harrington

Unmasking Suffering's Masks: Reflections on Old and New Memories of Nazi Medicine

EVEN WITH THE PASSAGE OF A HALF CENTURY, Nazi medical science continues to exist in the consciousness of today's medical profession as the ultimate morality play of our time: a stark and terrifying moment when medicine, at its most civilized and sophisticated, allowed its skills and resources to be deflected from the goals of healing and life and invested in a perverse ideology of death and suffering. At the same time, the tendency for memory to be infused by a larger-than-life sense of horror complicates scholarly efforts to look to the history of Nazi medicine for clearer insights into the processes that create and sustain the "medicalization" of human suffering. In our nightmares and consciences, the complex truths of the past are at risk of being sorted and pressed into the simplifying imperatives of the present. The act of "looking" is partly "pre-interpreted" through a range of intense personal and collective present meanings.

This means that even as the critics and moral consciences within the medical profession tell certain stories over and over again, in order that medicine may never repeat the mistakes of the past, other stories are less well told and less well remembered because they jar in one way or another with current sensibilities or perceived truths. In this sense, we fail to use the past as a resource as fully as we could. Our memory is fractured.

This essay is offered as a defense of this assertion, and a meditation on its implications for the larger concern of this issue of

Anne Harrington is Professor of the History of Science at Harvard University.

181

Dædalus: human suffering as a social problem, and how scholarship may illuminate the conditions that abet and sustain it. The essay reflects a sense of fracture in its form as well as its content. Its argument is organized around three stories—true but incomplete stories—that are juxtaposed but not clearly "integrated." The first story is about "us": it reconstructs the familiar templates of today that are regularly utilized to explain Nazi biomedicine, and it suggests that those templates are intricately associated with a certain ethical vision of clinical reform in the present. The second story is about "them," about the ways in which certain Nazi physicians and scientists created their own collective representations of what was wrong with both Germany and biomedicine, and of what reform would look like. The last story is still in progress: it asks what would happen if certain "us"/"them" distinctions created by the postwar community of medical practitioners and theorists, both in Germany and the United States, were to become unstable and our enemies began to sound like "us."

STORY ONE: NAZI BIOMEDICINE AS OBJECTIVITY RUN AMOK

Since 1945, Nazism, including Nazi medicine, has been written as a catastrophic chapter in a number of larger moral stories. Some talk about scientific racism, some about the evils of eugenicist thinking; some focus on anti-Semitism, or on militarism, or on extreme nationalistic, conservative politics, or on the German scholarly community's abdication of reason and responsibility. Each story tells a certain truth, and each may cause a society to view current moral issues in a different way. Within the American medical profession today, however, one of those true but partial stories strikes a particularly resonant chord. This is the story I call "Nazi biomedicine as objectivity run amok."

The story in question has its roots in the moral atmosphere of immediate postwar Germany and the unprecedented decision by the victorious Allied powers to try certain medical doctors for war crimes at the Nuremberg trials. The first account of those trials, *das Diktat der Menschenverachtung* (*Dictatorship of Disdain for Humanity*), was published in 1947. The authors of this book were not avenging Americans or other members of the Allied judges (although the 1949 English translation of this book, *Doctors of*

Infamy, did include additional statements by several American physicians who had been involved in the trial).[1] Instead, the authors of the book were two German physicians from the University of Heidelberg, Alexander Mitscherlich and Fred Mielke. Before the book's appearance, no one knew what kind of document they would produce; no one knew how they would interpret the responsibility of deciding what it would mean to write the history of these emerging revelations. Their reply, when it emerged, was clear and has become one of the most insistent recurring replies of our own postwar consciences: one writes the history of atrocities like the Nazi medical practices and experiments in order to *unmask,* to expose the suffering and sadism that were glossed over by pretensions of medical and scientific legitimacy and need. The voices of these first witness-bearers, Mitscherlich and Mielke, were unambiguous:

> An icy wind was sweeping over the rubble-heaps of Nuremberg when the trial began on December 9, 1946. It enveloped all of us in thick clouds of dust. The cold was oppressive—and the atmosphere too remained oppressive. Never once was suffering vouchsafed the boon of pity in that great dungeon from which the ensuing weeks brought news, bit by bit, ominously belated. Amid the growing desolation, each act of cruelty had merely served to wear away one more fragment of what had once been whole.[2]

In keeping with this simple but poignant goal of unmasking, most of *Doctors of Infamy* consists of excerpts, without commentary, from 1,471 documents received in evidence at the trial. The idea was that showing the truth, unvarnished and all the more eloquent for its stark simplicity, could help guarantee that such a situation would never happen again.

But Mitscherlich and Mielke also provided a way of conceiving what made it *possible* for Nazi medical practitioners to not see the suffering they were perpetuating. Again, many in the profession today who would act as guardians of humane values in medical practice and research have absorbed their message into their bones. These authors wrote:

> There is not much difference whether a human being is looked on as a "case," or as a number to be tattooed on the arm. These are but two aspects of the faceless approach of an age without mercy. . . .This is the alchemy of the modern age, the transmogrification of subject

into object, of man into thing against which the destructive urge may wreak its fury without restraint.[3]

In other words, for Mitscherlich and Mielke, the most pernicious energy driving the engine of Nazi medical science had *not* been its racism, anti-Semitism, political agendas, and so on; it had been its perverse fidelity to an obscene *objectivity* that ultimately found it possible to see all activities through the lens of expediency, scientific "interest," and efficiency. *"Objectivity"* had masked the suffering humans actually affected or destroyed by the activities in question. In this sense, *Doctors of Infamy* established a legacy in which the moral act of witness-bearing, of authentic *seeing,* became associated with an epistemological stance that denied scientific objectivity the capacity to *see* humanely. Those who would fight evil, those who would honor suffering must be prepared to rip through the pretenses of objectification in order to return subjectivity and voice to its victims.

Perhaps no one has been more explicit in affirming this dual moral-epistemological position than Benno Müller-Hill, German professor of genetics and author of *Tödliche Wissenschaft (Murderous Science).*[4] He concluded his testimony with the following words:

> I have come to the end of my account....You will not hear the screams of children as the chloroform injections reached their hearts in my sentences. Nor will you hear the cries of the resisting patient: "You will rue this with your blood," as the door closed behind him. I have not spoken of those who blew up the crematorium in Auschwitz and who were executed immediately. Who hears the cries of the last of these men hanged in front of fellow prisoners: "Comrades, I am the last." Any hope there was for mankind was not to be found in German scientists but in their resisting victims. The staring eyes of the murdered rest on us....[5]

How was it possible for the Nazis not to "hear the screams of children" or of their other victims? Müller-Hill's explanation returns us to the theme of our story:

> Scientists espouse objectivity and spurn value judgements. But pure objectivity leads to regarding everything as being feasible. The killing of mental patients? If it is objectively necessary on economic grounds, and if it can be objectively organized, why not? The use of

mental patients, the Jews, and the Gypsies as experimental animals before or after their necessary deaths? If the authorities allow it, why not?...For these scientists, objectivity opened the door to every conceivable form of barbarism.[6]

Is it an accident that such stories get written and read with such passion in today's era of high-tech medical treatment, relentless research, and fears that the voice of patients and the ethic of personal clinical care are being lost in a system that values "cure" as a dissociated end in itself? In other words, is it possible that the story of Nazi biomedicine as "objectivity run amok" resonates so readily for critics of modern biomedicine, not only because it is true on its own terms, but because the writers involved in the present-day critique already "know," from their own experiences, how true this particular reading of the past "must" be? When Arthur Kleinman argues that biomedicine is an epistemological system fundamentally constituted "to discount the moral reality of suffering"—to reduce, dehumanize, and objectify its human subject[7]—he is not compelled to evoke the specter of the "Nazi doctors." Nevertheless, images of their bloodless, merciless instrumentalism are always available, both to him and to his readers, as the final court of appeal when arguments about the dangers of "objectification" are made.[8]

Ironically, one of the effects of raising the story about Nazi medicine to "objectivity run amok" is that those who resonate to such critiques as outlined above discover that the world is full of dangers, but that nevertheless they personally belong to the community of good people who have "seen" a potential future in a dark past, and have made a commitment to averting it. It is therefore painful but perhaps not particularly destabilizing for critics of biomedicine to remember the historical story of Nazi biomedicine as "objectivity run amok."

STORY TWO: NAZI BIOMEDICINE AS HOLISM[9]

The challenge comes when one expands one's vision of the past to discover something unexpected. It turns out that a significant number of the architects of Nazi medical ideology also believed that they were protesting the reductionistic, objectifying, calculating "gaze" of scientistic medicine; they claimed to be committed to rescuing the "whole person" for clinical care and research. Certainly, there may be a temptation to dismiss that other protest as something "inauthentic," "disingenuous," and clearly different from the impulses that drive our own concerns, but it is worth lingering a little longer over that story to see if it may carry other lessons for our own self-consciousness.

Though it is convenient to call this story of protest and reform "Nazi holism," it is important to understand that holistic thinking in German medicine did not begin with Nazism and was not inevitably compelled to become part of Nazism. We are talking about developments in German science and culture that began long before Hitler, and that then went in a range of political and intellectual directions. The first stage in making sense of Nazi "holism" is to have a sense of its position in that bigger, politically more complex picture.

The picture presents itself as a montage of images from the period around World War I, and is framed and infused with a sense of crisis—in the sciences, in medicine, and not least in society and culture. People argued over the reasons, but there was widespread agreement that part of the blame must be borne, not only by the enemy outside and the politicians within, but by the ascendancy of a mechanistic natural science, whose nihilistic message of "technique" and instrumentalism over soul and integrity had led to existential despair and a steady degradation of community life and values. Science had declared humanity's life and soul a senseless product of mechanism. Thus, people treated one another as machines. Many believed that a misguided worship of the machine and its values had been at the heart of the lost war—the first war where technology had been the deciding factor. As one commentator would later put it: "Things had come to rule over men."[10]

The thing is, a not insignificant proportion of German scientists of the time, especially in the biomedical and psychological sciences, agreed with the diagnosis. In the course of studying processes of life and mind in the laboratory and the clinic, these men had concluded that both salvation and wholeness were possible after all, and that the sources of renewed hope were to be found in a revised understanding of living nature itself. Riding out under the banner of "wholeness," these scientists argued, in varying ways, that a *transformed* biology and psychology, one that had learned to see phenomena less atomistically and more "holistically," less mechanistically and more "intuitively," could lead to the rediscovery of a nurturing, meaningful relationship with the natural world.[11] What science had wrought, science would heal.

In the process of overcoming the influence of the "machine" in their laboratory and clinical work, these holistic life and mind scientists also found it possible to speak to the broader question of the "machine" in society and intellectual life. From Berlin to Prague, Vienna to Zurich, holistic life and mind scientists mingled their voices with those of cultural critics, crisis mongers, and would-be reformers. Those other voices, from outside the sciences, also typically used images of the "machine" and "wholeness" in order to articulate what they believed had gone wrong in politics, the community, and individual existence—and to identify roads to renewal.[12] In contrast to the explicit emphasis of the scientists, the "machine" in these other arguments rarely referred directly to a particular model of life and mind. Nor was it a clear pointer to any particular product of applied knowledge and engineering: railroads, factories, telegraphs, etc. The image of the "machine" functioned, rather, as a general, full-armed gesture to the entire problematic world of scientific instrumentalism, modernism, and industrialization. "Wholeness" in these larger arguments was an equally full-armed, pastoral alternative to the "machine"—not so much a rejection of the modern world in toto as a vision that demanded that science and modern concepts of progress not be allowed to undermine the centrality of spiritual, moral, and aesthetic values for both the individual and the community.[13]

What happened when science began to mix the language of its own critique of the "machine" with that of these other, full-time cultural critics—many of them known for their distinctly "antiscientific" biases? (The radical "life philosopher" Theodor Lessing called modern man "a species of robber-apes which has been infected with megalomania by science."[14]) Significantly, the result was less an open struggle over values and control, and more a subtle shift in the cultural logic that ruled the larger critique as a whole. Even though science (the "old" science) had been the enemy, nevertheless it had always been a *powerful* enemy, with an authority that would be useful to have on one's own side. Now that it was in the process of remaking itself (the "new science"),[15] now that its truths were in the service of "wholeness" rather than the "machine," few objected to letting it continue to claim a unique social and epistemological authority in the larger debate. Draping its findings in images that resonated of the same spiritual and cultural traditions defended by these other critics, holistic science blurred distinctions between perceived problems and perceived solutions, all the while carrying its unique epistemological authority through one level of debate to the next. For those with the culturally and politically sensitized ears to hear the messages, the new arguments in biology and psychology for "wholeness" and against the "machine" would gradually come to persuade simultaneously as natural truth, salvation mythology, and psychobiological guide to cultural and political survival.

For a while, the scientific perspectives of holism seemed capable of being reconciled with a range of political positions: from socialism and democratic republicanism on one side to monarchism and fascism on the other. Jewish scientists like the neurologist Kurt Goldstein and the psychologist Max Wertheimer for a while represented compelling and persuasive voices for wholeness. However, as the 1920s descended into greater depths of discontent, aspects of the "wholeness"/"mechanism" battle imagery began to go more consistently in directions that both Germany and the rest of the world would learn to regret; they would begin to fold into the goals and politics of National Socialism. At this point, one begins to find oneself confronted with an apparent paradox. One finds that the holistic rhetoric of rebellion and reform in German biomedicine is functioning as a means of legitimating an oppressive social order rather than serving as a challenge to that order. Under National Socialism, the rebellious and quasi-militaristic dimension of German holism's self-image would intensify in directions that more or less explicitly equated the holistic fight to reform science with the Nazi fight against everything racially foreign. In 1935, the Munich mathematician M. Casper spoke of science's history as a Manichaean conflict between men who sought to conceive "the world as a whole" and men who tried to reduce that wholeness to mechanistic first principles. "Is it coincidence," he asked disingenuously, "that within the first rank only German names appear?"[16] Gestalt psychologist Wolfgang Metzger (who stayed on in Germany after his Jewish colleagues fled or emigrated) spoke of holistic science as locked in a battle against the "chaotic," "mechanistic" spirit of the West. The violence of the present war, he declared in 1942, was a "visible and tangible sign" of this "spiritual struggle" that would in the end lead to the rise of a "new world age."[17]

This intensification of militaristic language in the literature was accompanied by an increasing explicit tendency to superimpose the terms of the holistic struggle against mechanism onto the idea of a racial struggle between Germans and Jews, popularized by people like Chamberlain, Rosenberg, and Hitler. Jews now began to appear in the discussions as flesh-and-blood metaphors of the "cold" epistemology of the "machine." This is something different from the well-known tendency in Nazi Germany to denounce this or that example of "Jewish science" (psychoanalysis, Einsteinian relativity, etc.). Here, rather, Jewishness as a *racial condition*—the Jewish way of thinking and being—was perceived as a disorganizing and sterilizing force to be contained and conquered by the answering racial power of German-Aryan "wholeness."

That metaphorical transformation had a number of consequences. It was increasingly said, or implied, that the very capacity to see nature as a "whole" (the art of *Ganzheitsbetrachtung*) was a trait peculiar to the "Indo-Germanic" mind, while the Jewish mind was fundamentally analytic, dissolutive, and materialistic. One study, for example, claimed to have discovered evidence of inferior spatial and compositional ("holistic-perceptual") skills in the drawings of Jewish schoolchildren as compared to their Aryan peers.[18] Another study analyzed the evidence that Jewish scientists suffer from a lack of spatial perceptual capacity, as evidenced by their failure to develop roentgen stereoscopy.[19] The "psychological anthropologist" Erich Jaensch—whose influence in German psychology may have been unparalleled before his death in 1939[20]—developed a biopsychological typology that opposed a superior "Northern integration type" (the "J" type) to an inferior "Jewish-liberal dissolution type" (the "S" type).[21] The "S" type, which after 1933 he also called the *Gegentyp* (anti-type), was described as intellectually rigid and abstract, with a tendency to become easily fragmented. In addition, it was described as artificial, untrustworthy, and biologically soft (with a tendency towards tuber-culosis and schizophrenia).[22]

If it was the case that the German and the Jewish races had radically different ways of experiencing and interacting with the natural world—apparently rooted in their different biologies—then one possible conclusion for Nazi holists was that no objective standard of truth could exist to which all peoples must submit. Truth, by definition, always carried the stamp of a particular culture and biology—a particular *Volk* and *Blut*—and served that *Volk*'s "political reality" and "fateful struggle."[23] Indeed, as Heinz Wolff, a Nazi student leader, put it, the very notion that there could exist an "objectivity" transcending national and racial needs was a self-serving ideology, rooted in a (Jewish) scientific liberal-ism, whose devious aim was to encourage people to forget that science was actually made by "living men," by "men of flesh and blood." Writing in 1935, the prominent Nazi holistic physician Karl Kötschau agreed:

> The freedom of science cannot exist in the right to concern one's self with things that are fully alien to the thinking of one's own *Volk*, and that possibly even serve the interests of another *Volk*. To be dependent on an international *Weltanschauung* alien to one's own *Volk* is intellectual slavery, not freedom.[24]

But the "racializing" of holism's struggle against mechanism did not stop with such "biologies of knowledge" as these. Nazis like Alfred Rosenberg had long advocated the idea that the struggle between Teuton and Jew corresponded in some ill-defined way to a struggle between the principles of life and death.[25] However, it took a 1935 article by the physician Alfred Böttcher to make the further connections and claim that actually the holistic struggle to overcome mechanism in *science* could be understood as a struggle between an Aryan life principle and a Jewish death principle; between Nature and something unnatural whose "blood came out of Chaos":

> The Jewish way of thinking carries, like his blood that came out of Chaos, a dissolutive character. For this reason, the Jew is always attempting to split all things, to break them down to their atoms and in this way to make them complicated and so incomprehensible that a healthy person can no longer find his way in the jumble of

contradictory theories. Thus does the Jew dissolve the miracle of creation, leaving behind him a pile of rubble, a "chaos" everywhere he penetrates with his corrosive mind.

The healthy non-Jew, in contrast, born out of creation, thinks simply, organically, creatively. He unifies, builds up—he thinks in terms of wholes. Briefly summarized, the blood law of the Jew advances: chaos, world revolution, death! And the blood law of the creative-heroic man advances: the organic worldview, world pacification, life![26]

From rhetoric like this, it seems only a short step to the pronouncement of the holistic psychologist Friedrich Sander that all races that are inherently alienated from the German values of wholeness and gestalt (the *Gestaltfremde)* must be "eliminated." The German word he used was "*ausschalten,*" the same euphemism later used to refer to the genocide of the Jews under the terms of the "Final Solution."[27]

This story is highly ironic, since actually, until 1933, some of the most important and influential German holistic critics of biomedicine were both Jewish in their ethnic origins and liberal in their politics. In the atmosphere of relative tolerance that prevailed during the Weimar years, "liberal," "Jewish" holism managed to share some common cultural goals with "conservative" and, in some cases, "anti-Semitic" holism. By the late 1920s, however, influential Jewish holistic scientists like Max Wertheimer, founder of Gestalt psychology, and Kurt Goldstein, founder of a psychosomatic, existentially-oriented neurology, were increasingly vilified as problems posing as solutions, as pathogens pretending to offer healing solutions to Germany's woes. Their visions of wholeness were false because the Jewish mind was incapable of grasping what a true holistic science would look like. As one tracks the varied arguments across the decade, one can see how, gradually, different defenders of "wholeness" were coming to be as much in a state of tension with one another as they were with their mechanistic rivals, each developing arguments designed to undermine or neutralize those pushed by the other.

Of course, the Jews were not the only perceived blot on the *Volksganze* (folk community or "whole") under Nazism: the congenitally weak, sick, and mentally disabled were also singled out as "ballast," "parasites," and diseases within the organismic body to be systematically eradicated through mass sterilization and, in later years, through "euthanasia" or enforced "mercy" killings. Holistic rhetoric used the trope of the supremacy of the whole over its parts to counter anti-eugenicist arguments that relied on the putative rights of individuals to reproduce or live their lives as they saw fit. Thus, holistic psychologist Felix Krueger declared sternly in 1935:

> It is given to people that they may recognize that which is *un-whole* in their being, that is to say, opposed to life and hostile to formation. They must make a sacrifice of their imperfection, by obeying their state and freely recognizing the ordered power above them.[28]

Holistic rhetoric found common cause with eugenicist thinking by further suggesting that the "un-whole"—the infirm, disabled, and genetically inferior—represented in their own way no less an offense to the values of "wholeness" than did the Jews. In this rhetoric, the infirm and disabled—somewhat like the Jews—were *themselves* transformed into metaphors of mechanism. "Machine-people" was the disdainful term used by Nazi physician Karl Kötschau—a reference to the fact that such individuals owed their survival to medical technology, and were incapable of surviving outside the shelter of an artificial environment. Kötschau was the director of a government-sponsored movement in the 1930s—about which little was known in the scholarship about Nazi medicine until quite recently—to establish a holistic and synthetic "new German therapy" that would integrate "alternative" and mainstream medicine under an anti-Cartesian, anti-reductionistic "biological" metaphysics.[29]

What should medicine be all about, once it had moved away from machines and focused on life in its wholeness? These are Kötschau's words:

> Biological medicine does not cast the person out of Nature, does not dissect and atomize him, but rather always examines the person in his holistic functioning and reacting. . . .Biological research methods impart understanding and application possibilities from old medicine and folk medicine. . . .It is a contribution of the National Socialist revolution to have freed the doctor from. . .[his former] mechanistic-materialistic imprisonment. The medical profession accordingly moves more and more away from the former overly fastidious

and one-sided mechanistic thinking that...must have devastating consequences for the health of the *Volk*.[30]

What happened then to medical practice when Nazi medicine was freed from its "one-sided mechanistic thinking" and began to consider "...health and disease in the context of the Nature-whole"? It discovered that its primary concern should *not* be those who were already sickly and useless, but rather the healthy who had the most to contribute to the *Volk*.[31] And it realized that prevention and education rather than care must dominate its policies. In keeping with this insight, Kötschau's "New German Therapy" was vigorous in the 1930s in its efforts to discourage the use of "genetic poisons" such as alcohol and tobacco, to fight environmental toxins in the workplace, and even to encourage bakeries to produce more whole-grain bread rather than less nourishing white varieties.[32]

In addition, when some form of intervention proved unavoidable, New German Therapy encouraged physicians to consider the use of such "natural," "folk" therapeutic approaches as herbal remedies, massage, fasting, and special diets of raw vegetables and fruits. The medieval mystic German physician Paracelsus was evoked as the guardian angel of this endeavor. As historian Robert Proctor has put it: "Paracelsean medicine was said to embody the natural, earthbound, experimental nature of German medicine—medicine that was 'close to the people' and not based on 'a lot of complicated theories.' It embraced 'the whole man,' not just particular organs or ailments."[33]

Ultimately, the attempt to systematically reorient Nazi medicine in holistic directions would flounder under opposition from other medical leaders within the Party, and especially the SS.[34] In the end, particularly as the war made holism less practical and efficient, a more systematic kind of mechanism did prevail in policy, and in the camps, out of which emerged the images that came to haunt the present age. Holism "lost" the struggle to speak for Nazi medicine and biology, but not for lack of trying. Although both "holists" and "mechanists" were, in their different ways, equally dedicated to the goals of racial "cleansing" and strengthening the "Master Race," in the end "organicism" and calls for a return to *Volk* (community) were no match for the militaristic Darwinian

194 Anne Harrington

ethic and the practical technologies of racial management that the mechanists could offer (racial screening, sterilization, castration, and ultimately methods of mass "euthanasia"). Nevertheless, certain manifestations of the original Nazi holistic vision would persist to the end. For example, the 1940s saw the founding of a huge plantation for the growing and experimental testing of herbal remedies at the Dachau concentration camp. Here, some eight hundred to twelve hundred prisoners (many of them pastors, after the Jews were selected out for extermination in 1941) labored and died under the supervision of brutal SS followers of Paracelsus and other healers. This project may in the end stand as one of the most perverse symbols of the Nazi medical dedication to "wholeness."[35]

Even where technocratic pragmatism overtly prevailed in the concentration camps, we know little about the ways in which a nostalgic sugarcoating of the rhetoric of "wholeness" and "organicism" may have continued to help make it more palatable for some of its perpetrators. The career of SS-Colonel Joachim Mrugowsky, chief of the Institute of Hygiene in the *Waffen-SS*, is a case in point. The Institute of Hygiene was, among other things, responsible for maintaining and distributing the Zyklon-B gas used at Auschwitz.[36] At Auschwitz and Sachsenhausen, Mrugowsky sent countless prisoners to their deaths, conducted "research" that involved injecting healthy people with lethal tubercular cultures, and executed Russian prisoners using poisoned bullets.[37] At Nuremberg in 1946, he was found guilty of war crimes and condemned to death. Yet, it is very likely that this same physician would have vigorously protested against the idea that his work at Auschwitz represented the "machine" face of medicine at its most perverse. In his own mind, such a characterization would have seemed absurd, because he saw *himself* as someone vigorously opposed to the mechanizing tendencies of modern medicine and deeply committed to a holistic biomedical perspective. After hours in Auschwitz, he often retired to his extensive private library, filled with books revering the age of Goethe and Alexander von Humboldt.[38] Did the two sides of this man simply coexist in separate, more or less dissociated spheres, an example of what Robert Jay Lifton has called psychological "doubling"?[39] Or did men like Mrugowsky find it possible actively to visualize a way in which lethal injections and Goethean holistic ideals could be reconciled in some higher salvationist story? Either way, "objectification" does not seem an adequate term to capture the full complexity of social and psychological processes that permitted Goethe and gas chambers to coexist in Auschwitz and in this man's mind.

STORY THREE: "WHAT DOES THIS HAVE TO DO WITH MY FATHER'S WORK?"

If one agrees that Nazi biomedicine was more than "objectification," nevertheless its own rhetoric that declared it to be in fact a thing *opposed* to objectification may still leave us unmoved in our own moral certainties. In particular, a case like that of Mrugowsky may appear to be so monstrous that one readily brushes the rhetoric aside, focuses on the crimes behind it, and is tempted to leave it at that. But is it possible that the story of Nazi holism— Nazism that believed it was working to overcome "objectivity run amok"—is more unsettling than it may seem? Are there any lessons here for our own attempts to recognize what promotes good and what must be fought as evil? This essay seeks an answer to that question by means of a final story about a man who came, for many in postwar Germany, to represent the antithesis of the objectifying, "technocratic" gaze that the medical profession believed to have been typical of Nazi medicine in the death camps. The man is the German psychosomaticist Viktor von Weizsäcker (1886– 1957). One of his students and colleagues at the University of Heidelberg was Alexander Mitscherlich, first author of *Doctors of Infamy*. It is no accident, but perhaps somewhat troubling in light of the story that follows, that a disciple of Weizsäcker should turn out to have been the man who helped set the post-World War II focus on "objectification" as the murderous "essence" of Nazi medicine. In postwar Germany, Weizsäcker, even more than Mitscherlich, would be a powerful voice protesting objectification in medicine, and visualizing more humane alternatives to it.

The core idea of Weizsäcker's alternative system of medicine was his concept of the "Gestalt circle." He envisioned disease and physiological malfunctioning as encompassing not only inputs and outputs—perceptions and reactions—but also a "third variable": the subject and his or her direct experience of illness. As Weizsäcker conceived things, a patient's understanding of the symbolic or practical *meaning* of a disease—what medical anthropologists to-day call the "illness narrative"—shaped its actual reality and course in a circular dialectic that brought biology and biography together into an indivisible, interactive unity.[40]

For Weizsäcker this meant that medicine ultimately had to become more than a natural science: it had to embrace also what Weizsäcker himself called an "anthropological" perspective that perceived disease as having not just a physiological significance but also a biographical significance, the final nature of which could only be elucidated through empathic dialogue with the patient. From the beginning, psychoanalytic concepts like "unconscious," "repressed," and "defensive" would become central tools for illuminating the dynamics of disease thus understood—even as Weizsäcker went further with these concepts than Freud himself was prepared to go.

In a 1927 essay, Weizsäcker told the famous story of how the French neurologist Jean-Martin Charcot had privately admitted to a young Freud that, in cases of hysteria, there was "always" a sexual issue at stake. In his autobiographical account, Freud recalled how he had said to himself: "If he knows that, why doesn't he say so?" Weizsäcker then described an encounter he had himself had with an aging Freud, many years later, in which the great man had admitted that the sudden intrusion of an accident or organic disease in the life of a patient can cure that patient of his or her neurosis. Weizsäcker had then said to *himself*: "If he knows that, why doesn't he say so?" Obviously, it was up to Weizsäcker to "say so," and to develop the full clinical implications of the insight that (as he would later put it) "nothing organic is without meaning." In his 1927 essay, he concluded: "It seems as if, in science, there is almost a law whereby one epoch only says the one thing, while remaining silent about the other thing, that it also knows."[41] There is a deep, unintended irony in Weizsäcker's comment here that ultimately, as one probes his story, begins to resonate on more than one level.

Because here was holism that the German postwar medical community had embraced as incorruptible, had hailed as an antidote to the calculating, impersonal attitude of medical expediency that had allowed Nazi medicine to support—as Kleinman puts it—a "routinization of evil."[42] Yet, there may be something incomplete still about our understanding of its potentialities. At a historic public forum on "Medicine and National Socialism" held in Berlin in 1980—the first of its kind in Germany—Tübingen sociologist Walter Wuttke-Groneberg took on Weizsäcker's past in a hard-hitting paper entitled "From Heidelberg to Dachau." The paper asserted that Weizsäcker had differentiated himself from the SS-physicians of the concentration camps, "not in his aim, but [only] in his method."[43]

Wuttke-Groneberg found cause for these shocking claims in two professional occasions in Weizsäcker's life: a lecture series on "medical professional questions" that the psychosomaticist had offered at Heidelberg in 1933,[44] just after Hitler's seizure of power, and a 1947 essay entitled "Euthanasia and Human Experimentation" that was written in reaction to the Nuremberg trials.[45] Wuttke-Groneberg pointed out that Weizsäcker, though he certainly did not try to absolve the convicted physicians of responsibility for their crimes, nevertheless failed to condemn outright the concept of "physician as exterminator." Instead, he went out of his way to defend both euthanasia and human experimentation as necessary parts of medicine, and to paint a picture of violence and human sacrifice as a necessary part of the tragedy of human history. The atrocities of Auschwitz and Dachau were caused, he said, *not* by the idea that physicians may rightly destroy the lives of their patients, but by an indiscriminate technocratism that had led physicians to exercise their power in the absence of any rational *ethic* that could have guided decisions about appropriate extermination.

What would such an ethics of extermination have represented for Weizsäcker? Wuttke-Groneberg pointed to the above-mentioned 1933 lecture series in which Weizsäcker had for the first time defended the medical appropriateness of extermination in cases of lives judged "not worth living." At that time, Weizsäcker seemed to suggest that physicians making such judgments may want to consider whether the lives in question were capable of productive work. At any rate, the physician's aim, Weizsäcker argued in 1933, should not and could not be life "at any price." Instead, the medical profession, working in cooperation with the state, must develop a rational "policy of extermination" to guide its practices.

At the Berlin conference, Wuttke-Groneberg's presentation provoked considerable heated discussion and protest, with no consensus or clarity. He was accused of having deliberately conflated Weizsäcker's intellectually sophisticated and humane attempt to reintroduce the "subject" into medicine with the vulgar, subjectivist "New German Therapy" of the Nazis; of citing Weizsäcker's discussions on death and euthanasia selectively and in a manipulative manner; and of glossing over the significance of central Weizsäcker concepts like "mutuality" and "solidarity" that dictated that the extermination of any subject in a clinical situation that was anything other than a therapeutic release would leave deadly traces on the other party.[46] These counterarguments were not fully successful in dispelling a general sense of unease in the audience, but they were sufficient to usher in a fragile truce on the question of Weizsäcker's "brown past" that would hold for several years.

Then the plot thickened. Six years later, at a symposium in Heidelberg in 1986 celebrating Weizsäcker's one hundredth birthday, Mechthilde Kütemeyer—a clinician at Cologne who had helped edit Weizsäcker's collected writings—declared that evidence recently unearthed in the military archives of Poland raised troubling new questions about Weizsäcker's brief career as Director of the Neurological Clinic and Research Institute at the University of Breslau from 1941 to 1945:

> In the military archive of Katowitz, Poland, over 200 patient files stemming from the years 1942 and 1943 were found, along with an explicit accompanying note containing the following content: "Neurological Research Institute, Prof. von Weizsäcker, Breslau, Neudorfer Street 118–120. Please find enclosed the fixed brain and spinal cord of child. . .(name and birthdate) that I am sending you in accordance with your letter from 25.3.1942, requesting an opportunity to investigate it neuropathologically. An excerpt from the case history is included. The supervising physician (Hecker), Province Medical Chief, Privy Councillor." We are dealing here with antisocial and handicapped children and youths from the Children's Division of the Loben Psychiatric Clinic for Youth (Lubliniec). The patient files make unmistakably clear that the brains in question were products of child euthanasia.[47]

The silence and foot shuffling after these remarks was palpable. People tried purposefully to deflect the conversation in other directions. Then, Frau Penselin, Weizsäcker's daughter, gained the floor and demanded to know more about the documents discussed by Kütemeyer, with which she said she was unfamiliar. Most of all, she demanded to know how she was supposed to understand the significance of these documents, what role her father had played in all this, and—above all—*what it all had to do with his work.* Before Kütemeyer could open her mouth, the moderator, Peter Hahn, moved in, "Unfortunately, I must now at this point interrupt. I think these questions are so important that they must be further discussed and clarified elsewhere." When a member of the audience shouted "let the questions be answered!" Hahn chose to deal with the interruption as a disciplinary issue, and the unruly outsider eventually quieted down.[48]

But the questions remain, particularly in the pained words of Weizsäcker's daughter, *"what does all this have to do with my father's work?"* What we are dealing with here is a question that is not only about the "objective" historical record. It is also a question about how collective memories of a traumatic past function in shaping present identities, how certain historical revelations are seen to have relevance for our *own* intellectual attractions and moral commitments.

The historian Christian Meier, writing about Auschwitz, declared that, "for a nation to appropriate its history," it must "look at it through the eyes of identity."[49] His concern, of course, was with the need of the German people to appropriate their own history. However, in light of the fact that Auschwitz haunts not just Germans but the "rest of us" as well, is there a moral responsibility to consider what it would mean—also for "us"—to look at Auschwitz, not from the perspective of an outsider's moral outrage, but through the "eyes of identity"?

The challenge of looking back at the Nazi past with the "eyes of identity" is the challenge of discovering that past images and phantasms of goodness *could* have seduced us too—not in the name of brutality and evil, but in the name of some vision of salvation and reform. In hindsight, we may be able to see, with chilling clarity, how a past vision became an illuminated end in itself, divorced from the concrete circumstances of its actualization, but are we certain that we would have "seen" so clearly then? And if not, how can we be so certain that our current commitments to the good causes and ideals around which we have built our professional lives are allowing us to see as clearly as we should?

The struggle to write new and less comfortable stories about the Nazi past, including stories told through the "eyes of identity" may be important for another reason. Recently, several historians have called attention to the ways in which the agendas of ecologically-oriented leftist groups like the Green Party have absorbed in refashioned form some of the ideals and ideologies of the same holistic and vitalistic biologies that at one time struck an alliance with the Third Reich.[50] Critics like Jean-Pierre Faye have also called attention to ways in which key pieces of the vocabulary of postmodernism ("deconstruction," "logocentrism") actually had their origins in protests against "objectification" written by Nazi and proto-fascist writers like Ernst Krieck and Lugwig Klages.[51] In other words, the part of Nazism that was not—in its own eyes— about "objectification" but rather saw itself as a protest *against* it, shows signs of being an early chapter in a story we are still in the process of writing today. The fact that it is a story that involves many today who actively abhor the agendas of Nazism is only surprising because our working memories of Nazism have left too many of us still vulnerable to surprises of this sort. To have a clearer understanding of the ways in which "their" stories may resonate with "our" own is almost certainly going to be uncomfortable. It would seem, however, to be a necessary expansion of consciousness if we accept that part of the task of confronting human suffering is to recognize that products of our own moral imagination—especially those that shine for us the most brightly— can, if we let them, become seductions, myths of goodness that we can be tempted to serve, even at the expense of the human beings in whose name they were allegedly first constructed.

ENDNOTES

[1]Alexander Mitscherlich and Fred Mielke, *Doctors of Infamy: The Story of the Nazi Medical Crimes (Diktat der Menschenverachtung)*, trans. Heinz Norden (New York: H. Schuman, 1949).

[2]Ibid., 151.

3Ibid., 152.

4Benno Müller-Hill, *Murderous Science: Elimination by Scientific Selection of Jews, Gypsies, and Others, Germany 1933–1945*, trans. George Fraser (Oxford and New York: Oxford University Press, 1988).

5Ibid., 104.

6Ibid., 89.

7See Arthur Kleinman, "A Critique of Objectivity in International Health," in *Writing at the Margin: Discourse Between Anthropology and Medicine* (Berkeley, Calif.: University of California Press, 1995).

8Cf. also Kleinman's discussion of the "medicalization" of terror, torture, and mass homicide in the Nazi death camps in *Rethinking Psychiatry: From Cultural Category to Personal Experience* (New York: The Free Press, 1988).

9Much of the material for this "story" and the next is taken from my forthcoming book, *Reenchanted Science: Holism in German Culture from Wilhelm II to Hitler* (Princeton, N.J.: Princeton University Press, 1996).

10The above quotation is by German socialist analyst Erich Wittenberg, writing in 1938 from abroad. Wittenberg went on to identify the drama of the Great War as a "high-point" of rationalistic, technological thinking, and the defeat of Germany as "the hour of reversal": "They found themselves at the end of the world war at the graveyard of their hopes. . . .Never before had a youth experienced such a total destruction of all values, sciences and arts; never before was the distance between the naive hope with which the youth were pulled into the field and the hard and cold reality so great and so unbridgeable." Erich Wittenberg, "Die wissenschaftskrisis in Deutschland im Jahre 1919: Ein Beitrag zur Wissenschaftsgeschichte," *Theoria: A Swedish Journal of Philosophy and Psychology* 4 (1938): 235–36.

11Examples include Hans Driesch, who resurrected teleological, vitalistic thinking in biology with his nonmaterial concept of the *entelechy* (guiding the embryo through its developments); Jakob von Uexküll, who called attention to the irreducible unity of an organism within an environment it had itself "created" from sense experience, and whose experienced features were meaningfully related to the organism's own existence (an orientation that would influence both ethology and psychosomatic medicine in Germany); the holistic (*Ganzheit*) school of biopsychology under Felix Krueger that emphasized the primacy of affect and irrationality in the unfolding of perception and cognition; the school of Gestalt psychology in Berlin under Wertheimer, Köhler, and Koffka that stressed the way in which perceived reality was ordered by active contributions of the perceiving mind/brain; the dynamic, teleological neurology of Constantin von Monakow that emphasized the regenerative capacities of the brain and its innate spiritual impulses; the psychosomatic "organismic" neuropsychiatry of Kurt Goldstein that celebrated health as biological "value" and stressed how life strived always for personal meaning; the "person"-oriented biologist and medicine of the internist Theodor Brugsch, and the "medical anthropology" of Viktor von Weizsäcker, discussed later in this essay.

12Fritz Ringer, *The Decline of the German Mandarins: The German Academic Community, 1890–1933* (Cambridge, Mass.: Harvard University Press, 1969), is still probably the best source for getting a sense of these broader debates as they developed in the universities, even though Ringer did not include the natural sciences in his study.

[13]Leo Marx who, speaking of the "fatalistic view of technology" in American literary culture, stresses that the world view of "pastoralism. . .should not be thought of as the logical antithesis of the modern belief in progress. That hypothetical role belongs to primitivism, the doctrine which holds that the environment most conducive to human well-being is the purest, least developed state of nature. The ideal situation that a true primitivist may be supposed to cherish is located as far away as possible, in space or time or both, from the urban centers of advanced civilization. The pastoral world-view, on the other hand. . .entails neither an uncritical embrace of material progress nor its total repudiation. What matters most in the pastoral dispensation is the proper subordination of all material concerns to the satisfactions of the inner life. . . ." Leo Marx, "Literary Culture and the Fatalistic View of Technology," *The Pilot and the Passenger: Essays on Literature, Technology, and Culture in the United States* (New York: Oxford University Press, 1988), 187.

[14]In Theodor Lessing's classic *Decline of the Earth under Mind (Untergang der Erde am Geist)*, cited in Herbert Schnädelbach, *Philosophy in Germany, 1831–1933* (Cambridge and New York: Cambridge University Press, 1984), 145.

[15]Erich von Kahler's *Der Beruf der Wissenschaft* (Berlin: Bondi, 1920) was an important monograph of the time that made a great deal of this presumed distinction between "old" and "new" science. Portions of this book were translated and reproduced in the volume edited by Peter Lassman and Irving Velody, *Max Weber's "Science as a Vocation"* (London: Unwin Hyman, 1989).

[16]Cited in Karl Lothar Wolf and Wilhelm Troll, *Goethes Morphologischer Auftrag* (Saale: Max Niemeyer, 1942), 60.

[17]Wolfgang Metzger, "Der Auftrag der Psychologie in der Auseinandersetzung mit dem Geist des Westens," *Volk im Werden—Zeitschrift für Erneuerung der Wissenschaften* 10 (1942): 143.

[18]Alexander von Senger, "Ergänzungen zu meiner Arbeit 'Rasse und Baukunft,'" *Ziel und Weg: Zeitschrift des Nationalsozialistischen Deutschen Ärzte-Bundes* 5 (1935): 564–69.

[19]Heinrich Chantraine, "Naturwissenschaft und Raumsichtigkeit," *Ziel und Weg* 6 (1) (1936): 7–16.

[20]Frederick Wyatt and Hans-Lukas Teuber, "German Psychology under the Nazi System—1933–1940," *Psychological Review* 51 (1944): 233.

[21]Ulfried Geuter, *The Professionalization of Psychology in Nazi Germany* (Cambridge: Cambridge University Press, 1992), 169; See also E. R. Jaensch, *Der Gegentypus: Psychologisch-anthropologische Grundlagen deutscher Kulturphilosophie, ausgehend von dem was wir überwinden wollen* (*Rassenkunde u. Psychologische Anthropologie* Nr. 2; *Beihefte* 75 zur *Zietschrift für angewandte Psychologie und Charakterkunde*) (Leipzig: Johann Ambrosius Barth, 1938).

[22]Jaensch, *Der Gegentypus*.

[23]Robert A. Pois, *National Socialism and the Religion of Nature* (New York: St. Martin's Press, 1986), 72.

[24]Karl Kötschau, "Die nationalsozialistische Revolution in der Medizin," *Ziel und Weg* 5 (1935): 135.

[25]Cf. Gyorgy Lukács, (1955) *Die Zerstorung der Vernunft: d. Weg d. Irrationalismus von Schelling zu Hitler* (Berlin: Aufbau-Verlag, 1984), 430.

[26]Alfred Böttcher, "Die Lösung der Judenfrage," *Ziel und Weg* 5 (1935): 226.

[27]Friedrich Sander, "Deutsche Psychologie und nationalsozialistische Weltanschauung," *Nationalsozialistisches Bildungswesen* 2 (1937): 642.

[28]Cited in Ulfried Geuter, "Das Ganze und die Gemeinschaft—Wissenschaftliches und politisches Denken in der Ganzheitspsychologie Felix Kruegers," in Carl Graumann, ed., *Psychologie im Nationalsozialismus* (New York/Berlin/Heidelberg/Tokyo: Springer Verlag, 1985), 72.

[29]Currently, the most comprehensive discussion of this movement exists in a medical history dissertation by Detlef Bothe, *Neue Deutsche Heilkunde, 1933–1945* (*Abhandlungen zur Geschichte der Medizin und der Naturwissenschaften*, vol. 62, eds. Rold Winau and H. Müller-Ditez) (Husum: Matthiesen Verlag, 1991).

[30]Kötschau, excerpt from *Zum nationalsozialistischen Umbruch in der Medizin* (1936), Doc. 83, 1–2, in Walter Wuttke-Groneberg, ed., *Medizin im Nationalsozialismus: Ein Arbeitsbuch* (Tübingen: Schwäbische Verlagsgesellschaft, 1980), 152.

[31]Ibid., 154–55.

[32]For some discussion, see Robert Proctor, *Racial Hygiene: Medicine under the Nazis* (Cambridge, Mass.: Harvard University Press, 1988), 235–38.

[33]Ibid., 233–34.

[34]The background to these developments lies in inherent methodological divisions in biology and medicine in Germany that went back many years, and had early led to the rise of two mutually antagonistic biomedical factions within the Nazi movement. The first of these, more Party dominated, was an ideologically-driven right-wing group that was sympathetic to holistic thinking and largely motivated by *völkisch* anti-Semitism and Aryan racial ideals. This group included people like ideologue Alfred Rosenberg, Gerhard Wagner, head of the Nazi Doctors' League, Julius Streicher, editor of the virulently anti-Semitic *Der Stürmer*, and holistic biologist Ernst Lehmann, editor of *Der Biologe*. The second faction was made up of pragmatic medical technocrats who wanted to use a hard-nosed form of Mendelian genetics, Darwinism, and racial biology as the basis for Nazi social policy and military strategy. This group had found a home for itself under the jurisdiction of Himmler's SS and its daughter racial organizations, the *Lebensborn* and *Ahnenerbe*. It included men like human geneticist Karl Astel and his assistant Lothar Stengel von Rutkowski at Jena, the botanist Heinz Brücher, and professor for law and race Falk Ruttke, who later took over SS training on race in occupied Poland. When Karl Kötschau was appointed to a chair in "nature therapy" at Jena in 1934, a plot was hatched to topple Kötschau, his allies, and ultimately the entire effort to make "holism" the framing metaphysical ideology of Nazi medical science and practice. Basically, the idea of the Astel group was to "expose" holism as a form of cleverly disguised

Roman Catholic dogmatism, the goal of which was to subvert the "empirical, factual" approach to nature that was now declared by this group to be central to the ethos of National Socialism.

[35]For details of the Dachau concentration camp herbal project, see documents 110, 1–6 in *Medizin im Nationalsozialismus: Ein Arbeitsbuch*, 199–202; and *Volk und Gesundheit: Heilen und Vernichten im Nationalsozialismus*, ed. Projektgruppe "Volk und Gesundheit," mit Beiträge von Martin Beutelspacher (Tübingen: Tübinger Vereinigung für Volkskunde, 1982), 52–54.

[36]Robert Jay Lifton, *The Nazi Doctors: Medical Killing and the Psychology of Genocide* (New York: Basic Books, 1986), 31–32.

[37]*Volk und Gesundheit: Heilen und Vernichten im Nationalsozialismus*, 39.

[38]See Walter Wuttke-Groneberg in *Medizin im Nationalsozialismus: Ein Arbeitsbuch*, 38.

[39]Lifton, *The Nazi Doctors*, 418–29.

[40]For a sense of the breadth, see Weizsäcker's collected works in ten volumes, *Gesammelte Schriften in 10 Bänden*, ed. Peter Achilles, Dieter Janz, Martin Schrenk, and Carl Friedrich von Weizsäcker (Frankfurt: Suhrkamp Verlag, 1986).

[41]Viktor von Weizsäcker, "Der Arzt und der Kranke: Stücke einer medizinischen Anthropologie," in Ibid., vol. 5, 177.

[42]Kleinman, *Rethinking Psychiatry*, 105.

[43]Wuttke-Groneberg, "Von Heidelberg nach Dachau," in G. Baader and U. Schultz, eds., *Medizin in Nationalsozialismus* (Berlin: Verlagsgesellschaft Gesundheit GmbH, 1980), 120.

[44]Viktor von Weizsäcker, "Ärztliche Fragen. Vorlesungen über allgemeine Therapie," in Achilles, Janz, Schrenk, and von Weizsäcker, eds., *Gesammelte Schriften in 10 Bänden*, book 5.

[45]Viktor von Weizsäcker, "'Euthanasie' und Menschenversuche," in *Gesammelte Schriften*, book 7: *Allgemeine Medizin: Grundfragen medizinischer Anthropologie*, 91–125.

[46][Discussion to] Wuttke-Groneberg, "Von Heidelberg nach Dachau," *Medizin in Nationalsozialismus*, 139–40.

[47]Kütemeyer, [Contribution to] "Podiumgespräch: Viktor von Weizsäcker—heute Viktor von Weizsäcker zum 100," in *Geburtstag (Beiträge zum Symposion der Universität Heidelberg, 1–3 May 1986)*, eds. P. Hahn and W. Jacob (Berlin, Heidelberg, New York: Springer-Verlag, 1986), 169.

[48]See Ibid., 187–88. The protest from the member of the audience is recorded on page 188.

[49]Christian Meier, *Vierzig Jahre nach Auschwitz: Deutsche Geschichtserringerung heute* (Munich: Deutschen Kunstverlag, 1987), cited in Ian Burma, *The Wages of Guilt: Memories of War in Germany and Japan* (New York: Farrar, Straus and Giroux, 1994), 69.

[50]For some references and discussion, see Anna Bramwell, *Ecology in the 20th Century: A History* (New Haven, Conn. and London: Yale University Press, 1989).

[51]I am indebted to Loren Goldner at the Center for European Studies, Harvard University, for bringing these details to my attention in an unpublished manuscript reviewing Faye's work.

We cannot accept the body as a simple assemblage of invariant natural facts, either in its actual structure and functioning or in its representation. . . .Thinking of the body as active, as something that asserts or presents itself, opens the way to conceptualizing a relation between self and body not simply as the culturally selected interpretation and representation of stimuli but as an active engagement that takes place in the very sinews, nerves, and bones of our bodies. . . .It is in response to this extraordinarily complex process of engagement that human beings create narratives to express the relations between biology, individual sentience, culture, and history. . .situated knowledge about the body is never benign or without political meaning. . .it is a negotiation about private space and the colonization of the body and person by society.

Margaret Lock

From *Encounters with Aging: Mythologies of Menopause in Japan and North America*

Berkeley, Calif.: University of California Press, 1993

Margaret Lock

Displacing Suffering: The Reconstruction of Death in North America and Japan

We all labor against our own cure;
for death is the cure of all diseases.

—Sir Thomas Browne, 1605–1682
"Urn Burial"

The boundaries which divide Life and Death are at
best shadowy and vague. Who shall say where the
one ends, and where the other begins?

—Edgar Allan Poe
"Premature Burial"

ONE VIVID MEMORY I RETAIN FROM WORLD WAR II is of an iron lung, massive and scary, that stood outside the hospital ward where I was taken after the family house was destroyed by a rocket fallen short of its London target. The iron lung was used, we kids knew all too well, for severe cases of polio, the infectious disease causing the greatest havoc at that time—scarlet fever and diphtheria having been brought largely under control, and tuberculosis confined (although only for the next forty years) to the "working classes" living in cities such as London, Birmingham, and Glasgow. Tales about the iron lung and who had died

___

Margaret Lock is Professor of Anthropology in the Departments of Social Studies of Medicine and Anthropology at McGill University, Canada.

207

encased inside it circulated amongst us as we traded our shrapnel collections. Together with the nightly air raids, this contraption signaled that death lurked close by, and we made sick jokes about the technologies of both war and medicine to hide our terror.

The history of technology has usually been transmitted as a heroic tale about the conquest of the enemy, whether it be human or the natural world—a narrative of progress, and of the betterment of humanity in general. Of course, this dominant ideology has, for the past century at least, been accompanied by a counter discourse replete with ambivalence and warnings about the consequences of technology gone wild. In novels by Mary Wollstonecraft Shelley, Charles Dickens, and Kurt Vonnegut, among many others, we read of the havoc and misery that technology can create. The humanities and social sciences have also sounded regular warnings: Jacques Ellul claimed, for example, that "Technique has become *autonomous*; it has fashioned an omnivorous world which obeys its own laws and which has renounced all tradition,"[1] a sentiment echoed by John Kenneth Galbraith, Rene DuBos, and Martin Heidegger, each from their very different vantage points. Autonomy in the Kantian tradition is, of course, associated with the notion of free will, of an individual no longer subject to externally created laws. As Langdon Winner has pointed out, the very idea of an autonomous technology raises an "unsettling irony, for the expected relationship of subject and object is exactly reversed."[2] We humans have apparently lost out to the monster, but nevertheless rush eagerly ahead creating new devices. Like Shiva in Hindu iconography, Bryan Pfaffenberger suggests, technology, as seen through a modernist lens at least, is both creator and destroyer, an agent of future promise and of culture's destruction.[3]

It has generally been assumed that the major driving force behind the creation of technologies is to meet universal human needs. Herbert Marcuse was one who accepted this position, and, although he was concerned about the way in which the products of technological progress could be subverted under the name of rationality for ideological purposes, he nevertheless emphasized that mastery of nature could, if properly applied, be associated with freedom and autonomy.[4] Jürgen Habermas, building in part on Marcuse, insisted that an apparent consensus created around the supposed rationality of technological progress veils the interests of powerful elites and removes debate from the public sphere.[5] Activities associated with technology are far from autonomous; on the contrary, they are intimately associated with the social and political order. Nevertheless, for both Marcuse and Habermas, since the creation of technology is a rational endeavor designed to meet universal human needs, there is nothing inherently questionable about the endeavor, provided that one goes about it in the right way.

G. Basalla and M. Sahlins take more radical positions, ones with which most anthropologists would agree; they stress that, aside from the fundamental requisites for sustaining life, it is culture and not nature that defines necessity. Necessity is not, after all, the mother of invention in any predetermined way; rather, human technology is a "material manifestation of the various ways men and women throughout time have chosen to define and pursue existence."[6] Technology is thus an integral part of the history of human aspirations and "the plethora of made things are a product of human minds replete with fantasies, longings, wants, and desires."[7] To simply link technology with power is to leave tacit the dominant modernist ideology of progress as an inherently rational pursuit to which culture makes no contribution.

It is easy to assume that among the many forms of technology those related to medicine exist, by definition, to meet basic human needs, in particular to reduce suffering and avert premature death. It is not surprising, perhaps, that aside from a concern about runaway expenditure and unwanted side effects on the body, there has been, until recently, relatively little resistance, in principle, to the development and application of medical technology. Despite the fact that the interests of powerful elites are often directly involved with the creation, manufacture, distribution, and application of medical technology,[8] the assumption that techniques that allow us to penetrate with increasing facility into the recesses of the body, together with those that supposedly relieve pain and prolong life, are inevitably for the good usually holds sway.

Over the past two decades it has become increasingly clear that biomedical technologies are by no means autonomous and, moreover, that the characterization of suffering, being culturally constructed, has a profound influence on their development, associated discourse, and application. It is in connection with the application of reproductive technologies, neonatal intensive care, genetic engineering, organ transplantation, and dying that contested domains have become most evident. That dispute has emerged around these dramatic manipulations should come as no surprise, for their application necessarily involves debate about tacit knowledge of what constitutes life and death.

In North America particularly, efforts to reduce suffering have habitually focused on control and repair of individual bodies. The social origins of suffering and distress, including poverty and discrimination, even if fleetingly recognized, are set aside, while effort is expended in controlling disease and averting death through biomedical manipulations.[9] Disputes with respect to biomedical technology usually revolve around the question of individual rights, autonomy, and justice. Activists have focused on abuse of individual patients by powerful elites, but very few commentators have stepped back and asked why, for example, infertility, menopause, and aging should be conceptualized as diseases, or why we struggle to save extremely premature infants but show little concern about the reasons for their premature birth or the social consequences of their continued existence.

This essay will focus on disputes in North America and Japan that are associated with the transplantation of major organs, together with the required redefinition of death necessary to implement this technology. Were it not for the development of the iron lung, an ostensibly autonomous, supremely utilitarian piece of technology, and its successor, the artificial respirator or ventilator, by means of which many people who can no longer breathe independently are kept alive, there would be no debate today about the reduction of suffering and the "saving" of lives through transplant technology. The artificial respirator clearly meets a basic need, but the uses to which it is put today have implications that reach far beyond the simple function of sustaining breathing on a temporary basis. Transplant technology, involving the removal of body fluids or parts from one person, and their insertion into a second person designated as needy, could never be mistaken for a value free endeavor—from its inception, at the very minimum, altruism was inevitably implicated.[10] Once certain patients on the artificial ventilator were harnessed to the heroic and showy technology of organ transplants, it became apparent, particularly to those involved in medical practice, that there was some urgency to clarify exactly what is meant by biological death.

It would seem that there can be very little room for ideological posturing in connection with defining death—most of us raised in the contemporary West believe, I suspect, that death is a rather easily definable point of no return about which there can be little argument. Japan, like North America, is in theory a predominantly secular society, and is similarly driven by principles of rational order and scientific progress, principles that are evident in many aspects of the health-care systems on both sides of the Pacific. However, in Japan the possibility of tinkering with death has opened up the floodgates of a concern that reaches far beyond the demise of individuals, whereas in North America, by contrast, death was quietly redefined in 1968 by an elite group of Harvard physicians, and further modified in 1981 so that the concept of "whole-brain death" is now recognized in the Uniform Determination of Death Act as equivalent to the end of life. There was a brief period in the late 1960s when public concern about these changes was evident, but today, in the great majority of North American hospitals, brain death is accepted as the end of life, and the "harvesting" of organs from brain dead bodies has become routinized.

This contrast between North America and Japan invites comparison of the different forms the search takes in late modernity for the relief of suffering and the creation of a just and moral order, together with an examination of the relationship this search has to the production and application of scientific and technological knowledge. It is now apparent in most corners of the world, except perhaps in the heart of Leviathan, that science, in particular biomedicine, has come to be thought of by many as one form of neo-imperialism. In an era of struggles to create and recreate cultural identities and establish the grounds of cultural difference, the self-conscious possession of scientific knowledge, or, alternatively, its repudiation as inauthentic or culturally inappropriate, is explicitly made use of as an ideological tool to establish local power bases and authority. The production and circulation of technologies are, therefore, not only far from autonomous but, on the contrary, incite and foster culturally infused political activity. Suffering becomes grist for the mill of ideological dispute, and individual misery either disappears from sight or else is appropriated in the interests of dominant others.

REMAKING DEATH

After the development of artificial respirators, attempts were made to clarify precisely what constitutes death in several international forums. In both a 1966 CIBA symposium held in London and a 1968 World Medical Association conference held in Sydney, delegates worked under the assumption that what they were participating in was an unprecedented response to new medical technologies that made it necessary for the first time to "define" death.[11] However, in an article entitled "Back from the Grave," Martin Pernick has shown that concern about establishing the time of death is not new but rather is the latest round in an ongoing historical debate, repeatedly revitalized in the wake of new medical discoveries.[12] Pernick cited a 1940 article in *Scientific American* as a relatively recent example of this concern, in which it was stated that "frequent" errors in diagnosing death remained the cause of cases of premature burial,[13] and concluded that it is not simply responses to specific medical discoveries that have shaped the content of debates about death, but that professional interests and cultural values are inevitably implicated, precluding the possibility of arriving at a rational, universally acceptable definition.

Phillipe Ariès, writing about the history of death in the *longue durée,* claims that for at least a millennium there existed in Europe, until the thirteenth century, what he terms "tamed death." A familiarity with death associated with neither fear nor despair, "halfway between passive resignation and mystical trust," was, Ariès claims, characteristic of the time.[14] Destiny was revealed through death, and the dying person participated in a public ceremony in which "his own personality was not annihilated but put to sleep."[15] Ariès suggests that from medieval times on, death gradually became more individualized; an awareness of personal mortality and of failure associated with death was apparent in medieval European iconography. After the Enlightenment, Ariès detects another shift in *mentalité* in which death "became challenged and furtively pushed out of the world of familiar things."

Interest shifted to the death of the other—to the "loved one"—and our own deaths became asocial and unnameable.

Ariès has been criticized, quite rightly I believe, for downplaying the individual "torment and pain" that must always have accompanied many deaths, and for giving undue emphasis to its social significance.[16] Ariès was, after all, primarily interested in the cultural representation of death, rather than in everyday experiences, individual or collective. Zygmunt Bauman has commented that, in principle at least, death was "tame" prior to the Age of Reason because it posed no challenge to the social order. Being preordained, the end of the life cycle and also eminently social, there was no need to fight death. For Bauman, shared knowledge about death, which he believes is incited by a universal awareness of mortality, provides the driving force for cultural creativity, a push for transcendence—"culture is about expanding temporal and spatial boundaries of being, with a view to dismantling them altogether. . .the first activity of culture relates to *survival*—pushing back the moment of death, extending the life-span."[17] Bauman suggests that the knowledge and fact of mortality drives the cultural construction of the idea of immortality—"mortality is ours without asking—but immortality is something we must build ourselves. Immortality is not a mere absence of death; it is *defiance* and denial of death."[18] Thus, the construction of immortality is, in Bauman's estimation, the major source of life's meaning in all societies, resulting in the transformation of biological death, "a fact of nature," into a cultural artifact, which in turn "offers the primary building material for social institutions and behavioral patterns crucial to the reproduction of societies in their distinctive forms."[19]

A contemporary scientific approach to death has, in theory, by painting itself into the cold corner where culture is no longer deemed relevant, done away with all meaning, save that a corpse indicates biological failure. Moreover, as is well known, from at least the time of Descartes, the living body gradually came to be understood in medicine as a kind of "animated corpse," since dissection was the primary means of aggregating facts about human biology.[20] Thus, mortality was medicalized in order to combat death and disease. Today death is "measurable" and legally recognizable as an absence of neuronal functioning or, alternatively, of respiration and a heartbeat. Having apparently been stripped of culture, death can no longer transcend biology to act as a touchstone for coming to terms with mortality. Instead, it is simply understood, in medicine at least, as biological failure, a waste:

> Death is primarily regarded as an illness or an aberration rather than something that is natural [and] the physician is supposed both to certify death and state its cause. . . .These certificates also illustrate the belief that although human beings die from many causes at once, it is always possible to isolate a single and precipitate cause of death. . . .Death is conceptualized as an ailment that is amenable to intervention.[21]

Narratives such as that of Ariès about a progression from a socially meaningful, preordained death to one where individual dying became the focus, and then to a vision of death as something to be conquered, are told from the vantage point of the *grand reçit*—as though cultures are monolithic, seamless wholes, and as though a neat cleavage exists between culture, a human creation, and nature, subject to timeless biological law. Ruth Richardson, in *Death, Dissection and the Destitute,* shows how in nineteenth-century England the "life strategies" of the common folk by no means coincided with the aspirations of those scientists who employed professional body snatchers to obtain corpses for dissection and autopsy. People went to great lengths to try to prevent the robbing of graves, anatomical dissection, and the commodification of corpses. For most citizens dissection was considered not only demeaning but literally cruel, and even in the medical literature there was much debate as to whether or not clinical detachment should be equated with inhumanity, although perhaps a "necessary inhumanity."[22] In *Middlemarch,* George Eliot has the townsfolk talk disparagingly and fearfully about Lydgate the "modern" doctor and his fascination with dissection.

The body in death *may* have been stripped of social and individual significance in the minds of pathologically oriented medical professionals but, for the majority of ordinary people living in nineteenth-century Europe, at least, death retained a meaning that transcended the physical demise of an individual. In theory, in the late twentieth century, by participating in the medicalization and sanitization of death—by virtually confining it to hospitals—we have capitulated to the view that death is essentially a biological event. This very capitulation is, of course, contingent upon a culturally created dominant ideology that understands the physical body as precultural, an aggregation of natural facts amenable to rational experiment and manipulation. Culture is left to deal, often rather peremptorily, with only the final disposal of the body, and the work of grief. Moreover, many writers confirm that we no longer know how to behave around those who are dying—the very process smells of failure and induces panic. Of course, a major paradox is evident because contemporary mass media is laden with images of violent deaths that leave nothing hidden or sanitized, but such garish endings belong to the other, not to ourselves, and perhaps actually facilitate the anesthetization of our own mortality. Nevertheless, there are now many signs of increasing public dispute about the confinement of death, and about the all-out battle to defeat it. As Martin Pernick points out, "Today, perhaps for the first time, public criticism involves both a fear of being wrongly declared dead, and a fear of being wrongly declared alive."[23]

MAKING DEATH USEFUL

In America the first major step in the most recent remaking of death was taken by an ad hoc committee of the Harvard Medical School in 1968. It is significant that this was accomplished shortly after the world's first heart transplant took place in South Africa in 1967. The group of physicians who comprised the committee declared unilaterally that individuals in a state of "irreversible coma," and diagnosed as having "brain death syndrome," could be declared dead.[24] Prior to this time, it was accepted simply by convention that death could only be medically established once the heart had stopped beating, but confusion arose when artificial respirators were brought into routine use, because they allow the heart to remain beating after integrated brain function has ceased. The committee gave two reasons for establishing a clear definition of death: *1)* that "increased burdens" on patients, families, and hospital resources were caused by "improvements in resuscitative and support measures," and *2)* that "obsolete criteria for the definition of death can lead to controversy in obtaining organs for transplantation."[25] Thus, reaching a medical consensus about a definition of brain death as the end of life was clearly linked from the outset to a demand for human organs. These debates captured some passing media and public attention.[26]

During the early 1970s, the concept of "brain death syndrome" was challenged in the courts. In one landmark case in Virginia in 1972 the jury ruled against the donor's family, who claimed that the transplant surgeons had been responsible for the death of their relative. Other court cases followed including several involving homicide victims, but none resulted in the prosecution of a doctor.[27] At the same time, a debate about medical practice was under way in the medical world itself as to which tests, if any, could be relied upon to confirm an individual doctor's opinion about brain death, and secondly as to who would act as "gatekeepers" to protect physicians from malpractice suits.[28] A Uniform Determination of Death Act was eventually declared in 1981, after extensive debate among the members of a President's Commission especially set up for that purpose. This Act was immediately supported by the American Medical Association and the American Bar Association, and was subsequently adopted over a number of years by the majority of state legislatures.

The President's Commission, in opposition to the position taken by a number of individual physicians, philosophers, and theologians (who were writing mostly in professional journals, rather than for the media), opted to further rationalize and update what they characterized as "obsolete" diagnostic criteria and to enshrine a definition of death in law, something that thus far had not been the situation.[29] The Commission recommended that a concept of "whole-brain death," equated with an "irreversible loss of all brain function," be adopted. This condition was carefully distinguished in the report from a "persistent vegetative state," as exemplified by patients such as Karen Ann Quinlan and Nancy Beth Cruzan, whose brain stems continued to function despite an irreversible loss of higher brain function. The earlier definition of "irreversible coma" left room for doubt as to whether patients such as these could be taken for dead, and the concept of whole-brain death sought specifically to clarify this point. Thus, physicians, in constructing a "uniform" death, deliberately set out to protect themselves against malpractice, while at the same time ensuring a source of organs for transplants from legally defined dead bodies.

Despite this effort, a number of publications appeared shortly after the Act was passed in which medical professionals, philosophers, and social scientists pointed out the numerous ways in which the wording of the Act is ambiguous. In particular, two criteria remain acceptable for the determination of death: irreversible cessation of circulatory and respiratory functions *or* irreversible cessation of all functions of the entire brain, including the brain stem. The philosopher David Lamb, in summarizing this controversy, suggests that ambiguity is present because the Commission wished to avoid a radical departure, a "paradigm shift," from what had been conventionally recognized as death prior to the invention of the artificial ventilator, while at the same time meeting the pragmatics demanded by the necessity of a legal definition.[30] One of the problems the Commission faced was to transform the *process* of dying into a clearly definable *event*—to establish death as a point in time. Pressure to remove organs as expediently as possible made the transformation of death into a recognizable, scientifically determinable event absolutely essential. As Roy Selby and Marilyn Selby had noted just prior to the Commission, "dying must never be confused with death."[31] Despite the apparent routinization of brain death as a diagnosis, and efforts to create uniformity in the determination of death, considerable doubt and debate continues to this day as to whether we are on an ethical slippery slope, and as to what actually constitutes death.[32] Thus, we remain, in Kuhn's terms, in a paradigm crisis, striving for commensurability but unable to achieve it.

This relatively quiet remaking of death has been masked throughout by a focus on the heroics of medicine and the prolongation of life. Two impending deaths are, of course, involved—that of the donor and that of the recipient—but the public imagination has been fired in North America by the idea of the "gift" of life. The life and death of the patient from whom organs will be "harvested" is left unmarked except as "donor" (although the use of anencephalic babies temporarily swayed this priority).[33] The media usually focuses our attention on the life that will be "saved," and particularly on the moments during and immediately after surgery when the proclamation of success is made; survival rates beyond the first few weeks fail to make more than serendipitous news coverage, and very few people indeed know about the prognosis for transplant patients, long-term outcomes, or about their "quality of life" after surgery.

Between 1982 and 1992, the number of transplants performed in the United States tripled, and it is estimated that over thirty-five thousand Americans are currently living with a donated organ in their body.[34] Transplants of all kinds, many of them repeat attempts after rejection, are routinized procedures; the "cutting edge" of transplant technology is concerned with "cluster" transplants, brain tissue implants, and the paring down of large organs for use in infants and children. The current drive to "maximize" the availability of organs is grounded in the utilitarian assumption that organs must be made available for the greatest good of all and includes a major debate about whether the buying and selling of organs should be established. Discussion is focused on organ procurement, including what type of contract with potential donors and their families is most appropriate for making them more readily available;[35] whether adoption of a market model for obtaining organs is appropriate;[36] and whether the body should be understood as a form of property.[37]

It is evident, therefore, that whatever discussion takes place about the remaking of death in North America is being carried out after the fact of the routinization of organ transplants from brain dead donors, and is colored by the pressures that a perceived escalating "shortage" of organs adds to the debate. Moreover, public consciousness, molded by the media, is focused almost without exception on the heroics of transplants and the "saving" of life, a situation that Ivan Illich has characterized as a fetishization of life.[38] The health "fad," particularly evident in the United States, requiring constant personal vigilance and body control, together with the imbibing of medications (such as hormone replacement therapy) purported, among other claims, to extend life, are other facets of this fetishization.[39]

In contrast to debates about death prior to the introduction of the artificial respirator, the issue today is infinitely more complex, because there are now *two* deaths inextricably linked through the coincidental failure of their body parts. It is not unreasonable to assume that public concern about the death of the donor should have been powerful enough to limit the rather rapid routinization of major organ transplants; current biomedical ethics in North America, and to a lesser extent in Europe, are, after all, grounded in respect for autonomous individuals and their welfare. These values inevitably become somewhat unraveled at the seams with two patients and their competing rights to consider, and one might expect to see some evidence in the media of this conflict of interest, perhaps even a national debate similar to the one about abortion. Clearly this has not happened. Organ donors, as a class of people, are praised for their generosity and altruism—for the "gift of life"—but as individuals their deaths remain essentially unnoticed. *Apparently* we equate lack of brain function with the end of life, and we trust the medical profession in their judgment as to when exactly this takes place. Perhaps this situation should come as no surprise in a rational, secular society where it makes little sense to dwell on the misfortune of "neomorts," to use Willard Gaylin's graphic neologism;[40] perhaps it is simply more "healthy" to think of individuals "living" on in others, and to recognize transplants as a life saving technology—a device that not only sidesteps the failure of death, but seemingly vanquishes it.

In 1991, more than two thousand people were on the waiting list for heart transplants in the United States, and the number of donors has decreased in recent years. One transplant surgeon has talked of the "alarming number of patients who die waiting,"[41] a situation described as a "public health crisis."[42] But by no means does everyone understand this crisis in the same way. Leon Kass, for example, characterized the problem very differently in a recent article on the selling of organs:

> Now, embarked on the journey, we cannot go back. Yet we are increasingly troubled by the growing awareness that there is neither a natural nor a rational place to stop. Precedent justifies extension, so does rational calculation: we are in a warm bath that warms up so imperceptibly that we don't know when to scream.[43]

Few cultural commentators are as explicit as Kass, but doubts, although rarely publicly discussed, apparently extend well beyond critics situated within the medical world, as was clearly also the case in the nineteenth century. Renée Fox's assessment of a Gallup

Poll taken in 1985, for example, is that "many respondents...
expressed anxiety about the possibility that if they signed a donor
card physicians might prematurely take steps to pronounce them
dead, to surgically excise their organs, or even to hasten their
death."[44] Another smaller survey revealed that the willingness of
people who perceive themselves to be on the margins of society (in
particular blacks) to become donors is lower than among the
middle classes.[45] This finding has a macabre irony to it, since, from
the point of view of surgeons, the "best" organs come from those
who die in traffic accidents, gunshot wounds, knifings, and so on,
among whom the numbers of young blacks and Hispanics are very
high.

A recent study from Scandinavia shows that among an age-
stratified, random sample of 1950 Swedish individuals, nearly 70
percent showed some discomfort about autopsy and organ donation. People reported, for example, that they were ill at ease at the
thought of cutting up a dead body, and many were concerned that
the patient might not be dead at the time of organ removal.[46] Not
only is the public cautious, but several studies have shown that, in
North America at least, many nurses and other medical staff are
conflicted when it comes to identifying donors and approaching
their families to obtain consent.[47] The fact that we cannot bring
ourselves to simply talk of "death" but refer consistently to "brain
death" clearly suggests that life is still present in the minds of most
people;[48] continued usage of the term brain death is in itself an
example of the ambiguity and uncertainty involved. These researchers have also pointed out that newspaper and television
accounts regularly report that patients who have been declared
brain dead later "die" when "life-support" measures are removed,
and health professionals, they claim, regularly use terminology
"that implies such patients die twice."[49]

THE SLIPPERY SLOPE OF PERSONHOOD

The President's Commission that culminated in the Death Act
stated clearly that for death to be diagnosed all brain function
must have ceased, including the reflexes controlled by the brain
stem. At this point there is a lack of "neurological integration,"
and what is left is "no longer a functional or *organic* unity, but

merely a *mechanical* complex.[50] Richard Zaner has pointed out that, for whole-brain advocates, "it is the biological organism (or, more specifically, the physiological/anatomical nervous system) which is definitive for life and death, not the *person* whose organism (or nervous system) it is."[51] Zaner and the majority of the contributors to the book *Death: Beyond Whole Brain Criteria* believe that the Commission put the cart before the horse by trying to develop a concept of death out of a set of standardized medical tests while evading the central issue of *who* had died. In order for there to be a uniform statutory definition of human death there must first be, according to Zaner, a general consensus over what constitutes "personhood" or "personal identity."[52] The Commission, recognizing that no such consensus exists, pointed out that the issue has been debated for centuries, and explicitly sought to circumvent the problem by making a biological argument in which rationally conceived operational criteria and medical tests provide the answer. The response of Edward Bartlett and Stuart Youngner was that neither operational criteria nor valid tests can be decided upon unless a working definition is first established—namely a concept of what it *means* to die.[53] Such a definition has to be "societal," not biological they argued, since a permanent loss of "personhood" should be of central concern, rather than the demise of the body physical. With this in mind, Zaner concluded that "at the very least. . .the central issues inherent to any definition of death must be kept rigorously open."[54]

Definitions grounded in the idea of a loss of personhood have been characterized as "ontological" and contrasted with what are taken to be narrowly defined scientific definitions based on the state of brain function.[55] Lamb, a philosopher, is concerned that those who argue for a redefinition based on ontological criteria are in actuality appealing to the idea that a loss of higher brain function is equivalent to death. He points out that such arguments are concerned only with criteria that describe "the minimum necessary qualities for personhood, defined in terms of psychological abilities," and he asserts that a Cartesian dualism is present in such arguments, which assume the ethical cutoff point to be the moment when the "ghost" leaves the machine.[56]

Karen Gervais criticized Lamb in turn for placing too much reliance on a biological definition; Lamb, she states, understands

death as "a fact awaiting discovery," and she characterizes the
ontological approach, in contrast, as based in ethical reflection.[57]
Lamb has countered this rebuttal by claiming that whole-brain
death is an "ethically superior formulation" because "in matters
of life and death, objective testable criteria concerning presence or
absence of vital functions are more reliable than indeterminate
assessments concerning the quality of residual life, or speculations
regarding personhood, or utilitarian requirements for transplant
organs."[58] Lamb is clearly concerned that overriding interests about
the supposed crisis precipitated by an "organ shortage" will seize
the day and send us on our way down the slippery slope to
redefining death in response to perceived needs. He adds that a
whole-brain death formulation does not dispute the loss of all
capacity for integrated mental activity, but because the "essence"
of personal identity is an elusive concept, which in any case resides
in a different logical space than the cessation of vital functions, it
is certainly not one on which doctors should rely in making decisions about death. Personal identity, after all, does not have any
specific anatomical location, insists Lamb, but is a quality akin to
"spirit," "will," or "soul," with religious, legal, and political associations. Loss of personhood or moral integrity are cultural conceptions and are, therefore, subject to a wide range of interpretation and open to easy manipulation and abuse where pragmatism
and utilitarianism hold sway. Norman Fost, arguing along similar
lines, has asserted that the problem with utilitarian justifications
for redefining death, exemplified by the recently enacted Uniform
Determination of Death, is that constant redefinition is invited
whenever utility requires it, creating "not only instability, but the
perception and possibility that unwanted persons can be defined
out of existence [whenever] it serves the greater good."[59]

Given this climate, Lamb and other supporters of whole-brain
death believe it is imperative to search out "precise" measurement
of neurological functioning because they are suspicious of a culturally produced, psychologically driven interpretation of life, and see
less of an opening for abuse when using a tightly defined, biologically based definition (provided in practice there is an under diagnosis of death whenever there is doubt). This argument assumes,
of course, not only that death is measurable, but also that such
measurements are accurate and unfailingly replicable. A recent

survey conducted among 195 physicians and nurses produced some disquieting results. Youngner and colleagues remind us that the concept of whole-brain death was initially accepted because it was assumed that "in the hands of competent physicians" a diagnosis of irreversible loss of all brain function is clinically practical and completely reliable. However, they found that only 35 percent of survey respondents both knew the whole brain criteria for death and were able to apply it correctly.[60] One fifth of these respondents were directly involved in making diagnoses about death at that time. Moreover, when asked to give their personal opinions about concepts of death and then apply them to hypothetical cases, 58 percent of the respondents did not use a concept of death consistently, and furthermore personal concepts varied widely among health-care professionals.[61]

Because of possible conflict of interest, neurosurgeons and neurologists are today expected to do nothing more than suggest to the families of their patients, once brain death has been declared, that they might think about donation of organs. Transplant surgeons and physicians, for their part, may not enter the scene until after brain death has been declared on two separate occasions. This ruling, not applied when transplants were first performed, seems eminently sensible, but it means that involved medical specialists know little of each other's interests and concerns in the application of these technologies. Of more importance, perhaps, it ensures that the failure of death is rapidly transformed, the bereaved family willing, into a celebration of immortality.

STRIVING FOR CONSENSUS: THE JAPANESE DEBATE

There are some remarkable differences at the present time between Japan and North America with respect to organ transplants: whereas, for example, in America nearly two thousand heart transplants took place in 1990, in Japan there were none. It is obvious that this difference cannot be explained by a lack of technology or skills, or by a shortage of economic resources on the part of the Japanese. So, cultural differences *must* be at work. Initially, my inclination was to ask what it is about Japanese and *not* North American culture, experience, and social organization that could account for this discrepancy. What widely shared knowledge do the Japanese possess that makes them resistant to the technologically aided extension of human life? This approach seemed particularly pertinent because Japan utilizes and exports more complex medical technology than any other nation in the world.[62] Is this cultural difference to be found at the level of attitudes towards the mastery of nature or, more specifically, to a concern about tinkering with the bodies of the dying and the dead? Is Japan perhaps not as secular and rational, not as "modern" as its outward appearance leads us to believe? Alternatively, is it perhaps due to cultural influences on the actual production of scientific discourse about death and dying in Japan? Or is the difference due largely to the way in which the power and interests of doctors are played out, and the form of institutionalization that medicine takes in Japan? Or is it some combination of the above?

It is relatively easy to take off from this point, embracing an implicit assumption that there is something inherently odd about not striving to "save" lives in a secular society with neither economic nor technological constraints; to set out, therefore, to scrutinize the relics of tradition, survivals from an archaic past lurking in Japanese late modernity that account for this anomaly. But such an approach violates the majority of interpretations given by Japanese on this subject, many of whom flatly deny that culture, that is, the "culture of tradition" is involved and argue instead for a more pragmatic explanation in which politics and power relations among the professions, and between the medical world and the public, are implicated.[63] Equally important, by focusing on Japan as the anomaly, North American assumptions about the good and just society remain unproblematized and thus, implicitly, the norm for the contemporary world, something that also concerns many Japanese participants as they argue their version of the brain death debate.

Shortly after the world's first heart transplant was conducted in South Africa, several attempts were made in other locations to carry out the same procedure, including Sapporo, Hokkaido in 1968. As in other parts of the world, the Sapporo procedure initially produced an accolade from the media, and was heralded as a dramatic medical triumph. However, several months later, the physician in charge, Dr. Wada, was arraigned on a murder charge and only acquitted after six years of wrangling. The majority of

Japanese believe in retrospect that the patient whose heart was removed was not brain dead, and that the recipient, who died two and a half months after the operation, was not sufficiently in need of a new heart to have undergone the procedure in the first place.[64] As part of the ongoing national debate about brain death, discussion of the case was formally reopened in 1991, and the chairman of the Japanese Medical Association, testifying before a government committee, reported that twenty-three years ago, right after the removal of the supposedly ineffective heart from the recipient patient, it had been tampered with, indicating that the involved doctors may have tried to exaggerate the degree of its deterioration.[65] The case is now considered in retrospect as a barbarous piece of medical experimentation carried out by a doctor who received a good portion of his training in America and is, moreover, described as self-aggrandizing.

There have been a good number of other cases in connection with organ transplants where the Japanese medical profession has not shown up in a good light. One, for example, involved a highly controversial kidney/pancreas transplant at Tsukuba University in which organs were removed from a young mentally retarded woman diagnosed as brain dead, but neither she nor her parents had given permission for her to be a donor.[66]

CONTESTED DEFINITIONS OF DEATH

The first definition of brain death in Japan was formulated by the Japan Electroencephaly Association in 1974. Probably in response to the much publicized case of the mentally retarded patient, the Life Ethics Problem Study Parliamentarians League, composed of twenty-eight Diet members and forty-five other professionals, was established in 1985, and after one year endorsed the need for legislation about brain death.[67] In the same year, the Ministry of Health and Welfare set up a Brain Death Advisory Council, the final report of which contained the definition of brain death made use of in Japan today.[68] This report is explicit, however, that "death cannot be judged by brain death." Nevertheless, the diagnosis is frequently applied, not as a signal to turn off the respirator, but to prepare relatives for an impending death.[69]

The report spurred other involved groups to make pronouncements about their positions. In January 1988, after two years of meetings by a working group, the directors of the Japanese Medical Association voted unanimously to accept brain death as the termination of human life. Despite this decision, there remains a lack of agreement among the representatives of medical specialties and also among individual physicians who are deeply divided on the issue. The politically outspoken Japan Association of Psychiatrists and Neurologists (some of the sixty-nine hundred members of whom are responsible for making brain death diagnoses) fear that if brain death is equated with death, the handicapped, mentally impaired, and disadvantaged will be at risk of being diagnosed prematurely in a greedy desire to get at their organs. In their 1988 report they state that a major problem is with the difficulty in deciding when brain function is irreversibly lost.[70]

Some physicians have joined members of the public to form the highly visible Patients' Rights Committee, whose interests range well beyond the question of brain death. Under the leadership of the flamboyant Dr. Honda from the prestigious department of internal medicine at Tokyo University, they have recently filed several lawsuits charging murder when organs have been removed from brain dead patients, one of which was in connection with the Tsukuba University case described above. The Public Prosecutor's Office has not thus far reached a decision in connection with any of these cases, but has thrown two of them out of court, stating that there is no public consensus in Japan as to how to define death.[71] Eric Feldman believes that because, after almost seven years, complaints made by the Patients' Rights Committee remain unresolved, hesitation on the part of doctors to forge ahead with transplantation is reinforced.[72]

As a result of the unresolved debate, copiously documented by the media, the government felt compelled in late 1989 to set up a Special Cabinet Committee on Brain Death and Organ Transplants in order to bring about closure. This committee, composed of fifteen members from various walks of life, was charged to make a report to the Prime Minister by 1991, and its very formation signaled to the public that the government was ready to support a move to legalize brain death as the termination of life. The group was so deeply divided that for a while it appeared that it would never produce anything more than an interim report, but in January 1992 a final report was forthcoming. In principle the members should have reached consensus, but this they could not achieve. The majority position is that brain death is equivalent to human death, that organ transplants from brain dead donors are acceptable, and that the current definition of brain death as formulated by the Ministry of Health is appropriate. The minority position made it clear that they wished to have the social and cultural aspects of the problem fully debated; in their opinion the discussion thus far had been largely confined to "scientific" information, which they believed to be inadequate.[73] The public was kept fully apprised of just who appeared before the committee. It was evident that many of those who testified, including certain scientists and doctors, argued against the acceptance of brain death, but nevertheless the majority of the committee eventually moved to support its approval.[74]

Throughout, the Japan Federation of Bar Associations (*Nichibenren*) has maintained its position against the acceptance of brain death as the termination of life. It has expressed concern for the "sanctity of life," and about possible medical "experimentation." The Federation has also pointed out that there may be unforeseen consequences in connection with inheritance claims, and a lack of public consensus on the issue was noted by them.[75] The day following the announcement of the Cabinet Committee report, the Ministry of Justice, the National Police Agency, and the Public Prosecutor's Office all reiterated their continued resistance to brain death.[76]

The Patients' Rights Committee, lawyers, the police, several television producers, and many authors of newspaper articles and books on the subject of brain death, and even a number of medical professionals appear to be publicly contesting the authority of transplant surgeons. What they usually cite as their principal cause for concern is a lack of trust in the medical teams who will make decisions about cases of brain death; they believe that in the rush to retrieve organs the process of dying will be curtailed or even misdiagnosed. The opposition is explicitly opposed to the secrecy and arrogance of some members of the medical profession, and points out that patients and their families are vulnerable to exploitation.

Certain of these same opponents of brain death are pushing for informed consent, together with a frank disclosure and discussion of diagnoses with patients, neither of which activities are by any means routinely established in Japan. This contest, therefore, although at one level a debate about the accuracy and replicability of scientific decision-making, is also a challenge to the hegemony of invested authority, exerted in what is characterized by several of the challengers as a traditionally Japanese way, whereby subjects are rendered passive and expected to comply with medical regimen without question.

One of the national newspapers, *Asahi Shinbun,* recently described the medical world as "irritated" with government dithering, and doctors sense that their international reputations as outstanding surgeons are fading. At the annual meeting of the Japanese Medical Association held in Kyoto in 1990, which I attended, two plenary sessions and several smaller panels were given over to brain death and organ transplants. The principal paper givers were physicians who had lived and worked for some time in the United States and who had practiced transplant surgery while there. Aside from the scientific part of their presentations, every one of them strongly asserted that Japanese medicine is suffering because of the national uproar over brain death. They all showed slides of themselves standing, usually in surgical garb, side by side with American transplant surgeons together with happy, lively patients who had recently received organ transplants. These presentations were one of the few occasions, until very recently, when attention was focused on the situation of patients whose lives might be prolonged, however temporarily, by transplant procedures.[77]

REACHING PUBLIC CONSENSUS

Taking place in concert with government, professional, and media discussion is the most persistent search for a national consensus (*kokuminteki gôi*) among the Japanese public that has taken place to date on any subject. There were at least ten national surveys about brain death and organ transplants between 1983 and 1992. Over the years the number of people who recognize brain death has increased from 29 percent to nearly 50 percent. In all of the surveys, a paradox is evident, however: many people approve of organ transplants from brain dead patients although they themselves do not accept brain death as the end of life. It seems that the Japanese public is willing to allow transplants to take place, even though they personally would not be comfortable with participating in such a procedure.

The results of opinion polls are usually used by those who are against brain death to support their arguments, since it has been frequently reiterated that public consensus must be reached before brain death can be nationally recognized. Nevertheless, one is left with the feeling, voiced by many members of the Japanese public, that the whole exercise of repeatedly surveying the nation is essentially a farce, and that the idea of trying to achieve a simple consensus on such an inflammatory subject is essentially without meaning.

CULTIVATING THE NATURAL

Clearly, the Japanese public's mistrust of physicians contributes to the brain death "problem," but why has *this* issue more than any of the other pressing problems in connection with biomedical technology captured the attention of the nation for nearly thirty years? Discussions about informed consent, euthanasia, and the new reproductive technologies appear in the media with increasing frequency today, but not nearly to the same extent as the topic of brain death and organ transplants, debate about which can become exceedingly vituperative.[78]

A perusal of the over five hundred articles, books, and newspaper editorials published on brain death and organ transplants since 1986 reveals that brain death is reported to be too "unnatural" *(fushizen)* to be called "death," for example,[79] or that it is "contrary to basic human feelings." The idea of "controlling" death is also described as going against nature.[80] Organ transplants are characterized in one book as *egetsu nai* (a powerful vernacular expression indicating that something is foul, ugly, or revolting) and *chi ma mire* (bloody).[81] Arguments against the institutionalization of organ transplants requiring a brain dead donor appear, therefore, to raise major concerns about interfering with the natural order. However, for the most part these concerns remain articulated only as emotion-laden adjectives or else by indirect allusions to the "cold," over-rational "West."

Contemporary Japanese attitudes towards scientific knowledge and its associated technology are difficult to pin down because of their intimate connection to a widespread ambivalence about the process of Japanese modernization. Moreover, Japanese attitudes towards modernization cannot be understood in isolation from ever changing interpretations, produced both inside and outside the country, about the relationship of Japan to the West. The form that current debate takes about body technologies in Japan, therefore—the feasibility of tinkering with the margins between culture and nature, and the very definition of those margins—reflect more general concerns about modernization, postmodernization, and "Westernization."

In Japan throughout the late nineteenth century, the eager quest for Western science and technology "was grounded in [a] sense of cultural certitude";[82] an awareness that the "core" or the bass note (*koso*) of Japanese culture would remain unaffected. Technology, self-consciously aligned with the other, was placed in opposition to culture in this discourse, and epitomized by the platitudes *wakon yōsai* (Japanese spirit and Western technology) and *tōyō dōtoku, seiyō gijutsu* (Eastern morality, Western technology). Tetsuo Najita and others have shown how this confidence in the endurance of "traditional" culture was gradually eroded. Early this century and again after World War II internal tension erupted over Japan's increasing technological sophistication and internationalization.[83] Fears about an imminent collapse of the nation's cultural heritage became commonplace, and one reaction was a reassertion of cultural essentialism.[84]

For many Japanese, the specter of Westernized individualism, utilitarianism, and super-rationalism triggers emotional responses that push them towards a rhetoric of difference, even as they buck at its inherently nationalistic underpinnings. This is the discursive background against which the brain death debate is taking place. Appellations such as "tradition" and "religion" smack of superstition and premodern sentimentality to a large number of people, but Japan is repeatedly described by internal commentators and outside observers alike as having undergone a unique form of modernization and hence of being quintessentially different.

Those who have doubts about the introduction of new technologies have to struggle very hard, therefore, to find a suitable language with which to articulate their discomfort. Criticizing a "Western," "scientific," interventionist approach to nature makes one vulnerable to accusations of Japanese essentialism and antirationalism. Equally difficult to voice is criticism of the epistemological grounds on which a scientific determination of death is constructed, for this smacks of antirationalism. Criticizing the unethical behavior of the Japanese press and activities of Japanese doctors as lacking standardization and quality control is rather easily justified and, almost everyone agrees, is a valid critical stance. Thus, the issue is politicized, but the possible contribution of culture to the argument is usually ignored or explicitly rejected.[85]

Those who choose to make a cultural argument about redefining death usually defend the status quo on the grounds that as a nation the Japanese do not like "unnatural" things, and posit an essential difference from the "West," leading to very dangerous territory. However, one or two attempts have been made to create a more nuanced argument based on the structure of Japanese social relationships. Masahiro Morioka suggests, for example, that rather than focusing on the standardization of brain death, as does so much of the literature, attention should be shifted to the brain dead person at the center of a nexus of characteristically Japanese human relations both familial and medical. He deliberately seeks to redefine the problem as social rather than clinical.[86] The anthropologist E. Namihira analyzes Japanese attitudes towards the dead body to account for resistance to brain death and organ transplants—an argument that highlights the cultural construction of nature, but one to which the majority of Japanese intellectuals with whom I have talked have reacted with a good deal of resistance.[87]

The entire commentary about tampering with definitions of death is, therefore, complex, emotional, and fraught with ideological pitfalls because debate cannot be divorced from other pressing issues of national import. A tension between technology as both creator and destroyer of culture is evident. Not surprisingly, negotiating a moral high ground has thus far proved impossible, not least when people try to shelter behind scientific justifications for their arguments.

DISCOURSE ON SOCIAL DEATH

In Japan biological death is usually understood as a process, not as a point in time.[88] Moreover, a distinction is made by many commentators between biological and social death, believed to take place some time after the demise of the physical body. Although few commentators talk explicitly about a Confucian-derived belief in the ancestors, its influence on the brain death debate is apparent. Preliminary interviews I conducted with fifty Japanese informants, men and women, made it clear that the fate of the body after biological death, together with a concern about the recently dead, may contribute to a reluctance both to donate and to receive organs. Everyone interviewed stated that they no longer believe in the elaborate prewar ancestor system, integral to the extended family. Nevertheless, over half of the respondents indicated that they carry out regular, often daily rituals in their homes and at the graves of their deceased parents and grandparents. Most pointed out that family and social obligations require that the bodies and memories of deceased family members be treated with respect.

A 1981 survey showed that the majority of Japanese (between 60 and 70 percent) believe that when and where one is born and dies is determined by destiny, and that this should not be changed by human intervention.[89] Appropriate separation of the soul from the body at the moment of death is central to the Japanese belief about dying;[90] in a recent survey, 40 percent responded that they believe in the continued existence after death of *reikon* (soul/ spirit).[91] This same survey showed that among young people between the ages of sixteen and twenty-nine, belief in the survival of the soul is particularly prevalent.[92]

From an analysis of the very moving narratives provided by relatives of victims of the Japan Air Lines crash in the mountains of Gunma prefecture in 1985, Namihira concluded that the spirit of the deceased is often anthropomorphized and is believed to experience the same feelings as the living. Hence, relatives have an obligation to make the spirit "happy" and "comfortable." People were in agreement that it is important for a dead body to be brought home, and that a corpse should be complete (*gotai manzoku*), otherwise the spirit will suffer and may cause harm to the living. Namihira cites the results of a 1983 questionnaire by a committee set up to encourage the donation of bodies for medical research: Of 690 respondents, 66 percent stated that cutting into dead bodies is repulsive and/or cruel, and also shows a lack of respect for the dead. Against these figures, the numbers of people agreeing to autopsies has steadily increased in recent years,[93] as has the number of people willing to go abroad to obtain organ transplants[94] as well as those willing to recognize brain death as the end of life. Clearly, the population is deeply divided about attitudes towards the dying and the recently dead, and many would, in any case, probably state one thing in response to a survey and actually do another when confronted with personal suffering.

In Japan the boundary between the social and the natural was never very rigidly defined—the ancestors were immortalized as entities who continue to act in the everyday world, but eventually become part of an animized natural order, forming a vital bridge between the spiritual, social, and natural domains. Despite the Confucian origins of the ancestors, the philosopher Akira Omine links the type of animism with which the ancestors are associated to Shinto, the indigenous religion of Japan, which represents, he believes, "quirky local beliefs cherished in our peculiarly unspiritual island country and incomprehensible to most of the world."[95] Shinto, associated with the Emperor and with nationalism, has an exceedingly delicate status among large numbers of liberal minded Japanese today. Omine goes on to claim that although animism affects attitudes about the dead, it "simply lacks the depth of vision to address a challenge like that of redefining the boundary between life and death."[96] It seems that Omine, in common with many of his intellectual colleagues, would like to keep formalized religious belief (but not necessarily spirituality) out of the brain death discussion.

Comments such as those of Omine make it evident that everyday discourse and practices about social death produce considerable anxiety among certain Japanese who wish their nation to be understood as eminently rational, in particular because such discourse is grist for the mill of commentators (both inside and outside Japan) who hope to signal that "tradition" and the "old moral order," including the ancestors who signify continuity above all else, is intact and functioning in the Japan of late modernity.

When it comes to discussing organ transplantation, many people point out that formalized gift giving remains central to ongoing relationships of reciprocity in Japan, and continues to contribute to the moral order. The idea of receiving an organ that had been anonymously donated would be very difficult for many to accept without incurring an enormous sense of guilt and without violating a sense of what is correct behavior.[97] In addition, a few people with whom I have talked have clearly been physically repulsed by the very idea of organ transplantation. For them, transfer of body parts among unrelated people extends beyond the bounds of what is "natural" and entails a completely unacceptable mixing of self and other. Certain scientists also see things this way, for transplant technology has explicitly been described by an eminent Japanese immunologist as the conjoining of the "self" and "nonself."[98] A similar, rather special, manifestation of this concern was demonstrated around the dying Emperor Shôwa, who received many blood transfusions during the last year of his life, all of which had to be supplied by family members. It should be noted that there is little or no opposition to organ transplants from living, related donors, suggesting that it is an inappropriate mixing of self and other beyond the "natural" bounds of the family that causes discomfort.

Although abortion is acceptable to most Japanese citizens, and is usually characterized as an unfortunate but necessary intervention at times, use of fetal tissue for research and transplants is not permitted. Fetuses are thought of by most people as living and conceptually inseparable from the body of the pregnant woman. However, since a fetus has no independent social or moral standing it is not fully human. Many Japanese are nevertheless concerned about mistreatment of fetal tissue, although its status is less problematic than that of a brain dead individual. Concern is evident about the traumatic death of a fetus, especially on the part of Japanese women, and lucrative Buddhist-based rituals are enacted all over Japan to appease the souls of aborted fetuses.[99] Thus, traumatic and sudden death, together with the mixing of self and other, both before birth and later in the life cycle, are culturally sensitive and contested events in Japan. However, the politics of solid organ transplants, coupled with a pervasive concern about respect for the deceased, means that the brain death debate takes center stage, whereas abortion continues to be accepted quite simply as an unfortunate but unavoidable part of human life.

LATE MODERNITY, CULTURAL IDENTITY, AND THE OTHER

It is striking that the culture and values of the "West" are scrutinized in the brain death debate in Japan. We hear and read much about Christianity (but nothing of Judaism), about rationality and the brain as the center of the body, about altruism, individualism, and even selfishness—all values associated with the "West." But, despite a call to move beyond a discussion of scientific decision-making, as noted above, Japanese values are not often examined explicitly. It has been suggested by some that if the original heart transplant, the Wada case, had not flared up into a legal battle, the entire brain death debate may never have surfaced, and the medical world would simply have gone ahead unilaterally as they did in North America. Others strongly disagree with this position, although many believe that brain death will be made legally acceptable in Japan fairly soon and that the search for a national consensus is simply a placatory exercise before those in power go ahead to institutionalize organ transplants; indeed, a private members bill has recently been submitted for consideration to the Diet.

Thoughtful people recognize that while brain death is obviously a sensitive topic, the definition of death, although clearly the nub of the debate, has a metaphorical significance that triggers a cascade of ideological repercussions reaching far beyond the medical world. The present dilemma for progressive thinkers in Japan is how to dispose of the remnants of patriarchal and patronage thinking—the reactionary part of the Confucian heritage—without drawing on a language that single-mindedly pursues the entrenchment of the "Western" values of individual autonomy and rights. It is in this context that the argument about brain death is taking place, and, as in the West, it is an overwhelmingly secular argument in which representatives of religious organizations are, for the most part, remarkably absent.[100] At its most abstract level, the current angst is a manifestation of the ceaseless, restless, contradictory debate about Japan and the West, a debate that has proceeded unabated for something approaching two hundred years, in which the "West" has come to be associated with ideas having

universal application, whereas Japanese ideas are linked to uniqueness. As one pediatrician has recently put it, "Why should we
mindlessly imitate Westerners? We would only be turning ourselves into white Westerners with Asian faces."[101]

Although a certain amount of genuine passion is aroused over
the fate of those individuals whose lives are directly involved, little
is heard from patients and their families, whether they be potential
donors or receivers. Recently, however, a woman whose daughter
will soon require a liver transplant, when interviewed by *Newsweek*
for its Japanese edition, complained, "Why do we have to suffer
just because we have the misfortune to be Japanese?"[102] Since the
beginning of 1994, the year in which an international conference
on organ transplantation was deliberately staged in Japan by surgeons keen to break through the current impasse, the fate of those
patients not able to receive transplants, together with those who
have gone abroad to obtain organs, has started to capture the
imaginations of the media and the Japanese public. An extraordinarily moving art exhibition, at which pictures created by Japanese children who had received organs were exhibited beside accounts of their medical histories, was held in Kyoto in conjunction
with the transplant conference.

Thus far, the debate has not been about individual human
suffering, but rather a manifestation of the struggle by citizens and
activists from a whole range of political persuasions about moral
order in contemporary Japan. Those who recognize brain death as
the end of life usually accept a modernist ideology of technologically driven progress in the relief of human suffering, while many
(but not all) of those against embrace an argument about the
essentialist difference of Japan and exhibit concerns about a perceived loss of moral order. Very slowly and painfully forced, it
seems to me as I interview and observe Japanese who are dealing
directly with this problem in ethics committees, citizens groups,
and so on, by a genuine concern about the suffering of individuals,
a middle ground is emerging. Nevertheless, extremists on both
sides remain highly vocal and influential. Those arguing for a
modulated position usually start with case studies rather than
from abstract propositions, or from the simple assumption that
biomedical technology is intrinsically good. Some people arguing
for a middle ground actively seek to avoid the silencing of indi-

vidual suffering in the name of nationalism, or professional or governmental interest, but these voices are only just becoming audible, and are not great in number as yet. It is notable, however, that even in modulated discussion grounded in everyday experience, the split between those for and against the acceptance of brain death remains strikingly evident. Even when the suffering of potential recipients is clearly recognized this does not mean that involved Japanese will necessarily agree that transplants are an unequivocal good. When I asked one pediatrician, often visible in the media, who deals with dying children every day, why she remains adamantly opposed to the introduction of organ transplants from brain dead donors, she acknowledged that Buddhism, although of no apparent consequence in her daily life, is probably an influence since she believes deeply that death is in some way preordained and that we humans should not play God. Although Buddhist related, the sentiments of this pediatrician may not be very far removed from those of people living in other parts of the world today, but when contextualized in the current debate about death in Japan they reveal the extent to which "needs" and "suffering" and our responses to those marked as "suffering" and "needy" remain shaped by culturally derived values.

The talk today in the United States is of "rewarded gifting" and "organ wastage," signs of the urgent need to procure more and more organs in a steady move towards the large-scale commodification of human parts. In our haste in North America we talk little about the flow of organs from the poor to the rich, from the Third World to the First World, and even less of possible atrocities, despite documentation of such by Amnesty International. Leon Kass has described this process as a "coarsening of sensibilities and attitudes" and adds that ". . .there is a sad irony in our biomedical project, accurately anticipated in Aldous Huxley's *Brave New World*: We expend enormous energy and vast sums of money to preserve and prolong bodily life, but in the process our embodied life is stripped of its gravity and much of its dignity. This is, in a word, progress as tragedy."[103] We also keep death firmly under wraps and, despite evidence of societal disagreement and misunderstanding about the new death we have created, refuse to debate this issue in public. Perhaps we can learn directly from the Japanese case on this point, if nothing else, and begin to recognize once again that mortality is not merely biological demise. In striving to make the brain dead immortal by stating that they live on in others as donated organs, we in fact collapse the very culture/nature distinction that made the yardstick for justifying brain death in the first place. Surely such a contradiction deserves debate.

The monster is amongst us, and we need more courage than Frankenstein exhibited if we are to use technology to relieve suffering in an equitable manner; a first step is to recognize how easily suffering can be used in the service of ideological and political ends. On both sides of the Pacific, if debate about technology and the body is reduced to a confirmation or otherwise of scientific accuracy, or to a discussion of political interest, or even, for that matter, to one of ethical correctness, we will consistently lose sight of the necessity to step further back so that more difficult questions can be posed. Prominent among them is a consideration of the relationship of tacit, culturally shaped knowledge to the production of scientific knowledge and its practices, together with the associated contests, within and among societies, about legitimization of such knowledge as truth. Most important, of course, is the effect of such discussion on the recognition of suffering and what, if any, condition should be assigned as beyond the realm of cultural intervention.

ACKNOWLEDGMENT

This research was funded by the Social Sciences and Humanities Research Council of Canada, grant number 410–93–0544.

ENDNOTES

[1] Jacques Ellul, *The Technological Society,* trans. John Wilkinson (New York: Alfred A. Knopf, 1964).

[2] Langdon Winner, *Autonomous Technology: Technics-out-of-Control as a Theme in Political Thought* (Cambridge, Mass.: The MIT Press, 1977), 16.

[3] Bryan Pfaffenberger, "Social Anthropology of Technology," *Annual Review of Anthropology* 21 (1992): 495.

[4]Herbert Marcuse, *One-Dimensional Man: Studies in the Ideology of Advanced Industrial Society* (Boston, Mass.: Beacon Press, 1964).

[5]Jürgen Habermas, *Toward a Rational Society* (Boston, Mass.: Beacon Press, 1970).

[6]G. Basalla, *The Evolution of Technology* (Cambridge: Cambridge University Press, 1988), 14.

[7]Ibid., 14.

[8]Andrew Kimbrell, *The Human Body Shop: The Engineering and Marketing of Life* (San Francisco, Calif.: Harper San Francisco, 1993). Margaret Lock, *Encounters With Aging: Mythologies of Menopause in Japan and North America* (Berkeley, Calif.: University of California Press, 1993), 341ff.

[9]Arthur Kleinman, *The Illness Narratives: Suffering, Healing and the Human Condition* (New York: Basic Books, 1988). Mary-Jo DelVecchio Good, Paul E. Brodwin, Byron J. Good, and Arthur Kleinman, eds., *Pain as Human Experience: An Anthropological Perspective* (Berkeley, Calif.: University of California Press, 1992).

[10]Renée C. Fox and Judith P. Swazey, *Spare Parts: Organ Replacement in American Society* (New York: Oxford University Press, 1992).

[11]L. A. Rado, "Death Redefined: Social and Cultural Influences on Legislation," *Journal of Communication* 31 (1981): 41–47.

[12]Martin Pernick, "Back from the Grave: Recurring Controversies Over Defining and Diagnosing Death in History," in Richard Zaner, ed., *Death: Beyond Whole-Brain Criteria* (Dordrecht: Kluwer Academic Publishers, 1988), 17.

[13]Ibid.

[14]Phillipe Ariès, *Western Attitudes Towards Death: From the Middle Ages to the Present,* trans. Patricia M. Ranum (Baltimore, Md.: The Johns Hopkins University Press, 1974), 103.

[15]Ibid., 104.

[16]Norbert Elias, *The Loneliness of the Dying,* trans. Edmund Jephcott (Oxford: Basil Blackwell Ltd., 1985).

[17]Zygmunt Bauman, *Mortality, Immortality and Other Life Strategies* (Stanford, Calif.: Stanford University Press, 1992), 5.

[18]Ibid., 7.

[19]Ibid., 9.

[20]Drew Leder, *The Absent Body* (Chicago, Ill.: The University of Chicago Press, 1990).

[21]Lindsay Prior, *The Social Organization of Death: Medical Discourse and Social Practices in Belfast* (London: Macmillan, 1989), 32, 33.

[22]Ruth Richardson, *Death, Dissection and the Destitute* (London: Penguin, 1988), 31.

[23]Pernick, "Back from the Grave: Recurring Controversies Over Defining and Diagnosing Death in History," 58.

240   *Margaret Lock*

[24] Ad Hoc Committee of the Harvard Medical School to Examine the Definition of Death, "A Definition of Irreversible Coma," *Journal of the American Medical Association* 205 (1968): 337–40.

[25] Ibid., 337.

[26] See, for example, "When is Death?," *Time*, 16 August 1968.

[27] R. Simmons et al., *Gift of Life: The Effect of Organ Transplantation on Individual, Family, and Societal Dynamics* (New Brunswick, N.J.: Transaction Books, 1987).

[28] Peter Black, "Brain Death," *The New England Journal of Medicine* 229 (1978): 338–44.

[29] George J. Annas, "Brain Death and Organ Donation: You Can Have One Without the Other," *Hastings Center Report* 18 (1988): 621.

[30] David Lamb, *Death, Brain Death and Ethics* (London: Croom Helm, 1985), 23.

[31] Roy Selby and Marilyn Selby, "Status of the Legal Definition of Death," *Neurosurgery* 5 (1979): 535.

[32] Paul Byrne and Richard Nilges, "The Brain Stem in Brain Death: A Critical Review," *Issues in Law and Medicine* 9 (1993): 3–21. Robert Veatch, "The Impending Collapse of the Whole-Brain Definition of Death," *Hastings Center Report* 23 (1993): 18–24.

[33] Margaret Lock, "Deadly Disputes: The Remaking of Death in Japan and North America," in Francis Zimmermann and Beatrice Pfleiderer, eds., *Medicine and Social Criticism* (Cambridge: Cambridge University Press, forthcoming).

[34] J. M. Prottas, *The Most Useful Gift: Altruism and the Public Policy of Organ Transplants* (San Francisco, Calif.: Jossey-Bass, 1994).

[35] M. Somerville, "Access to Organs for Transplantation: Overcoming Rejection," *Canadian Medical Association Journal* 132 (1985): 113–17.

[36] Prottas, *The Most Useful Gift: Altruism and the Public Policy of Organ Transplants*. J. R. Williams, "Human Organ Sales," *Annals of the Royal College of Physicians and Surgeons of Canada* 18 (1985): 401–404.

[37] L. B. Andrews, "My Body, My Property," *Hastings Center Report* 16 (1986): 28–38.

[38] Ivan Illich, *In the Mirror of the Past: Lectures and Addresses 1978–1990* (New York: Marion Boyars Publishers Ltd., 1992), 224.

[39] Robert Crawford, "Healthism and the Medicalization of Everyday Life," *International Journal of Health Services* 10 (1980): 365–88. Lock, *Encounters With Aging: Mythologies of Menopause in Japan and North America.*

[40] Willard Gaylin, "Harvesting the Dead," *Harpers Magazine* 52 (1974): 23–30.

[41] T. G. Peters, "Life or Death: The Issue of Payment in Cadaveric Organ Donation," *Journal of the American Medical Association* 265 (13 March 1991): 1302.

[42] T. Randall, "Too Few Human Organs for Transplantation, Too Many in Need...and the Gap Widens," *Journal of the American Medical Association* 265 (13 March 1991): 1223.

43Leon Kass, "Organs for Sale? Propriety, Property, and the Price of Progress," *The Public Interest,* April 1992, 84.

44Renée C. Fox and Judith P. Swazey, *Spare Parts: Organ Replacement in American Society* (New York: Oxford University Press, 1993), 57.

45J. F. Childress, "Ethical Criteria for Procuring and Distributing Organs for Transplantation," in J. F. Blumstein and F. A. Sloan, eds., *Organ Transplantation Policy: Issues and Prospects* (Durham, N.C.: Duke University Press, 1989), 87–113.

46Margareta Sanner, "A Comparison of Public Attitudes Toward Autopsy, Organ Donation and Anatomic Dissection," *JAMA* 271 (1994): 284–88.

47Arthur L. Caplan, "Professional Arrogance and Public Misunderstanding," *Hastings Center Report* 18 (1988): 34–37. J. M. Prottas and H. L. Batten, "Health Professionals and Hospital Administrators in Organ Procurement: Attitudes, Reservations, and their Resolutions," *American Journal of Public Health* 78 (1988): 642–45. S. J. Youngner, M. Allen, E. T. Bartlett et al., "Psychosocial and Ethical Implications of Organ Retrieval," *New England Journal of Medicine* 313 (1 August 1985): 321–24.

48Youngner, Allen, Bartlett et al., "Psychosocial and Ethical Implications of Organ Retrieval."

49S. J. Youngner, S. Landefeld, C. J. Coulton et al., "'Brain Death' and Organ Retrieval: A Cross-Sectional Survey of Knowledge and Concepts among Health-Care Professionals," *Journal of the American Medical Association* 261 (1989): 2205–210.

50J. L Bernat et al., "On the Definition and Criterion of Death," *Annals of Internal Medicine* 94 (1981): 391.

51Richard M. Zaner, "Introduction," in Richard Zaner, ed., *Death: Beyond Whole-Brain Criteria* (Dordrecht: Kluwer Academic Publishers, 1988), 7.

52Ibid., 5.

53Edward T. Bartlett and Stuart J. Youngner, "Human Death and the Destruction of the Neocortex," in Zaner, ed., *Death: Beyond Whole-Brain Criteria,* 199–216.

54Zaner, "Introduction," in Zaner, ed., *Death: Beyond Whole-Brain Criteria,* 13.

55Karen G. Gervais, *Redefining Death* (New Haven, Conn.: Yale University Press, 1987).

56David Lamb, *Organ Transplants and Ethics* (London: Routledge, 1990).

57Gervais, *Redefining Death,* 155.

58Lamb, *Death, Brain Death and Ethics.*

59Norman Fost, "Organs from Anencephalic Infants: An Idea Whose Time Has Not Yet Come," *Hastings Center Report* 18 (1988): 7.

60Youngner, Landefeld, Coulton et al., "'Brain Death' and Organ Retrieval," 2208.

61Ibid., 2209.

242　*Margaret Lock*

[62]Naoki Ikegami, "Health Technology Development in Japan," *International Journal of Technology Assessment in Health Care* 4 (1989): 239–54.

[63]Jiro Nudeshima, *Nôshi, zôkiishoku to nihon shakai* (Brain Death, Organ Transplants and Japanese Society) (Tokyo: Kôbundô, 1991).

[64]Masaharu Gôto, "Body and Soul: Organ Transplants," *Look Japan* 38 (1992): 32–33.

[65]"Cover-up suspected in first heart transplant," *Mainichi Shinbun,* 31 March 1991.

[66]"Organs removed from woman without consent," *Mainichi Daily News,* 24 December 1984.

[67]Eric A. Feldman, "Over My Dead Body: The Enigma and Economics of Death in Japan," in Naoko Ikegami and John C. Campbell, eds., *Containing Health Care Costs in Japan* (Ann Arbor, Mich.: University of Michigan Press, 1995).

[68]Kôseishô, "Kôseishô kenkyuhan ni yoru nôshi no hantei kijun" (Brain death determination criteria of the Ministry of Health and Welfare) (Tokyo: Kôseishô, 1985).

[69]Gen Ohi, Tomonori Hasegawa, Hiroyuki Kumano, Ichiro Kai, Nobuyuki Takenaga, Yoshio Taguchi, Hiroshi Saito, and Tsunamasa Ino, "Why are cadaveric renal transplants so hard to find in Japan? An analysis of economic and attitudinal aspects," *Health Policy* 6 (1986): 269–78.

[70]"Silence on Heart Transplant," *Asahi Shinbun,* 2 April 1991. Masaya Yamanchi, "Transplantation in Japan," *British Medical Journal* 301 (1990): 507.

[71]Taro Nakayama, *Nôshi to Zôki Ishoku* (Brain Death and Organ Transplants) (Tokyo: Saimaru Shippansha, 1989).

[72]Feldman, "Over My Dead Body: The Enigma and Economics of Death in Japan."

[73]Kantô Chiku Kôchôkai, "Rinji nôshi oyobi zôkiishoku chôsa kai," Tokyo, 1992. Yomiuri Shinbun, "Noshi ishoku yônin o saigo tôshin" (Final report approves of brain death, organ transplants), 23 January 1992.

[74]"'Nôshi Ishoku' michisuji nao futômei" (Brain Death and Transplants: The Way is Still Not Clear), *Nihon Keizai Shinbun,* 23 January 1992.

[75]"Giron fûjûbun to hihan no kenkai" (Insufficient debate is the critical opinion), *Asahi Shinbun,* 17 October 1991.

[76]"'Nôshi wa hito no shi,' tôshin" (Brain death is death, says report), *Asahi Shinbun,* 23 January 1992.

[77]See also Shumon Miura, "Attitudes Towards Death," *Japan Echo* 18 (1991): 67. "Zoki ishoku no saizensen" (The frontline in transplants), *Newsweek Nihon Han* (Japanese ed.), 25 February 1993.

[78]Takeshi Umehara and Michi Nakajima, "Soredeme nōshi wa shi dewa nai" (Still Brain Death is Not Death), *Bungeishunju* (March 1992): 302–12.

[79]Kôshichirô Hirosawa, "Tachiba kara mita nôshi to shinzô ishoku" (Brain death and heart transplants from the point of view of a circulatory system specialist),

in Takeshi Umehara, ed., *Nôshi to zôki-ishoku* (Brain Death and Organ Transplants) (Tokyo: Asahi Shinbunsha, 1992).

[80]Toyô Watanabe, *Ima naze shi ka* (Why Death Now?) (Tokyo: Niki Shuppan, 1988). Takeshi Umehara, ed., "Hajime ni" (Introduction), in '*Nôshi' to zôki-ishoku* (Brain Death and Organ Transplants) (Tokyo: Asahi Shinbunsha, 1992), 1–7.

[81]Eiko Fukumoto, *Seibutsugaku jidai sei to shi* (Life and Death in the Era of Biological Sciences) (Tokyo: Gijitsu to Ninjen sha, 1989).

[82]Tetsuo Najita, "On Culture and Technology in Postmodern Japan," in M. Miyoshi and H. D. Harootunian, eds., *Postmodernism and Japan* (Durham, N.C.: Duke University Press, 1989), 3–20.

[83]Najita, "On Culture and Technology in Postmodern Japan," in Miyoshi and Harootunian, eds., *Postmodernism and Japan*.

[84]H. D. Harootunian, "Visible Discourse/Invisible Ideologies," in Miyoshi and Harootunian, eds., *Postmodernism and Japan*, 63–92.

[85]M. Nakajima, *Mienai shi: Nôshi to zôki ishoku* (Invisible Death: Brain Death and Organ Transplants) (Tokyo: Bungei Shunju, 1985). Nudeshima, *Nôshi, zôkiishoku to nihon shakai*.

[86]Masahiro Morioka, *Nôshi no Hito* (Brain Dead People) (Tokyo: Fukutake Shoten, 1991).

[87]E. Namihira, *Nôshi, Zôki Ishoku, gan Kokuchi* (Brain Death, Organ Transplants, Truth-Telling about Cancer) (Tokyo: Fukubu Shoten, 1988).

[88]Tôru Uozumi, "Nôshi mondai ni kansuru shiken to teian" (My opinion and proposals on the brain death issue), in Takeshi Umehara, ed., *Nôshi to zôki-ishoku* (Brain Death and Organ Transplants) (Tokyo: Asahi Shinbunsha, 1992). Koshichirō Hirosawa, "Tachiba kara mita nôshi to shinzô ishoku" (Brain death and heart transplants from the point of view of a circulatory system specialist), in Takeshi Umehara, ed., *Nôshi to zôki-ishoku* (Brain Death and Organ Transplants). Yoshihiko Komatsu, "Sentaki gijutsu to nôshironsô no shikaku" (The blind spot in advanced technology and brain death debates), *Gendai Shisô* 21 (1993): 198–212.

[89]Kumiko Maruyama, Hayashi Fumi, and Kamisaka Hisashi, "A Multivariate Analysis of Japanese Attitudes Toward Life and Death," *Behaviormetrika* 10 (1981): 37–48.

[90]Fleur Woss, "When Blossoms Fall: Japanese Attitudes Towards Death and the Other-World: Opinion Polls 1953–1987," in R. Goodman and K. Refsing, eds., *Ideology and Practice in Modern Japan* (London: Routledge, 1992), 72–100.

[91]*Shôwa 61 nenpan yoron chôsa nenkan* (Yearbook of Opinion Polls), "Kokoro no jidai. Zenkoku yoron chôsa" (The era of heart. Opinion poll by the Mainichi publishing house for the whole of Japan), in Naikaku Sôri Daijin Kanbô Kôhôshitsu, ed. (Tokyo: Mainichi Shinbunsha, 1987), 508–10.

[92]*Shôwa 54 nenpan yoron chôsa nenkan* (Yearbook of Opinion Polls), "Zenkoku kenmin ishiki chôsa" (Research on the consciousness of the Japanese prefectural populations), in Naikaku Sôri Daijin Kanbô Kôhôshitsu, ed. (Tokyo: NHK hôsô yoron chôsasho, 1979), 585–91.

[93]Monbushô, *Kaibôtai shûshû sû to kontai hiritsu* (Total Number of Bodies Accumulated for Autopsy and Percentage of Anatomical Gifts) (Tokyo: Monbushô Igaku Kyôikuka Shirabe, 1993).

[94]Hiroshi Takaji, "Nôshi to zôki ishoku ni kansuru daii no shinpojûmu" (The First Symposium in Connection with Brain Death and Organ Transplants), in Nagoya Bengoshi Kai, eds., *Nôshi to zôki ishoku miezarushî o mochimete* (Tokyo: Roppo shuppansha, 1991).

[95]Akira Omine, "Right and Wrong in the Brain-Death Debate," *Japan Echo* 18 (1991): 69.

[96]Ibid.

[97]Emiko Ohnuki-Tierney, "Brain Death and Organ Transplantation: Culture Bases of Medical Technology," *Current Anthropology* 35 (1994): 233–54.

[98]Tomio Tada, *Meneki no Imi ron* (The Meaning of Immunity) (Tokyo: Seidosha, 1993).

[99]William LaFleur, *Liquid Life: Abortion and Buddhism in Japan* (Princeton, N.J.: Princeton University Press, 1992).

[100]Carl Becker, *Breaking the Circle: Death and the Afterlife in Buddhism* (Carbondale, Ill.: Southern Illinois University Press, 1993).

[101]"Zoki ishoku no saizensen" (The frontline in transplants), *Newsweek Nihon Han* (Japanese ed.), 25 February 1993.

[102]Ibid.

[103]Kass, "Organs for Sale? Propriety, Property, and the Price of Progress."

Allan Young

Suffering and the Origins of Traumatic Memory

T HE TERM "SUFFERING" HAS TWO BROAD MEANINGS as it is used in everyday discourse. First, the term identifies a disvalued state to which certain organisms are susceptible because of their biological makeup: suffering is associated with somatic pain and the moments of consciousness that accompany or anticipate this pain. To experience such suffering, an organism requires only a nervous system evolved to the point where we can say that it is conscious of its pain. The second kind of suffering includes states that are variously described as psychological, existential, or spiritual and that are identified by such words as "despairing" and "desolated." This second kind of suffering has a social or moral dimension, in the sense that it is understood locally, by identifiable groups and communities, in the context of ideas about redemption, merit, responsibility, justice, innocence, expiation, etc. Buddhists, Christians, and devotees of the Zar cult all experience suffering in its second meaning, but the quality of their suffering (in the sensibilities of their respective communities) is not the same.

The two kinds of suffering overlap rather than coincide. The first is based on a universal biology. (For the moment, set aside the fact that the boundary between suffering and nonsuffering in the first sense is culturally determined.) Therefore, it is pan-human and includes neurologically-evolved nonhuman species. The second kind of suffering is based on social codes (which include moral and religious codes), and these codes may reject the idea

Allan Young is Professor of Anthropology in the Departments of Social Studies of Medicine, Anthropology, and Psychiatry at McGill University, Canada.

that all human beings are eligible to suffer in this sense, even when they experience equal degrees of suffering in the first sense. Up until and into the nineteenth century, the idea of universal suffering, the eligibility of all people to suffer psychologically, existentially, or spiritually, was justified mainly on philosophical or theological grounds. This is not the case today (at least in the West): psychobiology and psychiatry have provided us with a new rhetoric of suffering, grounded in the authority of science and predicated on the mechanism called psychogenic trauma. (This rhetoric, I should add, complements, and does not challenge, the traditional religious and philosophic conceptions of universal suffering.)

The idea of psychogenic trauma is today widely understood among all classes and social groups. The underlying idea is an extension of much older conceptions, rooted in folk psychology, concerning the power of experiences to cause intense emotions that, in turn, cause pain and disease. Why "trauma" and "traumatic"? Why these particular words and not some others? The earliest entry for "traumatic" in the *Oxford English Dictionary* was in 1656: "belonging to wounds or the cure of wounds," a definition that mirrors the term's Greek root. This was the single use of the word until the nineteenth century, when it was first extended to include mental trauma. So the answer to my question, "Why 'trauma'?," might seem only too obvious. Trauma, originally a term for physical wounds causing pain and suffering, was extended, *via analogy*, to include cognitive-emotional states that cause psychological and existential pain and suffering. This commonsense view is historically incorrect, however: the two kinds of trauma, organic and psychological/existential, are connected through genealogy, not analogy.

It was the universality of the body and of physical pain, first mapped in surgical theaters and in experiments on animals in physiology laboratories, that provided science and medicine with its authority to talk about traumatic suffering of the mind. The extension of trauma from body to mind was not direct, though; it was mediated through either the discovery or the invention of a heretofore unidentified variety of memory—the *traumatic memory*. The traumatic memory, as we know it today, emerged in the closing decades of the nineteenth century, with the intersection of two chains of events. One chain begins with investigations of somnambulism in the late eighteenth century, leads through Ribot's speculations on hypermnesia and psychogenic amnesia, on to the clinical studies of Charcot, Janet, and Freud, and ends with the discovery of the "pathogenic secret," an act of self-deception in which a person hides a memory of a disturbing event from herself. Although out of consciousness, the memory continues to affect her behavior and is a source of suffering.[1] At about the same time, a second chain of events produces a related phenomenon, a traumatic memory rooted in anatomy and physiology. The two lines intersect at various points, beginning with Charcot's investigation of traumatic hysteria, and, more recently, in theories concerning the origins and chronicity of posttraumatic stress disorder. This essay provides a brief and necessarily incomplete account of only half of this story, namely the history of the embodied traumatic memory.[2]

NERVOUS SHOCK AND SURGICAL SHOCK

Historical accounts of the traumatic event routinely trace to the publication of *On Railway and Other Injuries of the Nervous System*, by John Erichsen, a professor of surgery.[3] Erichsen, like other British physicians responsible for diagnosing and assessing injuries and symptoms attributed to railway accidents, divided these patients into three categories: *1)* cases originating in powerful blows or "shocks" that damage neural tissue in ways that are visible to postmortem examination; *2)* cases resulting from shocks that originate in trivial blows or from shaking and jarring and that produce generally invisible damage; and *3)* cases in which people fabricate symptoms to collect compensation. In all three cases, the symptoms are outwardly the same.[4]

Like other early writers on traumatic injuries, Erichsen was also an authority on surgery, and his description of the symptoms of nervous shock parallels his account of surgical shock:

> [The effects of shock] consist in a disturbance of the functions of the circulatory, respiratory, and nervous systems, the harmony of action of the great organs being disarranged. On the receipt of a severe injury the sufferer becomes cold, faint, and trembling; the pulse is small and fluttering; there is a great mental depression and disquietude; the disturbed state of mind revealing itself in the counte-

nance, and in the incoherence of speech and thought; the surface
becomes covered by a cold sweat; there is nausea, perhaps vomiting,
and relaxation of the sphincters. . . .In extreme cases, the depression
of power characterizing shock may be so great as to terminate in
death.[5]

Erichsen's descriptions of nervous shock and surgical shock are
pathognomonic: they identify sets of characteristic symptoms but
indicate no causal mechanisms. Erichsen does not specify how the
organ systems—nervous, circulatory, and respiratory—are connected in cases of shock. However, knowledgeable physicians of
the period would have been able to supply the missing details.
What these ideas were likely to have been can be discerned from a
popular text on the topic of trauma, Edwin Morris's *A Practical
Treatise on Shock After Surgical Operations and Injuries*.[6] Like
Erichsen, Morris was a surgeon with a special interest in railway
accidents. He defines shock as an effect "produced by violent
injuries from any cause, or from violent emotions. . . ." The idea
that the effect of violence inflicted on one part of the body might
then be transmitted to other parts and to internal organs presup-
poses the existence of an anatomical structure that connects all of
these parts. Further, the structure must be able to perform its
function without leaving behind any obvious postmortem evidence, since shock can occur in the absence of lesions or hemor-
rhages. The only structure capable of all this is "the nervous
system, acting directly upon the great nervous centre, the brain. . . ."
Once nervous influences on the heart's action are suspended, the
flow of blood to the brain, nervous system, and respiratory organs
is interrupted, and a negative feedback is created, producing an
effect that accompanies surgical shock and, in the form of syncope, many cases of nervous shock: "the brain could not perform
its normal part without the blood any more than the heart could
beat without the brain."[7]

A satisfactory account of trauma also had to explain the part
that *fear* seemed to play in cases of both surgical shock and
nervous shock. Morris mentions fearful patients who died before
their surgery, and links their deaths to the power of their emotion.
But how does an emotion, acting alone, produce effects that dupli-
cate the consequences of a serious physical trauma? The puzzle is
solved once one accepts that fear is simply an assault, comparable

in its action to a physical blow or injury: "shock through the medium of the brain is such as to suspend the faculties of sense and volition, and to act directly upon the heart as a powerful sedative, producing a prostration of the nervous system. . . ."[8]

This is the background knowledge that Erichsen's readers would have brought to his account. Unlike Morris and other authorities, Erichsen implied that, in railway injuries, traumatic shock occurs exclusively through concussion to the spine. While the initial effects of the concussion are invisible, detectable organic changes gradually develop. These changes may take months and are characterized by the "softening and disorganization" of the cord, ruptures in its membranes, and inflammations—effects similar to the changes found in chronic meningitis and myelitis.[9]

Erichsen describes the typical "uninjured" patient as being initially calm and asymptomatic. The effects of his injury begin once he gets home. "A revulsion of feeling takes place. He bursts into tears, becomes unusually talkative, and is excited. He cannot sleep, or if he does, he wakes up suddenly with a vague sense of alarm. The next day he complains of feeling shaken or bruised all over. . . ." A week later he cannot exert himself or resume business. As the (hypothesized) spinal lesions develop, he grows pallid, careworn, and anxious; his memory suffers and his thoughts become confused; he is fretful and irritable; his head throbs and he is giddy; he suffers from double vision and photophobia; his hearing is either hypersensitive or dulled, and he is troubled by a loud and incessant noise; his posture alters and his gait becomes unsteady; the strength of his limbs diminishes, sometimes to the point of paralysis; he experiences a change or loss of sensation, such as numbness or tingling; his senses of taste and smell are likewise affected; his pulse is feeble, unnaturally slow in the earlier stages of his disorder and unnaturally fast in the later stages; he suffers from local pain and tenderness in the area of the spine.[10]

Erichsen's account mentions, in passing, the victim's mental state during railway collisions:

[I]n no ordinary accident can the shock be so great as in those that occur on Railways. The rapidity of the movement, the momentum of the person injured, the suddenness of its arrest, the helplessness of the sufferers, and that natural perturbation of mind that must disturb the bravest, are all circumstances that of necessity increase the severity of the resulting injury to the nervous system. . . .[11]

Once more, Erichsen fails to identify the mechanisms—psychological and physiological—through which states of helplessness and perturbation (fear, fright, confusion) might intensify the effects of physical injuries.

The most sustained criticism of Erichsen came from Herbert Page, a fellow of the Royal College of Surgeons and consulting physician for the London and Western Railway Company. In 1883, Page had published a monograph on railway accidents that summarized 234 case histories, many involving injuries "without apparent mechanical lesion." In his book, he criticizes Erichsen for attempting to explain the entire span of traumatic railway cases by a single mechanism—spinal concussion resulting in lesions—and also for underplaying or misunderstanding the role of mental factors, especially fear and the desire for compensation, in the onset of symptoms. In 1846, Parliament had passed the Campbell Act, for compensating families of persons killed in accidents resulting from the negligence of a second party. In 1864, an amendment to the Act extended its provisions to include victims of railway accidents. In the following year, juries awarded over £300,000 to people injured on the railways.[12] According to Page, the British public was fully aware of the provisions of the Campbell Act, and people involved in railway accidents were now unable to think of injuries in isolation from their possible monetary significance. He advises physicians to take care when diagnosing people with trivial or invisible injuries: to consider not only the possibility of conscious fraud, but also the possibility that the patient's state of mind might be affected in "wholly unconscious ways" by a desire for compensation.

Page's account of the physiology of shock is based on a surgical monograph by Edward Furneaux Jordan.[13] Like Morris, Furneaux Jordan argued that fear plays a determinative role in certain cases of shock, and this explains why surgical shock "is not always proportionate in its intensity to the severity of the wound."[14] According to Page, the "medical literature abounds in cases where the gravest disturbances of function, and even death. . .have been produced by fright and fright alone," and the same mental element explains why people who suffer broken and mangled limbs in railway accidents arrive at the hospital in a state of shock characteristically more severe than that suffered by people with similar injuries from other causes.[15]

A typical case of nervous shock involves "S. W.," a man who suffered a broken nose and bruises (relatively minor injuries) in "a very severe and destructive collision."

> [S. W.] lay for several days after the accident in a state of great nervous depression, with feeble and rapid pulse, and inability to eat or sleep. He suffered at the same time much distress from the fact that a friend sitting beside him in the carriage had been killed; and this seemed to prey constantly upon his mind. The bodily injuries progressed rapidly towards recovery. . . .[But even after two months] his mental condition showed extreme emotional disturbance. He complained that he had suffered continuously from depression of spirits, as if some great trouble were impending.[16]

At this point, S. W. suffered from shortness of breath, his pulse was weak, and he was too shaken and feeble to manage more than a bit of reading. His voice was weak and often inaudible, he cried easily, slept poorly, and was troubled by distressing dreams. His claims for compensation were settled two years later, but his medical problems continued. He remained depressed, tired easily, slept poorly, and suffered palpitations four years after the accident.[17]

A smaller number of Page's cases consist of "neuromimesis," instances of "purely functional disorders" imitating neurological disease.[18] A typical case concerns "R. C.," an army officer who had been pitched back and forth in his carriage during a nighttime collision. R. C. did not recall being injured,

> [but] the next morning he felt very ill and vomited, and he soon began to suffer from pain across the loins, queer sensations all over the body, nausea, giddiness, and want of sleep. On. . .the twelfth day after the accident he fell suddenly and struck his nose against the corner of a table. . . .His own description was that the "fit came on about three in the afternoon, I fell down and screamed, and then began to cry and sob violently. During it I was unconscious, although I knew that people were around me. . . ." He called this fit an "hysterical attack," and the doctor who saw him immediately afterwards, and who found him more or less unconscious, said that this

was its nature. Six weeks after the accident he complained of pain in the back, loss of memory, inability to apply himself, occasional giddiness, nausea, and want of sleep.[19]

According to Page, R. C.'s hysterical seizures originated in syncope, a temporary loss of consciousness that is caused when the heart fails to provide the brain with blood. Page traced R. C.'s symptoms (and, one supposes, S. W.'s) to "morbid changes of the nerve centres which underlie them." These changes were unlike those proposed by Erichsen, since they were not confined to the spinal cord nor could they be compared with the effects of meningitis. Indeed, Page disavowed any analogy:

> That there are changes is almost certain; what those changes are we do not know. One thing, however, may be said with some degree of confidence, that they differ very materially from the gross pathological changes in structure which we are accustomed to see upon the post-mortem table, or. . .[through] the microscope.[20]

THE PHYLOGENETIC MEMORY

Nervous shock, like surgical shock, travels along pathoanatomical pathways, but opinions differ as to whether these pathways are parallel or congruent. At the end of the nineteenth century, George W. Crile, an American surgeon-physiologist, proposed to connect fear to physical injury, and nervous shock to surgical shock, by introducing a new element into the equation, namely *pain*. Crile writes that pain announces itself in two ways: There is dumb pain, the intrinsically unpleasant experience that sensate organisms instinctively strive to avoid. But pain can also be a supremely important kind of bodily knowledge, a signal that locates injury and that is a portent of mortality. Nonhuman organisms do not fear injury per se, rather they must *learn* to fear the events that cause injury. And what they learn to fear is the pain that accompanies injury. It is precisely because pain is unpleasant that it is also a gift. Without the knowledge of pain, the organism and its species would be free to pursue their own destruction.[21]

The organism fears pain and it fears the things that will bring it pain. Thus, fear is constituted from two things: a bodily state and a memory. These memories are acquired ontogenetically through the organism's own experience with pain, and they are acquired phylogenetically through inherited fears. This conclusion, that fear is the memory of pain, did not originate with Crile. Charles Darwin made a similar suggestion in *The Expression of Emotions in Man and Animals*,[22] and the source of Darwin's idea is Herbert Spencer, whose account of fear is given in *The Principles of Psychology*.[23]

Spencer is the missing link in the genealogy of traumatic memory. What are the origins of fear? How do organisms know what things they must fear? The answers seem obvious: fear is an instinct and the organism's ability to recognize elemental dangers is likewise instinctive. For Spencer, however, that answer begs the question, "What is 'instinct' and what are *its* origins?" For many of Spencer's contemporaries, that question was simply unnecessary, since instinct was assumed to be the starting point for explaining behavior and not the object of explanations.

Spencer had started with a localizationist view of the brain. Like Gall and other phrenologists, he divided the cortex into regions, each the site of a mental faculty, among which fear could be included.[24] In *The Principles of Psychology,* he shifted to an associationist position: percepts and simple concepts agglutinate into complex ideas and cognitive-affective structures when they are linked through resemblance (analogy), contiguity (in time and space), causality, and sensation (pain and pleasure). Like David Hume, Spencer rejected the innateness of human knowledge and any suggestion that the repository of knowledge, the "self," is more than a fiction based on personal memories. But there is also an important difference between Spencer and Hume. Hume's position is that the self is a fiction constructed on personal memories: "Had we no memory, we never should have any notion of causation, nor consequently of that chain of causes and effects, which constitute our self or person."[25] This proposition is not good enough for Spencer because it fails to explain two truths: First, there is knowledge that is universal but cannot be traced to an individual's own experiences or instruction. The infant's "instinctive" fear of snakes is an instance of such knowledge. Second, "If, at birth, there exists nothing but a passive receptivity of impressions, why is not a horse as educable as a Man? Should it be said that language makes the difference, then why do not the cat and the dog, reared in the same household, arrive at equal degrees and kinds of intelligence?"[26]

Spencer answers his questions by introducing an evolutionary premise, in the guise of phylogenetic memory:

> [T]here are established in the structure of the nervous system absolute internal relations—relations that are potentially present before birth in the shape of definite nervous connexions; that are antecedent to, and independent of, individual experiences; and that are automatically disclosed along with the first cognitions. . . .But these pre-determined internal relations, though independent of the experiences of the individual, are not independent of experiences in general: they have been determined by the experiences of preceding organisms.[27]

Each phylogenetic memory begins as an individual experience. To say that an experience is remembered means that it has left a neurological trace. These traces (which include memorized action patterns) tend to fade over time unless they are periodically recalled and/or reenacted, in which case a trace evolves into a permanent neural pathway. Pathways grow progressively deeper as the organically registered experiences of multiple generations are accumulated. In time, such pathways permit impulses to move unimpeded, so that no cognitive effort is required to move from initial perception to completed response. On reaching this point, a phylogenetic memory is equivalent to what is called an instinct.[28]

One might argue that a phylogenetic memory is not really a memory, since it does not enter consciousness. However, the same objection might be raised concerning pathogenic secrets described by Ribot, Charcot, Janet, Breuer, Freud, and others (fixed ideas, repressed memories, and so on). In fact, the phylogenetic memory *does* enter consciousness: not through cognitive effort, it is true, but at the moment of reenactment. What is special about this conscious memory is that, at the moment of remembrance and reenactment, it collapses time, fusing the ancestral past and the experienced present.

Spencer's phylogenetic memory is cognate with Haeckel's notion of epigenesis, the idea that a species's evolutionary history is recapitulated in the embryological development of its individual members. Spencer's Lamarckian theory was subsequently elaborated upon by the British neurologist John Hughlings Jackson, who pictured the nervous system as an accretion of layers. Consciousness and active memories lie at the topmost level; more recently acquired ancestral memories, still requiring cognitive effort, make up the next layers; and the lower levels consist of the most ancient and "instinctive" memories.[29] The rediscovery of Mendel's genetic experiments at the turn of the century signaled the end of Lamarckian theories and the ascendance of Darwinian mechanisms: chance, mutation, and natural selection. The decline of use-inheritance was not immediate: Pavlov entertained the possibility of hereditary transmission of conditioned reflexes into the 1920s;[30] German and French researchers kept the door open to Lamarckianism for two more decades; and Freud continued to base the sexual etiology of the psychoneuroses on a phylogenetic (Oedipal) memory of the sort described by Spencer.[31]

However, there is no necessary link between phylogenetic memory and Lamarckian premises, and one could argue that simple kinds of phylogenetic memory might be inherited just as easily through Darwinian mechanisms. This is how Crile and his contemporary Walter B. Cannon think of fear. Fear looks to the past (memory of pain) and likewise to the future, to actions (fight or flight) that allow the organism to avoid pain, injury, and death. Here again, the key idea—that fear and its opposite, anger, are dual expressions of one physiological phenomenon—originates with Spencer.[32] What makes Cannon's account of fear different from Spencer's is that it moves elements of phylogenetic memory out of the brain and into the sympathetic nervous system and its functional extension, the adrenal glands.

Cannon represents fear and anger as phases of physiological mobilization within an internal environment (the organism) that is perpetually striving to adjust itself, through the regulative actions of the sympathetic nervous system and the endocrines, to changes and challenges originating in the external environment.[33] It would seem that Cannon, like Spencer and unlike Erichsen and Page, is depathologizing fear, shifting its traumatic associations to the field of evolutionary biology, and redefining its neurophysiology as a transient state of adaptive arousal. One has to follow him only one step further to see that this is not the whole story. A dramatic account of how a survival mechanism, physiological mobilization triggered by fear and anger, can be transformed into its opposite, a pathogenic process, is found in Cannon's article titled "'Voodoo' Death," published at the end of his career. According to Cannon, episodes of successful sorcery (voodoo death) go through a sequence: a curse is laid in public, the victim is isolated by his community, and then the community converges on the wretched man "in order to subject him to the fateful rite of mourning." Over the course of these events, the victim is filled with "powerless misery." Spurred by fear and anger, he is physically primed to either escape or attack the source of danger, but is unable to follow either course. "If these powerful emotions prevail, and the bodily forces are fully mobilized for action, and if this state of extreme perturbation continues in uncontrolled possession of the organism for a considerable period, without the occurrence of action, dire results [including death] may ensue."[34]

Cannon's ideas about the pathophysiology of voodoo death are based on research conducted on decorticated cats earlier in his career. In the experiments, Cannon severed connections between the cerebral cortex and the remainder of the nervous system, producing a state of excessive activity of the sympathetic-adrenal system that was allowed to continue unabated. Cannon called this state "sham rage" and claimed that it replicates the states of intense fear and anger that occur naturally in whole animals. After several hours of sham rage, the decorticated cat's blood pressure gradually dropped, to the point where its heart stopped beating. This process is Cannon's solution to the mystery of voodoo death and it likewise explains the nervous shock syndrome described by Erichsen and Page. Victims "die from a true state of shock, in the surgical sense—a shock induced by prolonged and intense emotion." Although the hocus-pocus of voodoo death is foreign to civilized societies, similar processes occur there too. Cannon mentions cases of World War I soldiers who fell into shock following "wounds. . .so trivial that they could not be reasonably regarded as the cause of the shock state."[35]

Cannon's idea of voodoo death is rooted in a universal biology, but it is a remarkably circumscribed phenomenon, found mainly among primitive peoples, "bewildered strangers in a hostile world. Instead of knowledge they have a fertile and unrestricted imagination, which fills their environment with all manner of evil spirits capable of affecting their lives disastrously."[36] Further, in his account, fear is inescapable and its effects unrelenting. But what happens when exposure to traumatic shock is intermittent? Cannon (and Crile) calls this phenomenon "summation"—a process during which the physical effects of multiple exposures accumulate and eventually lead to the progressive destabilization associated with voodoo death. Animal experiments conducted by Pavlov at about the same time pointed to a radically different possibility: during periods between exposures, the organism returned to homeostasis, but a state different from the *status quo ante*. In other words, recurrent trauma produces a transformation rather than a summation.

This is a critical moment in the genealogy of the traumatic memory. In Cannon's experiments, a distance had been preserved between the victim and the source of its pain and fear. The Pavlovians collapsed this space and interiorized the source of pain. In a classic conditioning experiment, an animal is exposed to a source of inescapable pain, such as electric shock. The animal is repeatedly reexposed to the shock, and each time it produces pain and physiological arousal. At the same time, the animal is aware of stimuli in its immediate environment that co-occur with the source of its pain but are incidental to it. The victim learns to associate these phenomena with the shock and they acquire a mnemonic power: whenever it encounters them, it is forced to remember and relive its distress and arousal. In time, the scope of the conditioned response is extended, through association, to objects and events located outside the original place of pain. Escape is now impossible: each reexposure revives the victim's pathogenic memory and the potency of the conditioned stimuli.

A properly conditioned victim has several ways of responding to its pathogenic memory. Pavlovians focused on two reactions: some victims develop routines (phobias) allowing them to avoid noxious stimuli, and others simply give up (learned helplessness). There is, however, a third possible reaction, let us call it *neo*-Pavlovian, since it emerges later, in connection with posttraumatic stress disorder. The basic idea is that victims of traumatic memory seek out circumstances that replicate their etiological events. This scenario is based on anecdotal and experimental evidence suggesting that endorphins (endogenous opioids) are released into a victim's bloodstream during moments of traumatic shock. This would be an adaptive response during fight-or-flight emergencies, since endorphins would produce a state in which the individual is undistracted and undeterred by pain. In cases of posttraumatic stress disorder, endorphins would produce a tranquilizing effect by reducing the feelings of anxiety, depression, and inadequacy that often accompany this syndrome. Over time, such people would become *addicted* both to their endorphins and to the memories that release these chemicals. When intervals between exposures grow too long, people can be expected to experience the symptoms of opiate withdrawal (which are, coincidentally, also criterial features of the posttraumatic stress disorder diagnostic classification): anxiety, irritability, explosive outbursts, insomnia, emotional lability, hyperalterness. These symptoms would exacerbate the ongoing distress intrinsic to this disorder and pain would build to the point where the individual is induced to self-dose with his endorphins. This would be accomplished by reexposing himself to situations that mimic his original traumatogenic event.[37]

FINIS

Spencer, Crile, and Cannon scripted an evolutionary narrative in which the inability to feel pain is represented as a dangerous kind of ignorance. The body was said to remember its pain, and "fear" was the name given to this memory. Fear, like pain, was transmuted into an evolutionary gift, enabling the organism to anticipate threats and to avoid its destruction. The account is positive and reassuring, signaling the beneficent wisdom of a higher pragmatism. Pain and fear have been normalized, turned into memories with which the individual can now make his way in the world. With the neo-Pavlovians, the meaning of memory is turned inside out, and transformed into a recognizably modern phenomenon: an affliction through which pain and fear colonize and degrade the sufferer's life-world.

ENDNOTES

[1]Henri F. Ellenberger, "The Pathogenic Secret and its Therapeutics," in Mark Micale, ed., *Beyond the Unconscious: Essays of Henri F. Ellenberger in the History of Psychiatry* (Princeton, N.J.: Princeton University Press, 1993), 341–59.

[2]Allan Young, *The Harmony of Illusions: Inventing Post-Traumatic Stress Disorder* (Princeton, N.J.: Princeton University Press, 1995).

[3]John E. Erichsen, *On Railway and Other Injuries of the Nervous System* (London: Walton and Maberly, 1866).

[4]Ibid., 10, 113–14.

[5]John E. Erichsen, *The Science and Art of Surgery*, 6th ed. (London: Longmans, Green, 1872), 106.

[6]Edwin Morris, *A Practical Treatise on Shock after Surgical Operations and Injuries, with Special Reference to Shock Caused by Railway Accidents* (London: Robert Hardwicke, 1867).

[7]Ibid., 9–10, 11, 17, 19.

[8]Ibid., 20–21.

[9]Erichsen, *On Railway and Other Injuries of the Nervous System*, 95, 112–14.

[10]Ibid., 95–110.

[11]Ibid., 9.

[12]Morris, *A Practical Treatise on Shock after Surgical Operations and Injuries, with Special Reference to Shock Caused by Railway Accidents*, 55.

[13]Edward Furneaux Jordan, *Surgical Inquiries; Including the Hastings Essay on Shock, the Treatment of Surgical Inflammations, and Clinical Lectures* (London: J. and A. Churchill, 1880).

[14]Ibid., 1–2, 10, 13.

[15]Herbert W. Page, *Injuries of the Spine and Spinal Cord without Apparent Mechanical Lesion, and Nervous Shock, in their Surgical and Medico-Legal Aspects* (London: J. and A. Churchill, 1883), 117.

[16]Ibid., 151–52.

[17]Ibid., 151–52.

[18]Ibid., 198–99.

[19]Ibid., 216–17.

[20]Ibid., 198–99.

[21]George W. Crile, *An Experimental Research into Surgical Shock* (Philadelphia, Pa.: Lippincott, 1899); George W. Crile, "Phylogenetic Association in Relation to Certain Medical Problems," *Boston Medical and Surgical Journal* 163 (1910): 893–904; and George W. Crile, *The Origin and Nature of the Emotions* (Philadelphia, Pa.: W. B. Saunders, 1915).

[22]Charles Darwin, *The Expression of the Emotions in Man and Animals* (Chicago, Ill.: University of Chicago Press, 1965).

[23]Herbert Spencer, *The Principles of Psychology* (London: Longman, Brown, Green, and Longmans, 1855), 594–600.

260   *Allan Young*

²⁴Edwin Clarke and L. S. Jacyna, *Nineteenth-Century Origins of Neuroscientific Concepts* (Berkeley, Calif.: University of California Press, 1987), 220–34, 238–44; Robert M. Young, *Mind, Brain and Adaptation in the Nineteenth Century* (New York: Oxford University Press, 1990), 173, 180–81.

²⁵David Hume, *A Treatise of Human Nature,* vol. 1 (Darmstadt: Scientia Verlag Aalen, 1964), 542.

²⁶Herbert Spencer, *The Principles of Psychology,* 2nd ed. (London: Longman, Brown, Green, and Longmans, 1880), 468.

²⁷Ibid., 470.

²⁸Ibid., 450–51.

²⁹Roger Smith, *Inhibition: History and Meaning in the Sciences of Mind and Brain* (Berkeley, Calif.: University of California Press, 1992), 76, 78–79; Young, *Mind, Brain and Adaptation in the Nineteenth Century,* 178, 182–83, 186–87.

³⁰Ivan P. Pavlov, *Conditioned Reflexes: An Account of the Physiological Activity of the Cerebral Cortex* (London: Oxford University Press, 1927), 285.

³¹Patricia Kitcher, *Freud's Dream: A Complete Interdisciplinary Theory of Mind* (Cambridge, Mass.: MIT Press, 1992), 67–74, 104–109, 174–90; Frank Sulloway, *Freud, Biologist of the Mind* (New York: Basic Books, 1983), chap. 4.

³²Spencer, *The Principles of Psychology,* 596. For similar observations, see Darwin, *The Expression of the Emotions in Man and Animals,* 74, 77.

³³Walter B. Cannon, "The Interrelations of Emotions as Suggested by Recent Physiological Researchers," *American Journal of Psychiatry* 25 (1914): 181–256; Walter B. Cannon, *Bodily Changes in Pain, Hunger, Fear and Rage* (Boston, Mass.: Charles T. Branford, 1929), chaps. 12, 14.

³⁴Walter B. Cannon, "'Voodoo' Death," *American Anthropologist* 44 (1942): 176.

³⁵Ibid., 179.

³⁶Ibid., 175.

³⁷B. A. van der Kolk, M. Greenberg, H. Boyd, and J. Krystal, "Inescapable Shock, Neurotransmitters, and Addiction to Trauma: Toward a Psychobiology of Posttraumatic Stress," *Biological Psychiatry* 20 (1985): 314–25; Roger K. Pitman, B. A. van der Kolk, S. P. Orr, and M. S. Greenberg, "Naloxone-Reversible Analgesic Response to Combat-Related Stimuli in Posttraumatic Stress Disorder," *Archives of General Psychiatry* 47 (1990): 541–44.

Paul Farmer

On Suffering and Structural Violence: A View from Below

E VERYONE KNOWS THAT SUFFERING EXISTS. The question is how
to define it. Given that each person's pain has a degree of
reality for him or her that the pain of others can surely
never approach, is widespread agreement on the subject possible?
Almost all of us would agree that premature and painful illness,
torture, and rape constitute extreme suffering. Most would also
agree that insidious assaults on dignity, such as institutionalized
racism and sexism, also cause great and unjust injury.

Given our consensus on some of the more conspicuous forms of
suffering, a number of corollary questions come to the fore. Can
we identify those most at risk of great suffering? Among those
whose suffering is not mortal, is it possible to identify those most
likely to sustain permanent and disabling damage? Are certain
"event" assaults, such as torture or rape, more likely to lead to late
sequelae than are sustained and insidious suffering, such as the
pain born of deep poverty or of racism? Under this latter rubric,
are certain forms of discrimination demonstrably more noxious
than others?

Anthropologists who take these as research questions study
both individual experience and the larger social matrix in which it
is embedded in order to see how various large-scale social forces
come to be translated into personal distress and disease. By what
mechanisms do social forces ranging from poverty to racism be-

*Paul Farmer, an Assistant Professor in the Department of Social Medicine at Harvard
Medical School, practices medicine at the Brigham and Women's Hospital in Boston and
at the Clinique Bon Sauveur in rural Haiti.*

come *embodied* as individual experience? This has been the focus of most of my own research in Haiti, where political and economic forces have structured risk for AIDS, tuberculosis, and, indeed, most other infectious and parasitic diseases. Social forces at work there have also structured risk for most forms of extreme suffering, from hunger to torture and rape.

Working in contemporary Haiti, where in recent years political violence has been added to the worst poverty in the hemisphere, one learns a great deal about suffering. In fact, the country has long constituted a sort of living laboratory for the study of affliction, no matter how it is defined. "Life for the Haitian peasant of today," observed anthropologist Jean Weise some twenty-five years ago, "is abject misery and a rank familiarity with death."[1] The situation has since worsened. When in 1991 international health and population experts devised a "human suffering index" by examining measures of human welfare ranging from life expectancy to political freedom, 27 of 141 countries were characterized by "extreme human suffering." Only one of them, Haiti, was located in the Western hemisphere. In only three countries in the world was suffering judged to be more extreme than that endured in Haiti; each of these three countries is currently in the midst of an internationally recognized civil war.

Suffering is certainly a recurrent and expected condition in Haiti's Central Plateau, where everyday life has felt like war. "You get up in the morning," observed one young widow with four children, "and it's the fight for food and wood and water." If initially struck by the austere beauty of the region's steep mountains and clement weather, long-term visitors come to see the Central Plateau in much the same manner as its inhabitants: a chalky and arid land hostile to the best efforts of the peasant farmers who live here. Landlessness is widespread and so, consequently, is hunger. All the standard measures reveal how tenuous the peasantry's hold on survival is. Life expectancy at birth is less than fifty years, in large part because as many as two of every ten infants die before their first birthday. Tuberculosis is the leading cause of death among adults; among children, diarrheal disease, measles, and tetanus ravage the undernourished.

But the experience of suffering, it is often noted, is not effectively conveyed by statistics or graphs. The "texture" of dire affliction is perhaps best felt in the gritty details of biography, and so I introduce the stories of Acéphie Joseph and Chouchou Louis.[2] The stories of Acéphie and Chouchou are anything but "anecdotal." For the epidemiologist as well as the political analyst, they suffered and died in exemplary fashion. Millions of people living in similar circumstances can expect to meet similar fates. What these victims, past and present, share are not personal or psychological attributes—they do not share culture, language, or race. Rather, what they share is the experience of occupying the bottom rung of the social ladder in inegalitarian societies.[3]

Acéphie Joseph's and Chouchou Louis's stories illustrate some of the mechanisms through which large-scale social forces crystallize into the sharp, hard surfaces of individual suffering. Such suffering is structured by historically given (and often economically driven) processes and forces that conspire—whether through routine, ritual, or, as is more commonly the case, these hard surfaces—to constrain agency.[4] For many, including most of my patients and informants, life choices are structured by racism, sexism, political violence, *and* grinding poverty.

ACÉPHIE'S STORY

For the wound of the daughter of my people is my heart wounded,
I mourn, and dismay has taken hold of me.
Is there no balm in Gilead? Is there no physician there?
Why then has the health of the daughter of my people not been restored?
O that my head were waters, and my eyes a fountain of tears, that I might weep day and night for the slain of the daughter of my people!
—*Jeremiah 8:22–9.1*

Kay, a community of fewer than fifteen hundred people, stretches along an unpaved road that cuts north and east into Haiti's Central Plateau. Striking out from Port-au-Prince, the capital, it can take several hours to reach Kay. The journey gives one an impression of isolation, insularity. The impression is misleading, as the village owes its existence to a project conceived in the Haitian capital and drafted in Washington, D.C.: Kay is a settlement of refugees, substantially composed of peasant farmers displaced more than thirty years ago by Haiti's largest dam.

Before 1956, the village of Kay was situated in a fertile valley, and through it ran the Rivière Artibonite. For generations, thousands of families had farmed the broad and gently sloping banks of the river, selling rice, bananas, millet, corn, and sugarcane in regional markets. Harvests were, by all reports, bountiful; life there is now recalled as idyllic. When the valley was flooded with the building of the dam, the majority of the local population was forced up into the stony hills on either side of the new reservoir. By all the standard measures, the "water refugees" became exceedingly poor; the older people often blame their poverty on the massive buttress dam a few miles away, and bitterly note that it brought them neither electricity nor water.

In 1983, when I began working in the Central Plateau, AIDS, although already afflicting an increasing number of city dwellers, was unknown in most areas as rural as Kay. Acéphie Joseph was one of the first villagers to die of the new syndrome. But her illness, which ended in 1991, was merely the latest in a string of tragedies that she and her parents readily linked together in a long lamentation, by now familiar to those who tend the region's sick.

The litany begins, usually, down in the valley hidden under the still surface of the lake. Acéphie's parents came from families making a decent living by farming fertile tracts of land—their "ancestors' gardens"—and selling much of their produce. M. Joseph tilled the soil, and his wife, a tall and wearily elegant woman not nearly as old as she looked, was a "Madame Sarah," a market woman. "If it weren't for the dam," M. Joseph assured me, "we'd be just fine now. Acéphie, too." The Josephs' home was drowned along with most of their belongings, their crops, and the graves of their ancestors.

Refugees from the rising water, the Josephs built a miserable lean-to on a knoll of high land jutting into the new reservoir. They remained poised on their knoll for some years; Acéphie and her twin brother were born there. I asked them what induced them to move up to Kay, to build a house on the hard stone embankment of a dusty road. "Our hut was too near the water," replied M. Joseph. "I was afraid one of the children would fall into the lake and drown. Their mother had to be away selling; I was trying to make a garden in this terrible soil. There was no one to keep an eye on them."

Acéphie attended primary school—a banana-thatched and open shelter in which children and young adults received the rudiments of literacy—in Kay. "She was the nicest of the Joseph sisters," recalled one of her classmates. "And she was as pretty as she was nice." Acéphie's beauty and her vulnerability may have sealed her fate as early as 1984. Though still in primary school, she was already nineteen years old; it was time for her to help generate income for her family, which was sinking deeper and deeper into poverty. Acéphie began to help her mother by carrying produce to a local market on Friday mornings. On foot or with a donkey it takes over an hour and a half to reach the market, and the road leads right through Péligre, the site of the dam and, until recently, a military barracks. The soldiers liked to watch the parade of women on Friday mornings. Sometimes they taxed them with haphazardly imposed fines; sometimes they taxed them with flirtatious banter.

Such flirtation is seldom unwelcome, at least to all appearances. In rural Haiti, entrenched poverty made the soldiers—the region's only salaried men—ever so much more attractive. Hunger was again a near-daily occurrence for the Joseph family; the times were as bad as those right after the flooding of the valley. And so when Acéphie's good looks caught the eye of Captain Jacques Honorat, a native of Belladère formerly stationed in Port-au-Prince, she returned his gaze.

Acéphie knew, as did everyone in the area, that Honorat had a wife and children. He was known, in fact, to have more than one regular partner. But Acéphie was taken in by his persistence, and when he went to speak to her parents, a long-term liaison was, from the outset, seriously considered:

> What would you have me do? I could tell that the old people were uncomfortable, worried; but they didn't say no. They didn't tell me to stay away from him. I wish they had, but how could they have known?. . .I knew it was a bad idea then, but I just didn't know why. I never dreamed he would give me a bad illness, never! I looked around and saw how poor we all were, how the old people were finished. . . .What would you have me do? It was a way out, that's how I saw it.

Acéphie and Honorat were sexual partners only briefly—for less than a month, according to Acéphie. Shortly thereafter, Honorat fell ill with unexplained fevers and kept to the company of his wife in Péligre. As Acéphie was looking for a *moun prensipal*—a "main man"—she tried to forget about the soldier. Still, it was shocking to hear, a few months after they parted, that he was dead.

Acéphie was at a crucial juncture in her life. Returning to school was out of the question. After some casting about, she went to Mirebalais, the nearest town, and began a course in what she euphemistically termed "cooking school." The school—really just an ambitious woman's courtyard—prepared poor girls like Acéphie for their inevitable turn as servants in the city. Indeed, domestic service was one of the rare growth industries in Haiti, and as much as Acéphie's proud mother hated to think of her daughter reduced to servitude, she could offer no viable alternative.

And so Acéphie, at age twenty-two, went off to Port-au-Prince, where she found a job as a housekeeper for a middle-class Haitian woman working for the US embassy. Acéphie's looks and manners kept her out of the backyard, the traditional milieu of Haitian servants: she was designated as the maid who, in addition to cleaning, answered the door and the telephone. Although Acéphie was not paid well—she received $30 each month—she tried to save a bit of money for her parents and siblings, recalling the hunger gnawing at her home village.

Still looking for a *moun prensipal*, Acéphie began seeing Blanco Nerette, a young man with origins identical to her own: Blanco's parents were also "water refugees" and Acéphie had known him when they were both attending the parochial school in Kay. Blanco had done well for himself, by Kay standards: he chauffeured a small bus between the Central Plateau and the capital. In a setting characterized by an unemployment rate of greater than 60 percent, his job commanded considerable respect. He easily won the attention of Acéphie. They planned to marry, and started pooling their resources.

Acéphie had worked as a maid for over three years when she discovered that she was pregnant. When she told Blanco, he became skittish. Nor was her employer pleased: it is considered unsightly to have a pregnant servant. So Acéphie returned to Kay, where she had a difficult pregnancy. Blanco came to see her once or twice; they had a disagreement, and then she heard nothing from him. Following the birth of her daughter, Acéphie was sapped by repeated infections. She was shortly thereafter diagnosed with AIDS.

Soon Acéphie's life was consumed with managing drenching night sweats and debilitating diarrhea, while attempting to care for her first child. "We both need diapers now," she remarked bitterly towards the end of her life, faced each day not only with diarrhea, but also with a persistent lassitude. As she became more and more gaunt, some villagers suggested that Acéphie was the victim of sorcery. Others recalled her liaison with the soldier and her work as a servant in the city, both locally considered risk factors for AIDS. Acéphie herself knew that she had AIDS, although she was more apt to refer to herself as suffering from a disorder brought on by her work as a servant: "All that ironing, and then opening a refrigerator."

But this is not simply the story of Acéphie and her daughter. There is Jacques Honorat's first wife, who each year grows thinner. After Honorat's death, she found herself desperate, with no means of feeding her five hungry children, two of whom were also ill. Her subsequent union was again with a soldier. Honorat had at least two other partners, both of them poor peasant women, in the Central Plateau. One is HIV positive and has two sickly children. Blanco is still a handsome young man, apparently in good health and plying the roads from Mirebalais to Port-au-Prince. Who knows if he carries the virus? As an attractive man with a paying job, he has plenty of girlfriends.

Nor is this simply the story of those infected with the virus. The pain of Mme. Joseph and Acéphie's twin brother was manifestly intense, but few understood the anguish of her father. Shortly after Acéphie's death, M. Joseph hanged himself.

CHOUCHOU'S STORY

"History shudders, pierced by events of massive public suffering. Memory is haunted, stalked by the ghosts of history's victims, capriciously severed from life in genocides, holocausts, and extermi-

*nation camps. The cries of the hungry, the shrieks of political
prisoners, and the silent voices of the oppressed echo slowly, painfully through daily existence."*

—*Rebecca Chopp*
The Praxis of Suffering

Chouchou Louis grew up not far from Kay in another small village
in the steep and infertile highlands of Haiti's Central Plateau. He
attended primary school for a couple of years but was obliged to
drop out when his mother died. Then in his early teens, Chouchou
joined his father and an older sister in tending their hillside gardens. In short, there was nothing remarkable about Chouchou's
childhood; it was brief and harsh, like most in rural Haiti.

Throughout the 1980s, church activities formed Chouchou's
sole distraction. These were hard years for the Haitian poor,
beaten down by a family dictatorship well into its third decade.
The Duvaliers, father and son, ruled through violence, largely
directed at people whose conditions of existence were similar to
that of Chouchou Louis. Although many of them tried to flee,
often by boat, US policy maintained that Haitian asylum-seekers
were "economic refugees." As part of a 1981 agreement between
the administrations of Ronald Reagan and Jean-Claude Duvalier,
refugees seized on the high seas were summarily returned to Haiti.
During the first ten years of the accord, 24,559 Haitians applied
for political asylum in the United States; eight applications were
approved.

A growing Haitian pro-democracy movement led, in February
1986, to the flight of Duvalier. Chouchou Louis must have been
about twenty years old when "Baby Doc" fell, and he shortly
thereafter acquired a small radio. "All he did," recalled his wife
years later, "was work the land, listen to the radio, and go to
church." It was on the radio that Chouchou heard about the
people who took over after Duvalier fled. Like many in rural
Haiti, Chouchou was distressed to hear that power had been
handed to the military, led by hardened *duvaliéristes*. It was this
army that the US government, which in 1916 had created the
modern Haitian army, termed "Haiti's best bet for democracy." In
the eighteen months following Duvalier's departure, over $200
million in US aid passed through the hands of the junta.

In early 1989, Chouchou moved in with Chantal Brisé, who was pregnant. They were living together when Father Jean-Bertrand Aristide—by then considered the leader of the pro-democracy movement—declared his candidacy for the presidency in the internationally monitored elections of 1990. In December of that year almost 70 percent of the voters chose Father Aristide from a field of ten presidential candidates.

Like most rural Haitians, Chouchou and Chantal welcomed Aristide's election with great joy. For the first time, the poor—Haiti's overwhelming majority, formerly silent—felt they had someone representing their interests in the presidential palace. These are the reasons why the military coup d'état of September 1991 stirred great anger in the countryside, where the majority of Haitians live. Anger was soon followed by sadness, then fear, as the country's repressive machinery, dismantled during the seven months of Aristide's tenure, was hastily reassembled under the patronage of the army.

In the month after the coup, Chouchou was sitting in a truck en route to the town of Hinche. Chouchou offered for the consideration of his fellow passengers what Haitians call a *pwen*, a pointed remark intended to say something other than what it literally means. As they bounced along, he began complaining about the conditions of the roads, observing that, "if things were as they should be, these roads would have been repaired already." One eyewitness later told me that at no point in the commentary was Aristide's name invoked. But Chouchou's complaints were recognized by his fellow passengers as veiled language deploring the coup. Unfortunately for Chouchou, one of the passengers was an out-of-uniform soldier. At the next checkpoint, the soldier had him seized and dragged from the truck. There, a group of soldiers and their lackeys—their *attachés,* to use the epithet then in favor—immediately began beating Chouchou, in front of the other passengers; they continued to beat him as they brought him to the military barracks in Hinche. A scar on his right temple was a souvenir of his stay in Hinche, which lasted several days.

Perhaps the worst aftereffect of such episodes of brutality was that, in general, they marked the beginning of persecution, not the end. In rural Haiti, during this time, any scrape with the law (i.e., the military) led to blacklisting. For men like Chouchou, staying out of jail involved keeping the local attachés happy, and he did this by avoiding his home village. But Chouchou lived in fear of a second arrest, his wife later told me, and his fears proved to be well-founded.

On January 22, 1992, Chouchou was visiting his sister when he was arrested by two attachés. No reason was given for the arrest, and Chouchou's sister regarded as ominous the seizure of the young man's watch and radio. He was roughly marched to the nearest military checkpoint, where he was tortured by soldiers and the attachés. One area resident later told us that the prisoner's screams made her children weep with terror.

On January 25, Chouchou was dumped in a ditch to die. The army scarcely took the trouble to circulate the canard that he had stolen some bananas. (The Haitian press, by then thoroughly muzzled, did not even broadcast this false version of events.) Relatives carried Chouchou back to Chantal and their daughter under the cover of night. By early on the morning of January 26, when I arrived, Chouchou was scarcely recognizable. His face, and especially his left temple, was misshapen, swollen, and lacerated; his right temple was also scarred. His mouth was a pool of dark, coagulated blood. His neck was peculiarly swollen, his throat collared with bruises, the traces of a gun butt. His chest and sides were badly bruised, and he had several fractured ribs. His genitals had been mutilated.

That was his front side; presumably, the brunt of the beatings came from behind. Chouchou's back and thighs were striped with deep lash marks. His buttocks were macerated, the skin flayed down to the exposed gluteal muscles. Some of these stigmata appeared to be infected.

Chouchou coughed up more than a liter of blood in his agonal moments. Given his respiratory difficulties and the amount of blood he coughed up, it is likely that the beatings caused him to bleed, slowly at first, then catastrophically, into his lungs. His head injuries had not robbed him of his faculties, although it might have been better for him had they done so. It took Chouchou three days to die.

EXPLAINING VERSUS MAKING SENSE OF SUFFERING

The pain in our shoulder comes
You say, from the damp; and this is also the reason
For the stain on the wall of our flat.
So tell us:
Where does the damp come from?
                                    —*Bertholt Brecht*

Are these stories of suffering emblematic of something other than two tragic and premature deaths? If so, how representative is each of these experiences? Little about Acéphie's story is unique; I have told it in detail because it brings into relief many of the forces constraining not only her options, but those of most Haitian women. Such, in any case, is my opinion after caring for dozens of poor women with AIDS. There is a deadly monotony in their stories: young women—or teenaged girls—who were driven to Port-au-Prince by the lure of an escape from the harshest poverty; once in the city, each worked as a domestic; none managed to find financial security. The women interviewed were straightforward about the nonvoluntary aspect of their sexual activity: in their opinions, they had been driven into unfavorable unions by poverty.[5] Indeed, such testimony should call into question facile notions of "consensual sex."

What about the murder of Chouchou Louis? International human rights groups estimate that more than three thousand Haitians were killed in the year after the September 1991 coup that overthrew Haiti's first democratically elected government. Nearly all of those killed were civilians who, like Chouchou, fell into the hands of military or paramilitary forces. The vast majority of victims were poor peasants, like Chouchou, or urban slum dwellers. (The figures cited here are conservative estimates; I am quite sure that no journalist or observer ever came to count the body of Chouchou Louis.[6])

Thus, the agony of Acéphie and Chouchou was, in a sense, "modal" suffering. In Haiti, AIDS and political violence are two leading causes of death among young adults. These afflictions were not the result of accident or of force majeure; they were the consequence, direct or indirect, of human agency. When the

Artibonite Valley was flooded, depriving families like the Josephs of their land, a human decision was behind it; when the Haitian army was endowed with money and unfettered power, human decisions were behind that, too. In fact, some of the same decisionmakers may have been involved in both cases.

If bureaucrats and soldiers seemed to have unconstrained sway over the lives of the rural poor, the agency of Acéphie and Chouchou was, correspondingly, curbed at every turn. These grim biographies suggest that the social and economic forces that have helped to shape the AIDS epidemic are, in every sense, the same forces that led to Chouchou's death and to the larger repression in which it was eclipsed. What is more, both were "at risk" of such a fate long before they met the soldiers who altered their destinies. They were both, from the outset, victims of structural violence.

While certain kinds of suffering are readily observable—and the subject of countless films, novels, and poems—structural violence all too often defeats those who would describe it. There are at least three reasons why this is so. First, there is the "exoticization" of suffering as lurid as that endured by Acéphie and Chouchou. The suffering of individuals whose lives and struggles recall our own tends to move us; the suffering of those who are distanced, whether by geography, gender, "race," or culture, is sometimes less affecting.

Second, there is the sheer weight of the suffering, which makes it all the more difficult to render: "Knowledge of suffering cannot be conveyed in pure facts and figures, reportings that objectify the suffering of countless persons. The horror of suffering is not only its immensity but the faces of the anonymous victims who have little voice, let alone rights, in history."[7]

Third, the dynamics and distribution of suffering are still poorly understood. Physicians, when fortunate, can alleviate the suffering of the sick. But explaining its distribution requires more minds, more resources. Case studies of individuals reveal suffering, they tell us what happens to one or many people; but to explain suffering, one must embed individual biography in the larger matrix of culture, history, and political economy.

In short, it is one thing to make sense of extreme suffering—a universal activity, surely—and quite another to explain it. Life experiences such as those of Acéphie and Chouchou—who as

Haitians living in poverty shared similar social conditions—must be embedded in ethnography if their representativeness is to be understood. These local understandings are to be embedded, in turn, in the larger-scale historical system of which the fieldwork site is a part.[8] The social and economic forces that dictate life choices in Haiti's Central Plateau affect many millions of individuals, and it is in the context of these global forces that the suffering of individuals receives its appropriate context of interpretation.

Similar insights are central to liberation theology, which takes the suffering of the poor as its central problematic. In *The Praxis of Suffering,* Rebecca Chopp notes that, "In a variety of forms, liberation theology speaks with those who, through their suffering, call into question the meaning and truth of human history."[9] Unlike most previous theologies, and unlike much modern philosophy, liberation theology has attempted to use social analysis to both explain and deplore human suffering. Its key texts bring into relief not merely the suffering of the wretched of the earth, but also the forces that promote that suffering. The theologian Leonardo Boff, in commenting on one of these texts, notes that it "moves immediately to the structural analysis of these forces and denounces the systems, structures, and mechanisms that 'create a situation where the rich get richer at the expense of the poor, who get even poorer.'"[10]

In short, few liberation theologians engage in reflection on suffering without attempting to understand its mechanisms. Theirs is a theology that underlines connections. Robert McAfee Brown has these connections and also the poor in mind when, paraphrasing the Uruguayan Jesuit Juan Luis Segundo, he observes that "the world that is satisfying to us is the same world that is utterly devastating to them."[11]

MULTIAXIAL MODELS OF SUFFERING

"Events of massive, public suffering defy quantitative analysis. How can one really understand statistics citing the death of six million Jews or graphs of third-world starvation? Do numbers really reveal the agony, the interruption, the questions that these victims put to the meaning and nature of our individual lives and life as a whole?"

—*Rebecca Chopp*
The Praxis of Suffering

How might we discern the nature of structural violence and explore its contribution to human suffering? Can we devise an analytic model, one with explanatory and predictive power, for understanding suffering in a global context? Some would argue that this task, though daunting, is both urgent and feasible. Our cursory examination of AIDS and political violence in Haiti suggests that analysis must, first, be *geographically broad*. As noted, the world as we know it is becoming increasingly interconnected. A corollary of this belief is that extreme suffering—especially when on a grand scale, as in genocide—is seldom divorced from the actions of the powerful.[12] The analysis must also be *historically deep*—not merely deep enough to remind us of events and decisions such as those which deprived Acéphie of her land and founded the Haitian military, but deep enough to remember that modern-day Haitians are the descendants of a people kidnapped from Africa in order to provide us with sugar, coffee, and cotton and to enrich a few in a mercantilist economy.

Factors including gender, ethnicity ("race"), and socioeconomic status may each be shown to play a role in rendering individuals and groups vulnerable to extreme human suffering. But in most settings these factors have limited explanatory power. *Simultaneous* consideration of various social "axes" is imperative in efforts to discern a political economy of brutality. Furthermore, such social factors are differentially weighted in different settings and at different times, as even brief consideration of their contributions to extreme suffering suggests.

The Axis of Gender

Acéphie Joseph and Chouchou Louis shared, as noted, a similar social status, and each died after contact with the Haitian military. But gender helps to explain why Acéphie died of AIDS whereas Chouchou died from torture. Gender inequality also helps to explain why the suffering of Acéphie is much more commonplace than that of Chouchou. Throughout the world, women are confronted with sexism, an ideology that designates them as inferior to men. When, in 1974, a group of feminist anthropologists surveyed the status of women living in several disparate settings, they found that, in every society studied, men dominated political, legal, and economic institutions to varying degrees; in no culture was the status of women genuinely coordinate, much less superior, to that of men.[13] This power differential has meant that women's rights may be violated in innumerable ways. Although male victims are clearly preponderant in studies of torture, the much more common crimes of domestic violence and rape are almost exclusively endured by females. In the United States, the number of such aggressions is staggering. When sexual assaults by both intimates and strangers are considered, "one in four women has been the victim of a completed rape and one in four women has been physically battered, according to the results of recent community-based studies."[14]

In most settings, however, gender alone does not define risk for such assaults on dignity. It is *poor* women who bear the brunt of these assaults.[15] This is true not only of domestic violence and rape, but also of AIDS and its distribution, as anthropologist Martha Ward points out:

> The collection of statistics by ethnicity rather than by socio-economic status obscures the fact that the majority of women with AIDS in the United States are poor. Women are at risk for HIV not because they are African-American or speak Spanish; women are at risk because poverty is the primary and determining condition of their lives.[16]

Similarly, only women can experience maternal mortality, a cause of anguish around the world. More than half a million women die each year in childbirth, but not all women are at increased risk of adverse outcomes in pregnancy. In 1985, the World Health Organization estimated that maternal mortality is, on average, approximately 150 times higher in developing countries than in developed nations. In Haiti, where maternal mortality is as high as fourteen hundred deaths per one hundred thousand live births—almost five hundred times higher than in the wealthy countries—these deaths are almost all registered among the poor.[17]

The Axis of "Race" or Ethnicity

The idea of race, which is considered to be a biologically insignificant term, has enormous social currency. Racial classifications have been used to deprive certain groups of basic rights, and therefore have an important place in considerations of human suffering. In South Africa, for years a living laboratory for the study of the long-term effects of racism, epidemiologists report that the infant mortality rate among blacks may be as much as ten times higher than among whites. For South African blacks, the proximate cause of increased rates of morbidity and mortality is lack of access to resources: "*Poverty* remains the primary cause of the prevalence of many diseases and widespread hunger and malnutrition among black South Africans."[18] And social inequality is seen in the uneven distribution of poverty.

Significant mortality differentials between blacks and whites are also registered in the United States, which shares with South Africa the distinction of being the only two industrialized countries failing to record mortality data by socioeconomic status. In the United States, in 1988, life expectancy at birth was 75.5 years for whites and 69.5 years for blacks. Accordingly, there has been a certain amount of discussion about race differentials in mortality, but public health expert Vicente Navarro recently complained about the "deafening silence" on the topic of class differentials in mortality in the United States, where "race is used as a *substitute* for class." But in 1986, on "one of the few occasions that the US government collected information on mortality rates (for heart and cerebrovascular disease) by class, the results showed that, by whatever indicators of class one might choose (level of education, income, or occupation), mortality rates are related to social class."[19] Indeed, for the major causes of death (heart disease and cerebrovascular disease), class differentials were significantly larger than race differentials. "The growing mortality differentials between whites and blacks," Navarro concludes, "cannot be understood by looking only at race; they are part and parcel of larger mortality differentials—class differentials."[20] The sociologist William Julius Wilson made a similar point in his landmark study, *The Declining Significance of Race*. He argues that "trained and educated blacks, like trained and educated whites, will continue to enjoy the advantages and privileges of their class status."[21] It is the black poor—and an analysis of the mechanisms of their impoverishment—that are being left out.

The Conflation of Structural Violence and Cultural Difference

Awareness of cultural differences has long complicated discussions of human suffering. Some anthropologists have argued that what seem to outside observers to be obvious assaults on dignity may in fact be long-standing cultural institutions highly valued by a society. Often-cited examples range from female circumcision in the Sudan to head-hunting in the Philippines. Such discussions are invariably linked to the concept of cultural relativism, which has a long and checkered history in anthropology. Is every culture a law unto itself and a law unto nothing other than itself? In recent decades, confidence in reflex cultural relativism faltered as anthropologists turned their attention to "complex societies" characterized by extremely inegalitarian social structures. Many found themselves unwilling to condone social inequity merely because it was buttressed by cultural beliefs, no matter how ancient. Cultural relativism was also questioned as a part of a broader critique of anthropology by citizens of the former colonies.[22]

But this rethinking has not yet eroded a tendency, registered in many of the social sciences but perhaps particularly in anthropology, to confuse structural violence with cultural difference. Many are the ethnographies in which poverty and inequality, the end results of a long process of impoverishment, are conflated with "otherness." Very often, such myopia is not really a question of motives, but rather, as Talal Asad has suggested, our "mode of perceiving and objectifying alien societies."[23] Part of the problem may be the ways in which the term "culture" is used. "The idea of culture," explains one authority approvingly in a book on the subject, "places the researcher in a position of equality with his subjects: each 'belongs to a culture.'"[24] The tragedy, of course, is that this equality, however comforting to the researcher, is entirely illusory. Anthropology has usually "studied down" steep gradients of power.

Such illusions suggest an important means by which other misreadings—most notably the conflation of poverty and cultural difference—are sustained. They suggest that the anthropologist and "his" subject, being *from* different cultures, are *of* different worlds and *of* different times.[25] These sorts of misreadings, innocent enough within academia, are finding a more insidious utility within elite culture, which is becoming increasingly *transnational.* Concepts of cultural relativism, and even arguments to reinstate the dignity of different cultures and "races," have been easily assimilated by some of the very agencies that perpetuate extreme suffering.[26] Abuses of cultural concepts are particularly insidious in discussions of suffering in general and of human rights abuses more specifically: cultural difference is one of several forms of essentialism used to explain away assaults on dignity and suffering in general. Practices, including torture, are said to be "in their culture" or "in their nature"—"their" designating either the victims or the perpetrators, or both, as may be expedient.

Such analytic abuses are rarely questioned, even though systemic studies of extreme suffering would suggest that the concept of culture should have an increasingly limited role in explaining the *distribution* of misery. The interpretation of—and justifications for—suffering is usually patterned along cultural lines, but this, I would argue, is another question.

STRUCTURAL VIOLENCE AND EXTREME SUFFERING

> *At night I listen to their phantoms*
> *shouting in my ear*
> *shaking me out of lethargy*
> *issuing me commands*
> *I think of their tattered lives*
> *of their feverish hands*
> *reaching out to seize ours.*
> *It's not that they're begging*
> *they're demanding*
> *they've earned the right to order us*
> *to break up our sleep*
> *to come awake*
> *to shake off once and for all*
> *this lassitude.*

> —Claribel Alegría
> *"Visitas Nocturnas"*

Any distinguishing characteristic, whether social or biological, can serve as pretext for discrimination, and thus as a cause of suffering. In discussing each of the above factors, however, it is clear that no single axis can fully define increased risk for extreme human suffering. Efforts to attribute explanatory efficacy to one variable lead to immodest claims of causality, for wealth and power have often protected individual women, gays, and ethnic minorities from the suffering and adverse outcomes associated with assaults on dignity. Similarly, poverty can often efface the "protective" effects of status based on gender, race, or sexual orientation. Leonardo Boff and Clodovis Boff, writing from Brazil, insist on the primacy of the economic:

> We have to observe that the socioeconomically oppressed (the poor) do not simply exist *alongside* other oppressed groups, such as blacks, indigenous peoples, women—to take the three major categories in the Third World. No, the "class-oppressed"—the socioeconomically poor—are the infrastructural expression of the process of oppression. The other groups represent "superstructural" expressions of oppression and because of this are deeply conditioned by the infrastructural. It is one thing to be a black taxi-driver, quite another to be a black football idol; it is one thing to be a woman working as a domestic servant, quite another to be the first lady of the land; it is one thing to be an Amerindian thrown off your land, quite another to be an Amerindian owning your own farm.[27]

None of this is to deny the ill effects of sexism or racism, even in the wealthy countries of North America and Europe. The point is merely to call for more fine-grained and systemic analyses of power and privilege in discussions of who is likely to suffer and in what ways.

The capacity to suffer is, clearly, part of being human. But not all suffering is equal, in spite of pernicious and often self-serving identity politics that suggest otherwise. One of the unfortunate sequelae of identity politics has been the obscuring of structural violence, which metes out injuries of vastly different severity. Careful assessment of severity is important, at least to physicians, who must practice triage and referral daily. What suffering needs to be taken care of first and with what resources? It *is* possible to speak of extreme human suffering, and an inordinate share of this sort of pain is currently endured by those living in poverty. Take, for example, illness and premature death, in many places in the world the leading cause of extreme suffering. In a striking departure from previous, staid reports, the World Health Organization now acknowledges that poverty is the world's greatest killer: "Poverty wields its destructive influence at every stage of human life, from the moment of conception to the grave. It conspires with the most deadly and painful diseases to bring a wretched existence to all those who suffer from it."[28]

As the twentieth century draws to a close, the world's poor are the chief victims of structural violence—a violence which has thus far defied the analysis of many seeking to understand the nature and distribution of extreme suffering. Why might this be so? One answer is that the poor are not only more likely to suffer, they are also more likely to have their suffering silenced. As Chilean theologian Pablo Richard, noting the fall of the Berlin Wall, has warned, "We are aware that another gigantic wall is being constructed in the Third World, to hide the reality of the poor majorities. A wall between the rich and poor is being built, so that poverty does not annoy the powerful and the poor are obliged to die in the silence of history."[29]

The task at hand, if this silence is to be broken, is to identify the forces conspiring to promote suffering, with the understanding that these will be differentially weighted in different settings. In so doing, we stand a chance to discern the *forces motrices* of extreme suffering. A sound analytic purchase on the dynamics and distribution of such affliction is, perhaps, a prerequisite to preventing or, at least, assuaging it. Then, at last, there may be hope of finding a balm in Gilead.[30]

ACKNOWLEDGMENTS

I have the usual debts to faithful readers such as Haun Saussy and Jim Yong Kim, but wish also to acknowledge the constructive criticisms of this issue's editors and of Didi Bertrand, Ophelia Dahl, Johanna Daily, Jonathan Mann, Joe Rhatigan, Joyce Bendremer, and Vinh Kim Nguyen.

ENDNOTES

[1]Jean Weise, "The Interaction of Western and Indigenous Medicine in Haiti in Regard to Tuberculosis," Ph.D. Dissertation, Department of Anthropology, University of North Carolina at Chapel Hill, 1971.

[2]The names of the Haitians cited here have been changed, as have the names of their home villages.

[3]For a recent review of the effects of inegalitarian social structures on the health of wealthier populations, see Michael Marmot, "Social Differentials in Health Within and Between Populations," *Dædalus* 123 (4) (Fall 1994): 197–216.

[4]Some would argue that the relationship between individual agency and supraindividual structures forms the central problematic of contemporary social theory. I have tried, in this essay, to avoid what Pierre Bourdieu has termed "the absurd opposition between individual and society," and I acknowledge the influence of Bourdieu, who has contributed enormously to the debate on structure and agency. For a concise statement of his (often revised) views on this subject, see Pierre Bourdieu, *In Other Words: Essays Towards a Reflexive Sociology* (Cambridge: Polity, 1990). That a supple and fundamentally non-deterministic model of agency would have such a deterministic—and pessimistic—"feel" is largely a reflection of my topic, suffering, and my fieldwork site.

[5]Paul Farmer, "Culture, Poverty, and the Dynamics of HIV Transmission in Rural Haiti," in Han ten Brummelhuis and Gilbert Herdt, eds., *Culture and Sexual Risk: Anthropological Perspectives on AIDS* (New York: Gordon and Breach, 1995), 3–28.

[6]For an overview of the human rights situation during the recent coup, see Americas Watch and the National Coalition for Haitian Refugees, *Silencing a People: The Destruction of Civil Society in Haiti* (New York: Human Rights Watch, 1993) and William O'Neill, "The Roots of Human Rights Violations in Haiti," *Georgetown Immigration Law Journal* 7 (1) (1993): 87–117. I have reviewed these and other reports in Paul Farmer, *The Uses of Haiti* (Monroe, Maine: Common Courage, 1994).

[7]Rebecca Chopp, *The Praxis of Suffering* (Maryknoll, N.Y.: Orbis, 1986), 2.

[8]This argument is made at greater length in "AIDS and the Anthropology of Suffering," in Paul Farmer, *AIDS and Accusation: Haiti and the Geography of Blame* (Berkeley, Calif.: University of California Press, 1992). The term "historical system" is used following Immanuel Wallerstein, who for many years has argued that even the most far-flung locales—Haiti's Central Plateau, for example—are part of the same social and economic nexus: "by the late nineteenth century, for the first time ever, there existed only one historical system on the globe. We are still in that situation today." See Immanuel Wallerstein, "World-Systems Analysis," in *Social Theory Today,* ed. Anthony Giddens and Jonathan Turner (Stanford, Calif.: Stanford University Press, 1985), 318. See also Immanuel Wallerstein, *The Modern World-System: Capitalist Agriculture and the Origins of the European World-Economy in the Sixteenth Century* (San Diego, Calif.: Academic Press, 1974). The weakness of these analyses is, of course, their extreme divorce from personal experience.

[9]Chopp, *The Praxis of Suffering,* 2. See also the works of Gustavo Gutiérrez, who has written a great deal about the meaning of suffering in the twentieth century: for example Gustavo Gutiérrez, *A Theology of Liberation* (Maryknoll, N.Y.: Orbis, 1973) and Gustavo Gutiérrez, *The Power of the Poor in History* (Maryknoll, N.Y.: Orbis, 1983). For anthropological studies of liberation theology in social context, see the ethnographies by John Burdick, *Looking for God*

in Brazil (Berkeley, Calif.: University of California Press, 1993) and Roger Lancaster, *Thanks to God and the Revolution* (New York: Columbia University Press, 1988).

[10]From the Puebla document, cited in Paul Farmer, "Medicine and Social Justice: Insights from Liberation Theology," *America* 173 (2) (1995): 14.

[11]Robert McAfee Brown, *Liberation Theology: An Introductory Guide* (Louisville, Ky.: Westminster, 1993), 44.

[12]The political economy of genocide is explored by Christopher Simpson in *The Splendid Blond Beast: Money, Law, and Genocide in the Twentieth Century* (New York: Grove Press, 1993). See also Gotz Aly, Peter Chroust, and Christian Pross, *Cleansing the Fatherland: Nazi Medicine and Racial Hygiene* (Baltimore, Md.: Johns Hopkins University Press, 1994). As regards the transnational political economy of human rights abuses, see the two-volume study by Noam Chomsky and Edward S. Herman, *The Washington Connection and Third World Fascism* and *After the Cataclysm* (Boston, Mass.: South End Press, 1979).

[13]Michelle Rosaldo and Louise Lamphere, eds., *Women, Culture, and Society* (Stanford, Calif.: Stanford University Press, 1974).

[14]Mary Koss, Paul Koss, and Joy Woodruff, "Deleterious Effects of Criminal Victimization on Women's Health and Medical Utilization," *Archives of Internal Medicine* 151 (1991): 342.

[15]It is important to note, however, that upper class/caste women are in many societies also subject to laws that virtually efface marital rape. The study by Koss, Koss, and Woodruff includes this crime with other forms of criminal victimization, but it is only through community-based surveys that such information is collected.

[16]Martha Ward, "A Different Disease: HIV/AIDS and Health Care for Women in Poverty," *Culture, Medicine and Psychiatry* 17 (4) (1993): 414.

[17]World Health Organization, "Maternal Mortality: Helping Women Off the Road to Death," *WHO Chronicle* 40 (1985): 175–83.

[18]Elena Nightingale, Kari Hannibal, Jack Geiger, Lawrence Hartmann, Robert Lawrence, and Jeanne Spurlock, "Apartheid Medicine: Health and Human Rights in South Africa," *Journal of the American Medical Association* 264 (16) (1990): 2098. The italics are mine. For a more in-depth account, and a more complicated view of the mechanisms by which apartheid and the South African economy are related to disease causation, see Randall Packard, *White Plague, Black Labor: Tuberculosis and the Political Economy of Health and Disease in South Africa* (Berkeley, Calif.: University of California Press, 1989).

[19]Vicente Navarro, "Race or Class versus Race and Class: Mortality Differentials in the United States," *The Lancet* 336 (1990): 1238.

[20]Ibid., 1240.

[21]William Julius Wilson, *The Declining Significance of Race: Blacks and Changing American Institutions*, 2nd ed. (Chicago, Ill.: University of Chicago Press, 1980), 178.

[22]See the studies by Elvin Hatch, *Culture and Morality: The Relativity of Values in Anthropology* (New York: Columbia University Press, 1983), and by Ernest Gellner, *Relativism and the Social Sciences* (Cambridge: Cambridge University Press, 1985).

[23]Talal Asad, ed., *Anthropology and the Colonial Encounter* (London: Ithaca Press, 1975), 17.

[24]Roy Wagner, *The Invention of Culture* (Englewood Cliffs, N.J.: Prentice-Hall, 1975), 2.

[25]Johannes Fabian has argued that this "denial of coevalness" is much ingrained in our discipline. Not to be dismissed as an issue of style, such a denial contributes to the blindness of the anthropologist: "Either he submits to the condition of coevalness and produces ethnographic knowledge, or he deludes himself into temporal distance and misses the object of his search." See Johannes Fabian, *Time and the Other: How Anthropology Makes its Object* (New York: Columbia University Press, 1983). See also the compelling essay by Orin Starn, "Missing the Revolution: Anthropologists and the War in Peru," in George Marcus, ed., *Rereading Cultural Anthropology* (Durham, N.C.: Duke University Press, 1992), 152–80.

[26]For a penetrating examination of the appropriation of identity politics by big business, see the essay by L. A. Kauffman, "The Diversity Game," *The Village Voice*, 31 August 1993.

[27]Leonardo Boff and Clodovis Boff, *Introducing Liberation Theology* (Maryknoll, N.Y.: Orbis Books, 1987), 29.

[28]World Health Organization, *Bridging the Gaps* (Geneva: World Health Organization, 1995), 5.

[29]Cited by Jack Nelson-Pallmeyer, *Brave New World Order: Must We Pledge Allegiance?* (Maryknoll, N.Y.: Orbis, 1992), 14.

Talal Asad

On Torture, or Cruel, Inhuman, and Degrading Treatment

THIS ESSAY DISCUSSES THE MODERN CONCEPTION of "cruelty," in particular as represented in Article 5 of the *Universal Declaration of Human Rights:* "No one shall be subjected to torture or to cruel, inhuman or degrading treatment or punishment." In this statement, the adjectives qualifying "treatment or punishment" seem to indicate forms of behavior that, if not quite equivalent to "torture," at least have a close affinity with it.

Moral and legal judgments that derive from this rule have an interesting history in the West, to which my discussion will refer. In this essay, I advance the thesis that the universal rules enshrined in the Declaration cover a wide range of qualitatively different kinds of behavior. More precisely, my argument contains four points. First, the modern history of "torture" is not only a record of the progressive prohibition of cruel, inhuman, and degrading practices. It is also part of a more complex story of the modern secular concept of what it means to be truly human. Second, although the phrase "torture or cruel, inhuman, or degrading treatment" serves today as a cross-cultural criterion for making moral and legal judgments about pain and suffering, it nevertheless derives much of its operative sense historically and culturally. My third point is linked to the first two: the new ways of conceptualizing *suffering* (which include the categories "mental torture" and "degrading treatment") and *sufferer* (a term that now refers also to nonhumans, and even to the natural environment) are increasingly universal in scope but particular in prescriptive content. The final point is that the modern dedication to eliminating pain and suffering often conflicts with other commitments and values: the right of individuals to choose and the duty of the state to maintain its interests.

Talal Asad is Professor of Anthropology at Johns Hopkins University.

Together, these four points underscore the unstable character of a central category deployed in modern Western society. The instability relates, in brief, to the fact that the ideas of torture, cruelty, inhumanity, and degrading treatment are intended to measure what are often incommensurable standards of behavior. In addition, they are applied in particular cases in a contradictory fashion.

I do not argue that there can be no such thing as cruelty. I am merely skeptical about *the universalist discourses* that have been generated around it. But my skepticism is intellectual, not moral. This paper is not concerned with attacking the reforms inspired by the United Nations condemnation of torture or cruel, inhuman, and degrading treatment. Rather, it focuses primarily on the way Western discourses about cruelty are constructed and the ways that the idea of torture can overlap with and substitute for ideas of cruel, inhuman, and degrading treatment. In my view, such inquiries are necessary if we seek to clarify our transcultural judgments.

TWO HISTORIES OF TORTURE

It is useful to first consider two books that together demonstrate very different ways of writing histories of cruelty. The first, by G. R. Scott, represents physical cruelty as a feature of barbaric societies—i.e., societies that haven't yet been humanized. The second, by Darius M. Rejali, distinguishes between two kinds of physical cruelty, one appropriate to premodern societies and the other to modern societies, and describes that difference in the context of contemporary Iran.

Scott was a Fellow of several British learned societies, including the Royal Anthropological Institute. His *History of Torture* is perhaps the first modern story of its kind.[1] It deals at length with "savage and primitive races," ancient and early modern European peoples, and Asian civilizations (China, Japan, and India). On the one hand, it tells a story of punishments now largely discontinued or suppressed; on the other, it speaks of motives for inflicting suffering that are deep-rooted and pervasive. Scott's indebtedness to Krafft-Ebing's ideas is evident not only in explicit form in his chapters on sadism and masochism but also in the general evolutionary scheme he employs, according to which the primitive urge to inflict pain remains a latent possibility (sometimes realized) in civilized society.

Scott is somewhat unusual for his time in including the mistreatment of animals in his account of torture and in describing their plight as a consequence of the nonrecognition of rights. Like other moderns, he sees the extension of rights to be crucial for the elimination of cruelty. But in the course of arguing this thesis, he hits on a profound and disturbing ambiguity. It is not entirely clear whether he thinks that human cruelty is merely an instance of *bestial* cruelty—i.e., a working out of the supposedly universal instinct of stronger animals to hunt or attack the weaker—or whether he believes that human cruelty is unique, not a characteristic of animal behavior at all, and that everyday human ruthlessness toward animals is essential for justifying the persecution of vulnerable people (defeated enemies, uninitiated children, and so on) on the grounds that they are *not fully human.* In either case, Scott disturbs liberal ideas of what it is to be truly human: either humans are essentially no different from other animals, or they are different by virtue of their unique capacity for cruelty.

It is worth noting that the instances of physical pain Scott describes as "torture" belong sometimes to the category of involuntary submission to punishment and sometimes to the category that includes the practices of personal discipline (e.g., rituals of endurance, asceticism). He makes no distinction between the two: pain is regarded as an isolable experience, to be condemned for what it is.

In the encounter between "savage races" and modern Euro-Americans, Scott has no doubt that "torture" is something the former do to the latter—perhaps because torture is synonymous with "barbarity." At any rate, the sufferings inflicted on Native Americans by white settlers and the expanding United States have no place in his history of torture.

This is not to say that Scott asserts torture to be entirely absent in the modern state. On the contrary, he is quite explicit about its use by the police to secure confessions ("the third degree"). His position is that the story of modernity is in part a story of the progressive elimination of all morally shocking social behavior—including what is now described in international law as "cruel, inhuman or degrading treatment or punishment." Scott does not claim that this intention has been fully realized, only that progress has been made. In this story of progress, he tells us, the state's definition and defense of rights are the most effective protection against cruelty.

In his important book *Torture and Modernity,* the Iranian political scientist Darius Rejali makes the interesting argument that, far from being a barbaric survival in the modern state, as Scott's story suggests, torture is in fact integral to the modern state.[2] Although he classifies torture into two types, modern and premodern, he shares with Scott the view that the term "torture" has a fixed referent. More precisely, both authors assume that to speak of torture is to refer to a practice in which the agent *forcibly* inflicts pain on another, regardless of the place the practice occupies within a larger moral economy.

Rejali offers a sophisticated account of the role of political punishments in Iran both before and after the inception of modernization in that country. Modern torture, he argues, is a form of physical suffering that is an inseparable part of a disciplinary society. In Iran the practice of torture is as essential to the Islamic Republic today as it was to the Pahlevi regime the republic replaced. Both in their own way are modern disciplinary societies.

Rejali believes that his book refutes what Foucault has to say about torture in *Discipline and Punish.*[3] Rejali maintains that torture does not give way to discipline in modern society, as Foucault claims, but persists in a major way. This belief, however, arises from a misreading of Foucault, whose central concern is not with torture but with power, and consequently with a contrast between sovereign power (which needs to exhibit itself publicly) and disciplinary power (which works through the normalization of everyday behavior).

Public rituals of torture are no longer deemed necessary to the maintenance of sovereign power. (Whether they were in fact functionally necessary to the maintenance of "social order" is, of course, another question.) But Foucault's thesis about disciplinary power is not subverted by evidence of *surreptitious* torture in the modern state. On the contrary, precisely because torture carried out in secret is said to be intimately connected with the extraction of information, it is an aspect of policing. Policing is a governmental activity directed at defending a fundamental "interest of society": the ordinary and extraordinary security of the state and its citizens. It is also an institution in which knowledge and power depend upon each other. Much of the activity of policing—and this point is curiously neglected by Rejali—circulates in secret.

Modern torture as part of policing is typically secret partly because inflicting physical pain on a prisoner to extract information, or for any purpose whatever, is "uncivilized" and therefore illegal. It is also secret because policing agents do not wish to advertise everything they learn from tortured prisoners. After all, the effectiveness of certain kinds of disciplinary knowledge depends upon its secrecy. The secret character of knowledge acquired in policing therefore relates both to the uncertainty of outside critics as to whether, and if so how often, something illegal has been done by a bureaucratic power to obtain that knowledge ("torture is intolerable in a civilized society") and also to how, when, and where law-enforcing power chooses to act once it possesses the secret information ("every society must protect itself against criminal conspiracies").

Rejali's definition of torture as "sanguinary violence condoned by public authorities" slips uneasily between the legitimate and public practice of classic torture, on the one hand, and, on the other hand, the *secret* (because "uncivilized") character of police torture in modernizing states like Iran. His fuller argument doesn't address this difference. Modern torture, he insists at length, is integral to what Foucault called disciplinary society. It is, if not identical to discipline, at least very close to it.

Rejali's book contains valuable insights relating to the brutalizing aspect of the process of modernization. Two objections might be made to his argument, however. First, his main example (twentieth-century Iran) represents what many readers will identify as a "modernizing" rather than a "fully modern" society. Whether all the transformations in Iran in the period covered by Rejali's book truly represent modernization in the sense of moral improvement is—these readers will say—an open question, but shocking evidence of blatant torture in that country does not prove that torture is integral to modernity. Rejali's argument at this point would have been stronger if he had referred to a modern society, such as Nazi Germany, rather than a society merely on the way to being modernized.[4] Although Nazi Germany was a notoriously *illiberal* state, it was certainly no less modern than any other.

The other objection is this: Rejali does not explain why, unlike discipline, *modern* state use of torture requires the rhetoric of denial. The brief answer to this question, surely, is that a new sensibility now exists regarding physical pain. Although it occurs frequently enough in our time, the modern conscience regards the inflicting of pain without "good reason" (to perform a medical operation, for instance) as reprehensible and therefore as an object of moral condemnation. It is this attitude toward pain that helps define the modern notion of cruelty.

The modern conscience is also a secular conscience, a category that subsumes what we now know as modern religion. Christianity, which was traditionally rooted in the doctrine of Christ's *passion*, consequently finds it difficult to make good sense of suffering today. Modern theologians have begun to concede that pain is essentially and entirely negative. "The secularist challenge," writes a modern Catholic theologian,

> even though separating many aspects of life from the religious field, brings with it a more sound, interpretive equilibrium; the natural phenomena, even though sometimes difficult to understand, have their cause and roots in processes that can and must be recognized. It is man's job, therefore, to enter into this cognitive analysis of the meaning of suffering, in order to be able to affront and conquer it. . . . Through his works, even before his words, Jesus of Nazareth proclaimed the goodness of life and of health, as the image of salvation. For Him pain is negativeness.[5]

The writer of this passage is clearly thinking of disease, but since pain can also be a consequence of human intention, it follows that such pain should be eliminated from the world of human interaction—even from religious disciplines and from the enactment of martyrdom, where it once had an effective and honored place. The secular Christian must now abjure passion and choose action. Pain is not merely negativeness. It is, literally, a scandal.

ABOLISHING TORTURE

Why has the infliction of physical pain now become scandalous? A well-known part of the answer is this progressivist story: two centuries ago, critics of torture such as Beccaria and Voltaire recognized how inhuman it was and how unreliable as a way of ascertaining the truth in a trial. Thus they saw and articulated what others before them had (unaccountably) failed to see. Their powerful case against judicial torture shocked Enlightenment rulers into abolishing it. The theme of torture's intolerable cruelty emerged more clearly because the pain inflicted in judicial torture was declared to be *gratuitous*. Pain inflicted on prisoners to make them confess was immoral, it was argued, particularly because it was grossly *inefficient* in identifying their guilt or innocence.[6] (Enlightenment reformers didn't necessarily condemn physical punishment as such, because it involved considerations other than simple instrumental ones, especially ideas of justice. Eventually, however, the evolution of modern ideas of justice were to contribute to growing hostility to painful punishment.) But why was this gratuitous pain not condemned by critics earlier? What had prevented people from seeing the truth until the Enlightenment?

In his brilliant study *Torture and the Law of Proof,* John Langbein provides a partial explanation. He demonstrates that torture was proscribed when the Roman canon law of proof—which required either confession or the testimony of two eyewitnesses to convict—declined in force in the seventeenth century. Increasing resort to circumstantial evidence secured convictions more easily and speedily. The abolition of judicial torture was thus, in effect, the moral condemnation and legal proscription of an extremely cumbersome and lengthy procedure that was coming to be regarded as more or less redundant. Langbein implies that the moral truth about judicial torture was linked to the prior construction of a new concept of legal truth.[7]

When torture became the object of vigorous polemic in the eighteenth century, Jeremy Bentham concluded that the pain of torture was sometimes easier to justify than the suffering inflicted in the name of punishment. In the course of this justification he maintained, for example, that courts of law resorting to imprisonment in cases of contempt might find that applying physical pain, or even threatening to apply it, would secure obedience in a way "less penal" than prison:

A man may have been lingering in prison for a month or two before he would make answer to a question which at the worst with one stroke of the rack, and therefore almost always with only knowing that he might be made to suffer the rack, he would have answered in a moment; just as a man will linger on a Month with the Toothach [*sic*] which he might have saved himself from at the expense of a momentary pang.[8]

It is not Bentham's apparent refusal to distinguish between voluntary and involuntary subjection to pain that should be noted here. Rather, it is the idea that subjective experiences of pain can be objectively compared. This idea is crucial for the modern understanding of cruel, inhuman, and degrading treatment in a cross-cultural context, although liberals today would strongly reject Bentham's view regarding the occasional preferability of torture to imprisonment. It is precisely some notion of comparability in suffering that makes of long years in prison (including solitary confinement) a "humane" punishment and of flogging an "inhumane" one, even though the *experiences* of imprisonment and flogging are qualitatively quite different.

In an interesting passage in *Discipline and Punish,* Foucault notes that in the nineteenth century imprisonment was compared favorably to other forms of legal punishment mainly because it was regarded as the most egalitarian.[9] This was a consequence of the philosophical doctrine that *freedom was the natural human condition.* Penal reformers reasoned that since the desire for liberty was implanted equally in every individual, depriving individuals of their liberty must be a way of striking at them equally—that is, regardless of their social status or physical constitution. Just as fines were easier for the rich to pay, physical pain was borne more easily by the sturdy and strong. No form of punishment accorded so precisely with our *essential humanity,* therefore, as imprisonment did. That legal incarceration was considered to be equitable contributed to the sense that physical punishment was gratuitous. For this reason, although modern liberals must disagree with the conclusion Bentham reached about torture, they must approve of his endorsement of a quantitative comparison of disparate kinds of suffering. It is not difficult to see how the utilitarian calculus of pleasure and pain has come to be central to cross-cultural judgment in modern thought and practice. By a reductive operation, the idea of a calculus has facilitated the comparative judgment of what would otherwise remain incommensurable qualities.[10]

HUMANIZING THE WORLD

The historical process of constructing a humane society, it is said, has aimed at eliminating cruelties. Thus it has often been observed that European rule in colonial countries, although not itself democratic, brought about moral improvements in behavior—i.e., the abandonment of practices that offend against the human.

Major instruments in this transformation were modern legal, administrative, and educational practices. And a central category deployed in these practices was the modern category of customary law. "Of all the restrictions upon the application of customary laws during the colonial period," writes James Read, "the test of repugnancy 'to justice or morality' was potentially the most sweeping: for customary laws could hardly be repugnant to the traditional sense of justice or morality of the community which still accepted them, and it is therefore clear that the justice or morality of the colonial power was to provide the standard to be applied." Read points out that the phrase "repugnant to justice and morality" does not have a precise legal meaning and that early legislation in the colonies sometimes employed other expressions, such as "not opposed to natural morality and humanity," to perform the same revolutionary work.[11]

But moral and social progress in those countries has been uneven. Although Europeans tried to suppress cruel practices and forms of suffering that were previously taken for granted in the non-European world by making the practitioners legally culpable, the suppression was not always completely successful. Today the struggle to eliminate social suffering is taken up by the United Nations. Or so the story goes.

I want to propose, however, that, in the attempt to outlaw customs the European rulers considered cruel, it was not concern with indigenous suffering that dominated the Europeans' thinking, but rather the desire to impose what they considered civilized standards of justice and humanity on a subject population—i.e., the desire to create new human subjects.[12] The anguish of subjects compelled under threat of punishment to abandon traditional practices—now legally branded as "repugnant to justice and morality" or as "opposed to natural morality and humanity," or even sometimes as "backward and childish"—could not therefore play a decisive part in the discourse of colonial reformers. On the contrary, as Lord Cromer put it with reference to the misery created among the Egyptian peasantry by legal reforms under British rule: "Civilisation must, unfortunately, have its victims." [13] In the process of learning to be "fully human," only some kinds of suffering were seen as an affront to humanity, and their elimination sought. These types of suffering were distinguished from suffering that was *necessary* to the process of realizing one's humanity—i.e., pain that was adequate to its end, not *wasteful* pain.

Inhuman suffering, typically associated with barbaric behavior, was a morally insufferable condition for which someone was therefore responsible; those requiring it (themselves inhuman enough to cause it to be inflicted) must be made to desist and, if necessary, punished. That, at any rate, is the discourse of progressive reform. What individual colonial administrators actually felt, thought, or did is another (though not entirely unrelated) matter. Most experienced administrators were prepared to tolerate various "uncivilized" practices locally for reasons of expediency, but all were no doubt aware of the dominant progressivist discourse rooted in "civilized" societies.[14]

A recent unpublished paper by Nicholas Dirks offers a nice example of this discourse in late nineteenth-century British India. His account of the inquiry conducted by the colonial authorities into the ritual of hookswinging contains this sober judgment by the presiding British official: [15]

> It is, in my opinion, unnecessary at the end of the nineteenth century and, having regard to the level to which civilisation in India has attained, to consider the motives by which the performers themselves are actuated when taking part in hook swinging, walking through fire, and other barbarities. From their own moral standpoint, their motives may be good or they may be bad; they may indulge in self-torture in satisfaction of pious vows fervently made in all sincerity and for the most disinterested reasons; or they may indulge in it from the lowest motives of personal aggrandisement, whether for the alms they might receive or for the personal distinction and local éclat that it may bring them; but the question is whether public opinion in this country is not opposed to the *external acts* of the performers, as being in fact repugnant to the dictates of humanity and demoralizing to themselves and to all who may witness their performances. I am of the opinion that the voice of India most entitled to be listened to with

respect, that is to say, not only the voice of the advanced school that has received some of the advantages of western education and has been permeated with non-Oriental ideas, but also the voice of those whose views of life and propriety of conduct have been mainly derived from Asiatic philosophy, would gladly proclaim that the time had arrived for the Government in the interests of its people to effectively put down all degrading exhibitions of self-torture.[16]

The fact that the performers themselves declared that they felt no pain was irrelevant. So, too, was the plea that this was a religious rite. Such claims to difference were not acceptable. It was the offense given by the performance to a particular concept of being human that reduced qualitatively different kinds of behavior to a single standard.

Confirmation of this offensiveness was obtained by listening to *some* colonized voices only. This group included Indians who were directly westernized. And, of greater significance, it also included those who accepted a westernized exegesis of their Asiatic philosophy.[17] From the point of view of moral progress, the voices of those who took a reactionary position could not be heeded.

Clearly, in the cause of moral progress, there was suffering and there was suffering. What is interesting is not merely that some forms of suffering were to be taken more seriously than others but that "inhuman" suffering as opposed to "necessary" or "inevitable" suffering was regarded as being essentially *gratuitous* and therefore legally punishable. Pain endured in the movement toward becoming "fully human," on the other hand, was seen as necessary because social or moral reasons justified why it must be suffered. This view is of a piece with the post-Enlightenment concern to construct through judicial punishment the most efficient means of reforming offenders and of guarding society's interests.[18]

As the idea of progress became increasingly dominant in the affairs of Europe and the world, the need for measuring suffering was felt and responded to with greater sophistication.

REPRESENTING "TORTURE," ACTING
WITH DELIBERATE CRUELTY

Pain is not always regarded as insufferable in modern Euro-American societies. In warfare, sports, and psychological experimentation—as well as in the domain of sexual pleasure—the inflicting of physical suffering is actively practiced and also legally condoned. This makes for contradictions that are exploited in public debate. When transitive pain is described as "cruel and inhuman," it is often referred to as "torture." And torture itself is condemned by public opinion and prohibited by international law.

It is hardly surprising, therefore, that the many liberal-democratic governments that have employed torture have attempted to do so in secret.[19] Sometimes they have also been concerned to redefine legally the category of pain-producing treatment in an attempt to avoid the label "torture." For example:

> Torture is forbidden by Israeli law. Israeli authorities say that torture is not authorized or condoned in the occupied territories but acknowledge that abuses occur and state that they are investigated. In 1987 the Landau Judicial Commission specifically condemned "torture" but allowed for "moderate physical and psychological pressure" to be used to secure confessions and to obtain information; a classified annex to the report defining permissible pressure has never been made public.[20]

Other governments in the Middle East (for example, Egypt, Turkey, and Iran) have also condoned torture, and, unlike liberal-democratic governments, they have used it freely against their own citizens. But the remarkable feature of the Israeli case cited here is the scrupulous concern of a liberal-democratic state with calibrating the amount of pain that is legally allowable. There is evidently a concern that *too much* pain should not be applied. It is assumed that "moderate physical and psychological pressure" is at once necessary and sufficient to secure a confession. Beyond that quantity, pressure is held to be excessive (gratuitous) and *therefore* presumably becomes "torture."[21] Other states in the Middle East are rarely so punctilious—or so modern in their reasoning.

The use of torture by liberal-democratic states relates to their attempt to control populations of those who are not citizens. In such cases, torture cannot be attributed to "primitive urges," as Scott suggests, nor to governmental techniques for disciplining citizens, as Rejali argues. It is to be understood as a practical logic integral to the maintenance of the nation state's sovereignty, much like warfare.

The category of torture is no longer limited to applications of physical pain: it now includes psychological coercion employing disorientation, isolation, and brainwashing. Indeed, the term "torture" in our day denotes not only behavior that is actually prohibited by law but also behavior that we desire to have so prohibited in accordance with changing concepts of "inhumane" treatment (e.g., from child abuse and the public execution or flogging of criminals to animal experiments, factory farming, and fox hunting).

This wider category of torture or cruel, inhuman, and degrading treatment could in theory be applied to the anguish and mental suffering experienced by people in societies obliged to give up their beliefs and "become fully human" (in the sense understood by Euro-Americans). But by a curious paradox it is a version of relativism that prevents such an application of the category. For the anguish is itself the consequence of a passionate investment in the truth of beliefs that guide behavior. The modern *skeptical* posture, in contrast, regards such passionate conviction as "uncivilized" as well as a perpetual source of danger to others and of pain to oneself. Beliefs should either have no direct connection to the way one lives or be held so lightly that they can be easily changed.

One might be inclined to think that at least in humanizing societies more sorts of inflicted pain come to be considered morally unacceptable with the passage of time. In some cases, however, pain-producing behavior that was once shocking no longer shocks— or, if it does, not in the way it did in the past. Putting large numbers of people in prison for more and more kinds of offenses is one example. Inflicting new forms of suffering in battle is another.

Some writers on pain have claimed that war is "the most obvious analogue to torture."[22] That may be, but it is significant that the general concept of "cruel, inhuman or degrading treatment or punishment" is not applied to the *normal* conduct of war even though modern technological warfare involves forms of suffering that are, in scope and in kind, without precedent. The Geneva Convention, it is true, seeks to regulate conduct in war.[23] But, paradoxically, this has had the effect of legalizing most of the new kinds of suffering endured in modern war by combatants and noncombatants alike.

The military historian John Keegan wrote of the new practices of "deliberate cruelty" nearly two decades ago when he described some of the weaponry employed in twentieth-century warfare:

Weapons have never been kind to human flesh, but the directing principle behind their design has usually not been that of maximizing the
pain and damage they can cause. Before the invention of explosives,
the limits of muscle power in itself constrained their hurtfulness;
but even for some time thereafter moral inhibitions, fuelled by a sense
of the unfairness of adding mechanical and chemical increments to
man's power to hurt his brother, served to restrain deliberate bar-
barities of design. Some of these inhibitions—against the use of poison gas and explosive bullets—were codified and given international
force by the Hague Convention of 1899;[24] but the rise of "thing-
killing" as opposed to man-killing weapons—heavy artillery is an
example—which by their side-effects inflicted gross suffering and dis-
figurement, invalidated these restraints. As a result restraints were
cast to the winds, and it is now a desired effect of many man-killing
weapons that they inflict wounds as terrible and terrifying as possible. The claymore mine, for instance, is filled with metal cubes . . . ,
the cluster bomb with jagged metal fragments, in both cases because
that shape of projectile tears and fractures more extensively than a
smooth-bodied one. The HEAT and HESH rounds fired by anti-tank
guns are designed to fill the interior of armoured vehicles with show-
ers of metal splinters or streams of molten metal, so disabling the
tank by disabling its crew. And napalm, disliked for ethical reasons
even by many tough minded soldiers, contains an ingredient which
increases the adhesion of the burning petrol to human skin surfaces.
Military surgeons, so successful over the past century in resuscitating
wounded soldiers and repairing wounds of growing severity, have
thus now to meet a challenge of wounding agents deliberately conceived to defeat their skills.[25]

One might add to this that the manufacture, possession, and de-
ployment of weapons of mass destruction (chemical, nuclear, and
biological) must be counted as instances of declared governmental
readiness to engage in cruel, inhuman, and degrading treatment
against civilian populations even when these weapons are not actually used. In brief, cruel modern technologies of destruction are
integral to modern warfare, and modern warfare is an activity essential to the security and power of the modern state, on which the
welfare and identity of its citizens depends. In war, the modern
state demands from its citizens not only that they kill and maim
others but also that they themselves suffer cruel pain and death.[26]
So how can the *calculated* cruelties of modern battle be recon-

ciled with the modern sensibility regarding pain? Precisely by treating pain as a *quantifiable essence*. As in state torture, an attempt can be made to measure the physical suffering inflicted in modern warfare in accordance with the proportionality of means to ends. The human destruction inflicted should not outweigh the strategic advantage gained. But given the aim of ultimate victory, the notion of "military necessity" can be extended indefinitely. Any measure that is intended as a contribution to that aim, no matter how much suffering it creates, may be justified in terms of "military necessity." The standard of acceptability in such cases is set by public opinion, and that standard varies as opinion moves in response to contingent circumstances (e.g., who the enemy is, how the war is going).

I want to stress that I am making no moral judgment here. My concern is to identify the paradoxes of modern thought and practice that relate to the deliberate infliction of pain between states as well as within them. If I focus on state-condoned cruelty, this is not because I assume that the state is its only source today, but because our moral discourse about cruel, inhuman, and degrading treatment or punishment is closely linked to legal concepts and political interventions.

In the instances discussed so far, I have suggested that the instability of the concept of physical suffering is the source both of ideological contradictions and of strategies available for evading them. If we now shift our attention to the domain of interpersonal relations that the modern state defines as "private," we meet with a contradiction that has deeper roots, one that cannot be resolved simply by, say, redefining the concept of torture or by prohibiting calculated cruelty in military combat.

SUBJECTING ONESELF TO "CRUEL AND DEGRADING TREATMENT"

While the category of "torture" has in recent times been expanded to include cases of induced suffering that are primarily or entirely psychological, it has also been narrowed to exclude certain cases of the calculated infliction of physical pain. This sometimes leads to contradictions. But another kind of contradiction also exists in modern social life.

Moderns are aware of situations in which the negative experience of pain and the positive experience of pleasure are inseparable. Sadomasochism is disturbing to many people precisely because it confronts them with suffering that is no longer simply painful: it is at once pain and the opposite of pain. Two centuries of powerful criticism directed at the utilitarian's calculus of pleasure versus pain has not destroyed the commonsense view that these two experiences should be mutually exclusive. Yet in the eroticization of suffering the two are intimately linked, and this link is actively sought by some.

Here is an extract from a sadomasochist handbook published recently in New York:

> Because I consider any attempt to define SM in a single concise phrase to be the ultimate exercise in futility—or masochism—I shall forego the temptation to add yet another version to the great discarded stack of unsuccessful, inadequate verbal garbage. Instead let me suggest a short list of characteristics I find to be present in most scenes which I would classify as SM:
>
> 1) A dominant-submissive relationship.
> 2) A giving and receiving of pain that is pleasurable to both parties.
> 3) Fantasy and/or role playing on the part of one or both partners.
> 4) A conscious humbling of one partner by the other (humiliation).
> 5) Some form of fetish involvement.
> 6) The acting out of one or more ritualized interactions (bondage, flagellation, etc.).[27]

Notice that this text speaks not about *expressions* of pain, and still less about conventional play-acting, but about pain experienced and inflicted, in which both partners, the active and the passive, are jointly agents. So why is sadomasochism not rejected by all moderns who condemn pain as a negative experience?

One answer, according to some interpreters, is that not everyone "confuses the distinction between unbridled sadism and the social subculture of consensual fetishism. To argue that in consensual S/M the 'dominant' has power, and the slave has not, is to read theater for reality."[28]

However, the point of my question is not to dismiss the distinction between "unbridled sadism" and the "subculture of consensual fetishism." Rather, it is to ask what happens when individual self-fashioning embraces every difference—including the difference between "pain" and "pleasure"—within an aesthetic whole. We are sometimes told that the hybridization of categories, including those that organize our sensual experience, is a mode by which stable authority may be subverted in the name of liberty. But it is possible also that the eroticization of pain is merely one of the ways in which the modern self attempts to secure its elusive foundation.

Recently, an article in a London newspaper gave the following account of a local performance by an American artist at the Institute of Contemporary Arts:

> With his face set in a mask of concentration, Ron Athey allows his head to be pierced with a six-inch needle just above the eyebrow. You watch, transfixed, as the needle snakes along beneath the skin like water pulsing through an empty hosepipe. A droplet of blood wells up at the point where steel meets scalp. This is the first spike of Athey's crown of thorns—a body piercer's tribute to the power of Christian iconography, an ex-junkie's flirtation with the needle, and a gay man's defiance of infection with HIV.
>
> By the time the macabre "sketch" is finished, Athey is encrusted with needles, garlanded with wire and oozing blood, in what appears to be a parody of the crucifixion. Ah, but is it a parody, defined in the dictionary as "an imitation so poor as to seem a deliberate mockery of the original"? Or is it—as Athey's supporters would claim—an exploration of the nature of martyrdom, as manifest to a worldwide gay community in the era of AIDS?[29]

What is remarkable about these paragraphs is that the writer finds herself having to put the familiar theatrical word "sketch" in quotation marks—but not so the equally familiar theological expression "martyrdom." The reader is given to understand that this is a *real* tribute to the power of Christian iconography, a *real* exploration of the nature of (Christian) martyrdom, but that it only "appears" to be a form of theater, an "imitation."[30]

I stress that I am not here challenging this claim but rather underlining the writer's recognition that in the discourse of modern self-fashioning, the tension holding "real" and "theatrical" apart can collapse. Especially in a modern culture, where the split be-

tween the real and its mere representation has become institutionalized, it becomes necessary to assert from time to time that a given
performance is *merely* theatrical or that another performance is *not
really* theater. My point, however, is that it is the *difference* between
"the real" and "the mimetic"—like the difference between "pain"
and "pleasure"—that is available to modern self-fashioning. And
consequently the tension between "real" and "pretend" bondage is
itself aestheticized, and the clear distinction between consent and
coercion problematized.

Of course, S/M as defined in the text quoted earlier differs from
this performance at the ICA. In the latter case, for example, a separation exists between performers and observers; no experience of
giving and receiving pain binds the two together in mutual pleasure. We find only a one-sided representation (presentation?) of an
evocative image of suffering, which is preceded by a painful construction of that image on the stage. Furthermore, the intention of
the performance is not the production of private pleasure. We can't
know whether the various members of Athey's audience respond
primarily to the icon of Christ's last passion or to the painful construction of that icon on the stage—or to both. Nor can we tell
what difference it would make to those who would like to ban this
performance if they were to be told that Athey suffers from a malfunctioning of the nervous system that prevents him from feeling
pain—or, more tellingly, if they were to be told that like a religious
virtuoso he has learned to experience it *positively*.

Think of the Shi'a Muslim flagellants mourning the martyrdom
of the Prophet's grandson Hussain annually every Muharram. That
instance of self-inflicted pain is at once real *and* dramatic (not "theatrical"). It has even less to do with "pleasure" than does Athey's
performance. It differs from the performance in being a collective
rite of religious suffering and redemption; it is not a secular act that
borrows a religious metaphor to make a political statement about
prejudice. Nor is it premised on the right to self-fashioning and the
autonomy of individual choice. Yet both strike against the modern
sensibility that recoils from a willing, positive engagement with suffering. For ascetics, as for sadomasochists, pain is not merely a
means that can be measured and pronounced excessive or gratuitous in relation to an end. Pain is not action but passion.

These brief references to pain willingly endured in modern society help us to raise some questions at the transcultural level.

The interesting feature about the criteria enumerated in the S/M text quoted earlier is that they come up against Article 5 of the *Universal Declaration of Human Rights:* "No one shall be subjected to torture or to cruel, inhuman or degrading treatment or punishment." This rule is not qualified by the phrase "unless the parties concerned are consenting adults." In the same way and for the same reason, one may not consent to sell oneself into slavery, even for a limited period, not even if the parties concerned find the relationship of bondage erotic.

So, too, the liberalized church strongly disapproves of monks being whipped at the command of their abbot for penalizable faults—even when the penance has a ritual closure and a dramatic character, and even if the monks have taken monastic vows of obedience voluntarily. This follows from the modern rejection of physical pain in general, and of "gratuitous" suffering in particular. But it is more precise to put it this way: the modern hostility is not simply to pain; it is to pain that does not accord with a particular conception of being human—*and that is therefore in excess.* "Excess" is a concept of measure. An essential aspect of the modern attitude to pain rests on a calculus that defines appropriate actions.

Nothing I have said so far is an argument against S/M. I am not denouncing a "dangerous" sexual practice.[31] Nor I am concerned to celebrate its "emancipatory" social potential.[32] These antagonistic positions—mirror images of each other—seem to assume that sadomasochism has an essence. But the *essence* of what legal and moral discourse constructs, polices, and contests as S/M is not the object of my analysis. As in the field of "abnormal and unnatural" sexual practices generally, state power is of course directly and vitally involved, helping to define and regulate normality. My concern here, however, is with the structure of public debate over the valorization of painful experience in a culture that regards it negatively. In that debate, argument is sharpened because, on the one hand, moderns disapprove of physical pain as "degrading." On the other hand, they are committed to every individual's right to pursue unlimited physical pleasure "in private," so long as that conforms to the legal principle of consenting adults and does not lead to death or serious injury. One way that moderns attempt to resolve this contradiction is by defining cruelty in relation to the principle of individual autonomy, which is the necessary basis of free choice. But if the concept of cruel, inhuman, and degrading treatment cannot be consistently deployed without reference to the principle of individual freedom, it becomes relativized.

This becomes clearer in the transcultural domain. Here it is not simply a matter of eliminating particular cruelties, but of imposing an entire modern discourse of "being human," central to which are its ideas about individualism and detachment from passionate belief. Thus, while at home the principle of consenting adults acting within the bounds of the law works by invoking the idea of free choice based on individual autonomy, the presence of consenting adults abroad may often be taken to indicate mere false consciousness, a fanatical commitment to outmoded beliefs, which invites forcible correction.

Yet only the suspicious individual—suspicious of others and of oneself—can be truly autonomous, truly free of fanatical convictions. But continual suspicion introduces instability at another level: that of the subject.

CONCLUDING COMMENT

This essay has questioned and explored the basic idea underlying the United Nations declaration cited at the beginning: "No one shall be subjected to torture or to cruel, inhuman or degrading treatment or punishment." I have suggested that this idea is unstable, mainly because the aspirations and practices to which it is attached are themselves contradictory, ambiguous, or changing. Of course, the fact that an idea is unstable may not, in itself, be reason enough for abandoning it. But neither the attempt by Euro-Americans to impose their standards by force on others nor the willing invocation of these standards by weaker peoples in the Third World makes the standards stable or universal. It merely globalizes them.

We need ethnographies of pain and cruelty that can provide a better understanding of how relevant practices are actually conducted in different traditions. Such ethnographies will certainly show us that cruelty can be experienced and addressed in ways other than as a violation of rights—for example, as a failure of specific virtues or as an expression of particular vices. They will also show us that if cruelty is increasingly represented in the language of rights (and especially of human rights), this is because *perpetual legal struggle* has now become the dominant mode of moral engagement in an interconnected, uncertain, and rapidly changing world.

ENDNOTES

[1] G. R. Scott, *The History of Torture Throughout the Ages* (London: T. Werner Laurie, 1940).

[2] Darius M. Rejali, *Torture and Modernity: Self, Society, and State in Modern Iran* (Boulder, Colo.: Westview Press, 1994).

[3] In this, Rejali agrees with Page DuBois; see Page DuBois, *Torture and Truth* (New York: Routledge, 1991), 153–57. See Michel Foucault, *Discipline and Punish: The Birth of the Prison*, trans. Alan Sheridan (New York: Vintage, 1979).

[4] Z. Bauman has explored the structures and processes of the modern state that made possible the distinctive modes of cruelty under Nazism in *Modernity and the Holocaust* (Ithaca, N.Y.: Cornell University Press, 1989).

[5] A. Autiero, "The Interpretation of Pain: The Point of View of Catholic Theology," in J. Brihaye, F. Loew, and H. W. Pia, eds., *Pain* (Vienna/New York: Springer-Verlag, 1987), 24. Incidentally, there is a curious paradox in invoking a metaphor of military violence ("to affront and conquer") to describe the compassionate work of healing. But such paradoxes abound in Christian history.

[6] Thus Beccaria denounces "the barbarous and useless tortures multiplied with prodigal and useless severity for crimes that are either unproven or chimerical." Cesare Beccaria, *On Crimes and Punishments*, ed. and trans. D. Young (Indianapolis, Ind.: Hackett, 1986), 4. And Voltaire, with characteristic sarcasm, remarks: "On a dit souvent que la question [i.e., torture] était un moyen de sauver un coupable robuste, et de perdre un innocent trop faible." François-Marie Arouet de Voltaire, *Oeuvres complètes de Voltaire,* new ed. (Paris, 1818), vol. XXVI, 314.

[7] John H. Langbein, *Torture and the Law of Proof: Europe and England in the Ancien Regime* (Chicago, Ill.: University of Chicago Press, 1977).

[8] See the two fragments first published as "Bentham on Torture," in M. H. James, ed., *Bentham and Legal Theory* (Belfast: Northern Ireland Legal Quarterly, 1973), 45.

[9] See Foucault, *Discipline and Punish: The Birth of the Prison,* 232.

[10] In her important work *Classical Probability in the Enlightenment* (Princeton, N.J.: Princeton University Press, 1988), Lorraine Daston has described how, over two centuries, Enlightenment mathematicians struggled to produce a model that would provide a moral calculus for the "reasonable man" in conditions of uncertainty. Although modern probability theory has become entirely divorced from this moral project since about 1840, the idea of a calculus continues to be powerful in liberal welfare discourse.

11 See James S. Read, "Customary Law Under Colonial Rule," in H. F. Morris and James S. Read, eds., *Indirect Rule and the Search for Justice* (Oxford: Clarendon Press, 1972), 175.

12 Lord Milner, Undersecretary for Finance during the British occupation of Egypt, which began in 1882, described Britain's imperial task in that country as follows: "This then, and no less than this, was meant by 'restoring order.' It meant reforming the Egyptian administration root and branch. Nay, it meant more. For what was the good of recasting the system, if it were left to be worked by officials of the old type, animated by the old spirit? 'Men, not measures' is a good watch-word anywhere, but to no country is it more profoundly applicable than to Egypt. Our task, therefore, included something more than new principles and new methods. *It ultimately involved new men.* It involved 'the education of the people to know, and therefore to expect, orderly and honest government—the education of a body of rulers capable of supplying it.'" Lord Milner, *England in Egypt* (London: Edward Arnold, 1899), 23 (italics added). Here Milner enunciates the government's need to create subjects (in both senses) as well as rulers informed by new standards of human behavior and political justice. That this would involve the application of some force and suffering was a secondary consideration. I stress that my point is not that colonial administrators like Milner lacked "humanitarian" motives, but that they were guided by a particular concept of "humanness."

13 Lord Cromer, "The Government of Subject Races," in *Political and Literary Essays, 1908–1913* (London: Macmillan, 1913), 44.

14 I am grateful to Jon Wilson for informing me that "the word *expediency* is one that we find again and again in Imperial India's official documents, from the 1820s to the *Royal Commission on Agriculture of 1928*." Resort to expediency, as to "interest," indicated a distrust of passionate belief. See A. O. Hirschman, *The Passions and the Interests* (Princeton, N.J.: Princeton University Press, 1977).

15 Hookswinging involves a ceremony in which the celebrant swings from a crossbeam built for the purpose on a cart, suspended by two steel hooks thrust into the small of his back. See D. D. Kosambe, "Living Prehistory in India," *Scientific American* 216 (2) (1967).

16 Nicholas Dirks, "The Policing of Tradition: Colonialism and Anthropology in Southern India" (University of Michigan, typescript), 9–10.

17 In relation to the more celebrated British prohibition of *sati* (the self-immolation of a Hindu widow on the funeral pyre of her husband) in 1829, Lata Mani notes: "Rather than arguing for the outlawing of *sati* as a cruel and barbarous act, as one might expect of a true 'moderniser,' officials in favour of abolition were at pains to illustrate that such a move was entirely consonant with the principle of upgrading indigenous tradition. Their strategy was to point to the questionable scriptural sanction for *sati* and to the fact that, for one reason or another, they believed its contemporary practice transgressed its original and therefore 'true' scriptural meaning." Lata Mani, "The Production of an Official Discourse on *Sati* in Early Nineteenth-Century Bengal," in F. Barker et al., eds., *Europe and Its Others* (Colchester: University of Essex, 1985), vol. I, 107. Thus it was a modernized "Hinduism" that was made to yield the judgment that *sati* was a cruel and barbarous act.

18 "Reformative theory presented punishment to offenders as being 'in their best interests' while utilitarian theory cast it as an impartial act of social necessity. In rejecting retributive theory, the reformers sought, in effect, to take the anger out of punishment. As it was legitimized to the prisoner, punishment was no longer to be, in Bentham's words, 'an act of wrath or vengeance,' but an act of calculation, disciplined by considerations of the social good and the offenders' needs." M. Ignatieff, *A Just Measure of Pain* (Harmondsworth: Penguin Books, 1989), 75.

19 For example, France in Algeria, the United States in Vietnam, Israel in Gaza and the West Bank, and Britain in Aden, Cyprus, and Northern Ireland.

20 U.S. Department of State, *Country Reports on Human Rights Practices for 1993* (Washington, D.C.: U.S. Government Printing Office, 1994), 1204.

21 This is precisely Bentham's argument about the rationality of torture in comparison with punishment: "The purpose to which Torture is applied is such that whenever that purpose is actually attained it may plainly be seen to be attained; and as soon as ever it is seen to be attained it may immediately be made to cease. With punishment it is necessarily otherwise. Of punishment, in order to make sure of applying as much as is necessary you must commonly run a risque [*sic*] of applying considerably more: of Torture there need never be a grain more applied than what is necessary." Jeremy Bentham, in James, *Bentham and Legal Theory*, 45.

22 Elaine Scarry, *The Body in Pain* (New York: Oxford University Press, 1985), 61.

23 It should not be forgotten that medieval warfare also had its rules; see, e.g., P. Contamine, *War in the Middle Ages* (Oxford: Basil Blackwell, 1984). In one sense, the moral regulation of conduct in warfare was even stricter in the early Middle Ages: killing and maiming, even in battle, were regarded as sins for which the church demanded penance. See F. H. Russell, *The Just War in the Middle Ages* (Cambridge: Cambridge University Press, 1975).

24 Of the mushrooming, or "dum-dum," bullet, invented in British India in 1897, Daniel Headrick observes: "This particular invention was so vicious, for it tore great holes in the flesh, that Europeans thought it too cruel to inflict upon one another, and used it only against Asians and Africans." Daniel Headrick, "The Tools of Imperialism: Technology and the Expansion of European Colonial Empires in the Nineteenth Century," *The Journal of Modern History* 51 (1979): 256.

25 John Keegan, *The Face of Battle* (Harmondsworth: Penguin Books, 1978), 329–30.

26 The paradox here is that the modern citizen is a free individual and yet is obliged to forego the most important choice a free human being can make—that affecting one's own life or death. The modern state can send its citizens to their unwilling deaths in war and forbid them from willing to end their own lives in peace.

27 Larry Townsend, *The Leatherman's Handbook II* (New York: Carlyle Communications, 1989), 15.

28 A. McClintock, "Maid to Order: Commercial Fetishism and Gender Power," *Social Text* 11 (4) (Winter 1993): 87.

[29] Claire Armistead, "Piercing Thoughts," *Guardian Weekly*, 17 July 1994, 26.

[30] Cf. McClintock's statement: "S/M is the most liturgical of forms, sharing with Christianity a theatrical iconography of punishment and expiation: washing rituals, bondage, flagellation, body-piercing, and symbolic torture." McClintock, "Maid to Order: Commercial Fetishism and Gender Power," 106. But why only symbolic?

[31] See, for example, R. R. Linden et al., eds., *Against Sadomasochism: A Radical Feminist Analysis* (San Francisco: Frog in the Well, 1982). See also the legal judgments in the Spanner case in England, now being appealed against in the European Court.

[32] The radical social criticism allegedly expressed by S/M is eloquently argued in McClintock, "Maid to Order: Commercial Fetishism and Gender Power"; but the liberatory implications of S/M are explicitly retracted at the end of the article. See also the clever book by Angela Carter entitled *The Sadeian Woman* (London: Virago, 1979). While such writings typically provide radical political decodings of S/M narratives, they also seem to be saying that, as a mode of obtaining orgasm, S/M is the product of socially distorted and sexually repressive relations.

E. Valentine Daniel

Suffering Nation and Alienation

Gatherings of exiles and émigrés and refugees,
gathering on the edge of "foreign" cultures;
gathering in the half-life, half-light of foreign
tongues, or in the uncanny fluency of another's
language; gathering the signs of approval and
acceptance, degrees, discourses, disciplines;
gathering the memories of underdevelopment,
of other worlds lived retroactively; gathering the
past in a ritual of revival; gathering the present.

　　　　　　　　　　　　　　—Homi Bhabha

The modes of conspicuousness, obtrusiveness,
and obstinacy all have the function of bringing
to the fore the characteristic of occurrentness in
what is available.

　　　　　　　　　　　　　　—Martin Heidegger

Narcotics cannot still the tooth
That nibbles at the soul.

　　　　　　　　　　　　　　—Emily Dickinson

A T THE HEART OF THE NATION-STATE lies an aestheticizing impulse.[1] Like other aesthetic forms, the nation-state too promises to bring forth order out of disorder, mold form from that in which form is absent. But even though this order may be posited only as a future hope—as in the writings of Hegel— something to be achieved in the making, this hope is drenched in

E. Valentine Daniel is Professor of Anthropology and Philosophy at Columbia University.

nostalgia, the imagined glory that once was. In South Asia in particular, the Orientalists' contribution to this nostalgia has been massive. Thus many South Asians find such books as A. L. Basham's *The Wonder That Was India* or Jawaharlal Nehru's *The Discovery of India* quite stirring.[2] Western nations have their own nationalized pasts. The nation-state promises to soothe and heal, but its healing comforts are expressed in the language of recovery and restoration, through an orientation toward the past. The nation-state promises to restore to the chords of collective discontent atunement with a collective consciousness, to recover for its people a moral order where there is only disorder, and to return its nationals to the path of their intended destiny. And above all, as part of its aestheticizing and healing mission, the modern nation-state has promised to provide refuge to those whose lives have been rendered chaotic by catastrophic events, of either natural or human origin. It is claimed that this too is a legacy from the past, attributed to Buddhist or Hindu hospitality or to what a Christian nation ought to do. In short, the nation-state is aestheticized by the nationalization of its past, which is projected onto the future—by which act the present is appeased.

This essay will argue, employing the example of the plight of Sri Lankan Tamils in Sri Lanka and (mainly) in the United Kingdom, that in the late twentieth century the nation-state has proved to be a mere narcotic at least in one respect and that in this it has failed to soothe the soul. I am referring to what nation-states do with those who are displaced within and into their national boundaries, with that class of persons who bear the label "refugees." Beyond the suffering of pain that many of these refugees' bodies have borne and of which I have written elsewhere,[3] there is a kind of suffering that is diffuse and lasting that refugees and asylum seekers endure. It is this suffering that I hope to bring to light.

It is noteworthy that wherever the question of nation has been introduced into studies of exiles and refugees, it has been done in a manner that has never been alert to the interrogation of the nation's reality in the lived experience of these people. A particular nation might be criticized for its treatment of its own citizens or its treatment of those who seek refuge within its borders, and even the experience of the loss of nationhood might be delineated in the experiences of refugees and exiles, but this is done with the tacit agenda of restoring to the nation and the displaced national what they have lost and also restoring them to the ideal of the nation-state itself as if it were an ontological fact, given and irrevocable. What further contributes to such omissions or slights is that in working with refugees and exiles the self-selectivity of informants and information is overdetermined in favor of the nation. That is, the most articulate and even vociferous informants who are self-selected to serve as the researcher's interlocutors are, in one way or another, implicated in the national project. Because of their investment in nation-bound identity politics, they rarely fail to remind the researcher of the integral place the nation-state has in the identity of every exile and refugee. What is thrown within the scope of the researcher may question the validity of this or that nation or nationality but never the very concept of nationhood. What goes unnoticed are those displaced persons who have opted out of the project of the nation— any and every nation.

It is about these kinds of refugees and exiles that I have chosen to write. With respect to my own ethnographic research, I have found such displaced persons in the most abundant numbers among what I describe as Phase 3 Tamil refugees in the United Kingdom. And I suggest that this kind of displaced person is likely to be found in increasing numbers among refugees of all peoples and places. Although the nineteenth and twentieth centuries were the centuries of the nation, we have no reason to believe that the twenty-first century will follow suit. I submit that the nation-averse displaced person is likely to become the rule rather than the exception. This particular sample of asylum seekers is but a token of a far wider, if hidden, category of displaced persons, hidden in the interstices of the nation and its far-extending labyrinthine structures.

This essay is based mainly on research conducted over the summer of 1993 in London, in which I sought to find out how Sri Lankan Tamil immigrants to the United Kingdom are disposed toward the nation, whether they nationalize their past, and, if so, how. These immigrants include asylum seekers as well as various shades of bona fide British subjects of Ceylonese and (later) Sri Lankan origin. I was interested not only in how these Tamils *imagined* their past but also in how this past, imagined or otherwise, entered into their way of being-in-the-world, how they folded it into their "background practices." I argue that Tamils came to Britain in three phases and that in each phase came immigrants whose comportment toward nationalism in general and a nationalized past in particular took, roughly, three distinguishable forms.[4] In order to do this, I have invoked Homi Bhabha to set the tone and Martin Heidegger to provide the type, and I offer the ethnographic token.[5]

TAMILS IN BRITAIN

Phase 1: The Elite

By the time Sri Lankan Tamils began to arrive in Britain in the early 1980s seeking asylum from the civil war in Sri Lanka, an earlier group of Tamils, who had preceded them under quite different circumstances, was already living in the United Kingdom. The 1980s group represented but the third phase of Tamil migration to Britain.

The first generation of Ceylonese (as they were then called) who emigrated to Britain was an odd assortment of Sinhalas, Tamils, and Burghers,[6] women and men who came to Britain in the early years surrounding Ceylon's independence from British colonial power. Most of them had in common an upper-class or upper-middle-class background, an education in the elite high schools of Ceylon, a self-identification as Ceylonese, and a cultivated ease with Western ways and tastes. Many came to Britain to obtain professional degrees in law, medicine, or engineering or to obtain graduate degrees that would ease them into the faculties of the universities and the ranks of the civil service at home. They cultivated a blend of nostalgia for the colonial days and a sense of national pride for the nation that was theirs. Few had any intention of staying on in Britain, for too many were the comforts of home that they would thereby relinquish. And, more important, to sever the link with Ceylon would be to sever the link with a nation, their nation. A survey of this generation's home libraries is a telling revelation: the books they had purchased in the 1950s through the 1980s were, aside from those covering the fields of their primary interest or specialization, national histories of Ceylon. A typical collection in these home libraries included R. L. Brohier's *Discovering Ceylon;* John Davy's *An Account of the Interior of Ceylon and of Its Inhabitants, with Travels in That Island;* Wilhelm Geiger's *The Ma-*

havamsa, or *The Great Chronicle of Ceylon;* Robert Knox's *An Historical Relation of Ceylon;* H. Parker's *Ancient Ceylon;* and, more recently, K. M. de Silva's *A History of Sri Lanka.*[7]

For these immigrants, Britain began as a rite of passage. As is true in all such cases, the children who were born in Britain found their parents' vestige of cultural and national loyalties to Ceylon quaint and queer. And yet, provoked by the British context in which emblems of nation were overwhelmingly and insistently present—emblems and a nationhood from which they were alienated—even this generation counteracted British nationalism with an assertion of their own national past. If they could remember and recite only one fact, it was that their nation was more than a thousand years older than England and Scotland.

What these immigrants deeply held and tried to inculcate in their children was the belief that they, among South Asians, were special. They were not Indians. They were certainly not "Pakis."[8] They were Ceylonese. They flaunted their "uncanny fluency of another's language," a high-pedigree dialect of British English, far removed from the kind that was spoken by the Indo-Pakistani immigrants of Southhall and Wembley. They had gone to the best of Ceylon's schools, and their children went to the better ("public," if possible) schools in Britain; they were professionals, as their children ought to be some day. The Tamils among this first phase of immigrants came largely from the highest Tamil caste in Ceylon, the Vellalas. They made sure that their children knew this. There were almost no Estate Tamils among them.[9] The Sinhalas also came from the upper classes, even if not all of them were from the uppermost caste of Sinhala society, the Goyigamas. The "cultured" comportment that these immigrants adopted vis-à-vis their fellow Asians as well as vis-à-vis white Britons was inscribed with "*national* pride." "We did not want to let down the name of our country," said a retired Tamil surgeon in Nottingham in an interview with me. Although Tamils of this generation had found sufficient cause for being ambivalent about Sri Lankan nationalism and its increasingly Sinhala-Buddhist shading, they nevertheless chose the company and cultural deportment toward the world not of South Indian Tamils living in Britain but of fellow Ceylonese.

Their living room walls sported Sri Lankan "Devil Dancing" masks, nineteenth-century originals or reproductions of paintings of various Ceylonese landscapes or the Kandy Äsələ Perehärə, and Sri Lankan batik. Brass and silver trays rested on ebony elephant tripods, all of them made in Ceylon. A few South Indian touches were to be found in Hindu homes, where a shrine was often set up in an inconspicuous corner with an image of Ganesh or a picture of Saraswathi, the goddess of learning. Occasionally—in a more recent trend—a picture of the holy man from Karnataka, Satya Sai Baba, looked down from a wall. In dining-room cabinets, china (increasingly, china made in Sri Lanka's new free trade zones by Noritake and others) was the rule, the South Indian "ever-silver" plates and tumblers the exception. As for musical instruments, one was more likely to find a piano, an electric guitar, bongos, and snare drums—instruments of Westernized Ceylonese—than a veena, sitar, tabla, or the South Indian drum, the mṛdangam. Very few among this generation appeared to be connoisseurs of Indian classical music, northern or southern. But many were aficionados of Western classical music and even jazz, another market of Ceylon's English-educated elite. On the "strictly indigenous side" in their record collection, one was more likely to find recordings of *baila* (the music of Iberian origin with a 3/4 beat and a melody confined to three chords) than a recording of the classical vocalist M. S. Subalakshmi singing the "Sri Venkateshwara Subrapadham," that devotional invocation so familiar to South Indian Hindus. A number of individuals of this generation and their children still recall and use the derogatory epithet "*thosai kade* music" to describe Indian classical music. The epithet derives from the days of Indian-run eateries in Ceylon that served *dosas* or *tocais* and customarily played recordings of Indian classical or devotional music on their radios.

A countercurrent also exited among these Tamils, however. While the Sinhalas were actively nationalizing their past, the Tamils were recovering and reasserting a heritage that stressed the cultural over the political, the cultural tending to be Tamil and Hindu. And even though the monuments of this heritage were more richly distributed in South India than in Sri Lanka, these Tamils had come to hold that the best of this heritage was alive in Jaffna, the northernmost peninsula of Sri Lanka, and was to be found in the dialect of Tamil spoken and the kind of Hinduism practiced (Saiva Siddhanta) in their corner of the island. Nevertheless, the overall impression one gets from this generation of Tamils in Britain is that Tamil cultural heritage often received lip service rather than being "transparently" incorporated into their background practices and habits.

At some point in the first half of the twentieth century, a nationalized past, and nationalism itself, had progressed from being an instrumental entity employed at the service of national independence to becoming a part of what Heidegger called an "equipmental whole." In his inimitable prose, Heidegger remarks that "equipment—in accordance with its equipmentality—always is *in terms of* its belonging to other equipment: inkstand, pen, ink, paper, blotting pad, table, lamp, furniture, windows, doors, room."[10] Like a piece of furniture, which is a piece of furniture only insofar as it belongs to an equipmental nexus, in Ceylon the national past became part of an equipmental whole called nationalism to which also belonged such entities as development projects, history, archaeology, newspapers, voters, citizens, diplomacy, literature, chronicles, foreign relations, official languages, courts, parliaments, postal stamps, the armed forces, national monuments, national universities, and national costumes. Heidegger saw the way of being of those entities that are defined by their place *in the whole* as characterized by "availableness." For the Ceylonese of the immediate prewar and postwar years, a national past had become not only available but also transparent. For something to become transparent—that is, nonobtrusive—it has to become fully and genuinely appropriated equipment. As part of an equipmental whole, nationalism as well as an increasingly nationalized past became part of a suavely efficient and transparent habit of comportment in the world. "In the indifferent imperturbability of our customary commerce with [things surrounding us]," Heidegger notes, "[those entities that are transparent] become accessible precisely with regard to their unobtrusive presence. The presupposition for the possible equanimity of our dealing with things is, among others, the uninterrupted quality of that commerce."[11]

Even during preindependence negotiations with the British, Tamil politicians began to fear the possible tyranny of a Sinhala majority in a new independent nation. But the "availableness" of a nation or a national past itself was never called into question. This was certainly true of the Tamil immigrants of Phase 1 in Britain. All peoples belonged to nations and thereby possessed nationalities. Tamils, like their Sinhala counterparts, belonged to a nation known as Ceylon.

The first clear signs of disturbance of the "availableness" of a nationalized past made their presence felt with the passage of the Sinhala Only Act of 1956, whereby Sinhala was made the sole official language. The late leader of the Tamil United Liberation Front (TULF), Appapillai Amirdhalingam, indirectly concurred with this assessment when he told me in an interview in December 1983 that "not until 1956 did we really believe that we were second-class citizens. Until then all we were engaged in were preventive measures, which we thought would hold." Some of the Jaffna Tamils I spoke to said that they began to realize that they had no nation of their own when the Tamils of recent Indian origin who were brought to the island to work on its plantations were disenfranchised and made stateless in two consecutive acts of Ceylon's postindependence Parliament in 1948 and 1949. For many Tamils of this generation who saw signs of Sinhala domination, their claim to a Ceylonese nation and its national past may indeed have run into doubt. Even so, this did not, as Heidegger might have put it, throw into "occurrentness" the "facticity" of nation, nationality, or a nationalized past. ("Occurrentness" refers to the presencing of an entity as an isolate, disarticulated from the background practices to which it belongs.) They continued to inhabit a world in which the nation was not something alongside which they lived but something that had become part of them and pervaded their relation to other objects of their world. In this respect, it is worth noting that "the concept of 'facticity' implies that an 'intraworldly' being has being-in-the-world in such a way that it can understand itself as bound up in its 'destiny' with the being of those beings which it encounters within its own world." [12]

A Ceylonese was such a being and was bound up, as a national, in his or her destiny with, among other beings, the nation and nationalism. When Phase 1 Tamil immigrants and members of their generation who remained in Ceylon were initially confronted with the possible transformation of the nation from something "available" into something "occurrent," the perceived options did not include the renunciation of a nationalized past but rather the search for and the discovery of a different nationalized past. In my interviews with more than fifty Tamils of this generation, only three claimed that they had always—that is, even as early as the 1950s—doubted the very premise of a nationalized past. Such doubts should not be taken in their customary mentalistic sense. Rather, the form in which such doubts were expressed was strikingly kinesthetic. A statement of a Tamil woman from Wimbledon was typical: "I never *felt* comfortable saying that Ceylon was my country." It is hard to tell how much of this particular assertion is intelligent hindsight rather than accurate recall of radical doubt or its absence, since my interviews with this woman and others like her were largely carried out in 1992. We may, however, safely concede that the signs of the "unavailability" of a nationalized past began to make their faint appearance in the mid-1950s, and possibly earlier, in the form of what the Heideggerian scholar Hubert Dreyfus calls a "malfunction" in the available. When equipment malfunctions, Dreyfus observes, it becomes "conspicuous." [13] "Tradition," when zealously invoked, is one of those noteworthy signs of equipment that has become conspicuous, thanks to its malfunction. "Conspicuousness presents the available equipment as in a certain unavailableness," wrote Heidegger. [14]

In the case of the nation, as we will see, with time this unavailability of the nation to Tamils was to disturb the availability of the Sinhalas' own nationalized past—or, at the very least, its raison d'être became debatable. There was a time when these Tamils' cultural past and the Sinhalas' national past found no parallax. From a Tamil, even those aspects of a pointedly Sinhala national past issued forth from a South Indian (ergo, Hindu) cultural past and therefore with minor adjustments the two were brought into line with each other. Dreyfus observes that "for most . . . forms of malfunction we have ready ways of coping, so that after a moment of being startled, and seeing a meaningless object, we shift to a new way of coping and go on. 'Pure occurrentness announces itself in such equipment, but only to withdraw to the availableness of something with which one concerns oneself.'" [15]

Phase 2: Students

The second phase of Tamil migration to Britain heralded a more serious disturbance of the availableness of the nation, making coping more difficult and the occurrentness of a nationalized past more

318   E. Valentine Daniel

obdurate. These immigrants consisted of a wider spectrum of class and caste, for in the 1960s and 1970s the universities and schools back home had opened up to and educated a more diverse population of students. The opening up of the universities, however, made education a more, rather than a less, precious commodity. The sociopolitical processes that brought about this state of affairs had been well rehearsed. Tamils were bound to face increasing competition from the Sinhalas, whose interest in and access to education was beginning to catch up with the proportion of Sinhalas in the population as a whole. But the competition in and corresponding value of education were further intensified by two policies of the Sri Lankan government. The first was the institution of a quota system that adversely affected the Tamils, and the second was the systematic closing of the civil services and the armed forces to Tamils.[16] Under these conditions, England became the escape route for many students, and most who migrated in this phase were students. But more to the point of our theoretical concern with nationalizing the past was a realization among educated Tamil youth that their nation's history—a national history—was not theirs. This unavailability deprived them of the privileges that were part of the equipmental whole of which the nationalized past was a part.

Class and caste barriers also existed between the first and the second phases of migrants. Many more students were choosing to attend the more recently established "polytechnics" rather than the older British universities, filled with pomp and tradition, that had been the choice of their predecessors. But education and the similarities in professional ambitions lessened these differences. The second generation trusted those who had preceded them and accepted their freely given help in the form of guidance, advice, contacts, and tips on how to make it in Britain. Phase 2 immigrants were, on the average, poorer than Phase 1 immigrants because they came from a poorer class, but even when they did have resources at home, the newly imposed exchange controls in Ceylon, now renamed Sri Lanka, made it difficult for them to transfer funds out of the country. Exacerbating this financial difficulty, Britain increased the fees it charged its foreign students to three times what domestic students paid. This meant that more students had to support their studies by working, and most chose jobs that were congenial to studying, such as night security guards and petrol station attendants. Women found jobs as cashiers in tourist memento shops and as clerks in grocery stores. In short, this generation of students was thrown into the rough-and-tumble of the host nation and exposed to its grubby bigotries and prejudices in a manner and to an extent not experienced by their predecessors.

Furthermore, these immigrants' nostalgia for their home country differed qualitatively from that of the first generation. They had no illusions about belonging to a ruling elite (becoming potential national leaders) or claiming all the comforts and privileges that went with that status. The political climate they had fled soured them on the Sri Lankan state as well as on most aspects of civil society. Unlike their predecessors, they had not gone to school with Sinhala classmates and studied in the English medium[17] but had, as a consequence of the language act of 1956, been schooled in an exclusively Tamil medium and had thereby come to consider their Sinhala compatriots as virtual strangers at best and enemies at worst. Their nostalgia is best described as basic homesickness: the missing of family, temple or church, friends, home-cooked food, and language. In Britain, they gathered in each others' homes to eat, chat, and, by the early 1980s, watch Tamil films on their VCRs rather than meeting in public places because in such places, especially in pubs, they felt that they were being laughed at, talked about, and even stalked by their English neighbors. Pubs were sites where native and stranger become subjects of "the half-light of foreign tongues." Nonetheless, many in this group who completed their education before the late 1970s found jobs in the United Kingdom or elsewhere in the world and chose not to return to Sri Lanka.

Great Britain's heavily nationalized past and the racist indignities issuing from it helped throw into clear relief Sri Lanka's own nationalized past and its own forces of comparable exclusion. On the bookshelves of those Phase 2 immigrants who were given to reading and collecting books, one was either unlikely to find Ceylonese or Sri Lankan history books in any significant number or likely to find them only as part of a genre of books and pamphlets that reflected a radically new concern with history. In the latter case, the few who allowed themselves to be preoccupied with history were engaged in writing a different history, obsessed with discovering a nationalized past that was distinctively Tamil, with Tamil chieftains and Tamil kings ruling justly over a nation of loyal subjects, if not citizens. For many in this subgroup, Prabhakaran, the leader of the Liberation Tigers of Tamil Eelam (LTTE),[18] was seen as fitting a uniquely Tamil notion of kingship: the king as dispenser of justice, as strong, compassionate, and, if necessary, brutal; not as a negotiating, compromising, vacillating, talk-prone politician. For most Phase 2 Tamils and the asylum seekers who were to follow, democracy had proven to be a farce, and monarchy presented itself as the ideal polity.

COPING WITH THE UNAVAILABLENESS OF THE NATION

To the extent that Ceylon's and (later) Sri Lanka's nationalized past presented itself in its unavailableness to the Tamils, and in being precipitated in its occurrentness as isolated and determinate rather than as belonging to an equipmental whole, the experiences of the Phase 1 and Phase 2 Tamils were similar. But the two groups coped differently with the disturbances to their world—a difference of degree if not kind.

The earlier generation had, despite its interest in the history of Ceylon, bracketed it away as a thing worthy of curiosity and yet, as they say, as only history.[19] They chose to emphasize the significance of culture, and even a common culture, as the basis of their common nationality. To be sure, differences between Tamils and Sinhalas were acknowledged, but so were the differences between Tamils and Burghers or Sinhalas and Muslims. These differences, however, were secondary to the primacy of a common nation based on a common culture. In this respect, we may note that the nemesis of a series of Sri Lankan (Sinhala) governments and prime ministers, the founder of the Federal party and (later) of the Tamil United Liberation Front (TULF), Mr. S. J. V. Chelvanayakam, had not asked for a separate nation-state for the Tamils but only for a federated state, sufficient to account for the lesser differences and to acknowledge the greater commonality.

The coping employed by this generation of immigrants can be best described as "absorbed coping." In absorbed coping, after a moment of surprise at the disturbance to one's habitual comportment in the world, one shifts to a new way of coping and goes on as if nothing has changed. In such a mode of coping, transparent circumspection—the grasp of one's environment in one's everyday way of getting around—is recovered without any need for a radically new stance in the world. In his passionate "political tract," the Sri Lankan Tamil anthropologist S. J. Tambiah recalls his own experience of being caught in the anti-Tamil riots of 1958, the first of their kind in the new nation's history.[20] His recovery from that experience—despite its traumatic quality—is an example of absorbed coping. Indeed, some may argue that his entire book, which was triggered by the anti-Tamil riots of 1983 and which offers solutions for reconciliation, continues to exemplify "absorbed coping." (Note that Tambiah belongs to the generation of Phase 1 Tamils.)

In the case of the second generation of immigrants, and among some of those in Phase 3 who were to follow, a shift occurred, from "absorbed coping" to "deliberate coping" and deliberation. This was especially true of those who were committed to finding the nationalized past of the Tamils in the last king of Jaffna, in the Cholas of South India, or in the persons of strongmen such as Prabhakaran. This enterprise entails a deliberate activity, with attention paid to what is being done and with an awareness of the consequences of one's actions.

Deliberate coping may also entail deliberation—the act of reflective planning. This was true not only of those who were obsessed with recovering a Tamil nationalized past but also of those who did not care for the distant past but who were deliberative in how they interacted with the Sinhalas they encountered, either in Britain or elsewhere. Contrast the following two statements, the first by a Phase 1 barrister and the second by a Phase 2 accountant:

> When I meet my Sinhala friends, I rarely think, "Ah, he is a Sinhala and I am a Tamil; we are different; I better watch out." I can even say I never think that way, and I am sure he does not either. The issue comes up only when we start discussing Sri Lankan politics, the recent stuff. And anyway, my Tamil is only little better than his Sinhala. His is mostly nonexistent.

> Friendships. Yes, there are friendships. It is funny. In the U.K., you know what all Sri Lankans now are called? "Tamils." Even the Sinhalas are called Tamils. Some of them get mad. Feel insulted. Most of those who have been around for some time think it is funny. That is how the whole racism bit is so funny: the anti-Tamil Sinhala racism in Sri Lanka with all the Aryan/non-Aryan talk of Sinhala racists. Some of these Sinhalas are my good friends. But however close we

are being friends, I can never forget that he is a Sinhala. And he can never forget that I am a Tamil. That is always there. Fundamental.

To speak of "deliberation," like "imagination" in Benedict Anderson's *Imagined Communities,* may strike one as succumbing to the kind of Cartesian mentalism I have tried assiduously to avoid.[21] What deliberates is not the mind as distinct from the body—even though "mind" in such a phrase may be used as Charles Peirce did, as "a sop to Cerberus."[22] Deliberation is more accurately understood as the action of a mindful body or an embodied mind. In deliberation, human beings experience the exercise of their habits' being subjected to habit-change. What habits do we speak of in this instance? The habit of nationhood, of belonging, of being with rather than merely being in or being as. Deliberation is a moment in which such habits are disturbed and rise to the threshold of habit-change. Is intentionality involved in deliberation (even if not in "imagination")? As Heidegger puts it, "intentionality is not an occurrent relation between an occurrent subject and an occurrent object but is constitutive for the relational character of the subject's comportment as such . . . Intentionality is neither something objective nor something subjective in the traditional sense."[23]

The wife of a Tamil physician in London told me the following: "I have always put [on] a *poṭṭu* when we go to parties. To me it is as natural as drinking water or wearing my *tālikkoṭi.* But after 1983, I *feel* [her emphasis] my *poṭṭu.* Even here in England, slightly afraid [when wearing it]. At the same time, slightly proud."[24] Here we see an example of the "deliberation" of a mindful body: a moment of habit-change.

Phase 3: Refugees

Among the immigrants of this third phase, especially in its latter half, we not only find the "national past" as equipment completely missing; we also find its absence transforming the entire equipmental whole to which it belonged from the available to the occurrent. Of such a transformation Heidegger writes: "The more urgently we need what is missing, and the more authentically it is encountered in its unavailableness, all the more obtrusive does that which is available become—so much so, indeed, that it seems to lose its character of availableness. It reveals itself as something just occurrent and no more."[25] In order to appreciate the total break-down of nationalism resulting from the disturbance of the unavail-able, the nation, which had once been a part of ongoing activity and a being-in-reality, we need to sift through some of the trials of these immigrants before and upon their entry into Britain.

The third phase of Tamil emigration to Britain and the West in general began with the Sri Lankan government's imposition of the draconian Prevention of Terrorism Act (PTA) in 1979, instituted in response to a campaign for a separate state on the part of a certain section of the Tamil population.[26] To appreciate the scale of the government's excessive and indiscriminate use of force, one can only sadly recite that prior to the 1983 anti-Tamil riots, which left thousands of Tamils dead and thousands more homeless, there were no more than a dozen members of the LTTE, the separatist group that was to grow subsequently into one of the most dreaded mili-tant organizations in the world. By the late 1970s and early 1980s, for the average Sinhala soldier, every Tamil was not only anti-Sinhala but antinationalist. The PTA fell hardest upon the Tamil youth. Every Tamil between the ages of sixteen and forty was con-sidered to be a terrorist whose tactic was surprise. For many young Tamil men (and later, women), the choice was flight from the atroc-ity of the Sri Lankan armed forces or flight into the membership of one of the many militant separatist groups.

The immigrants of this phase, which extends from the late 1970s to the present, were not a homogenous lot. Apart from the fact that all Phase 3 Tamils are asylum seekers, this phase is characterized by its continuously changing social and economic profile. It may be divided into two parts: the first consisting of those who left before the full-fledged civil war of post-1987, and the second of those who left thereafter. Among the latter, one is likely to find those for whom everything that is national—including a nationalized past—has broken down. Initially Phase 3 immigrants came as students either because that was the only way they knew to get to Britain or because they were too embarrassed to seek asylum right away. Once the student route was choked off by Britain's increasingly re-strictive policies, they openly sought asylum.

For Phase 2 Tamils, this development was something they had feared, had expected, and now understood. So they went all out to assist these Phase 3 Tamils by serving as sponsors, by providing them with places to stay, and by finding them jobs. Phase 2 Tamils were also more in touch than their Phase 1 counterparts with the constant changes in immigration laws, their interpretation, and enforcement—all set up as obstacles to immigration by the British authorities—and the ways of overcoming or circumventing them. The first generation's advice in these matters was outdated and irrelevant, as indeed the second generation's was soon to become.

What these Tamils gained from their acquaintance with Britain's immigration laws and its treatment of refugees was a sense of cynicism toward all things "national," especially national laws and even international laws. They saw, for instance, that international refugee laws did not serve to ameliorate the plight of refugees as much as they did to protect the sovereignty of nation-states and often to protect these nation-states from embarrassment. These nation-states were constituted of nationalized cultures and claims to hoary nationalized pasts that set up barriers to refugees at their borders. When it came to the question of immigrants—especially refugees—Phase 1 Tamils believed in the primacy of national sovereignty, especially the sovereignty of their adopted nation. Phase 3 Tamils, the later arrivals in particular, viewed it with cynicism, dread, or utter disregard. The sentiment of Phase 2 Tamils fell somewhere in between.

Once Phase 3 Tamils had been admitted into the country, Phase 2 and Phase 1 Tamils—especially those of Phase 1[27]—attempted to fit what they saw into a picture that they either knew, remembered, or had heard of: a class/caste-based social order in which the upper castes, when at their best, were helpers and patrons of the lower castes. When advice was extended to these newcomers, it was purportedly done with ultimate democratic intentions—in the words of a Tamil lawyer in Britain, "to help them become fit for a free and equal society." Initially there was even a sense of urgency in their gestures of help because, among other things, they had the "image of the Ceylon Tamil in Britain to protect."[28] If nothing more, they had to preserve their identity as "not 'Pakis,' and certainly not Afro-Caribbean." Before the mid-1980s, much help was given and much received. Phase 1 Tamils expected the newcomers to conform, to continue to take their advice, to move up rapidly in British society (as they themselves had done) by turning to education, and above all to keep a low profile until they were fit enough to ensure that the dignity of the Ceylon Tamil would not be tarnished by their visibility.

After the July riots of 1983, Phase 1 Tamils realized that they were fighting a losing battle against their decimated illusion of the "dignified Ceylon Tamil." By then, those who were arriving were not necessarily young men but older people who were dependents of the post-1979 asylum seekers. In the beginning, renewed attempts were made to cajole the young men and women of Phase 3 to fall into line with class/caste-based expectations. The Phase 1 Tamils employed subtle assertions of caste prerogatives on the one hand and overt encouragement of old-country gerontocracy on the other, both exercises of tradition. What they had not realized is that, with the rise of the Tamil militant movements in Sri Lanka, gerontocracy had been overthrown by a generalized neocracy. In the wake of the July riots, entire families arrived in Britain. When unaccompanied individuals came, their dependents soon followed. Marriages were made, and in-laws followed spouses. Some Phase 1 immigrants saw the "Paki phenomenon" taking shape in the Tamil community before their very eyes. The character of the Tamil immigrant community in Britain was never to be the same. It did not take long for matters to sour or require radical reframing. Those of Phase 1 who refused to reframe their world withdrew from helping the asylum seekers, declaring, at least among their own classes, that these "riffraff" were untrustworthy "tree climbers." [29]

PHASE I IMMIGRANTS' DISCOMFITURE

Phase 1 immigrants, most of whom were politically conservative and socioeconomically well-to-do, found it extremely discomfiting to witness the arrival of Tamils from the lower ends of caste and class, with their poor—even zero—command of English and their off-the-boat dress and demeanor. But they were most aghast at the "ungentlemanly political tactics they employed": some male asylum seekers stripped themselves down to their underwear at Heathrow airport to protest their threatened deportation. Above all, the Phase 1 immigrants found it difficult to come to terms with the fact that they were seeing "Tamils as refugees."

Many of them turned to help instead those young men and women who had never left Sri Lanka but had "chosen" to stay behind and fight the Sri Lankan and Indian armies. Ironically, that these fighters were also predominantly drawn from the lower castes of Tamil Sri Lanka did not matter to Phase 1 Tamils, who provided considerable financial and material support to the militant "liberation groups" back home. Some of the wealthiest of this class in Britain and in the United States—more in the United States than in Britain—expected their "boys," as these militants were called, to establish a separate nation-state called Eelam in short order, and a few expressed their hope of some day becoming ambassadors of this new nation in some of the leading European and North American capitals. In the meantime, they were gallant warriors in a proxy war. One wealthy Tamil physician in America offered me an advance of sixty thousand dollars to write a book on the ancient Tamil nation that had once extended to the lost continents of Atlantis and Lamuria. When I told this to a Phase 3 immigrant who had fled both the Sri Lankan state and the militant group to which he briefly belonged, he suggested, only half in jest, that in my place he would take the money and hire a Buddhist priest for thirty thousand dollars to write the same history. He justified his suggestion by noting that only a Buddhist priest could write a convincing history—for was it not a Buddhist priest who wrote the *Mahavamsa,* the ancient Sinhala-Buddhist chronicle? The remark is only one indication of the scorn with which many Phase 3 immigrants were willing to regard the national past.

Whereas some Phase 1 immigrants entertained fantasies and hopes of nationhood and ambassadorships, they also came to read, witness, and even experience open racism from Britain's whites. Not that Phase 1 Tamils had denied British racism before—but they had assumed that it kicked in only when promotion to upper-level managerial positions in corporations was at issue. "At a day-to-day level, the Brits," it was said, "are a decent lot. They keep their prejudices to themselves; we keep ours within us." In short, various forms of equivocation seemed to qualify British racism. But their own trust in the British was shaken when they saw Tamils being called "Pakis." Reports and stories that smarted even more began to reach the self-assured British Tamils. They heard that some young Tamils, when accused of being Tamil and threatened with physical violence by white youths, claimed to be Indians or Pakistanis. They heard that in the Netherlands Tamils in trouble tried to pass as British Guyanese or Africans. In Germany, it was said, "Tamil" was the worst insult a German could extend to a swarthy foreigner, from Turk to Vietnamese. Some blamed the asylum seekers for having robbed Tamils of their dignity. "They cannot even speak proper English. Some cannot even speak a word," complained one of the first-generation Tamils. But others realized that although they had imagined that their white fellow Britons knew the difference, the fact was that these whites neither knew nor cared. A sense of identification with all other nonwhites in Britain had begun to develop among some of the Phase 1 Tamils, mainly among the children of this generation.

Those Phase 1 immigrants who did not want their habits of body, mind, and heart shaken withdrew, either into themselves, their worlds, or the arcane recesses of their fancies. The awkward presence and practices of Phase 3 immigrants appeared to these earlier settlers as mere aberrations, "misfirings of the collective enterprise [of what it was to be a Ceylon Tamil in Great Britain] tending to produce habitus that are capable of generating practices regulated without regulation or any institutionalized call to order." [30] Phase 2 Tamils, few of whom had the luxury of withdrawal, witnessed the dark fog of their fellow Tamils' suffering gather itself into a thickness that surrounded them without evaporating.

Some Phase 1 immigrants continued to insist on playing the part of patron to client vis-à-vis the newcomers: advising, helping, instructing, meddling. As Phase 3 immigrants saw matters, all Phase 1 types could say was, "Don't do this, *tambi;* don't do that, *tambi;* and be careful, *tambi.*" [31] The male asylum seekers found their advice largely a recitation of irrelevant civilities. Many of the female asylum seekers were invited to work as domestic servants in the homes of Phase 1 immigrants; surprisingly few accepted such offers. Unconfirmed rumors abounded that some Phase 1 immigrants were in collusion with the Home Office, playing the part of loyal British subjects, feeding the government information that could result in the deportation of asylum seekers. [32] Here are typical statements gathered from Phase 3 asylum seekers about their Phase 1 predecessors: "They want us to go back and fight for *their* Eelam." "They want us to take orders from them, be their bearers." "They are jealous that we can drive cars here. Of course, they don't know that we drove cars even in Sri Lanka. They remember the days when the only cars in that country belonged to their grandfathers, and their great-grandfathers sucked up to the colonial white man." "They cheated us then, they'll cheat us now."

The only route to dignified settlement that Phase 1 and Phase 2 Tamils had known was education. For Phase 3 Tamils, this was neither their first nor their easiest choice, for several reasons. First, they were escaping a civil war that had wreaked havoc on their progress in education. Second, they had spent almost all of their families' resources to come to the United Kingdom, money that had to be replaced. Third, they had to earn and save more money to bring their parents, siblings, brides (or bridegrooms, in some instances), and spouses out of their strife-torn homeland. Unlike the students who preceded them in Phase 2, many of the male asylum seekers were married. Fourth, given the paucity of the earning potential of their fathers and brothers back home under civil war conditions and their consequent inability to save for their sisters' and daughters' marriages, it fell to these refugees to save money for those dowries. Lucky indeed was the woman whose prospective groom lived in the West and had permanent residency status—but such a man required a higher dowry. In essence, the times were too urgent to permit these immigrants to settle for the deferred gratification education had to offer. The Phase 3 immigrants needed cash, and they needed it fast.

The move from a land-centered rural Sri Lanka on a cash-bound quest to a cash-centered urban England seems to have had an effect on the Tamil nation. The nationalized past in which the Tamil nation figured was territorially grounded. Even the current civil war, in which Tamil separatists are fighting for a "traditional homeland," has increasingly become a war over territory rather than one over civil rights. For Phase 3 immigrants, the shift from the solidity of land to the liquidity of cash seems, in its small way, to have undermined the land-bound nation as well as a grounded nationalized past. In this regard, it is interesting to note that many Phase 1 Tamils had either bought or hoped to buy large English homes with spacious gardens in the exclusive outskirts of London. They called them estates. Those among Phase 2 and Phase 3 Tamils who did invest in real estate in the 1980s preferred to buy flats and referred to them as their "liquid assets." Flats in London were considered liquid, land in Jaffna considered a beautiful lodestone. As one asylum seeker put it, "It is even more important to be solvent than to get asylum in England." He elaborated: "Tomorrow I might get a chance to go to Canada. Then why would I want to be stuck here or miss the chance only because I was not solvent? Even the U.S., I understand, is now giving out green cards for those who have a million dollars." Fluid metaphors such as solvency and liquidity figure prominently in the speech of these immigrants, especially among those who escaped the ravages of the civil war by the skin of their teeth and those who saw their fellow Tamils stuck in undesirable second countries, abandoned en route to a country of asylum for lack of money. "I am told," another informant announced, "that in Toronto and Montreal there are places called 'Little Jaffna.' That is enough of a Tamil nation for me. Wherever there are enough Tamils, there is a Tamil nation." A far cry indeed from a nationalized past that was determined by solid boundaries! The future is to be fluid, in more respects than one.

PHASE 3 AND UNEXPECTED DESTINATIONS

The early arrivals of Phase 3 had been those with at least some means—the means to leave Sri Lanka before Britain began tightening her laws, before the Immigration Carriers' Liability Act was passed,[33] before racketeers got into the act of facilitating the asylum seeker's escape with false papers at high cost, before the price for getting to Heathrow went from less than four hundred British pounds to more than five thousand. The "success stories" involving petrol stations and retail stores that one is likely to hear from asylum seekers apply mainly to those early arrivals who came to Britain before 1985. For the very poor—increasingly the profile of the average Tamil arriving at Heathrow during the latter part of the 1980s—the new exorbitant passage was bought for only one family member through his or her family going deeply into debt, in some instances after selling house and possessions. No longer could the one who entered Britain raise enough money to pay back his or her own debt, let alone raise enough to pay the going price for chancy "illegal" exits and entries of other family members. And even if and when this was possible, the pitfalls and snares were many and very hazardous.

The London-based Joint Council for the Welfare of Immigrants has knowledge of cases in which middlemen—also Tamils—have abandoned groups of Tamils at "transit points" in such faraway places as Bangkok and Nairobi, absconding with the five thousand pounds plus "set-up money" received from their charges. Such a middleman takes the refugees to an apartment or a room, tells them to stay put—lest they be caught by the authorities—until arrangements can be made for the next leg of the journey en route to London or some other Western capital. The room or apartment in question is locked from the outside to ensure double protection. The anxious and frightened group waits, at times for days, until hunger or suspicion gets the better of them, and they break loose or start screaming for help. The desperate and penniless escapees are then sometimes offered, by yet another set of racketeers, the opportunity to become drug couriers as a means of buying their way back onto the road to asylum. A refugee who gave me such an account concluded it by saying:

> You ask me about Tamil nationalism. There is only Tamil internationalism. No Tamil nationals. Never was. Never will be. This is Tamil internationalism. Being stuck in a windowless room in Thailand, or a jail in Nairobi or Accra or Lagos or Cairo or America. Or being a domestic servant in Singapore or Malaysia for a rich Tamil relative. Being part of a credit card racket in London. Crossing Niagara Falls into Canada. I am told there is even a Tamil fisherman on a Norwegian island near the North Pole. All internationals. And don't forget the briefless barrister at Charing Cross who tries to hawk his specialty as an immigration lawyer to anyone who is gullible enough to believe him. He is a Tamil too.

The African destinations were explained to me as follows by yet another informant: "No one plans on ending up in Africa. This happens because of drug-pushing middlemen. Customs in African airports are not that strict. And most of the airport officials are bribed by other agents." When I asked whether these agents were Tamils, he replied, "They are. Mainly members of PLOTE [People's Liberation Organization of Tamil Eelam].[34] They are caught and deported from European ports back to their last stop, usually Nigeria."

The African connection was widely described in the following manner: Middlemen in Thailand or Pakistan buy tickets to African destinations for desperate Tamils, giving them a package of drugs and a promise of a final European or Canadian destination. The Tamils' only obligation is to hand over the package to an African courier in Africa. Unlike Tamils, Africans are willing to carry drugs in a form undetectable by European customs: stuffed in a condom that is then swallowed. Because of this method, Africans passed through customs with ease until recently, when a swallowed condom burst in a courier's stomach. The courier was rushed to the hospital, where he died, and an autopsy exposed the game. Even though the Tamil role in the Africans' trafficking of drugs has achieved the status of commonly repeated folkloric truth, I have not been able to either confirm or disconfirm this story with any Tamil who has directly participated in this dangerous activity. It is known, however, that the use of drugs is strictly prohibited not only by the general Tamil cultural strictures and the opprobrium it could bring upon those who violate them but also by the moral policing of the LTTE. Drugs are meant for Europeans. The money that is believed to result from the sale of drugs is meant for the war effort in Eelam.

The story of Tamil asylum seekers ending up in the United States is a curious one. Only very few asylum seekers have been granted asylum in the United States over the past decade, and more than half of them are Sinhalas who had fled the government's crackdown on dissidents in the south of the island. It is widely known in the Tamil community that it is virtually impossible to get asylum in the United States. Of those who attempt to do so, almost none intended to seek asylum in that country in the first place. But they were trapped in transit, as it were, on their way to Canada. The story of Shanmugam is both unique and typical and is worth recalling in some detail.

Shanmugam was a twenty-eight-year-old Tamil whom I came to know in 1989 through a human rights attorney in Seattle, who asked me to serve as an expert witness at his hearing before an immigration judge. According to Shanmugam and affidavits sent on his behalf by justices of the peace and other prominent citizens of Jaffna, he was the son of a farmer. He had an older sister and a younger brother. He was unconnected with any of the several Tamil militant groups operating in Jaffna. But he was persecuted by two Tamil militant groups, by members of the Indian Peace-Keeping Forces, and by the Sri Lankan army. He had bullet marks on his foot and shoulder where he had been shot by an EPRLF (Eelam

Peoples Revolutionary Liberation Front) guard.[35] He finally fled Sri Lanka, fearing for his life. Now let me continue his narrative based on his account to his attorney and me and to the court.

From 1980 until the riots of 1983, Shanmugam had lived with his married sister in a suburb of Colombo. He had moved from Jaffna to Colombo because he wanted to prepare himself for the GCE (advanced level) exams by attending a private "tutory" in Colombo. In 1983, Sinhala mobs attacked his brother-in-law's home and set fire to it. His sister had left for Jaffna to deliver her first child in her mother's home, as is customary. His brother-in-law, who tried to face the mob and dissuade them from attacking his house, was killed. Shanmugam jumped out a back window and over the garden wall and fled the scene. After spending several weeks in refugee camps in Colombo, he joined an exodus of Tamil refugees and went to Jaffna by boat.

Back in Jaffna, he and his younger brother tried their best to hide from recruiters for the various Tamil militant groups who were combing Jaffna for volunteers to join their groups and be trained to fight the Sri Lankan state. In 1985, his seventeen-year-old brother disappeared, leaving behind a note informing his parents that he was joining the liberation struggle. In 1986, Shanmugam was taken in for questioning by members of the Sri Lankan army. After two weeks of considerable beating and torture, and interventions by the then Government Agent and his pleading mother, he was released to his parents.

Then came the Indo–Sri Lankan Peace Accord, under the terms of which the Indian army occupied northern and eastern Sri Lanka so as to restore peace between the Tamils and the Sri Lankan state. A few months after the LTTE declared its battle against the Indian army, members of the Indian army took Shanmugam in for questioning. The solitary confinement and beatings lasted for a week. Again, he was released. Again, Shanmugam attributes his release to his mother's indefatigable pleadings with the Indian commander. No sooner was he released than he was captured by the LTTE and taken in for questioning. This time, the questions were about what he had told the Indians and what he knew about the whereabouts of his brother. In response to the first question, he told them all that he remembered. As for his brother's whereabouts, he said that he knew nothing, not even which militant group he had joined. During the first week of his confinement, he was relentlessly tortured.

During the second week, even though the questions continued, he was treated well by the Tigers.

The very day he was released by the Tigers, he was recaptured by the Eelam Peoples Revolutionary Liberation Front. This Tamil militant group had come under the good graces of the Indian forces and had been given a certain measure of civil and military authority over the citizens of Jaffna. But members of this group also had abused their authority, had alienated many Tamils of the north, and came to be seen as the lackeys of the occupying Indians. According to Shanmugam, the torture under the EPRLF was the most severe. First, they were convinced that he had gone voluntarily to the LTTE to divulge details of the interrogation by the Indians, and they wanted to know what he had told them. Second, convinced that his younger brother was with the Tigers, they were keen on capturing him for the Indians, who were by now at war with the Tigers.

After several weeks of incarceration, torture, and interrogation, Shanmugam managed to escape. He fled Jaffna, and, after several days of walking through the jungle, he reached Mannar. From there, he bought his passage on a speedboat and reached India. From India, he informed his parents of his safety and his whereabouts. He knew that it would be only a matter of time before one of the militant groups, if not the Indian authorities, caught up with him.

While in Madras, he learned that he could get a forged passport and a ticket to Canada. Through labyrinthine means he informed his parents of his plans to buy a passport and leave for Canada. A month later, his mother and sister sold all their jewelry, and his father sold most of their land; through equally labyrinthine means they sent him five thousand dollars. With this money, he was able to buy a forged passport at a discounted price and pay a travel agent, who supplied an air ticket, arranged the route of his flight, and provided him with a contact who knew someone in Vancouver, B.C. The contact would show him the ropes so that he could apply for and obtain asylum in Canada. He was told that the only thing he needed to remember was to destroy his passport and flush it down the toilet of the airplane just before landing in Vancouver. His passport was red in color, Malaysian, and was quite worn from considerable use. It seemed as if it had belonged to a Malaysian businessman.

Shanmugam was routed through Hong Kong and, unlike his

compatriots who were stranded in Bangkok, did not have to leave any of the airports en route until he reached Seattle. All that he had seen of the countries through which his flight pattern took him were the airports' transit lounges. In Seattle, all passengers had to disembark and go through U.S. Customs before continuing on their flight to Vancouver. No one had warned him of this wrinkle in his itinerary. Even before he got to the long line in front of the customs officer's high table, with his tin trunk in hand, he was apprehended by another officer and taken in for questioning. He told them his story. He told them that he had no intention of remaining in the United States but wanted to reach Canada. When given the choice of either being sent back by the next available flight or being incarcerated until he received a hearing, in which the odds of his being repatriated to Sri Lanka were almost assured, Shanmugam chose the latter. This is the short and sweet version of the more detailed, horrendous tale he told his lawyer and me, and later told the judge who presided over the court hearing.

A particular episode of the court hearing merits retelling because it illustrates yet another aspect of refugees' predicament that goes unreported. Shanmugam spoke no English and understood almost none. To assist him, the court hired a South Asian living in Seattle who had been certified by Berlitz as qualified to translate English into Tamil and vice versa. Under cross-examination, Shanmugam had just finished describing the burning of his sister's house in Colombo and the murder of his brother-in-law.

DEFENDANT: And then I ran through the side streets, to avoid the mobs.

PROSECUTOR: Who were these mobs made up of?

TRANSLATOR: (*Renders an intelligible translation in a form of Tamil heavily accented by Malayalam.*)

DEFENDANT: Singalavar [Sinhalas].

TRANSLATOR: Sinhalas.

JUDGE: Were there policemen on the street?

TRANSLATOR: (*Translates the question correctly in Malayalam. The defendant strains to follow him and then answers.*)

DEFENDANT: Police and army.

TRANSLATOR: Yes.

JUDGE: Did they help you?

TRANSLATOR: (*Translates the question in Malayalamized Tamil, but the defendant seems to follow the drift of the question and responds.*)

DEFENDANT: No. They hit me with their rifles. And when I fell down, they kicked me with their boots and said, "Run, Tamil, run."

TRANSLATOR: Yes.

At this point, I told the defense attorney that the translation was incorrect, and he conveyed this to the judge.

JUDGE: (*to defense attorney*): Your expert witness is an expert on Sri Lanka. But the translator is an expert in the language spoken and accordingly has been certified by Berlitz. Is your expert witness certified by Berlitz as an expert in . . . Tamil?

DEFENSE ATTORNEY: (*after seeing me shake my head*): No, your honor.

Almost immediately after asking the prosecutor to continue, the judge interrupted the prosecutor, asking the court recorder to stop recording the proceedings and turn off the tape recorder. Off the record, the judge asked me to render what I thought was the correct translation of the defendant's response to his question.

EXPERT WITNESS: He said that the police and soldiers did not help him but hit him with the butts of their rifles, and when he fell down, kicked him with their boots and said, "Run, Tamil, run."

JUDGE   (*to Berlitz translator*): Is that correct?

TRANSLATOR   (*now realizing that there is a native speaker of Tamil in the court room*): Yes, your honor.

At another point in the hearing:

PROSECUTOR: Are you a Malaysian?

TRANSLATOR: (*Renders an intelligible translation.*)

DEFENDANT: No.

PROSECUTOR: What is your nationality?

TRANSLATOR: Tamil or Sinhala?

DEFENDANT: Tamil.

TRANSLATOR: Tamil.

PROSECUTOR: So you believe in a separate Tamil nation in Sri Lanka?

TRANSLATOR: Do you want a Tamil nation?

DEFENDANT: I don't even have a country [translatable as "nation"] to which I belong.

TRANSLATOR: No.

Malayalam is a language spoken in southwest India. Linguists estimate that its breakaway from early Tamil occurred around the thirteenth century. The mutual intelligibility between modern Malayalam and modern Tamil is akin to that between Italian and Spanish. Imagine a monolingual Italian speaker certified by Berlitz as one who speaks and understands Spanish, who is appointed to serve as translator in a court of law between English-speaking attorneys and judge and a monolingual Spanish-speaking defendant. Such was Shanmugam's predicament.

I might add, as a postscript to my account of this memorable trial, that the judge rendered his judgment against the defendant. In his judgment, he thanked me for my testimony and for educating the court on the recent history of the ethnic tensions in Sri Lanka. But he declared that in the final analysis he was compelled to take the word of his State Department in meting out his judgment. According to the U.S. State Department, "There was no fear of persecution in Sri Lanka."

After two years, we learned that this judgment had been upheld by higher courts. Shanmugam was sent back to Sri Lanka. His family came to meet him at the Colombo airport. They claim to have seen him arrive at customs and then to have waited for him to emerge. But he never came out. After several hours of waiting and inquiries and receiving different kinds of answers, they tried to console themselves by saying that their experience of having seen him briefly must have been only an illusion. Other inquiries pointed toward Sri Lanka's Special Defense Forces, who, it was said, had whisked him off to the notorious Fourth Floor for interrogation. Whatever the case may be, Shanmugam has been neither seen nor heard from since that day.

Far fewer women than men were apprehended at the border, and when they were, most of them chose to return to Sri Lanka or managed to get themselves bailed out by relatives in the United States and then found their way to Canada. But children were also arrested and detained, and their story also needs to be told, if only because of the uniquely dangerous situation into which they are thrown by a well-meaning legal system. Two such cases merit our attention.

CHILDREN

Karunaharan was sixteen years old. Like Shanmugam, he had his asylum-seeking trip to Canada cut short at U.S. Customs in Seattle. He came from a middle-class family in Jaffna and had, until his escape, attended the prestigious secondary school of Jaffna College along with his older sister. One day, when he and his sister were walking home from school, they were stopped by a Sikh soldier of the Indian Peace-Keeping Forces. Karunaharan was told to wait on the road while his sister was taken into a house occupied by some Indian army officers. Within minutes of her disappearance behind the closed door of the house, he heard her screams. He ran to the side window of the house, and through a crack he saw his sister "being shamed." [36] He ran to the front door, which was being guarded by two grinning Indian soldiers, and tried to gain access. He was kicked by one of them, and he fell to the ground, unable to breathe. He heard his sister's screams become muffled and then grow fainter and fainter, until he heard her no more. He thought he was dying. Then he thought his sister was dead. He sat up and wiped his mouth. There was blood. Two other soldiers had replaced the two who had been guarding the door. Finding them engrossed in their own conversation, he crept back to the window just in time to see his sister being shot in the back. He sneaked back to the main road, and when he reached it, he heard a second shot. He ran home sobbing and screaming. After this incident, his parents managed to get him on a flight to Canada, which brought him into Seattle's detention center instead.

Karunaharan was not an adult and therefore was put in a detention center for children, where his co-detainees were streetwise American teenagers, incarcerated for crimes that ranged from selling drugs to aggravated assault, robbery, and even rape. Bright as he was and as much as he tried to adjust to the ethos of the place, his middle-class village background in conservative Jaffna had not prepared him for this. He was gang-raped the very first night and beaten up the next. His attorney succeeded in persuading the judge to release him to the custody of a Tamil citizen in the Seattle area in whose charges he was to be kept until his next hearing. He eventually crossed the border into Canada and was granted asylum there.

Shoba was ten years old when the Indian troops came to Jaffna to "keep the peace." When I interviewed her with her attorney in Seattle, she was thirteen. According to her, the Indian soldiers whom the citizens of Jaffna had welcomed with garlands had, within a few months, become enemies of all the people, except those who had joined the "EP" or supported them. People in her neighborhood secretly called the EPRLF the "EP" and rhymed it with *Nai Pee* ("dog shit"). The EPRLF ranked foremost in its conception a state based on socialist principles of equality: equality for all castes, both sexes, the Tamils of the various regions, and the Sinhalas. But when given the power of the gun and command by their Indian superiors, low-ranking EPRLF cadres in particular became drunk with power and patrolled the streets intimidating the citizens. When an EPRLF officer rode in his car, other vehicles had to pull over to the edge of the road; when an EPRLF cadre walked along a street, ordinary citizens had to step aside, even into a ditch if need be. Those who refused were taken in and punished or even beaten on the spot. Schoolchildren whose parents were not open supporters of the EP were especially afraid of running into uniformed members of the movement. They usually rode their bikes and chose side lanes and byways to make their way between home and school.

One day, Shoba and her friends were returning from school on their bikes, laughing over a joke that her friend had cracked, when they suddenly ran into an EP commander with his assistants. They all quickly got off their bikes. The girl who had cracked the joke was Shoba's best friend, the class comic and very smart. She was so taken aback by the armed "soldiers" that she simply rose from the bike seat and did not have time to wheel the bike to the side of the road. She stood astride her bike as if in shock—but still had a smile on her face because of her joke. One of the EP man jerked her off her bike. While the other threw the bike to the side of the road and smashed it, the commander ordered the man who had hold of her to take her to the field and make her kneel down. While Shoba and her schoolmates looked on in terror, the commander gave them a lecture about respect and the EPRLF and then turned toward her kneeling friend and shot her in the head. Then he put his gun in his holster, saying, "Let this be a lesson to you." The children pushed their bikes home, sobbing in silence for fear of being heard by the "soldiers," who continued on their promenade.

When Shoba reached home, she broke into hysterical sobs. Her mother and father shook her to make her speak and tell them what had happened. Finally, her father, who had never spanked her, slapped her in order to calm her down. Then she told them what had happened. Her father warned them to expect more trouble. "An old woman has shot an Indian officer," he told her. The Indian army had ordered the residents of a neighborhood to vacate their houses so that the soldiers, in response to a tip-off, could carry out a search for Tigers and their weapons. The old woman had refused to leave; she merely huddled in a corner and whimpered in terror. Since the North Indian soldiers did not know Tamil, a compassionate South Indian officer—a Malayalee—went into the woman's low-doored hut and bent down to assure her in the little Tamil he knew that she would be safe under his protection, and he pleaded with her to leave with him. The woman pulled out a machine gun that had been concealed by the drape of her skirt and shot the officer to death. She in turn was riddled with bullets by the two Indian *jawans* who had been waiting outside.

Even though the killing of the officer had taken place in another area of the peninsula, it was widely known that whenever a soldier was killed, the army went on a rampage. This had been more the case with the Sri Lankan army during its earlier occupation, but it happened with the Indians as well. Shoba's father also had heard that those neighborhoods which "stole electricity" by jerry-rigging connections to the main line were thought to be LTTE sympathizers who were rewarded with LTTE expertise. Shoba maintained to us that this was not true, that ever since the onset of fuel and electricity rationing, citizens all over Jaffna had resorted to such devices for beating the restrictions.

As predicted by her father, soldiers came to the neighborhood that afternoon around four o'clock. Most men had been tipped off to the Indians' arrival and had fled. The soldiers ordered everybody to step out of their homes, and the houses were searched. After the search was finished, the residents, all of them women, were told to go back in. Then a soldier came out of a house dragging a woman and her infant son. Shoba ran into the backyard to peek through the palm-frond fence and see what was happening. The senior officer asked the woman where the man of the house was. When she said she did not know, he shot her dead. She fell backward, still holding her infant. When her hands loosened the grip on her child and fell to her side, the child, still seated on her stomach, started to scream. The soldiers first left the child and his dead mother on the ground and walked out the front gate. But a few moments later, one of the soldiers returned and shot the infant with one bullet. Suddenly not a sound could be heard.

That was the night Shoba's parents decided to send her out of the country. She had a cousin in Canada, and that would be her destination. But she had no passport. They managed to get her a forged passport, in which her age was recorded as eighteen rather than thirteen. Because she was too young to travel alone, they found a naturalized Canadian relative and changed her name to read as if she were his wife; the two then traveled to Canada as husband and wife. When they were apprehended in Seattle, it was clear that she was younger than eighteen and much too young to be married. Confessions were wrung out of them with ease, and Shoba and her partner were arrested. The partner posted bail and left for Canada.

Fortunately for Shoba, a guard who sensed the danger she faced in juvenile detention pleaded with the judge to release her to the custody of someone—the guard herself was willing—who would take care of her until her hearing. (In several instances, guards who have seen the danger these children are in have volunteered to take them into their own homes.) The attorney assigned to defend Shoba got in touch with a Tamil family he knew and asked them if he might request that the judge release her to their custody. The male head of the family said that they would have been glad to help but feared being drawn into anything that could signal their presence to the LTTE members who were operating in Europe and Canada and who were very aggressive fund-risers for the cause of Eelam. They did not want their name to appear on any LTTE list for fear that this would instigate the Sri Lankan government to harass and persecute family members who still remained on the island.

Next the lawyer contacted an Estate Tamil family that had intermarried with the Sinhalas. This family willingly and gladly took in Shoba, saying that Estate Tamils were still Indian Tamils and therefore had nothing to fear from a Sri Lankan movement such as the LTTE. After two weeks, they flew with her to Ithaca, where she was handed over to a Sri Lankan Tamil Catholic priest, who took her across the Niagara bridge into Canada; there she applied for asylum and was met by her cousin. Before she crossed over, the priest asked her what she planned to do in Canada. Her answer: "Keep away from anyone who talks about Eelam or Sri Lanka or motherland."

Children much younger than Karunaharan and Shoba, even as young as five years old, have been put onto planes unaccompanied by any adult and sent to Germany and Switzerland. The German and Swiss news media have featured these arrivals in headline stories. Although some kind German and Swiss citizens rushed to adopt the children, others described this as a new "wave" and called the children "economic refugees." I expressed my puzzlement at this description to a German woman. She saw the situation as quite straightforward, based on "confessions" by the children themselves. When most of these arriving children were asked where their parents were, they would say, "Mommy said for me to go and that she will come soon and join me." That was the supposed evidence: a mother's ruse to claim the right to emigrate to the country as a parent, once the child was naturalized! That the children would have to grow to adulthood before being able to sponsor their parents, which would take as many as thirteen more years, did not seem like much of an issue. What this woman told me in an interview in Heidelberg was of course repeated more than once over the German and Swiss media. Even many of the kind souls who offered to adopt these children could not believe the cruelty of their parents, that they could lie to their children when they knew that they had neither plans nor the possibility of following the children. The second group is no closer to the truth than the first.

Unfortunately or otherwise, most South Asian parents choose to hide the truth when they deem it likely to cause instant pain, sorrow, and sadness. This is so with terminally ill patients, from whom both physician and relatives conceal the nature of their illness as long as possible. And it is especially true of parents and children. A mother who is about to administer some bitter medicine to her child will not hesitate to lie about its bitterness. The mother who sent her unaccompanied child to Switzerland or Germany probably did not have the luxury of reflecting on the long-range psychological trauma such deceptions would wreak on her child. The story of one woman who had dispatched her child in such a manner and whom I had the opportunity to interview in Sri Lanka is likely to have been a typical variant of the accounts of other mothers (and, in a few instances, fathers) who resorted to such desperate actions.

Punitham had lost her father, both brothers, and two of her four children. Left with only a son and a daughter, she decided to somehow get at least her son to safety. She knew that it would be only a matter of time before the next shell would fall or the next bullet would hit. She was determined to send her child to any country and have fate take over. Her choice for him was between certain death in Sri Lanka and a chancy life somewhere else. The only country that would not return her child, she had heard, was Germany. So she sold all her possessions and got her son a ticket. She could not bring herself to tell her son the truth. How could she be so cruel? How could she tell him that he was never going to see her again, that she would probably be killed while he would be able to live? If she had told him, how could he have left her behind and gone with the stranger he called "uncle," who took him to the airport? The only gift she thought she could give him was the gift of life. And she is glad that she gave it to him. But otherwise, she says, "There isn't a day that goes by that I don't pray for him, and weep for him. He was my only son. He is my only son. I am glad he did not die for Sri Lanka or for Eelam. Maybe he will remember Tamil. That is enough. He will be a German-Tamil. That is enough." Economic refugee, indeed!

THE DISAGGREGATION OF IDENTITY

Many of the men who left their wives and children and fled to great Britain after 1985 came to escape death. Now they hold little hope of seeing their families again. They live in a state of heightened anxiety as they await the seven-year limit: by the end of the seventh year they must, by law, be notified as to whether their application for asylum has been accepted. Many, unable to bear the strain, have returned home regardless of the consequences awaiting them. Some have met their death there. Others have returned to Sri Lanka after learning that the reason they left in the first place no longer exists: their families have been wiped out by one armed group or another. The intransigence of British authorities and the scale of British xenophobia and racism vis-à-vis refugees (as evidenced by frequent headlines in London's tabloids) are astounding when one realizes that between 1979 and 1989 Great Britain, with a population of almost 58,000,000, admitted only 54,935 refugees, a mere 0.09 percent of the total population. Of these, only 7,910 were Sri Lankans.[37]

If white Britain's reluctance to give refuge to asylum seekers is astounding, Phase 1 Tamils' willingness to share in this sentiment is ironic, but also understandable. They, like the white Britons, believed in a nation and a nationalized past. In the case of the Phase 3 refugees, the more urgently they needed a nation or a national past, the more authentically they encountered its unavailableness. The more obtrusively this unavailableness pressed itself upon the lives of these refugees, the more the nation and a national past revealed itself as something only occurrent and nothing more. The national past had been loosened from its hitherto unexpressed inclusion in the background practices of these Tamils. The nationalized past became an isolated property, a cipher.

By the beginning of the 1990s, further changes were observed in the composition of the more recent asylum-seeking cohort. Now not only did young men and women who had escaped the Sri Lankan and Indian armies seek asylum in Britain, but also warhardened and disenchanted militants, escaping tyrannous militant groups of their own, were arriving in London. This group introduced a climate of suspicion on the one hand and a pervasive cynicism on the other. The most prominent target of this cynicism was the nation. I have witnessed arguments between these Tamils and other Tamils who had embarked on the project of finding and establishing their national past, in which the former group considered the distant past that obsessed their fellow nationalists to be irrelevant at best and a sign of derangement at worst. The only past they knew and cared about—and did not want to be caught in— was the recent past of war, rape, torture, and death that they had just escaped. Phase 3 Tamils have also begun to establish new alliances and adopt new attitudes toward identity and difference that are now marking them off from Phase 1 Tamils in unprecedented ways. A series of examples will illustrate my point.

A number of Phase 3 Tamils who began working at the petrol pump moved up to managing petrol stations and the attached "mini-markets" and then on to acquiring small grocery stores formerly run by Ugandan Indians whose children now have no interest in inheriting their parents' businesses. Along with entailing late hours and hard work, running these shops presents a unique problem in customer relations. In Sivapalan's case, for instance, one of his customers is an older English woman who comes to his shop every day to ask him why he sells these nasty-smelling and strange-looking things and why he does not take it all and go back where he came from. Sivapalan smiles and checks out the items she buys— because they are inexpensive in his shop—and wishes her a good day. I asked him what he felt. He said, "Hate!" And then he added, "But I also know we will win and they will lose."

Sivapalan and other Tamil shopowners like him have another interesting customer in the young Afro-Caribbean British male. Some of these young men—"at least one per night"—walk into his shop and pick up a pack or two of beer, presenting, however, only a packet of chewing gum at the cash register. When asked about the beer, the young man boldly declares, knowing full well that everyone knows otherwise, that he brought the beer from outside and owes money only for the gum he bought at this store. Sivapalan takes the money for the chewing gum and lets him go. This practice is so well known that it even piques the sympathetic ire of Phase 1 Tamils, who wonder why the Tamil shopkeeper does not inform the police. Phase 3 Tamils consider this kind of advice a sign of the utter ignorance of Phase 1 Tamils and of the distance that separates the two groups. For one, the police are their foremost enemy. In support of these sentiments, Phase 3 Tamils supplied me with stories of police racism, injustice, and violence too numerous to recount here. As one Tamil put it, "The policemen of the world should have a county of their own." For another, the shopkeepers find the rage of their "law-abiding" Phase 1 counterparts amusing and out of place. Even I was impressed by the equanimity with which these shopkeepers reacted to these blatant acts of shoplifting. Even though these Tamils did not extend alliances of interper sonal relations to the Afro-Caribbean Britons, they extended them alliances of understanding. They did not see them as breaking the law but as having broken *with* the law. To this extent, their experience was a common one.

Tamils have little to do with the Afro-Caribbean community, a group whose "urban ways" they cannot relate to, people who, in their view, "give the family low priority." However, they find African immigrants much more compatible allies. Many of these immigrants not only share Phase 3 Tamils' asylum-seeking status, they also have "rural values." That these new links of affect have materialized may be illustrated by the following incident.

Sahitharan was a twenty-nine-year-old asylum seeker from Sri Lanka. He was waylaid by a group of young whites and bashed to death in London's Eastham. Several of the London-based organizations working for refugees organized a protest march. More than four thousand people of all ethnic groups joined the march. But only one hundred fifty Tamils attended, all from Phase 3. The largest non-Tamil representation at the rally was made up of black Africans. It is interesting to note that the trustees—all Phase I Tamils—of the Wimbledon Hindu temple denied the organizers of the march the right to hang posters on the temple premises. Their reason? "We do not want to antagonize the white community."

Other alliances have been forged among Phase 3 Tamils that have become more vital than any they ever had with their fellow Tamils of the other phases or the separatists/nationalists at home. Most of these alliances span national boundaries to include fellow asylum seekers in other European countries who have fled both the nationalist Sri Lankan army and the equally nationalist Tamil militant groups. To the immigrant Tamils, the nationalized past that these groups are frantically trying to construct is something they have broken away from, just as they feel they have broken with the law. Alliances have also extended to other refugees fleeing other national pasts, and a keen interest is shown in organizations such as Amnesty International, whose scrutiny transcends national boundaries.

DISPLACED PERSONS AND AN AGENTIVE MOMENT

But questions persist. In what sense can we say that these refugees have transcended the nation and the grip it has over their daily lives and preoccupations? And to what extent have these asylum seekers been able to draw from their suffering, from their alienation from nation, the ability to simultaneously dissolve the nation from its occurrentness in their lives in a boundless sea—the dissolver of all, especially boundaries—whose waves they can defy and in whose flows they can find moments of subversive pleasure? Will the last word belong to the nation-state and those who believe in it, live for it, fight and die for it, or to those who subvert it? Only time will tell. But what we do see are moments in which individuals and groups of individuals exercise their agency not so much against the structures of the nation-state but in indifference toward it. The transformation of their diffuse and enduring suffering into something positive and productive seems to rest on such agentive moments. But what do we mean by agency—or, rather, an agentive moment? To answer these corollary questions, we must take a necessary detour.

When historians and anthropologists speak of agency, the image brought to mind is that of the individual actor, the pioneer, the bold and reflective subject who acts, if not from authority and power, then out of determination. Even those who overtly reject such a reduction of agency to the individual do not renounce the covert paradigmatic status of the individual agent in their analysis. This is a testimony to the success of the Cartesianization of much of the modern world, in which the myth of the intuiting cogito has been naturalized. From here it is only one step to Cartesian dualism, in which the intuiting, self-contained self is set against a radical outside, a radical other. Thus we find formulations of the question of agency rendered in such oppositional terms as agency versus structure or agent versus patient. An agent is seen as one who takes one's future into one's own hands. Such an autonomous and unary self, as I have indicated, can only be intuited and can exist nowhere else but in the impossible world of the Cartesian cogito. And, furthermore, as Peirce, among others, has clearly demonstrated, "because we have no power of intuition, every cognition is necessarily determined logically by previous cognitions."[38] Thus historicity is an integral part of the symbol and the self. A semeiotic[39] perspective on the self, on life, and on being human is unavoidably historic and incorrigibly trinary. The core of Peirce's anti-Cartesianism, at least insofar as it pertains to questions about the individual and agency, is contained in his assertion that "man is a sign" (or a cluster of signs). An individual is but an illusion, be it the individual person or the individual point in mathematics, even if at times a necessary illusion.[40] The only thing that is real is process. A sign can never be an individual or a monad. It is a triadically constituted process. So is the self.

Self-awareness is not the product of intuition but of inference. Consciousness is a *process* in which "the self becomes aware of itself on becoming aware of what it is not, of the non-self, of the external Other."[41] Without the precipitation of self against the Other, there is nothing to infer and therefore no reason for self-awareness or self-consciousness to be; and, conversely, without self-consciousness, the self remains unrealized, as a mere potential, a pre-self, if you will. It is this triadically correlative relationship— among the self, the Other, and the awareness of the relationship of identity/difference that brings the two together—in process that constitutes a self. The triadicity of the self, then, is no different from the triadicity of the sign. Indeed, the self is a sign, mainly on the order of a symbol. The self and the sign are in time, and, like Derrida's signified,[42] they are always on the move. And if the self is constantly being inferred—and it can be inferred only in time— then "there is no time in the 'present instant' for an inference, least of all for an inference concerning that very instant."[43]

What we call a person or limit by calling him or her an "individual" is but an infelicitous shorthand for describing a relatively dense cluster of signs or sign-activities, whose density is owed to the property of signs to take habits. If a person can take habits, he or she can also lose habits and change habits. But the locus of habit-change is not necessarily confined to an individualized person: "the box of flesh and blood," as James described the self. It can occur in interpersonal space as well as intrapersonal space. An internal dialogue (which is what Peirce understands a thought to be) could be the locus of the agentive moment. It can occur between two or among a group or a throng of people. Hence I consider the Gandhian Self-Rule Movement or the civil rights marches of the 1960s as loci of agentive moments. Institutions can generate an agentive moment as long as they contain within them the signs of human being. So can any human creation. Thus the U.S. Constitution may be described as agentive, for it carries not only the traces of the authors and signatories of the document but also traces of the human habit of habit-change that is alive in the interstices of that document. In the case of the Tamil refugees, their very globalization—held together perhaps by the Internet, among other things—could be the locus of agency. Such a semeiotic view of the self positions the question of agency quite differently from the way it is positioned in a Cartesian world. For this reason, the semeiotic perspective is more at home with the notion of an agentive moment than with that of agency per se. What, then, is an agentive moment?

Before answering this question and bringing it within the ambit of the substance of this essay, I must first revisit the semeiotic concept of habit. If the self is part and parcel of semeiosis, and semeiosis is an ongoing process of making inferences from experience, from encounters with the non-self, then inferences also generate expectations, and expectations are of the nature of habit. The more our expectations—conscious and unconscious—are satisfied, the more regularized and ramified our habits become. "Habit" describes patterns of feeling, action, and thought. Or, as Marjorie Miller puts it: "a habit is a thoughtful mediation between feelings and actions through the development of a meaningful relation: a future imperfect conditional rule for action *in case*. The habit, as a rule, solidifies as it is ramified in mental rehearsal and/or practical action—repetition reveals the antecedents, conditions and implications of the 'associations, "transociations," or . . . dissociations' (see Peirce MS 318,351) established. Meaning *emerges*."[44] Habit describes a relatively settled period or state in semeiosis.

Habits are not confined to "individuals" alone but characterize semeiosic collectivities of various dimensions: a connubial partnership, a family, a department, a discipline, a congregation, an institution, a society, or a culture. And the agentive moment—to anticipate—can be located in any one of these semeiosic configurations as long as there lies in this configuration the human habit of habit-change. To be sure, inorganic matter has habits, plants have habits, and animals have habits. But only humans have the additional habit of or capacity for habit-change.[45]

In our ordinary lives, in our everyday commerce with the world around us, we are, by and large, protected from caprice and shock, from the "bruteness" of Secondness by the Thirdness of habit. Or, to put it more precisely, the interruptions of the reverie of the Thirdness of habit by instances of Secondness are but fleeting moments, infinitesimal tests, as it were, to see if semeiosis is active and to determine whether the prevailing "habits" are agentive. That is, are they sufficiently alive (nonpetrified) and capable of activating the habit of habit-change if necessary, capable of generating new meaning to life under new circumstances when called upon to do so? Most of the time they are, and human habits are indeed rife with life, "with things new born," to quote a line from Shakespeare's *Winter's Tale,* where life and death are juxtaposed.[46] But these minor events and consequent copings do not merit the term "agentive." There are, however, times in life when interruptions of habit or a breach in the order of things is of such magnitude that prevailing habits are not up to the task of providing the inferential appeasement for soothing the resulting shock by providing emergent meanings. The lives of many of those who figure in this essay have been held in the grip of such crises of meaning, where existing habits have proved to be unhelpful, where the abyss of a breached moment of Secondness holds its place. Such moments of Secondness are what I call agentive moments.

In this essay, the nation has proved to be an inadequate habit, introducing into the lives of many an agentive moment. It is agentive because the only way of escape or resumption of semeiosis and a meaningful life is through the generation of radically new habits that lead in radically new directions. Have new habits emerged under these circumstances? In most cases, the answer is a tentative and timorous yes. But where there have been no redeeming habits, where "deliberate coping" has not given meaning to life, death—corporeal (usually suicide) or psychic—has been the result, the terminus of semeiosis.

If human habit is rife with life—"with things new born"—it is also rife with death. What is the future of the nascent habits of those who, as individuals or as collectivities, have had to choose against familiar habits? They have one of two futures. They may, in time, be reabsorbed into the currents of older habits. For instance, those who have been displaced by the nation-state of Sri Lanka and alienated from the very habit of "nation" may, in new countries, under new assurances, return to being nationals once more by either becoming faithful citizens of their adopted nation-state or by appealing to a nostalgia for the nation of their birth, childhood, and early childhood—or both simultaneously. In such a case, we can say that the habit-change was short-lived. Most Tamil students I have met in North American universities who continue to be part of the discourse of nation have told me that this is what they expect to happen to their thoroughly alienated fellow Tamils. They may well be proven right. But it is also possible that the familiar habit of nation—an overwhelmingly pervasive and powerful habit—will have to yield to a thoroughly new constellation of habit, to be found through the "venturing into the diaspora of the spirit, as the only path for reaching something like home."[47] Is this moment in the lives of these displaced Tamils agentive, a moment at the threshold of such a new habit formation? This question can be answered only in retrospect, when the effects of this moment are fully realized and when it can be determined whether or not the habit of nation has undergone a habit-change in order to appease the radical interruption at and of this agentive moment.

CONCLUSION

In the modern world, we have come to view the nation-state as the ultimate unit of protection. What is it that renders a nation-state legitimate? John Herz's view is typical, combining nostalgic realism and nostalgic idealism: "Legitimacy originates from feelings and attitudes of the people within as well as neighbors and others abroad in regard to the unit, its identity and coherence, its political and general 'way of life.'"[48]

Herz further holds that a nation-state's internal politics require it to be grounded upon a contiguous expanse of territory,[49] its "physical corporeal capacity."[50] What Herz fails to add is that the physical corporeal capacity in question is a thoroughly temporalized one in the modern nation-state, temporalized with the past. Michael Walzer in his *Spheres of Justice* subsumes all plurality under the caption of "shared understandings" that make a modern nation-state possible, despite diversity.[51] This, I presume, includes a shared understanding of the past. What political theorists of the modern nation-state such as Walzer and Herz, and Schumpeter before them,[52] fail to appreciate is how problematic a phenomenon "shared understanding" is, and how it has become increasingly so in late modernity.

On the one hand there is the LTTE gallantly and ruthlessly fighting for its Eelam, and the Sri Lankan army fighting for its Sri Lanka. On the other hand there is the mother who simply wants her son to remember Tamil and could not care less for Eelam or Sri Lanka, as well as the ex-militant who almost lost his or her life for Eelam who comes to share that mother's outlook. A child expresses her wish not to be around people who speak of their motherland, even as children who are drafted and who volunteer bear arms for the motherland. One generation of Tamils entertains fantasies of being ambassadors of their victorious nation, while another generation wants little or nothing to do with their nation. While some fight for solid land and fixed boundaries, others strive for liquid assets and fluid boundaries.

This case study of Tamil immigrants to Britain probes only one instance in which nationalism and the national past have become such contested categories. I am certain that many more exist, and that some are being spawned at this moment in other parts of the world. By "contestation," I do not mean the arguments that abound as to whose nation a particular territory is and whose nationalized past is a valid one. I do not deny the existence of such debates, but I claim that they conceal a far more radical contestation: a contestation that has been made possible by the unavailableness and occurrentness of the categories in question. Shared understandings and principles of common membership in nations and national pasts are not only highly ephemeral affairs, but they also deny the reality of counternationalist currents that flow through and over the dikes of the territorial nation and the national imaginary. Refugees—not only Tamil refugees—are one of the many embodiments of this overflow that disturb "established priorities of identity/difference through which social relations are organized." [53] The transformation of the Tamil immigrant in Britain is one among many representations of "a social process through which fixed identities and naturalized conventions are pressed . . . to come to terms with their constructed characters, as newly emergent social identities disturb settled conventions and denaturalize social networks of identity and difference." [54]

A final note. Several readers of this essay have remarked on the irony of my having drawn on the work of Martin Heidegger for a contribution to a volume on social suffering, a man who at one time supported the Nazi cultural vision and who never publicly confronted his past. Despite my close reading and re-reading of Heidegger as well as my reading of the several deeply critical books that have most energetically taken Heidegger to task for his unforgivable involvement with Nazism,[55] I continue to believe that attempts to systematically link all or even most of his writings to prefigurations of the ideology of National Socialism remain unconvincing. This is not the place to insert my own position on the debate that has come to be known as the "Heidegger crisis." Suffice it to say that if I were to have delineated my own position it would have been heavily indebted to the careful sifting of the evidence and argument put forth by Joseph Kockelmans, Fred Dallmayr, Hans Sluga, and, to a lesser extent, Jacques Derrida.[56] If I were to draw only one moral from the sad and sordid *l'affair Heidegger,* it is the following.

In *Being in Time* and in *What Is Metaphysics?,* which followed a few years later, *Dasein* refers to the entity that each of us himself or herself is. It does not oblige us to see a human being as a biological entity, nor as essentially rational, nor again as consciousness. *Dasein* is anything but a self-contained subject or ego or a Cartesian cogito. *Dasein* is, literally, "being there." In "being there," *Dasein* is marked by an engagement with "being together" or co-being or being-with. However, the Heideggerian co-being was never intended to be or become coterminous with the Rousseauean or Hegelian state—the former the embodiment of the general will and the latter the actualization of reason. Nor was co-being a form of communitarianism of any sort. When the state or quasi-state, in any of these three forms, and the self-contained subject—to which Peirce was so averse—become coeval models of each other, xenophobic nationalism—which is but human subjectivity totalized—is the result. Nazism, no less than Sinhala chauvinism, no less than Tamil Tigerism, is a manifestation of inauthentic being. The irony, then, is that Heidegger himself, in his anxious quest for authentic being, courted and briefly surrendered himself to such an inauthentic being in one of its ugliest manifestations.

For the Phase 3 Tamil refugees of whom I have written, the unavailability of the nation-state has provided an opportunity for pursuing greater authenticity of being. To many of these refugees, the encounter with the radical other—nonbeing or death—has given being a fresh chance at authenticity. If *Dasein* is marked by engagement in being with and among other beings, it should also, in its move toward greater authenticity, be marked by what Heidegger called a "caring for." Fred Dallmayr characterizes this caring as a "reciprocal 'letting-be.'"[57] He warns, however, that such "letting-be" must not be equaled with an attitude of indifference or the escapist vacuity of a Deleuzian "nomadism." It is likely that some among these refugees will have chosen these inauthentic options. By "letting-be," Heidegger had in mind an attitude that is "strikingly captured in the notion of 'anticipating-emancipatory solicitude' (*vorspringend-befreiende Fursorge*), a solicitude that aids the other in pursuing his or her potential for being and nonbeing." It is a kind of solicitude that "'does not so much displace the other as anticipate his/her existential potentiality for being' and which 'helps the other to become transparent in his/her care to become *free for it*.'"[58] There are more among these Phase 3 immigrants, and among several members of host countries who have come to know such individuals, who are closer to such an authenticity of *Dasein* than are to be found among the LTTE, the Sri Lankan state, or the bureaucracies of refugee management. In the very social suffering endured in the face of death—physical and cultural—is to be found an agentive moment where a quest for greater authenticity of socially being-with becomes possible.

ENDNOTES

[1] This essay appears, in a slightly different form, as chapter 6 in my book *Charred Lullabies: Chapters in an Anthropography of Violence* (Princeton, N.J.: Princeton University Press, 1997).

[2] A. L. Basham, *The Wonder That Was India* (London: Sidgwick and Jackson, 1968); Jawaharlal Nehru, *The Discovery of India* (Garden City, N.Y.: Anchor Books, 1960).

[3] Daniel, *Charred Lullabies: Chapters in an Anthropography of Violence.*

[4] The three phases and the Tamils of these phases are herein typified. There are conspicuous exceptions in which Tamils of one phase have acted more like Tamils of a different phase.

[5] Tone, token, and type correspond to Charles Peirce's three phenomenological categories of Firstness, Secondness, and Thirdness. Very briefly, Firstness, or in-

itselfness, is associated with potentiality. Secondness, or over-againstness, is associated with actuality or the here-and-now; and Thirdness, or in-betweenness, is associated with mediation or generality.

6 Burghers are persons of some Dutch or Portuguese ancestry.

7 Richard Leslie Brohier, *Discovering Ceylon* (Colombo, Sri Lanka: Lake House Investments, 1973); John Davy, *An Account of the Interior of Ceylon and of Its Inhabitants, with Travels in That Island* (Dehiwala, Sri Lanka: Tisara Prakasakayo, 1969); Mahanama, *The Mahavamsa, or The Great Chronicle of Ceylon,* trans. Wilhelm Geiger (London: Luzac, for the Pali Text Society, 1964); Robert Knox, *An Historical Relation of Ceylon* (Colombo, Sri Lanka: M. D. Gunasena, 1956–57); H. Parker, *Ancient Ceylon* (London: Luzak & Co., 1909); K. M. de Silva, *A History of Sri Lanka* (Berkeley, Calif.: University of California Press, 1981).

8 "Paki" is a common pejorative term used for referring to South Asians in Britain. It is intended to conjure up an image of poor South Asian Muslims (presumably from Pakistan) who perform menial jobs, who speak a strange language, who practice a strange religion that requires them to prostrate themselves toward Mecca during prayer time wherever they happen to be—and, above all, whose women dress in strange clothes.

9 Estate Tamils are Tamils of Indian origin who were brought to Sri Lanka by the British in the nineteenth century and the first half of the twentieth century to work on coffee and (later) tea plantations. When Ceylon gained its independence from Britain, the new Ceylonese government, by an act of Parliament, disenfranchised these Tamils and made them stateless.

10 Martin Heidegger, *Being and Time* (New York: Harper and Row, 1962), 97.

11 Ibid., 309.

12 Ibid., 82.

13 Hubert L. Dreyfus, *Being-in-the-World: A Commentary on Heidegger's* Being and Time, *Division I* (Cambridge, Mass.: MIT Press, 1991).

14 Heidegger, *Being and Time,* 102–3.

15 Dreyfus, *Being-in-the-World: A Commentary on Heidegger's* Being and Time, 71–72.

16 For a more detailed discussion of facts and figures pertaining to the discrimination against Tamils in these two areas, see C. R. de Silva, "The Impact of Nationalism on Education: The Schools Takeover (1961) and the University Admissions Crisis (1970–1975)," in Michael Roberts, ed., *Collective Identities, Nationalisms, and Protest in Modern Sri Lanka* (Colombo, Sri Lanka: Marga Institute, 1979), 474–99; and S. Ponnambalam, *Sri Lanka: The National Question and the Tamil Struggle* (London: Zed Books, 1983).

17 In an English medium class or school, all subjects (with the exception of the student's mother tongue, if it is different) are taught in English. The case is analogous for the Tamil and Sinhala media.

18 The Liberation Tigers of Tamil Eelam (LTTE) is the primary Tamil militant separatist group that is currently fighting a war with the Sri Lankan army.

19 The Tamil word for "history" employed in this context is *sarittiram*. When Tamils refer to a narrative by using the words "That is a history" (*adu oru sarittiram*), the phrase is tinged with sarcasm and is better translated as "Now, that's a story."

20 S. J. Tambiah, *Sri Lanka: Ethnic Fratricide and the Dismantling of Democracy* (Chicago, Ill.: University of Chicago Press, 1986).

21 Benedict R. O'Gorman Anderson, *Imagined Communities: Reflections on the Origin and Spread of Nationalism* (New York: Verso, 1991).

22 Charles S. Hardwick, *Semiotic and Significs: The Correspondence Between Charles S. Peirce and Victoria Lady Welby* (Bloomington, Ind.: Indiana University Press, 1977), 80–81.

23 Cited in Dreyfus, *Being-in-the-World: A Commentary on Heidegger's* Being and Time, 76.

24 A *poṭṭu* is the vermilion mark that a Hindu woman who is not widowed wears on her forehead. During the riots, Sinhala rioters took this as a mark identifying Tamils. The *tālikkoṭi* is the emblem of marriage, worn as a pendant on a chain.

25 Heidegger, *Being and Time*, 103.

26 Among other things, the Prevention of Terrorism Act provides for arrest without warrant for "unlawful activity" (Articles 2 and 31); detention in "any place," incommunicado and without trial for eighteen months (Sections 6, 7, 11); detention without trial (Section 15A); and the treatment of confessions made while in detention as admissible evidence (Section 16). See Patricia Hyndman, *Sri Lanka: Serendipity Under Siege* (Nottingham: Spokesman, 1988).

27 Many of the Phase 1 immigrants, especially barristers and those schooled in the social sciences, were articulate critics of racism, classism, and casteism. The most prominent figure among them was the current editor of the journal *Race and Class,* A. Sivanandan. My characterization of Phase 1 immigrants in this essay best fits those who chose the professions of medicine, engineering, and the hard sciences.

28 This and all other statements quoted in this section of the essay are excerpts from interviews with Phase 1 Tamils obtained during field research in London carried out by either Y. Thangaraj or myself.

29 The phrase "tree climbers" is an allusion to a low caste from northern Sri Lanka whose traditional occupation was the tapping of toddy from palm trees. Not all Phase 3 refugees were members of the lower castes. The early Phase 3 immigrants were of modest means. With the passage of time, however, each month of the late 1980s and early 1990s brought poorer and more desperate refugees. They truly had nothing to return to; many had sold their last goat or brass pot to buy their passage.

30 Pierre Bourdieu, *Outline of a Theory of Practice* (Cambridge: Cambridge University Press, 1977), 17.

31 *Tambi* means "younger brother." It can be used as a term of endearment but can also be used patronizingly.

[32] Only one individual confided to me his role in informing for the Home Office and having a Phase 3 family deported. I was unable to find any documentary confirmation of this claim, and I am not sure whether it represented fact or misplaced but mendacious bravado.

[33] The Immigration Carriers' Liability Act made it the responsibility of air and sea carriers to ensure that their passengers carried valid papers. Failure to do so made a carrier liable to heavy fines.

[34] The People's Liberation Organization of Tamil Eelam (PLOTE) is one of several Tamil "liberation movements" born in the mid-1980s. This group never did engage in combat, either with the Indian or with the Sri Lankan state. But it became quite wealthy through investments made in Bombay and through running a passport-forging shop in that same city. The drug-pushing charge is quite widely leveled against this group, but I have been unable to either confirm or disconfirm it. Its leader, Uma Maheswaran, was killed by a member of the LTTE in 1989, after which any activities of his group directed toward the liberation of Eelam became extinct for all intents and purposes. The fragmented financial empire, I understand, continues to flourish.

[35] The Eelam Peoples Revolutionary Liberation Front (EPRLF) is a militant separatist group that, since the 1987 pact between India and Sri Lanka, has given up its demand for a separate state and has participated in government-arranged elections.

[36] The word *kevalappatuttinarkal* ("being shamed") is a euphemism for rape.

[37] See Stuart Turner, "Torture, Refugee, and Trust," in E. Valentine Daniel and John Knudsen, eds., *Mistrusting Refugees* (Berkeley, Calif.: University of California Press, 1996), 56–72.

[38] Charles S. Peirce, *The Collected Papers of Charles Sanders Peirce*, vols. 1–6, ed. C. Hartshorne and P. Weiss (Cambridge, Mass.: Harvard University Press, 1938), 5.265. In this section of my essay, I also quote from Charles S. Peirce, *The Collected Papers of Charles Sanders Peirce*, vols. 7–8, ed. A. Burks (Cambridge, Mass.: Harvard University Press, 1958). In keeping with the standard convention of citing from Peirce's *Collected Papers,* I do not cite page numbers; instead, the number to the left of the decimal point indicates the volume and the number to the right indicates the paragraph.

[39] Peirce's (and my) rationale for the spelling of "semeiotic" is twofold: "(1) There is no more reason for *semeiotics* or *semiotics* than for *logics* or *rhetorics*. (2) Both the spelling and the pronunciation should (in this case at least) be signs of etymology; that is, should make it evident that the derivation is from Greek *semeion,* sign, not from Latin *semi-* (half). There is nothing halfway about semeiotic; it is all about signs, and it is about all signs. And the *o* in semeiotic should be long because it has behind it a Greek omega, not an omicron." Max H. Fisch, "Peirce's General Theory of Signs," in Thomas Sebeok, ed., *Sight, Sound, and Sense* (Bloomington, Ind.: Indiana University Press, 1978), 32.

[40] Peirce, *Collected Papers,* 3.93n.1.

[41] Ibid., 1.324.

42 Jacques Derrida, *Of Grammatology*, trans. G. C. Spivak (Baltimore, Md.: Johns Hopkins University Press, 1974), 49.

43 Floyd Merrell, "Vagueness, Generality, and Undeciding Otherness," in Vincent H. Colapietro and Thomas M. Olshewsky, eds., *Peirce's Doctrine of Signs* (Berlin: Mouton de Gruyter, 1996), 39.

44 Marjorie Miller, "Peirce's Conception of Habits," in Colapietro and Olshewsky, eds., *Peirce's Doctrine of Signs,* 74. Miller is quoting from Peirce's unpublished manuscripts at the Houghton Library at Harvard University, MS 318, 351.

45 Vincent Colapietro, *Peirce's Approach to the Self* (Albany, N.Y.: State University of New York Press, 1989), 111–12.

46 Recall the great pivot line in *The Winter's Tale,* when the shepherd, who has rescued and exposed the infant Perdita, tells the clown, who has just witnessed simultaneous disasters—a shipwreck (by sea) and the bear devouring Antigonous (by land): "thou met'st with things dying, I with things new born." (Regarding Peirce's categories of Secondness and Thirdness, see note 5.)

47 Fred Dallmayr, *The Other Heidegger* (Ithaca, N.Y.: Cornell University Press, 1993), 48.

48 John H. Herz, "The Territorial State Revisited: Reflections on the Future of the Nation-State," *Polity* 1 (1) (1968):24.

49 Ibid., 25.

50 John H. Herz, *International Politics in the Atomic Age* (New York: Columbia University Press, 1959), 40.

51 Michael Walzer, *Spheres of Justice: A Defense of Pluralism and Equality* (New York: Basic Books, 1983).

52 Joseph Schumpeter, *Capitalism, Socialism, and Democracy* (New York: Harper and Row, 1942).

53 William E. Connolly, "Democracy and Territoriality," *The Journal of International Studies* 20 (3) (1991):477.

54 Ibid.

55 See especially Victor Farias, *Heidegger and Nazism* (Philadelphia, Pa.: Temple University Press, 1989); Tom Rockmore and Joseph Margolis, eds., *The Heidegger Case: On Philosophy and Politics* (Philadelphia, Pa.: Temple University Press, 1992); Richard Wolin, ed., *The Politics of Being: The Political Thought of Martin Heidegger* (New York: Columbia University Press, 1990); Richard Wolin, *The Heidegger Controversy: A Critical Reader* (New York: Columbia University Press, 1991); Philippe Lacoue-Labarthe, *Art and Politics: The Fiction of the Political* (Oxford: Blackwell, 1990); Luc Ferry and Alain Renaut, *Heidegger and Modernity* (Chicago, Ill.: University of Chicago Press, 1990); and Elzbieta Ettinger, *Hannah Arendt/Martin Heidegger* (New Haven, Conn.: Yale University Press, 1995).

56 Joseph J. Kockelmans, *On the Truth of Being: Reflections on Heidegger's Later Philosophy* (Bloomington, Ind.: Indiana University Press, 1984); Dallmayr, *The Other Heidegger;* Hans Sluga, *Heidegger's Crisis: Philosophy and Politics*

in Nazi Germany (Cambridge, Mass.: Harvard University Press, 1993); and Jacques Derrida, *Of Spirit: Heidegger and the Question* (Chicago, Ill.: University of Chicago Press, 1989).

[57] Dallmayr, *The Other Heidegger*, 64.

[58] Ibid.

J. W. Bowker

Religions, Society, and Suffering

FROM IGNORANCE TO TECHNOLOGY: THE INCREASING ISOLATION OF MEDICAL CARE

SIXTY YEARS AGO, LEWIS THOMAS was a medical student at Harvard. As he later recalled in *The Youngest Science,* he and his fellow students were taught "Osler's medicine." Sir William Osler had been a revolutionary in his day, forming part of what became known as "therapeutic nihilism." [1] Therapeutic nihilism meant abandoning what Osler called "popgun pharmacy," with the physician trying out haphazardly anything that might make a difference, "hitting now the malady and again the patient, he himself not knowing which." [2] As Thomas commented:

> The medical literature of those years makes horrifying reading today: paper after learned paper recounts the benefits of bleeding, cupping, violent purging, the raising of blisters by vesciant ointments, the immersion of the body in either ice water or intolerably hot water, endless lists of botanical extracts cooked up and mixed together under the influence of nothing more than pure whim. [3]

Nothing much, it would seem, had changed from a day in 1685 when Charles II fell ill. As MacPhail summarized the matter:

> For a perfect sight of the old medicine, let me conduct you to the bedside of Charles II. With a cry he fell. Dr. King, who, fortunately, happened to be present, bled him with a pocket knife. Fourteen physicians were quickly in attendance. They bled him more thoroughly; they scarified and cupped him; they shaved and blistered his head; they gave him an emetic, a clyster and two pills. During the next eight days they threw in fifty-seven separate drugs; and towards the end, a

John W. Bowker was Dean and Fellow of Trinity College, Cambridge, and is now Gresham Professor of Religious Studies at Gresham College in London and Adjunct Professor at the University of Pennsylvania and at North Carolina State University.

cordial containing forty more. This availing nothing, they tried Goa stone, which was a calculus obtained from a species of Indian goat; and as a final remedy, the distillate of human skull. In the case report it is recorded that the emetic and purge worked so mightily well that it was a wonder the patient died.[4]

Two hundred years later, Osler and his colleagues were beginning to point out that most such remedies (many of which were still in use) were more likely to cause harm than benefit and that the number of genuinely therapeutic drugs was extremely small. Thomas's father was himself a doctor and carried round in his doctor's bag virtually nothing—only morphine, digitalis, insulin, and adrenaline, the last of which he never used in his entire career. When Lewis Thomas set out on his own medical career—and this is only sixty years ago—the aims were not so much cure as diagnosis, prognosis, and explanation to the patient of what was going on:

> The successes possible in diagnosis and prognosis were regarded as the triumph of medical science, and so they were. . . . By the 1930s we thought we knew as much as could ever be known about the dominant clinical problems of the time: syphilis, tuberculosis, lobar pneumonia, typhoid, rheumatic fever, crysipelas, poliomyelitis. Most of the known varieties of cancer had been meticulously classified, and estimates of the duration of life could be made with some accuracy. . . . But during the third and fourth years of school we also began to learn something that worried us all, although it was not much talked about. . . . It gradually dawned on us that we didn't know much that was really useful, that we could do nothing to change the course of the great majority of the diseases we were so busy analyzing, that medicine, for all its facade as a learned profession, was in real life a profoundly ignorant occupation.[5]

Sixty years on, we still die, and many illnesses have to run their course. But ignorance is dramatically reduced, and successful interventions have multiplied—and not just interventions by way of surgery. A consequence, in many societies, has been the increasing isolation of high-cost, high-technology medicine from the general context of human life: we go to doctors (or hospitals), whereas once doctors came to us and performed their operations on the kitchen table. When we ask, as this volume does, whether the boundaries of medicine and public health should be reformulated to include issues of poverty, violence, and social breakdown, we are asking in effect whether there would be any gain in returning medicine to society in its much wider experience of suffering, and not just in the individual experiences of somatic disorder, which are then abstracted into a narrower definition of public health.

THEODICY AND THE FORMS OF SOCIETY

To make that move would certainly be to return to a religious perspective. When Anglican Christians recited the Litany (as they were supposed to do after Morning Prayer every Sunday, Wednesday, and Friday), they implored the good Lord to deliver them from all evil and mischief. Illness was embedded in a much wider understanding of social suffering.

> From lightning and tempest; from plague, pestilence, and famine; from battle and murder, and from sudden death, *Good Lord, deliver us*. From all sedition, privy conspiracy, and rebellion; from all false doctrine, heresy and schism; from hardness of heart, and contempt of thy Word and Commandment, *Good Lord, deliver us*.

The question of whether such prayer was any more effective than the medicine available at that time is not the point. Rather, the point is that religions are a consequence and a context of shared experience, in which the reality of all kinds of suffering—not only the suffering of illness in isolation—is a central concern. Indeed, it is *so* central that Max Weber regarded the whole character and style of different societies as being determined by their religious understanding of suffering, by what he called their "theodicies." In his view, religions offer theodicies not simply as abstract solutions to intellectual puzzles but as programs for action, or as substitutes for it.

Weber gave a much more general sense to the term "theodicy" than is usual. In other words, he did not confine his understanding of theodicy to the classical problem of how suffering can exist in the world if God is both omnipotent and all-loving. Of course Weber knew that this problem has been an important part of the human struggle to find a meaning for existence and experience. But he used the concept of theodicy to refer more extensively to the ways in which religions interpret the many inequalities that all people observe and experience and also to the ways in which, on the basis of those interpretations, religions create and legitimize different forms of society. In *The Sociology of Religion,* Weber first described the classical issue: "the more the development tends toward the conception of a transcendental unitary god who is universal, the more there arises the problem of how the extraordinary power of such a god may be reconciled with the imperfection of the world that he has created and rules over."[6] But then he moved on at once to the human experience of inequalities as the problem "which belongs everywhere among the factors determining religious evolution and the need for salvation." Referring to a questionnaire "submitted to thousands of German workers," he stated that it "disclosed the fact that their rejection of the god-idea was motivated, not by scientific arguments, but by their difficulty in reconciling the idea of providence with the injustice and imperfection of the social order."[7]

Thus, in Weber's argument, all humans experience great inequalities, which carry with them much suffering, unequally distributed: you are wise, I am foolish; you are well, I am sick; you are male, I am female; you are rich, I am poor. Why have these things come about? Religions pour explanation and meaning (i.e., theodicies) into these gaps of commonplace experience, and these theodicies create very different forms of society. Weber discerned three pure types of theodicy (in Weber's analysis, pure types are rarely found in unadulterated form but can be discerned as characteristic nevertheless):

> These three gave rationally satisfactory answers to the questioning for the basis of the incongruity between destiny and merit: the Indian doctrine of Karma, Zoroastrian dualism, and the predestination decree of the *deus absconditus.* These solutions are rationally closed; in pure form they are found only as exceptions.[8]

From the adopted theodicy of a particular religion, social consequences flow, which give to different societies their characteristic forms and actions (or lack of actions). Thus Weber concluded of "the pious Hindu and the Asiatic Buddhist":

> That these religions lack virtually any kind of social-revolutionary ethics can be explained by reference to their theodicy of rebirth, according to which the caste system itself is eternal and absolutely just.

The virtues or sins of a former life determine birth into a particular caste, and one's behaviour in the present life determines one's chances of improvement in the next rebirth.[9]

No one would now defend the detail of Weber's account of religions. Rather, the importance of his work lies in his discernment of the different styles in which religions have in the past constructed social meaning out of the experience of social suffering: no matter how true it is that there must be an individual *locus* of suffering, the meaning of suffering arises out of the relations of individuals together in society, so that in consequence the social fact of suffering is more than the sum of its parts. Suffering and its treatment, therefore, are not "added on" to the general pattern of social life: the reality of gap-induced suffering is so central that it evokes an organization of society on the basis of the meaning attributed to it. Weber's point remains, that any extension or reformulation of the boundary of medicine and public health is, first and foremost, an exercise in hermeneutics.

SOMATIC EXPLORATION AND EXEGESIS

But in that case, what is, so to speak, the text that demands exegesis and interpretation? It is the experience of pain, disorder, and dis-ease that occurs physiologically in the human body, or *soma*. However, even if the basic text is written in broadly universal terms (of somatic process in general, and of such items as nerve endings, neural wiring, and chemical and electrical activity in the brain), the exegesis, and thus the actual experience, is not. Shylock may well ask:

> Hath not a Jew eyes? hath not a Jew hands, organs, dimensions, senses, affections, passions? fed with the same food, hurt with the same weapons, subject to the same diseases, healed by the same means, warmed and cooled by the same winter and summer, as a Christian is? If you prick us, do we not bleed? If you tickle us, do we not laugh? If you poison us, do we not die? and if you wrong us, shall we not revenge? (*The Merchant of Venice*, 3.1.63).

It is indeed true that the somatic text is, broadly speaking, held in common: organs can be transplanted across the boundaries of religions, even though some religions would not approve. But the exegeses, which issue eventually in different religious systems, are profoundly different—so much so that there is a sense in which the Jewish experience of suffering (the appropriation of pain, illness, and so on) is *not* the same as that of a Christian. The exegeses of the somatic text amount, in effect, to divergent anthropologies—divergent accounts, that is, of what it is to be human.

These divergent anthropologies are not arbitrary. They have been formed and tested through many centuries (indeed, in most cases, through millennia) of somatic exploration and exegesis—exploration of what this body is capable of doing, of experiencing, of being, and of becoming and exploration of the environment it inhabits and the latent possibilities of that environment. Religions exploit behaviors and possibilities inherent in the human body and its environment and develop them in ways that bind the body (*religio*) to the meanings and values designated in the system in which its life is embedded.

This means that at their most basic level, religions can best be understood as systems organized (in, again, very different ways) for the coding, protection, and transmission of information (some of it verbal, but a great deal of it, in the religious case, nonverbal) that has proved to be of worth and that has been tested through many generations. In other words, religions are systems organized for the protection and transmission of the achieved discoveries of human competence, discoveries that have been truly prodigious. Religions are the resource and inspiration of virtually all the most enduring and value-laden human achievements (think only of the obvious, in art, architecture, music, dance, drama, agriculture, astronomy, poetry, ethics), quite apart from what they have secured in the interior experiences of the brain and in the designations of absolute value, culminating in God.

But these discoveries and achievements have not been identical in all religions: religions, therefore, have come, through the centuries, to set different priorities, goals, and values and to employ different techniques.

To offer only one brief example: religions may give priority in somatic exploration to either inversive or extraversive objectives and techniques. An inversive religion exploits and reinforces the astonishing consequences of finding truth *within* the somatic system. Thus many forms of Mahayana Buddhism have developed different techniques of meditation that lead to the realization (not just as a proposition but as a fact) that nothing exists other than the Buddha-nature and that we, as much as all other appearance, are simply what that nature is; all things, therefore, are devoid of differentiating characteristics once they are properly understood. Truth is discovered within the body, by transcending the superficial appearance of distinctions and differences in the external world.

An extraversive system, in contrast, not only explores what occurs and what is possible and what is experienced within the body but also considers what must, at least inferentially, be the case in the external environment for such somatic consequence to take the form that it does. It therefore gives value to the experience of relationship, not as something to be transcended but as something to be endorsed and pursued. In contrast to inversive systems, extraversive systems affirm that the condition of relationship with that which is external to one's own center of awareness is real and is indeed *the* ontological truth with which we must deal—so much so that the claim is made, both by Hindus and Christians, that interrelatedness must necessarily belong within the very nature of God (without any compromise of the condition of what Muslims would call *tawhid,* absolute unity), in the Trinity in Christianity and the Trimurti among Hindus.

On the basis, therefore, of exploration of the soma (which is not disjunctively different in its basic physiology wherever it is found), very different discoveries were made, which led eventually to different exegeses of the human text and to different religions. Thus any account of "religions and . . ." (no matter what topic completes the phrase—for example, "religions and social suffering") must begin with *differences,* not with superficial similarities. Virtually all generalizations about religions (except this one) turn out to be subverted by evidence.

Thus even Weber's apparently secure claim that what he classified as Karma-religions "lack virtually any kind of social-revolutionary ethics" turns out to be incorrect. "Pious Hindus and Asiatic Buddhists" have effected many social revolutions, though not necessarily along the lines of Marx in theory or the Year of Revolutions in practice—or even along the lines of the Protestant Reformation—which Weber may have had in mind. But think instead of the social revolutions of Asoka; of the Nara period of Buddhism in Japan, especially under the emperor Shomu (*Jen-wang-ching* [The Sutra of the Virtuous King] brings the application of the Buddhist revolution even down to the individual level of cures for illnesses and diseases); or of the overthrow of Indian culture and aristocracy in Burma after the return of the Mon Chapata from Sri Lanka, bringing with him the reformed Buddhism of Parakrambahu I (a social revolution that spread far beyond Burma). Think also of the return of P'raya Chakri to Bangkok in 1782, establishing the new Chakri dynasty, which led to the extensive social revolution of King Mongkut (Rama IV), culminating in the abolition of slavery under his successor (Mongkut had reluctantly left his life in a monastery to succeed his brother and regarded his reforms as specifically "Buddhist"—i.e., as based upon *dhamma,* hence their name, *th'ammayut,* or *dhammayuttika*); or of the Hindu renaissance, which led ultimately to Gandhi and of which M. L. Stackhouse observed, "It was neither a 'revolution of the saints' in the Puritan sense nor a 'revolution of the masses' in the Marxist sense. It was first of all a revolution of cultural consciousness." [10] As always, there is no Archimedean point of definition: social revolutions can take many different forms, and it is certainly not true that those who hold beliefs about *karma/kamma* and about rebirth or reappearance cannot have an interest in social revolution—or, for that matter, in social suffering. In fact, all religions have a strong sense of the nature of, and necessity for, society. But those accounts are not the same in each case.

RELIGIONS, SUFFERING, AND SOCIAL CONTEXT

It is clearly impossible to summarize here the different ways in which each major religion relates suffering to the wider context of society. The general characteristics of the understanding of suffering in each religion are reviewed in my books *Problems of Suffering in Religions of the World* and *The Meanings of Death.* [11] On the basis of those general descriptions, and also on the basis of what has been argued so far, we can see that both the nature of society and the nature of social suffering are indeed *defined:* there is no independent account of society that is objectively correct; all accounts are themselves social constructions, the secular as much as the religious. Thus the questions raised by this conference are an invitation to exactly that work of social construction/reconstruction which has been a major part of the history of religions.

What, if anything, can we learn from the religious enterprise of somatic exegesis applied to suffering and society? The most obvious point is that although particular kinds of suffering are recognized as being distinct, they are also seen as unable to be isolated from each other. Thus conditions that we might isolate as matters of health and illness are recognized for what they are (no one could mistake Shakespeare's "rotten diseases of the South, the guts-griping, ruptures, catarrhs, loads o'gravel i' the back, lethargies, cold palsies, raw eyes, dirt-rotten livers, whissing lungs, bladders full of imposthume, sciaticas, limekilns i' the palm, incurable bone-ache" [*Troilus and Cressida*, 5.1.20]), but they are understood as being embedded in the entire complexity of human suffering, as one aspect of it.

In part, of course, this is a consequence of ignorance. What we now regard as the specific causes of illnesses were not known at the time religious systems were forming their accounts of the human condition. Thus Augustine observed succinctly that "all diseases of Christians are to be ascribed to demons"; and the contest with demons is familiar in the descriptions of the healing of particular disorders in the ministry of Jesus. He was living and operating in a context in which the view was widespread that "where you see sickness, there you see sin." "R. Ammi [third century C.E.] said, 'There is no death without sin, there is no sickness without sin'" (*Babli Shabbat* 55a); "Raba [fourth century] said, 'If a man sees that painful suffering visits him, let him examine his conduct'" (*Babli Berakhot* 5a). Jesus contested that view (see, e.g., *Luke* 13.1–5, *John* 9.1–7), but he did not contest the sense in which all suffering is "of a piece": Jesus wept.

In a comparable way, Hindus saw a connection between health and conduct, although they believed that the causes of ill health might lie in bad actions that had occurred in previous births; for that reason, a moral stigma attached to people with leprosy or other visibly deforming diseases. But health matters are not isolated from the general condition of life. *Carakasamhita*, for example, is a classic text on medicine, but it combines health and medical matters with general instructions for achieving a good and satisfactory life.[12] That is why Rene Dubos could conclude the following:

An intriguing characteristic of ancient medicine is that it incorporated most aspects of knowledge. Ancient physicians were concerned with the physiological effects of music, astronomical events, and religious beliefs, just as they were interested in anatomical structure, surgical techniques or the activities of drugs. Through the catholicism of their attitude, ancient medicine became the mother of the sciences, the inspiration of humanism and the integrating force of culture.[13]

The same catholicity of attitude is evident in China, where the quest for immortality in religious Taoism (Daojiao/Tao-chiao) is not restricted to an endeavor to emancipate a self from society or a soul from a body. Taoists seek to relate the microcosm—which is present in the body in the three life-principles of breath (*qi/ch'i*), vitality, especially in semen (*jing/ching*), and spirit (*shen*)—to the macrocosm so that the whole of life, internal and external, becomes an unresistant (*wu-wei*) expression of that which alone truly is, namely, the Tao. It would thus be impossible to isolate some part of disease or disorder from its context. As early as the sixth century B.C.E., a text that surely rests on even earlier traditions, *Huang-ti Nei-ching* (The Inner Classic of the Yellow Emperor), was offering advice on health and healing that is entirely holistic: before healing comes proper nutrition, but before nutrition comes the calming and securing of the spirit. Since every aspect of nature is united in Tao, it follows that no suffering or distress can be isolated; nor can the alleviation of suffering be broken up into disparate parts. Thus the quest for immortality (even if conceived of only as longevity) takes many forms, some individual and some social: it may be addressed to inner hygiene and to control of the breath and of sexuality, but it may also be addressed to moral behavior in harmony with the way of Tao.

THE AETIOLOGY OF DISTRESS

Earlier I argued that the embedding of illness and health in the whole social structure came about, at least in part, through ignorance of the causes of many illnesses. While it is important not to overstress the point (since within limits the observation and diagnosis of illness were impressive, as much in India or China as in the New England of Lewis Thomas's youth), the fact remains that there were no particular grounds for viewing illness as in some way isolated from suffering in general. Illness might occur for many reasons, some of them entirely social and not at all within the control of the affected individuals. It is characteristic of the Deuteronomic understanding of kingship in Judah and Israel that the behavior of the king leads to direct consequences in the lives of the people—hence the repeated note in the books of Kings (in the Jewish Bible) that such-and-such a king did that which was evil in the sight of the Lord and thus provoked the anger of the Lord against Israel. That anger might take the form of a plague. When David was incited (by God himself in *II Samuel* 24.1ff., but by Satan in *I Chron.* 21.1ff.) to take a census of Israel and was offered a choice of three punishments for his presumption, he chose a plague in which seventy thousand died.

The same point, about the health of a society affecting the health of individuals, is made in one of the Jataka (previous birth) stories in the very different tradition of Buddhism. A wise and virtuous king once ruled in Banaras. But as he was unsure whether people really flourished under his rule, he disguised himself and went far and wide, asking whether people prospered under the rule of the king. Everyone assured him that the king was good and wise and that in consequence the kingdom prospered. At last he came to a hermit who lived in a remote part of the Himalayas, a hermit who was in fact the Bodhisattva, the future Buddha. The hermit gave the king a fig and asked him to taste it. It was the sweetest the king had ever tasted. The hermit said, "The fruit is sweet because the king rules with justice and impartiality; if the king were unjust, not only wild fruit but crops and oil and honey and all such things would lose their sweetness." The king went away delighted. But when he returned home, he could not resist an experiment, and so he began to rule with cruelty and injustice. In time he went back to the hermit, and this time the fig was bitter and dry. "The king must now be ruling unjustly," said the hermit, "for when a king's justice goes sour, the whole kingdom goes sour with it."

These, of course, are elementary stories, and we do not link illness to social order in those ways. But the pressure nevertheless remains on us to tell some other story to make the same point, that issues of health and illness remain embedded in social decisions and actions, not only in medical decisions about transmission and cure.

Enacted policies on transportation, housing, energy, education, and agriculture have both direct and indirect consequences for health; yet in most governments or administrations, health policies are only haphazardly integrated with those of other departments—strongly, for example, in the case of providing clean water; scarcely at all in the case of transportation. Conversely, in the relation of individuals to the health of a society, an equal ambiguity exists. All societies (including religious societies) allow or require the intentional killing of others in some circumstances—for example, in a defensive war. Yet in most societies, the voluntary taking of one's own life in the controlled circumstances of voluntary euthanasia is not allowed, even though that action might be to the overall advantage of a society by removing the necessity for extending life and thereby releasing funds for other medical care. In the United Kingdom in 1994, the House of Lords Select Committee on Medical Ethics unanimously rejected arguments for voluntary euthanasia on these grounds:

> Ultimately, we do not believe that these arguments [in favor of voluntary euthanasia] are sufficient reason to weaken society's prohibition of intentional killing. That prohibition is the cornerstone of law and social relationships. It protects each one of us impartially, embodying the belief that all are equal. . . . We acknowledge that there are individual cases in which euthanasia may be seen by some to be appropriate. But individual cases cannot reasonably establish the foundation of a policy which would have such serious and widespread repercussions. The death of a person affects the lives of others, often in ways and to an extent which cannot be foreseen. We believe that the issue of euthanasia is one in which the interest of the individual cannot be separated from the interest of society as a whole.[14]

The purpose of quoting this is not to introduce a debate about euthanasia, but to illustrate in contemporary terms the perennial religious emphasis, that the interest of the individual cannot be separated from the interest of society as a whole. If we apply this to our theme, the illness of the individual cannot be separated from the wider context of social suffering because the network of constraints that control the transformation of an eventuality into its outcome (into being the illness that presents itself) is always extremely large, even though we may single out one or a few of those constraints as "the cause." It may be that religious systems embedded illness in a wider social context because they were ignorant of the true aetiology of most illnesses, but they at least constructed aetiologies of disorder that were sensitive to the complexities of causation.

Thus while we would not speak of "kings causing plagues" by their own bad behavior, we are well aware that decisions about the economy have direct consequences for health. Religions serve as a reminder that Ockham's razor is a poor instrument to use if, instead of shaving, you end up cutting your own throat.

CAUSES AND CONSTRAINTS

The point here is simple but nevertheless essential (and often overlooked) in understanding and accounting for complex human behaviors. As we have seen, the spectacular advances in medical knowledge and interventions have led to their increasing isolation as a human activity. This has carried with it a corresponding isolation in the specification of the causes of illness or ill health. This is dramatically clear in the case of gene-based or gene-related illnesses because it seems so obvious that the cause of a disorder lies in a defective gene; more than four thousand disorders of this kind have now been identified. A well-known example is PKU (phenylketonuria), an inherited autosomal recessive error of metabolism, in which the enzyme phenylalanine hydroxlase is defective. Whereas this enzyme ordinarily catalyzes the conversion of the amino acid phenylalanine to tyrosine, when the enzyme is defective the conversion is critically slowed, with elevated plasma phenylalanine resulting. In childhood, these elevated levels have a toxic effect on neuron mylenization, which leads to gross cognitive impairment, fits, and microcephaly.

A comparable example is hepatolenticular degeneration, usually known as Wilson's disease. This again is an autosomal recessive defect, which causes excessive intestinal absorption of the copper that is consumed (in minute amounts) by everyone in food. If the copper accumulates in the body, it causes nervous degeneration and eventually premature death. In cases of this kind, the relation between cause and effect seems so obvious that it becomes a kind of paradigm for the explanation of other illnesses.

This is not surprising. Living as we do in a post-Newtonian world, we simply assume a notion of causality in which an active force coerces an otherwise passive or pliant object into a new outcome. Force is a vector quantity, with both a magnitude and a direction; in an interaction between objects, one exerts a force upon another. Despite the caution of Hume (that we never observe "cause," but only a constancy of conjunction from which we infer "cause"), the consistency of action and reaction is such that the sense of force remains dominant. Thus we take it for granted that defective genes cause particular disorders, and we rarely look further for relevant or salient constraints. To consider reformulating the boundaries of medicine and public health then becomes a frivolous distraction from the "real" work of attending to immediate causes and dealing with them in a strictly medical context. "Cause" as "the force that brings things about" leads to a selection and identification of the truly coercive and operative forces that have brought about the consequence in question. Backed up by a version of Ockham's razor ("where one explanation is sufficient, don't multiply explanations"), we arrive at the situation in which we at present find ourselves: specify the immediate cause if that is known, and deal with it if that can be done.

Yet in fact we know perfectly well that genes (to stay with those two examples) are embedded in a developmental process, not only of cells but of the entire soma, and that events in those environments (as also in the wider environments in which the body is set) causatively affect gene transcription and expression. Development depends not simply on what has been inherited from parents (genes and other materials in sperm and egg) but on cell activity, cell division, ambience, nutrition, and eventually the sensory inputs the developing organism experiences. It is now, for example, well known that the environment inside the womb is vital in controlling fetal weight—it is not simply a matter of unfolding gene programs. Thus different organs mature at different times, during periods of rapid cell division, before birth and during infancy (e.g., the pancreas continues to develop after birth, the kidneys develop during the last three months of pregnancy). The time of rapid cell division is known as the "sensitive period." Although the initiation of this period may be in part under genetic control, the unfolding of the process is not. Interference with the fetus or infant, e.g., through malnutrition, during the sensitive period has permanent effects, so much so that the phenomenon has been called "programming": these consequences are clearly *not* a result of genetic programs.

A well-known example of this kind of programming is the effect of injecting female rats with a single injection of the male sex hormone testosterone on the fifth day after birth: the result is that the rats never ovulate, and they fail to exhibit other marks of female sexual behavior. The same injection only a day or two later does not have the same marked effect. At the moment, we do not know in what ways many of these "programming" consequences work; but among the possibilities is a permanent change in the way the genes are transcribed. If that is so, then the genes are subordinate to the environment in which they are set.

Even at the simplest and most elementary levels, it becomes obvious that the gene cannot be isolated from the entire activity of the cell and that the evocation or suppression of gene transcription or gene expression depends on the many environments in which cellular activity is set. For example, the cleaner fish, *Laproides dimidiatus,* is a territorial fish, with the male owner of a territory controlling a harem of five or six females. The male is the largest fish, but the females also form a size-based hierarchy. When the male dies, the largest dominant female takes over the territory and within hours is controlling the harem. Within two weeks, the now-male fish is producing sperm.

The social context of somatic events, including suffering, is thus already apparent, even at the most elementary levels of observation. Far from following an invariable and inevitable trajectory from gene to death, the two earlier examples of PKU and Wilson's disease can be modified in the social context in which they occur. In the case of PKU, a screening test for the condition in newborn infants exists, which allows homozygous recessive individuals to be identified and placed on restricted phenylalanine diets, thereby preventing the elevated levels of plasma phenylalanine from occurring. It is now possible for 75 percent of such homozygous recessives to attend normal schools. In the case of Wilson's disease, patients can take pyridoxine and D-penicillamine throughout their lives to mobilize copper from the tissues and promote its excretion in the urine.

Those are highly specific and extremely local examples, still contained within the conventional medical boundary. Even so, they make it clear that the social context of an illness is a part of its history and that it is extremely rare for single causes to constrain eventualities into their outcomes. Even in the specific linkage between genes and particular disorders, the relation of the genes to the wider environment will affect the process and history of those disorders.

In general, therefore, this point must be emphasized: when we are trying to explain any complex phenomenon, we will always be wiser to think of *sets of constraints,* even if we wish to isolate some among them as being proximate causes of particular outcomes. An explanation will then be an adequate specification of those constraints that have brought about the eventuality (or outcome) in question. In the case of biology, the task is, as H. H. Pattee states it, "to explain the origin and operation (including the reliability and persistence) of the hierarchical constraints which harness matter to perform coherent functions." [15] If we keep "causes" in the context of "constraints" in this way, then we remain open to the reality that outcomes (that which presents itself evidentially before us) are brought into being not by one cause coercing the consequence, but rather by elaborate networks of constraints, including many that occur in the social environment.

This is not to deny that the specification of proximate causes (e.g., the defective gene) is of paramount importance. But it should never be *so* important that the possibility of additional constraints is ignored. The simplest relationships are not difficult to isolate, even if only as examples of sufficient constancies of conjunction: rain causes wetness, fire causes warmth, ice causes you to slip and fall—and, so it would seem but obvious to continue, genes cause cystic fibrosis. But even in those apparently simple instances, there is a much wider network of "cause" bringing those eventualities into their outcome: why is it ice and not fire that causes you to slip, and why fall rather than fly, and why you at this particular moment? In fact, if we wish to specify what it is that has delivered you into that predicament, we would have to specify so elaborate a network of constraints that we would never in practice have time to complete the task. The cause of your falling goes down eventually into the laws of motion; it extends contingently to details of your own life, which cannot be repeated in any other instance. So in practice we select the constraints that we believe will provide reasons (sufficient reasons) to account for the outcome. But to repeat the warning: Ockham's razor has virtue so long as you do not use it to cut off your own head; where additional constraints *must* be specified in order to account for an eventuality (or outcome), nothing is gained by insisting in the name of Ockham on only one. A better principle is this: be sufficiently, but not recklessly, generous in the specification of constraints, or at least otherwise be modest in what you claim to be "the true and only explanation."

The relevance of all this to the issue of social suffering is clear: if we habitually think of eventualities being brought into their outcomes (into being what they are) by networks of constraints, instead of continuing our more usual habit of looking for immediate causes alone, we will be more sensitive to the possibility that a great deal in a social context will be acting by way of constraint, even if it is not the most immediate cause of a disorder or illness. It is important to remember that not all constraints are active. Some are passive and are simply setting the boundary conditions of possibility; others are permissive, allowing the possibility of outcome but requiring some further sequence in the developmental process to be activated. But even though they are not immediate and active, operating as direct causes on a particular outcome, they are nevertheless necessary conditions for the eventuality (or outcome) in question to occur.

But of course, left like that, the task of explanation clearly becomes impossible. There is no way to specify the entire network of relevant constraints in the case of each and every outcome. It would mean accounting for one thing by everything. Not surprisingly, therefore, we separate out the task of explanation, by attending to the word "adequate"—an *adequate* description of those causes that have brought about the eventuality (or outcome) in question. This involves selecting from the whole network of constraints the items that relate specifically (specifiably) to the question we have in mind. The questions may be physical, chemical, biological, historical, cultural, sociological, genetic, biographical, medical, ethical— all the way through to gossip in the pub. In each case, we isolate from the entire network of existing constraints those items we take to be directly causative in producing the outcome in which we happen to be interested.

If we are then exhilarated by the explanatory success of what we have isolated (for example, if it seems recurrent across human examples, if it seems almost invariably linked to outcomes, if it allows predictions, and so on), we may lose our heads (as we wield that famous razor) and suppose that we have found "*the* cause" of some particular eventuality (or outcome)—as *in part* we may well have done. But by losing our sensitivity to the wider context of salient constraints, we may ironically become *a* cause of great suffering to others, as a consequence of the social or economic or educational policies we then enact.

The value, therefore, of "reformulating the boundaries of medicine and public health to include social problems such as poverty, violence . . . , refugeeship, chronic starvation, and family and community breakdown" should not be in order to make these problems "part of the established health agenda along with epidemics, chronic illnesses, and disability," because that would simply extend the current methodologies to a wider area, insofar as they can be made relevant to it. The point of reformulating the boundaries should be to shake loose the narrow concentration on single causes (important and successful though it may often be) in order to realize how profoundly the wider circumstances of existence constrain human lives into distress, some of which presents itself in what we now define as medical symptoms.

It will remain the case that what is required in practice is an adequate specification or description of those underlying constraints which have, with some immediacy, brought about the phenomenon to be explained. The relevance of "some immediacy" is that some limit must be set on the specification of constraints, since otherwise, as already pointed out, we will be explaining everything by everything. But no general rules should determine in advance what, in each instance, we must specify. If, as loss adjusters for an insurance firm, we ask, "What caused that fire?" we are unlikely to specify the presence of oxygen. Yet if we are evaluating the outbreak of fire in a space capsule, we will undoubtedly want to include the presence of oxygen in the specification of constraints.

At the same time, the list of *possible* constraints is not limitless. Some are frivolous, even though they may have been seen as causative in the past. A character in one of Aristophanes's plays maintains that rain is caused by Zeus urinating through a sieve. As an explanation, it certainly has *something* going for it: it accounts for the irregularity of rainfall and the space between the drops; in early Judaism, there was an attempt to measure the space between drops and to calculate what size holes must be in the canopy of the sky for rain to fall in that way. Observation rules out many claims and supplies a basis on which Ockham's razor can be applied: if gold-fish are disappearing from your pond, it makes more sense to look for cats or herons than for fish-loving angels or visitors from outer space.

But still the point remains: the observable and/or specifiable net-work of constraints over human behaviors is, as a matter of fact, extremely large. And while *some* proposed constraints may be ex-cised as frivolous or false, many, belonging to social context, per-sonal history, contingency, and consciousness, cannot. For that rea-son, the ambition to find covering laws that eliminate the need to specify any of those other constraints in accounting for human be-havior (i.e., strong reductionism) will never be fulfilled.

SOCIAL SUFFERING AND RELIGIONS

From this review, it will be obvious that religions set the occurrence and nature of suffering in a wide network of constraints: they may well be interested in identifying proximate causes, but they also rec-ognize that constraints in the much wider context of particular events belong causatively to their explanation as well. Characteris-tically, religions set the boundaries of constraint far wider than even the most sociologically-minded secular analyst will do, be-cause they set them in terms of God and Karma.

This is not an easy perspective for the contemporary world to share, not simply because the implicit propositions of religious sys-tems may happen to seem doubtful (insofar as they are propositions about putative matters of fact), but also because the nearest secular equivalent has collapsed in most parts of the world. In Marxist theory, events (including much human suffering) are constrained into their outcome not just by proximate causes but also by the dialectical laws of history. The failure of Marxism-Leninism in practice has reinforced our skepticism about "laws of history," or about any other larger constraints, in theory.

Yet social facts do act as constraints, often controlling eventualities into circumstances of health and illness: examples are the social acceptability of alcohol in some societies, the legal standards for car emissions, socially endorsed sexual behaviors. On an even larger scale, the nearest continuing secular equivalent of a general constraint is the development of the rules of exchange elaborated in economic theories and practices, over which even governments have, at times, extremely little control—or, to put it the other way around, economics set nonnegotiable constraints that control the political will. In a memorable report in *The New York Times,* when the Russians seemed likely to reassert control over Poland in 1980, some economists held that this would be a great contribution to the Polish economy. Under the headline "Soviet Intervention Could Aid Poland's Credit Position," the report began:

> Because of the spectacular expansion of lending to Poland and other Communist countries in the last decade, both the Communist authorities and the capitalist bankers recognize a convergence of interest in stability—so much so that one Western banker who asked not to be cited by name said that if the Russians actually did intervene in Poland, the nation's creditworthiness might actually increase. "Banks shrink from change," said Prof. Raymond Vernon of the Harvard Business School. "They prefer not to have to deal with the unexpected." [16]

But just as in this secular case of economics we can see that we are not *entirely* helpless and that there are ways of working with the constraints of economics to social and individual advantage, so also in the case of religions. Although the strongest of religious constraints seem to be irresistible, religions actually require a human cooperation with those constraints in order to act rightly or wisely in immediate and local circumstances. Indeed, it is *only* when the wider network of constraints is properly understood that we can attack particular instances of suffering and hope to do something about them.

Take, for example, the two instances of God and Karma. The Qur'an places much emphasis on the overriding power (*qadar*) of God to determine all things: "This is nothing but a reminder to all who dwell in the world for the benefit of those who will to go straight—and you do not will except as Gods wills [*illa 'an yasha'a 'llahu*—hence the familiar phrase accompanying any intention, *'in sha' Allah,* 'if God wills it']" (81.28–29). Not surprisingly, one of the earliest intellectual disputes in Islam was over the issue of how human responsibility and free will can be reconciled with the absolute sovereignty of God; and Islam is still frequently described as fatalistic. Yet in fact a solution was achieved, which reconciles both, in the doctrine of *kasb* or *iktisab* (acquisition): God does indeed create all possibilities, but humans have the responsibility to acquire their actions out of the many possibilities before them; and since the balance of good works against bad will on *yaum ud-Din* (the Day of Judgment) be exact, this doctrine actually constrains toward the performance of good actions, not to some fatalistic indifference.

In a comparable way, the doctrine of Karma might be interpreted as fatalistic. In an 1897 review of the contribution of Christian missions to social progress, James Dennis pointed out what he took to be the contrast with the Buddhist understanding of Karma:

> By existence is understood our career here upon earth, involving as it does sorrow and suffering as an inevitable lot, and also our continued existence in the interminable cycles of rebirth. Death is, therefore, simply a phase in the changes of existence, to be followed by rebirth in accordance with the good or evil we have done in this life, or, in other words, in accordance with our Karma, by which our present state has been determined and which will decide hereafter the character of future rebirths. Karma simply represents the inexorable workings of the law of causality, by which absolute justice is meted out to every human being, as determined by his deserts, whether they be good or evil. The problem of Buddhism is, therefore, how to escape from existence with its attendant miseries. It offers no help in securing this deliverance from any source other than man's unaided power to master himself. Man must in his own strength enter alone upon a desperate struggle to suppress his "will to live," to annihilate his desires and passions, reverse the constitutional tendencies of his nature, triumph over everything in his earthly environment which would attract or chain him to life, and become superior in his mental state to everything earthly and material. It is part of his victory to loathe his physical self, to despise every pleasant and desirable thing connected with ordinary earthly life, and become separated from his fellow-men in a realm of shadowy and colorless mental exaltation.[17]

It is not exactly a program on which a Democratic candidate might run for office. Yet in fact that account contains the seeds of its own contradiction: if the status in rebirth depends on actions now, "whether they be good or evil," there is an obvious incentive and constraint to follow the extremely clear and specific precepts of Buddhist morality (*pañca-sila*). In any case, Buddhism made an extremely sophisticated analysis of causality and rejected the view that any eventuality is constrained into its outcome by a single constraint (i.e., Karma). In one such analysis, we find five possible sources of constraint, any one or more of which might be operative in any particular instance: *1) bija-niyama,* biological or hereditary constraints; *2) mano-niyama* or *citta-niyama,* the unwilled operations of the mental order; *3) karma-niyama,* the consequences of volitional dispositions; *4) uti-niyama,* constraints in the physical environment; *5) dharma-niyama,* constraints derived from the transcendental order.

Applying these to an example, let us suppose that a bus crashes and all the passengers are killed. A naive understanding (misunderstanding) of Karma might suppose that the accumulation of bad Karma in each case brought all those individuals onto that particular bus in order to punish them. In fact, it might be the first source of constraint, a genetic defect leading to the sudden death of the driver; or the second source, an unwilled error by the driver, caused by sudden glare from the sun; or the third source, the driver deliberately drinking while driving; or the fourth source, a failure of the braking system; or the fifth source, the malice of Mara distracting the driver's attention. And in the case of *some* of the passengers, the eventuality (or outcome) might be karmically appropriate.

In general, the point to be emphasized is that while all religions require a commitment to alleviate suffering, they are generous in the specification of what may contribute to that alleviation. To be an enclosed nun is not to opt out of the world: it is to have more time to feel the pulse of the world and sustain its steady beat. It is not *ad rem* to ask whether a street in Calcutta or Bangkok, or for that matter in Rome or Karachi, exemplifies what religions say ought to be the case; the question of why there is a gap between theory and practice is to be asked not at Bellagio but on the Day of Judgment. What religions bring to the theme of the definition of social suffering is an insistence that while some items of suffering can indeed be isolated and treated in abstraction, this should not distract us from remaining alert to the far wider networks of constraints that contribute causatively to human suffering. Perhaps the ways in which religions looked to the wider context of society in their attempts to account for illness arose initially from ignorance, but the other side of the coin of ignorance bears the imprint of concern.

ENDNOTES

[1] Lewis Thomas, *The Youngest Science* (Oxford: Oxford University Press, 1984), 28.

[2] Sir William Osler, "Teaching and Thinking," in *Aequanimitas: With Other Addresses to Medical Students, Nurses, and Practitioners* (Philadelphia, Pa.: Blackiston, 1904).

[3] Thomas, *The Youngest Science*, 19.

[4] MacPhail, *British Medical Journal* (1993): 445.

[5] Thomas, *The Youngest Science*, 28–29.

[6] Max Weber, *The Sociology of Religion,* trans. E. Fischoff (London: Metheun, 1971), 138.

[7] Ibid., 139.

[8] Ibid., 113.

[9] Ibid.

[10] M. L. Stackhouse, *Creeds, Societies, and Human Rights* (Grand Rapids, Mich.: Eerdmans, 1984), 248.

[11] J. W. Bowker, *Problems of Suffering in Religions of the World* (Cambridge: Cambridge University Press, 1970); J. W. Bowker, *The Meanings of Death* (Cambridge: Cambridge University Press, 1991).

[12] T. Y. Sarma, ed., *Carakasamhita* (Bombay: Nirnaya Sagara Press, 1963).

[13] Rene Dubos, *Man, Medicine, and Environment* (Harmondsworth.: Penguin Books, 1970), 161–62.

[14] House of Lords Select Committee on Medical Ethics, United Kingdom, February 1994.

[15] H. H. Pattee, "Laws and Constraints, Symbols and Language," in C. H. Waddington, ed., *Towards a Theoretical Biology* (Edinburgh: Edinburgh University Press, 1972), vol. IV, 248.

[16] "Soviet Intervention Could Aid Poland's Credit Position," *The New York Times,* 31 August 1980.

[17] James Dennis, *Christian Missions and Social Progress: A Sociological Study of Foreign Missions* (New York: Fleming H. Revell, 1897), vol. I, 428–29.

Index

Abbas, Khwja Ahmad, 90
abortion, 234–35
Account of the Interior of Ceylon and of Its Inhabitants (Davy), 312
acknowledgment of pain, xiii, 70, 109, 111, 114; moral communities and, xxi, 38–42, 245–46; vs. silence, xvi–xvii, 94–95. *See also* responses to suffering
addiction, to traumatic memories, 258
advertising, Benetton, 23
Aeneid (Virgil), 40–41
aetiology, of distress, 368–71
Africa: famine, 4, 7–8, 21; Haitians from, 274; Tamils in, 330–31; UK immigrants from, 345; vulture-child photograph, 3–8; widows/widowers, 100; women's health, 22. *See also* Rwanda; South Africa
African National Congress (ANC), 104–5, 107, 108, 109, 112–13
Afro-Caribbeans: in UK, 345. *See also* Haiti
agentive moment, 345–50, 353
Aghori sect, 78
AIDS, xx, 11, 264, 267, 271–75 passim
alarmed vision, xvii, 47–65
Alegría, Claribel, 278
alienation: of Tamils, xxiii–xxiv, 345–58. *See also* aloneness; detachment; isolation
aloneness, 7–8, 28–32; of sorrow, 129; of survivors, 57–58, 61, 69. *See also* alienation
altruism, and transplantation, 210–11, 219, 235
ambiguities: about cruelty, 287; in death definition, 217, 220; about killing, 370; in personal suffering in public life, xviii–xix, 101–17, 119. *See also* dichotomies; extremes
American Bar Association, 216
American Chronic Pain Association, 44
American Medical Association, 216
Amerindians, xxvi, 287
Amirdhalingam, Appapillai, 316
Ammi, R., 367
Amnesty International, 237, 345
Analects (Confucius), 130–31, 140

anamorphic transformation, xiii
ancestors, 232–33, 255
Ancient Ceylon (Parker), 313
Anderson, Benedict, 322
anger, and pathogenetic memory, 255–56
animals: cruelty issues, 287; in moral communities, 40
animism, Japanese, 233
anthropocentrism, China, 175, 177
anthropology: and diversity in suffering, 2, 364; feminist, 274–75; focus on collective vs. individual, 105–6; on individual-social suffering, 261–62; mode of intimacy in here and now, 102; Nazi medicine and, 189–90, 196, 201; and necessity of technology, 209; and otherness, 277–78, 283. *See also* culture; ethnography
Antigone, 35, 87–88
Anti-Rightist Campaign, China, 135, 151, 162–63, 166–67, 175, 176
appropriations, xi, xvii–xix, xxvi, 1–23; of individual suffering, 119–48; of nation, 82–83; valid, 17–18; of women's bodies, 67–91, 101. *See also* mediatization; medicalization
Apter, David, 152, 156–57
Argentina, 53
Ariès, Philippe, 105, 212–14
Aristide, Father Jean-Bertrand, 269
aristocracy: Sade pornography, 41; in tragedy, 35–36, 39
Aristophanes, 376–77
Aristotle, 35–36, 37, 45
art: Tamil choices, 313–14. *See also* literature; performance art
artificial respirators, 210, 212, 215, 217
Asad, Talal, xxii–xxiii, 277, 285–308
Asahi Shinbun, 228
asceticism, self-inflicted pain, 302
Astel, Karl, 203–4
asthma, 11–12
Athey, Ron, 301–2
atrocity, xvii, 2; Holocaust, 47–65, 197; Sri Lankan armed forces, 323, 332; and transplantation, 237; unmasking, 183

383

Campbell Act, British, 250

camps, 48–52 passim, 57, 58, 64, 194–99 passim; Auschwitz, 48, 62, 184, 194–99 passim. *See also* Holocaust

Canada, Tamils and, 329–41 passim

cancer, 11–12, 32

cannibalism, in China, 17, 176

Cannon, Walter B., 255–57, 258

capitalism: China and, 168, 169; disordered, 8, 10–11, 19

Carakasamhita, 367

"caring for," in Heidegger, 353

Carter, Kevin, 3–7, 8, 9

Cartesianism, 97, 213, 221, 322, 346–47, 348

Casper, M., 188

Castoriadis, C., 69

catharsis, Aristotelian, 45

causes, and constraints, 371–77, 380

Cavell, Stanley, xvi, 21, 67, 68, 89, 93–98

Cawnpore massacre, 83

Ceylon, 312–17, 324–29, 354. *See also* Sri Lanka; Tamils

Chakri dynasty, 366

Chamberlain, Harold, 189

Char Adhyaya (Tagore), 71

Charcot, Jean-Martin, 196, 247, 254

charisma, Mao's, 170, 173–74, 177

Charles II, 359–60

Chatterji, Partha, 90

Chelmo, Poland, 49–50

Chelvanayakam, S. J. V., 320

Chen Duxiu, 123, 124–25, 126, 132

Chen Zhang-yu, 17

Chiang Kai-shek, 154, 158, 173

childbirth, death in, 275

"child of sorrow," 128–35

children: euthanized, 198–99; Haiti, 262; infant mortality rates, 262, 276; nature programs for, 15; photographs of, 3–8, 11, 22; sexual abuse of, 11, 66; Tamil, 337–42

Chile, 53

China, xiv; Maoism as source of social suffering in, 149–79; mass starvation, 16–17, 152, 175; People's Republic founded, 158; public uses of personal grief, 119–48; religion and illness, 368; Republican Revolution, 123, 124, 137; war with Japan, 124, 135, 153–61 passim, 169

Chinese Communist Party (CCP), xiv, 16–17, 120–29 passim, 150–79 passim

Chopp, Rebecca, 268, 273

Christ. *See* Jesus

Christianity: Anglican, 361; attitude toward pain, 127, 290; demon-caused diseases,

367; differences in suffering in, 364; and interrelatedness, 365; Japan and, 235; metaphors in, 305; monk whipping, 303; S/M and, 301–2, 308; suffering in, 30, 245

CIBA symposium, 212

Ci Jiwei, 126

"City of Sorrow" (Hussain), 86–87

civility, China and, 168–69, 177

civilized being: colonialists and, xxii–xxiii, 293–95, 306; revising myth of, 58–59. *See also* human

class. *See* social class

class struggle, China and, 165, 166, 169, 176, 177

cleansings, political, 129

Clément, Catherine, 97–98

Clifford, James, 105

clothes, of political widow, 110

Coetzee, Dirk, 109

Cohen, Ralph, 33

Cold War, 22

collectivity, xi, 2; of individual suffering, 38–39, 158, 162, 167; of mourning, 105–9; of violence, 151–58. *See also* communities; culture; societies

colonialism, 8, 293; in Ceylon, 312; in India, xv, 71–76, 83, 90, 294–95, 306; legitimating pain, xxii–xxiii, 293–95, 306. *See also* nationalism

comic spirit: of novels, 36. *See also* mirth

commodity: corpse as, 214; death as, xx, 10–11; experience as, 2, 7, 8; images of suffering as, 23; organ for transplant as, 218, 237; suffering as, xi, 8, 19; valid appropriations and, 18

communalism: Chinese intellectual, 155, 160, 170, 178; Indian, 75

Communists: Chinese, xiv, 16–17, 120–29 passim, 150–79 passim; South African, 107–8, 117

communities: different values for suffering, 2, 42; healthy, 54; matrilineal, 100; and media violence, 19; mourning of, 105; Nazi *Volkganze,* 191–94. *See also* culture; discourse communities; moral communities; societies

comparability, in suffering, 292, 293–95

conditioning, pathogenic memory, 257–58

Confucianism, xiv, 165, 235; on ancestors, 232, 233; attack on, 123, 158–59; and filial piety, 145, 167; on people and agriculture, 174; "sage-king," 171, 172–73; and suppressed emotions, 122

Confucius, 128; *Analects,* 130–31, 140; Madman of Qu, 130–31, 139–40, 144